PRAISE FOR *PRINCIPLES OF MARKETING ANALYTICS*

"This book is a timely and insightful guide to how data-driven thinking is reshaping modern marketing. It blends academic depth with practical relevance, making complex analytics approachable for both students and professionals. A strong contribution to the evolving field of marketing analytics."
Chidinma Ndukwe, Manager, Planning Reporting and Risk, TotalEnergies E&P Nigeria Ltd

"*Principles of Marketing Analytics* is a clear, authoritative and highly practical guide to understanding data-driven decision-making. What truly sets this text apart is its balance of theory and application, supported by exercises, real-world scenarios and actionable frameworks. A valuable resource for anyone committed to modern, evidence-based marketing."
Dr Raymond Webilor, Engineer, Spirax Sarco, Canada

"*Principles of Marketing Analytics* bridges analytical insight and creative strategy, helping students and academics understand how evidence-based decision-making shapes modern marketing practice. With clear learning outcomes, real-world examples, and practical exercises, it equips future marketers to turn data into meaningful actions that drive customer engagement and business growth. Highly recommended for those seeking to understand how analytics is reshaping the marketing discipline."
Dr Morolake Dairo, Lecturer in Fashion Marketing and Business, Manchester Fashion Institute, Manchester Metropolitan University, UK

"*Principles of Marketing Analytics* is a compelling and insightful book that illuminates the complexities of data-driven marketing with clarity and precision. The book's strength lies in its practical orientation and well-structured pedagogy using contemporary case studies, applied exercises, and real-world examples. *Principles of Marketing Analytics* stands as an essential reference for students, educators, and professionals eager to excel in evidence-based marketing within today's data-focused environment."
Dr Tahera Kalsoom, Lecturer in Fashion Business Analytics, Manchester Fashion Institute, Manchester Metropolitan University, UK

"An insightful and practical guide that truly captures how data-driven decision-making can transform brand strategy. It connects real-world marketing challenges with analytical solutions in a way that's both engaging and actionable. A valuable read for anyone passionate about using data to drive smarter marketing outcomes."
Lovina Uwerikowe, Marketing and Brand Strategy Professional, Graduate Assistant, University of Houston, US

"This book offers a timely and insightful contribution to contemporary debates in its field, skilfully bridging rigorous scholarship with real-world relevance. It will be an invaluable resource for students, practitioners and researchers who want to think more deeply and act more strategically in a rapidly changing environment."
Dr Sharon Nunoo, Lecturer in Fashion Marketing, Manchester Fashion Institute, Manchester Metropolitan University, UK

"*Principles of Marketing Analytics* successfully bridges academic insight with practical, real-world strategy. Ijeoma Onwumere's illustration of how data-driven customer segmentation can shape more targeted and effective marketing decisions makes the content both accessible and actionable. This book is a valuable resource for professionals seeking to elevate their marketing impact through analytics."
Diepiriye Adeline Akene, Technology Issue Management & GRC (Government, Risk Management and Compliance) Professional, CGI, US

"The book stands out for its simplified explanations, analytical debate and addressing practical real-world developments. For academic research, it offers a well-justified foundation grounded in scholarly work, making it a reliable reference for instigating further research. Students will find this edition useful for its accessible approach, step-by-step guidance and learning activities that demystify complex academic concepts."
Dr Farag Edghiem, Senior Lecturer in Digital Marketing Communications, Manchester Fashion Institute, Manchester Metropolitan University, UK

"This textbook is a practical guide for students and professionals seeking insights into data-driven marketing. With the inclusion of real-world examples and cutting-edge tools such as generative AI, the text equips readers with analytical skills to turn data into marketing insights for an evolving world of work."
Dr Ijeoma Ukeni, Lecturer in Management, University of Huddersfield, UK

"A must-read for modern marketers, this book demystifies the world of marketing analytics and translates complex data concepts into practical insights that drive real results. An essential guide for students, professionals and leaders looking to stay ahead in a data-driven marketing landscape."
Professor Gianpaolo Vignali, Professor of Sustainable Fashion Business, Manchester Fashion Institute, Manchester Metropolitan University, UK

"*Principles of Marketing Analytics* is an outstanding guide for any organization aiming to master data-driven decision-making."
Dr Abdul Jabbar, Associate Professor in Data Strategy and Analytics, University of Leicester, UK

Principles of Marketing Analytics

Understanding data-driven decision-making

Ijeoma Onwumere

First published in Great Britain and the United States in 2026 by Kogan Page Limited

Kogan Page
Kogan Page Ltd, 2nd Floor, 45 Gee Street, London EC1V 3RS, United Kingdom
Kogan Page Inc, 8 W 38th Street, Suite 902, New York, NY 10018, USA
www.koganpage.com

EU Representative (GPSR)
eucomply OÜ, Pärnu mnt 139b–14 11317, Tallinn, Estonia
www.eucompliancepartner.com

Kogan Page books are printed on paper from sustainable forests.

© Kogan Page, 2026

The moral rights of the author have been asserted in accordance with the Copyright, Designs and Patents Act 1988.

ISBNs
Hardback   978 1 3986 2329 3
Paperback   978 1 3986 2327 9
Ebook   978 1 3986 2328 6

British Library Cataloguing-in-Publication Data
A CIP record for this book is available from the British Library.

Library of Congress Cataloging in Publication Data
A CIP record for this book is available from the Library of Congress.

Typeset by Integra Software Services, Pondicherry
Printed and bound by CPI Group (UK) Ltd, Croydon CR0 4YY

CONTENTS

PART TWO Marketing analytics in action

LIST OF FIGURES AND TABLES

Figures

Tables

ABOUT THIS BOOK

Walkthrough of textbook features and online resources

Chapter outlines

Highlights the main topics that will be covered in the chapter.

CHAPTER OUTLINE

6.1 Overview of social media analytics

6.2 Measuring engagement and reach

6.3 Tools for analysing social media performance

Learning outcomes

Key goals that you should be able to grasp, understand and/or do when you have finished studying the chapter.

LEARNING OUTCOMES

- Understand the strategic value of social media analytics in marketing decision-making.
- Evaluate key performance indicators (KPIs) for social media platforms, including reach, engagement and conversion metrics.
- Use social listening and sentiment analysis tools to monitor brand perception.

Real-world/brand examples

A range of real-world examples from different industries to illustrate how key ideas and theories are operating in practice to help you to place the concepts discussed in a real-life context.

REAL-WORLD EXAMPLE Sephora's multi-platform engagement strategy

---

Sephora, a leading beauty retailer, employs a sophisticated strategy for measuring and optimizing engagement across platforms. For example, on Instagram, the brand uses carousel posts and stories to feature tutorials, boosting save and share rates. Meanwhile, on YouTube, Sephora tracks watch time and video completion rate as key engagement metrics for product demo content. By analysing the comparative performance of different content types, Sephora identified that short-form Reels had three times more engagement than static posts, leading it to reallocate resources accordingly (Sephora Digital Report, 2022).

Examples

Various short paragraphs that illustrate or emphasize a point, topic or concept.

EXAMPLE

During the launch of the Apple Vision Pro, social listening revealed polarized sentiment. Positive sentiment highlighted innovation and excitement, while negative sentiment focused on price and privacy concerns. Apple adjusted its messaging by emphasizing professional use cases and developer tools in follow-up campaigns (Apple, 2023).

Activities and practical exercises

Questions and activities throughout the text that encourage you to reflect on what you have learned and to apply your knowledge and skills in practice.

EXERCISE ⬀

Use Talkwalker or Sprout Social to create a dashboard analysing sentiment for a brand launch (e.g. Spotify Wrapped, H&M Conscious Collection)

These dashboards can help marketing teams identify perception risks, such as negative reviews gaining traction, or opportunities, like viral UGC that can be amplified.

Key terms

Important terms and concepts boxes/tables at the beginning of the chapter to highlight essential vocabulary of the chapter and act as a useful revision tool.

KEY TERMS

Social listening: The process of monitoring digital conversations to understand consumer sentiment and brand perception.

Social listening tools: Tools that track and analyse online mentions, trends and sentiment (e.g. Brandwatch, Talkwalker).

Social media dashboard: A visual interface used to track, measure, and analyse social media performance metrics.

User-generated content (UGC): Content created by customers and shared on social media platforms, often reflecting brand engagement.

References

Detailed references provide quick and easy access to the research and underpinning sources behind the chapter.

Online resources

This book includes access to online resources comprising lecturer PowerPoint slides and further reading lists.

Downloadable resources are available at www.koganpage.com

Key Takeaways and Concepts

Summarized points and concepts of the chapter, ideal for when you need to a quick reminder of the content or idea.

KEY TAKEAWAYS

- Marketing analytics is about using data to improve decision-making, not just reporting numbers.
- The discipline has evolved from intuition-based decisions to advanced AI-driven insights.
- Effective marketing analytics integrates **data collection, analysis** and **interpretation**.
- Benefits include improved ROI, customer retention, efficiency and competitive advantage.
- Challenges include **data quality, privacy, alignment with goals** and **organizational culture**.
- Future trends point towards **AI, big data, cross-channel analytics, predictive modelling** and **customer experience analytics**.
- Real-world examples (like Netflix) show that analytics impacts not only marketing campaigns but also **product strategy, personalization** and **customer loyalty**.

Questions

These questions can be used in classes and in independent study, to broaden understanding of chapter topics.

QUESTIONS

Discussion questions

1 In what ways has marketing analytics transformed from traditional approaches to modern data-driven practices?
2 How does marketing analytics enhance customer relationships and loyalty? Provide examples from real companies.

3 What are the main challenges organizations face when implementing marketing analytics, and how can they overcome them?

4 How can predictive analytics influence strategic decision-making in marketing campaigns?

5 Using the Netflix case, explain how marketing analytics can go beyond marketing to influence product innovation and business strategy.

6 To what extent should businesses rely on AI and machine learning in marketing analytics? What ethical considerations should be addressed?

Introduction

Part One Foundations of marketing analytics

Part One establishes the groundwork for understanding marketing analytics by presenting its definition, scope, methodologies and practical tools that enable evidence-based decision-making. Across three chapters, it introduces the field, emphasizes the role of data collection and management, and explains key marketing metrics that form the backbone of performance measurement.

Chapter 1 Introduction to marketing analytics

The opening chapter defines marketing analytics as the systematic use of data, statistical models and technology to evaluate and optimize marketing performance. It emphasizes why marketing analytics is increasingly critical in today's dynamic and data-rich environment. The chapter outlines the benefits, including improved customer insights, more accurate attribution of marketing investments and enhanced ability to optimize campaigns. Importantly, it demonstrates that marketing analytics is not just about measurement but about turning raw data into actionable intelligence. Readers gain an appreciation of the shift from intuition-based decision-making to evidence-based strategy, a theme that recurs throughout the book.

Chapter 2 Data collection and measurement – best practices for collecting, organizing and storing marketing data

This chapter explores the processes and challenges of collecting, organizing and storing marketing data. It highlights best practices in ensuring data quality, reliability and ethical compliance. Both online and offline data sources are covered, such as customer transactions, website analytics, CRM systems, surveys and social media platforms. A key theme is the integration of disparate datasets into unified databases to enable holistic insights. The exercise asks readers to design a data collection plan for a new product launch, ensuring that data flows from both digital channels (e.g. search engines, social media ads, email) and traditional offline channels (e.g. in-store

surveys, point-of-sale systems). To reinforce this, a simple database schema is introduced as a model, illustrating how entities like customer, purchase, campaign and
channel can be structured with key fields and relationships. This ensures students
understand how organized storage underpins effective analytics.

Chapter 3 Key marketing metrics

This chapter addresses the core metrics that measure marketing performance, categorized into acquisition, conversion and engagement. It details widely used measures
such as customer acquisition cost (CAC), conversion rate (CR), customer lifetime value
(CLTV), return on marketing investment (ROMI) and engagement metrics like click-
through rate (CTR), bounce rate and social media interaction rates. The exercise
provided asks readers to calculate customer lifetime value (CLTV) for a hypothetical
customer segment using sample data, reinforcing how metrics support forecasting and
long-term planning. Additionally, the awareness, interest, desire, action (AIDA) model
is introduced as a conceptual framework for tracking the customer journey. This shows
how marketing analytics can map metrics to each stage, for example impressions and
reach at the awareness stage, click-throughs and dwell time at the interest stage, repeat
visits or lead form fills at the desire stage, and conversions or purchases at the action
stage. This linkage between theoretical models and measurable KPIs underscores how
analytics bridges abstract marketing concepts and operational decision-making.

Overall contribution of Part One

Part One equips readers with the foundational skills and concepts needed for more
advanced marketing analytics covered in later sections. It establishes a logical progression: first defining the field (Chapter 1), then explaining how to systematically
gather and structure data (Chapter 2), and finally, interpreting performance through
key metrics (Chapter 3). Practical exercises and models ensure that readers not only
understand theoretical principles but can also apply them to real-world scenarios. By
the end of Part One readers are prepared to move beyond data collection towards
more sophisticated analyses, modelling and optimization strategies.

Part Two Marketing analytics in action

Part Two moves from foundational principles into the practical application of
analytics across core marketing functions. It demonstrates how data-driven insights
can guide segmentation, campaign optimization, social media strategies and web

experience improvements. Through exercises and models, the section emphasizes the importance of applying analytical methods to real-world challenges, ensuring that marketers can make actionable decisions.

Chapter 4 Marketing analytics in action – customer segmentation and targeting

This chapter emphasizes the strategic importance of identifying and prioritizing high-value customer groups. It introduces segmentation techniques ranging from traditional demographic clustering to advanced behavioural and psychographic methods. The exercise applies recency, frequency, monetary (RFM) analysis to segment customers of an e-commerce store, allowing students to classify buyers into actionable categories such as champions, loyal customers, at-risk buyers and hibernating customers. Such analysis helps pinpoint target groups for tailored campaigns. The model of customer personas is then introduced, showing how segments can be humanized by integrating demographic (e.g. age, income), behavioural (e.g. purchase frequency) and psychographic (e.g. lifestyle, values) attributes. This ensures marketers understand both the quantitative and qualitative aspects of segmentation, improving the precision of targeting strategies.

Chapter 5 Marketing campaign optimization

This chapter explores how analytics can enhance campaign design, execution and evaluation. It highlights techniques such as A/B testing, multivariate testing, predictive modelling and conversion tracking to refine messaging, creative elements and channel selection. The exercise asks readers to analyse the results of an A/B test for email subject lines, drawing conclusions about the winning variation based on open rates, click-through rates and conversions. The marketing funnel model is presented as a conceptual framework, breaking down the stages of awareness, consideration, conversion and retention. By linking metrics to each funnel stage, marketers can identify bottlenecks and optimize resource allocation, ensuring campaigns drive measurable impact across the customer journey.

Chapter 6 Social media analytics

This chapter focuses on social media as both a communication and performance measurement channel. It introduces metrics such as reach, impressions, engagement rate, share of voice, sentiment and influencer impact. The exercise requires students to use social listening tools to track brand mentions and perform a sentiment analysis for a specific campaign, illustrating how brands can gauge public perception in real time. To operationalize this, the chapter introduces a social media dashboard model, which integrates key performance indicators (KPIs) into a single view. The template demonstrates how marketers can monitor follower growth, engagement ratios, campaign performance and customer sentiment simultaneously. The chapter underscores the importance of aligning social media metrics with broader business objectives, such as brand equity, customer loyalty and revenue generation.

Chapter 7 Web analytics

This chapter covers website and digital platform performance analysis, focusing on understanding user behaviour and optimizing the customer experience. It explains key metrics such as sessions, page views, bounce rate, average session duration, exit rate and goal completions. The exercise involves interpreting a Google Analytics report to identify strengths and weaknesses in website performance, such as high-traffic pages with low conversions or elevated bounce rates on landing pages. The model of heatmaps and click tracking is introduced, showing how visual analytics tools reveal patterns of user interaction, such as where users click, how far they scroll and which sections capture the most attention. These insights guide website redesigns, navigation improvements and content placement to boost user satisfaction and conversion rates.

Overall contribution of Part Two

Part Two demonstrates how marketing analytics becomes actionable in day-to-day decision-making. While Part One established the conceptual foundation, this part emphasizes hands-on application: segmenting customers, testing campaigns, monitoring social media and analysing web traffic. Exercises bridge theory and practice, while models (customer personas, marketing funnel, social dashboards and heatmaps) give readers structured frameworks for implementation.

By the end of Part Two, readers are equipped not only to measure performance but also to act on insights – improving targeting, refining campaigns, engaging customers online and enhancing the digital experience. This positions analytics as a driver of continuous improvement, enabling businesses to remain competitive in fast-changing markets.

Part Three Advanced marketing analytics: Predictive modelling and beyond

Part Three, on advanced marketing analytics, delves into the core analytical techniques that empower marketers to make data-driven decisions about future trends, customer behaviour and marketing effectiveness. The section focuses on predictive modelling, regression analysis, forecasting and machine learning, offering a comprehensive toolkit for modern marketing strategy. It presents a robust, interconnected framework for advanced marketing analytics. From modelling individual customer behaviours to evaluating holistic campaign performance across channels, these tools empower marketers to make smarter, faster and more personalized decisions. The focus on continuous validation, adaptation and integration of analytics into business systems ensures strategies remain effective in an ever-evolving market landscape.

Chapter 8 Predictive modelling – forecasting trends and customer behaviour

Predictive modelling leverages historical data to forecast future outcomes, such as customer churn, sales or engagement. Logistic regression is widely used to estimate the likelihood of events (e.g. churn) based on variables like purchase frequency, complaints and customer service interactions. Regression analysis further quantifies how changes in marketing levers – like advertising spend or pricing – impact key outcomes, enabling resource optimization. Forecasting methods (e.g. SARIMA, neural networks) extend this approach to predict demand, customer lifetime value or campaign responses, with model accuracy validated using real-time data. These insights allow businesses to proactively tailor strategies and improve planning agility.

Chapter 9 Marketing attribution – evaluating channels and touchpoints

Marketing attribution models assess the effectiveness of different customer touchpoints. Traditional models, like first-click, last-click and linear, provide varying perspectives on how conversions are credited. More advanced models, such as Markov chains, consider the full sequence of interactions and compute transition probabilities to identify the true influence of each channel. This approach reveals how the removal of a touchpoint would affect conversion rates, offering a more accurate picture of multichannel effectiveness. Multi-touch analysis tools like path analysis and sequence mining uncover synergistic effects across channels, enabling smarter allocation of marketing budgets and refined customer journey optimization.

Chapter 10 Machine learning for marketing – automating and enhancing decisions

Machine learning automates complex marketing tasks and delivers actionable insights. Clustering algorithms (e.g. K-means, DBSCAN) enable dynamic customer segmentation based on behavioural patterns rather than static demographics. Recommendation engines, using collaborative or content-based filtering, personalize product suggestions to boost engagement and sales. AI-driven tools support lead scoring, content generation and campaign automation, enhancing operational efficiency. These systems adapt in real time, allowing businesses to respond swiftly to shifting consumer behaviours. Crucially, model interpretability and continuous monitoring are vital to maintain reliability and trust in automated decisions.

Chapter 11 The rise of generative AI in marketing

Generative AI is transforming marketing content creation and personalization. Tools powered by large language models (LLMs) can generate customer-specific email campaigns, product descriptions, social media posts and even chat responses at scale. This technology enhances creativity while preserving brand tone and consistency. When combined with predictive analytics and segmentation, generative AI can tailor messaging to micro-audiences, improving conversion rates. However, ethical considerations, data governance and transparency remain essential when deploying these tools to ensure responsible and sustainable AI usage.

PART ONE
Foundations of marketing analytics

01 | Introduction to marketing analytics

LEARNING OUTCOMES

By the end of this chapter, students should be able to:

- Define marketing analytics and explain its role in modern marketing.
- Trace the historical evolution of marketing analytics from qualitative methods to data-driven approaches.
- Understand the importance of marketing analytics in today's business environment.
- Identify the key components and benefits of marketing analytics.
- Recognize challenges and considerations in implementing analytics.
- Evaluate the impact of future trends such as AI, big data and predictive modelling.
- Apply theoretical frameworks to connect analytics with marketing decision-making.

CHAPTER OUTLINE

1.1 Defining marketing analytics

1.2 Historical evolution of marketing analytics

1.3 The importance of marketing analytics in today's business landscape

1.4 Key components of marketing analytics

1.5 Key benefits of marketing analytics

1.6 Challenges and considerations in marketing analytics

1.7 The future of marketing analytics

1.8 Real-world example and activity

Conclusion

References

1.1 Defining marketing analytics

Marketing analytics is defined as the practice of measuring, managing and analysing marketing performance. This discipline encompasses a range of methodologies and tools designed to decipher complex data related to customer behaviour, market trends and campaign effectiveness. By applying statistical analysis and data visualization techniques, marketers can assess various aspects of their campaigns, such as engagement rates, conversion metrics and return on investment (ROI). The insights gathered from marketing analytics not only streamline decision-making processes but also enhance the alignment between marketing efforts and business objectives. Through this systematic approach, organizations can establish meaningful connections between their marketing strategies and the real-world outcomes they aim to achieve (Chaffey and Ellis-Chadwick, 2019; Kumar and Rajan, 2019).

Marketing analytics is the systematic collection, measurement, analysis and interpretation of data related to marketing activities. It involves leveraging various data sources, such as customer interactions, market trends and campaign performance, to gain insights into consumer behaviour, evaluate the effectiveness of marketing strategies, and make data-driven decisions to improve marketing outcomes (Kumar et al, 2013). At its core, marketing analytics aims to bridge the gap between marketing theory and real-world application. It moves beyond traditional marketing intuition and relies on empirical evidence to guide decision-making. By analysing data, marketers can understand what resonates with their target audience, identify areas for improvement and ultimately optimize their marketing efforts for maximum return on investment (ROI).

The significance of marketing analytics cannot be overstated in today's competitive business landscape. It plays a pivotal role in driving informed business decisions and optimizing marketing strategies. By analysing data, companies can identify which marketing channels yield the best results, enabling them to allocate resources more effectively. These data-driven insights also support the development of personalized marketing messages, enhancing consumer engagement and fostering customer loyalty. Additionally, the ability to track performance in real time allows businesses to adapt quickly to changing market conditions or consumer preferences, ensuring they remain agile and relevant. In essence, marketing analytics transforms raw data into actionable strategies, equipping organizations with the knowledge to navigate complexities and capitalize on opportunities (Chaffey and Ellis-Chadwick, 2019; Kumar and Rajan, 2019).

Understanding and leveraging marketing analytics creates a framework for sustained organizational growth. It empowers marketers to adopt a proactive approach by continuously monitoring key performance indicators (KPIs) and adjusting strategies based on empirical evidence rather than assumptions. This ongoing cycle of analysis and refinement not only promotes efficiency but also enhances the overall effectiveness of marketing initiatives. For aspiring marketers and business leaders, familiarizing themselves with the tools and techniques of marketing analytics is essential. Engaging with analytics fosters a deeper understanding of market dynamics and cultivates the ability to make strategic decisions that drive long-term success. A practical tip for leveraging marketing analytics effectively is to integrate various data sources, such as social media metrics, website traffic and customer feedback, to obtain a comprehensive view of the marketing landscape (Wedel and Kannan, 2016; Davenport and Harris, 2017).

1.2 Historical evolution of marketing analytics

The origins of marketing analytics can be traced back to traditional methods that relied heavily on qualitative insights and anecdotal evidence. In the early 20th century, marketers primarily depended on intuition, experience and rudimentary tools such as surveys, focus groups and sales data to gauge consumer behaviour and market trends. These methods, while useful, were often limited in scope and accuracy, as they lacked the ability to capture the full complexity of consumer preferences and market dynamics (Kotler and Keller, 2016).

The mid-20th century marked a significant shift in marketing practices with the advent of more structured approaches. The introduction of market research techniques, such as statistical sampling and regression analysis, allowed marketers to move beyond intuition and base their decisions on empirical data. This period also saw the rise of customer segmentation, where businesses began categorizing consumers based on demographics, psychographics and purchasing behaviour. These advancements laid the groundwork for more sophisticated analytical methods (Sheth and Sisodia, 2015).

The digital revolution of the late 20th and early 21st centuries transformed marketing analytics into a data-driven discipline. The proliferation of websites, e-commerce platforms and social media generated vast amounts of consumer data, enabling marketers to track and analyse behaviour in real time. Tools like customer relationship management (CRM) systems, web analytics and big data technologies emerged, allowing businesses to gain deeper insights into customer journeys and preferences (Wedel and Kannan, 2016). This era also saw the rise of predictive analytics, which uses historical data to forecast future trends and behaviours, further enhancing the precision of marketing strategies.

Today, marketing analytics has evolved into a multifaceted field that integrates advanced technologies, such as artificial intelligence (AI), machine learning and automation. These tools enable marketers to process large datasets, identify patterns and deliver personalized experiences at scale. For instance, AI-powered algorithms can analyse consumer interactions across multiple touchpoints, providing actionable insights that drive engagement and conversion (Davenport and Harris, 2017). Moreover, the emphasis on real-time analytics has empowered businesses to respond swiftly to market changes, ensuring they remain competitive in a fast-paced environment.

The historical evolution of marketing analytics reflects a broader trend towards data-driven decision-making in business. From its humble beginnings in qualitative research to its current state as a technology-driven discipline, marketing analytics has continually adapted to meet the demands of an increasingly complex and interconnected marketplace. As organizations continue to embrace digital transformation, the role of marketing analytics will only grow in importance, shaping the future of how businesses understand and engage with their audiences (Kumar and Rajan, 2019).

1.3 The importance of marketing analytics in today's business landscape

In today's data-driven world, marketing analytics has become indispensable for businesses of all sizes. Its importance stems from several key factors that highlight its role in driving growth, enhancing customer relationships and ensuring competitiveness in an ever-evolving marketplace.

Increased competition

The modern marketplace is highly competitive, with businesses vying for consumer attention across multiple channels. To gain a competitive edge, companies must understand their customers deeply and tailor their marketing messages with precision. Marketing analytics provides the insights necessary to identify market trends, understand customer preferences and anticipate their needs. For example, by analysing customer data, businesses can segment their audience and deliver personalized campaigns that resonate with specific demographics, thereby increasing engagement and conversion rates (Kotler and Keller, 2016). This level of precision is critical in a crowded market where consumers are bombarded with information and choices.

Rapid technological advancements

The emergence of new technologies, such as social media, mobile devices and artificial intelligence (AI), has created a wealth of data. Marketing analytics provides the tools and techniques to harness this data effectively, allowing businesses to leverage these technologies to their advantage. For instance, AI-powered analytics can process vast amounts of data in real time, enabling marketers to predict consumer behaviour and optimize campaigns dynamically (Davenport and Harris, 2017).

Figure 1.1   Theoretical frameworks in marketing analytics

THEORETICAL FRAMEWORKS
IN MARKETING ANALYTICS

Resource-based view (RBV)
(Barney, 1991)
Analytics capabilities as a strategic
resource

Dynamic capabilities theory
(Teece, Pisano and Shuen, 1997)
Firms must adapt their analytics
practices to remain competitive

Technology acceptance model (TAM)
(Davis, 1989)
Explains adoption of analytics tools
by marketers

**Customer relationship management
(CRM) theory**
Links analytics with customer loyalty
and long-term value creation

Balanced scorecard
(Kaplan and Norton, 1996)
Using analytics to measure marketing's
contribution to organizational
performance

Additionally, tools like Google Analytics and CRM platforms allow businesses to track customer interactions across multiple touchpoints, providing a holistic view of the customer journey.

Changing consumer behaviour

Consumer behaviour is constantly evolving, driven by technological advances and shifting societal norms. Traditional marketing tactics may no longer be effective in reaching today's digitally savvy consumers. Marketing analytics helps businesses adapt to these changes by providing insights into how consumers interact with brands across different channels and platforms. For example, analytics can reveal which social media platforms are most effective for engaging specific demographics or which types of content drive the most conversions (Wedel and Kannan, 2016). This adaptability is crucial for staying relevant in a rapidly changing environment.

Data-driven decision-making

Marketing analytics empowers businesses to make data-driven decisions, reducing reliance on intuition or guesswork. By analysing data, marketers can identify which campaigns are performing well and which are not, allocate budgets effectively and optimize their marketing strategies for maximum impact. For instance, A/B testing and multivariate analysis allow businesses to experiment with different marketing approaches and determine the most effective strategies (Kumar and Rajan, 2019). This evidence-based approach not only improves efficiency but also maximizes return on investment.

Improved customer relationships

Marketing analytics provides valuable insights into customer behaviour, preferences and needs. By understanding their customers better, businesses can build stronger relationships, improve customer satisfaction and foster loyalty. For example, predictive analytics can help identify customers at risk of churn, enabling businesses to take proactive measures to retain them (Sheth and Sisodia, 2015). Additionally, analytics can inform personalized marketing efforts, such as tailored recommendations or targeted promotions, which enhance the customer experience and strengthen brand loyalty.

Strategic advantage in a dynamic environment

In an era where market conditions and consumer preferences can change overnight, marketing analytics equips businesses with the agility to respond quickly. Real-time analytics, for instance, allows companies to monitor campaign performance and make adjustments dynamically, ensuring they remain aligned with their goals (Chaffey and Ellis-Chadwick, 2019). This ability to adapt swiftly is a significant strategic advantage in today's fast-paced business environment.

1.4 Key components of marketing analytics

Marketing analytics is a multifaceted discipline that revolves around the systematic collection, analysis and interpretation of data relevant to marketing efforts. One of the essential elements of marketing analytics is **data collection**, which serves as the foundation for any analytical endeavour. Data can be gathered from diverse sources, such as customer interactions across digital platforms, purchase histories, social media engagement and surveys (Kotler and Keller, 2016). The effectiveness of marketing strategies heavily depends on the quality and comprehensiveness of the data collected. Furthermore, the process of **data analysis** involves not only statistical evaluations but also the use of advanced techniques like data mining and predictive analytics (Wedel and Kannan, 2016). These methods help to uncover patterns and trends that inform marketing decisions. **Interpretation** of this data is equally crucial, as it transforms raw numbers into actionable insights. Understanding these insights allows marketers to tailor their strategies to better align with consumer behaviour and preferences (Hair et al, 2019).

Integrating these components – data collection, analysis and interpretation – into cohesive marketing strategies enhances their overall effectiveness. A well-rounded marketing strategy takes the insights gained from analytics and applies them to real-world campaigns. For instance, by analysing customer data, marketers can segment their audience more effectively, crafting personalized messages that resonate with specific groups (Lilien et al, 2013). Additionally, this integration allows for real-time adjustments to campaigns. By constantly monitoring analytics, businesses can adapt their strategies to changing market conditions or customer feedback (Hanssens et al, 2014). This dynamic approach ensures that marketing efforts remain relevant and impactful. Companies that successfully weave these analytical components into their strategies often see improved engagement rates and higher returns on investment (Rust et al, 2010).

Understanding the key components of marketing analytics and their integration into strategies is not only vital for students studying marketing but also for professionals aiming to refine their approaches. One practical tip is to establish a regular review schedule for your analytics. By revisiting your data consistently, you can spot trends that might not be immediately visible and adjust your tactics promptly (Davenport and Harris, 2007). This ongoing engagement with analytics fosters a responsive marketing environment, ultimately leading to more successful outcomes.

1.5 Key benefits of marketing analytics

Implementing a robust marketing analytics framework offers numerous advantages that can significantly enhance a business's marketing efforts and overall performance. Listed next are the key benefits of marketing analytics, supported by academic research and industry insights.

Enhanced return on investment (ROI)

Marketing analytics enables businesses to measure the effectiveness of their campaigns with precision. By analysing data on campaign performance, companies can identify which strategies yield the highest returns and allocate resources more effectively (Rust et al, 2010). This data-driven approach ensures that marketing budgets are spent on initiatives that deliver the best results, ultimately improving ROI. For example, by tracking metrics such as customer acquisition costs (CAC) and customer lifetime value (CLV), businesses can optimize their spending and maximize the impact of their marketing investments (Hanssens et al, 2014).

Improved customer acquisition and retention

Marketing analytics provides deep insights into customer behaviour, preferences and purchasing patterns. By leveraging these insights, businesses can identify and target potential customers more effectively, leading to higher acquisition rates (Kotler and Keller, 2016). Additionally, understanding customer needs and preferences allows companies to tailor their marketing messages and offers, fostering stronger customer relationships and improving retention rates (Hair et al, 2019). For instance, personalized marketing campaigns based on customer data have been shown to increase engagement and loyalty (Lilien et al, 2013).

Competitive advantage

In today's highly competitive market, businesses that leverage data-driven insights gain a significant edge over their rivals. Marketing analytics allows companies to understand their customers better than competitors, enabling them to differentiate their offerings and build stronger brand loyalty (Wedel and Kannan, 2016). By identifying emerging trends and customer preferences early, businesses can adapt their strategies proactively, capturing a larger market share and staying ahead of the competition (Davenport and Harris, 2007).

Data-driven decision-making

One of the most significant benefits of marketing analytics is its ability to empower businesses to make informed decisions based on data rather than intuition or guesswork. This shift from subjective decision-making to an evidence-based approach leads to more effective marketing strategies and improved campaign performance (Hanssens et al, 2014). For example, predictive analytics can help businesses forecast future trends and customer behaviour, enabling them to design campaigns that resonate with their target audience (Rust et al, 2010).

Increased efficiency

Marketing analytics streamlines data collection and analysis processes, often through automation, which significantly improves the efficiency of marketing operations. By automating repetitive tasks such as data aggregation and reporting, marketers can focus on more strategic activities, such as developing innovative campaigns and build-ing stronger customer relationships (Davenport and Harris, 2007). This increased efficiency not only reduces operational costs but also allows businesses to respond more quickly to market changes and customer needs (Wedel and Kannan, 2016).

Real-time adjustments and agility

Another critical benefit of marketing analytics is the ability to monitor campaigns in real time and make adjustments as needed. By continuously tracking KPIs, busi-nesses can identify underperforming campaigns and optimize them as needed (Hanssens et al, 2014). This agility ensures that marketing efforts remain relevant and effective, even in rapidly changing market conditions.

Improved customer segmentation and personalization

Marketing analytics enables businesses to segment their audience more effectively based on demographics, behaviour and preferences. This segmentation allows for highly personalized marketing campaigns that resonate with specific customer groups, leading to higher engagement and conversion rates (Lilien et al, 2013). For example, businesses can use analytics to create targeted email campaigns or personalized prod-uct recommendations, enhancing the customer experience and driving sales.

Better resource allocation

By identifying which marketing channels and strategies deliver the best results, busi-nesses can allocate their resources more efficiently. This ensures that time, money and effort are directed towards the most impactful initiatives, reducing waste and improving overall marketing effectiveness (Kotler and Keller, 2016).

1.6 Challenges and considerations in marketing analytics

The field of marketing analytics is rapidly evolving, driven by technological advance-ments and changing consumer behaviours. Listed next are the key trends shaping the future of marketing analytics.

Artificial intelligence (AI) and machine learning

AI and machine learning are revolutionizing marketing analytics by automating data analysis, identifying patterns and making predictions. These technologies enable marketers to personalize customer experiences, optimize campaigns in real time and gain deeper insights into customer behaviour (Rust et al, 2010). For example, AI-powered chatbots can analyse customer interactions to provide personalized recommendations, enhancing customer satisfaction and engagement (Wedel and Kannan, 2016).

Big data and data visualization

While the exponential growth of marketing analytics offers significant benefits, businesses must navigate several challenges to fully leverage its potential. Some of the key challenges and considerations follow, supported by academic research and industry insights.

Data quality and integrity

Ensuring the accuracy, consistency and reliability of data is fundamental to effective marketing analytics. Poor data quality, such as missing data, inconsistent formats or errors, can lead to inaccurate insights and flawed decision-making (Davenport and Harris, 2007). For example, duplicate or incomplete customer records can skew segmentation efforts, leading to ineffective targeting. Businesses must implement robust data governance frameworks to maintain data integrity and ensure that analytics outputs are trustworthy (Hair et al, 2019).

Data privacy and security

With the increasing volume of customer data being collected, privacy and security have become critical concerns. Businesses must comply with data protection regulations, such as the **General Data Protection Regulation (GDPR)** in the EU or the **California Consumer Privacy Act (CCPA)** in the US, to avoid legal repercussions and maintain customer trust (Wedel and Kannan, 2016). Failure to secure customer data can result in breaches, damaging a brand's reputation and leading to financial penalties. Companies must invest in secure data storage solutions and adopt best practices for data encryption and access control (Kotler and Keller, 2016).

Data analysis and interpretation

Analysing and interpreting large volumes of data can be complex and resource-intensive. Businesses need advanced tools, such as **machine learning algorithms** and **data visualization platforms,** to process and make sense of the data effectively (Rust et al, 2010). Additionally, organizations must invest in skilled analysts who can translate raw data into actionable insights. Without the right expertise, businesses risk misinterpreting data, leading to suboptimal marketing strategies (Hanssens et al, 2014).

Integration with business goals

Marketing analytics must align with the organization's overall strategic objectives. This requires defining clear **key performance indicators (KPIs)** that reflect the business's goals, such as increasing customer lifetime value (CLV) or improving conversion rates (Lilien et al, 2013). Without alignment, analytics efforts may focus on irrelevant metrics, leading to wasted resources and missed opportunities. Regularly reviewing and updating KPIs ensures that marketing analytics remains relevant and impactful (Davenport and Harris, 2007).

Organizational culture

A data-driven culture is essential for the successful implementation of marketing analytics. Organizations must foster an environment where data is valued and employees are encouraged to make decisions based on evidence rather than intuition (Wedel and Kannan, 2016). This requires training employees to become data-literate and providing them with the tools and resources needed to access and analyse data. Leadership plays a critical role in promoting this culture by setting an example and prioritizing data-driven decision-making (Hair et al, 2019).

1.7 The future of marketing analytics

The field of marketing analytics is rapidly evolving, driven by technological advancements and changing consumer behaviours. The following are the key trends shaping the future of marketing analytics.

Artificial intelligence (AI) and machine learning

AI and machine learning are revolutionizing marketing analytics by automating data analysis, identifying patterns and making predictions. These technologies enable marketers to personalize customer experiences, optimize campaigns in real time and gain deeper insights into customer behaviour (Rust et al, 2010). For example, AI-powered chatbots can analyse customer interactions to provide personalized recommendations, enhancing customer satisfaction and engagement (Wedel and Kannan, 2016).

Big data and data visualization

The exponential growth of data generated by businesses and consumers has made **big data** technologies essential for marketing analytics. Advanced data visualization tools, such as Tableau and Power BI, help marketers interpret complex datasets and communicate insights effectively (Davenport and Harris, 2007). These tools enable businesses to identify trends and patterns that would otherwise go unnoticed, improving decision-making and strategy development.

Customer experience (CX) analytics

As customer experience becomes a key differentiator, businesses are increasingly focusing on **CX analytics** to understand customer journeys, identify pain points and improve satisfaction (Hanssens et al, 2014). By analysing customer interactions across touchpoints, companies can create seamless and personalized experiences that drive loyalty and retention (Kotler and Keller, 2016).

Cross-channel analytics

With consumers interacting with brands across multiple channels – such as social media, email and in-store – **cross-channel analytics** is crucial for understanding customer behaviour and delivering consistent experiences (Lilien et al, 2013). This approach allows businesses to track customer journeys across platforms, ensuring that marketing efforts are cohesive and aligned with customer expectations.

Predictive analytics

Predictive analytics uses historical data to forecast future trends and customer behaviour, enabling businesses to anticipate needs and develop proactive strategies (Rust et al, 2010). For example, predictive models can identify customers at risk of churn, allowing businesses to implement retention strategies before losing them. This forward-looking approach enhances decision-making and improves marketing effectiveness.

Conclusion

In today's data-driven world, marketing analytics has evolved from a luxury to an essential tool for businesses aiming to achieve sustainable growth. By leveraging the power of data, organizations can make informed decisions, optimize marketing campaigns and secure a competitive advantage in their respective industries.

The key benefits of marketing analytics are substantial, including **increased return on investment (ROI), enhanced customer acquisition and retention,** and the ability to make **data-driven decisions.** These advantages enable businesses to allocate resources more effectively, tailor their strategies to meet customer needs and stay ahead of competitors. However, to fully realize these benefits, organizations must address several challenges, such as ensuring **data quality**, navigating **privacy concerns** and aligning analytics efforts with broader **organizational goals**.

Looking to the future, the field of marketing analytics is poised for further transformation, driven by advancements in **artificial intelligence (AI)**, **big data technologies** and **predictive analytics**. These innovations will enable businesses to gain deeper insights, automate complex processes and anticipate customer behaviour with greater accuracy. Companies that embrace these advancements, invest in the necessary tools and expertise, and foster a **data-driven culture** will be best positioned to thrive in the increasingly dynamic and competitive marketplace of the future. By staying ahead of these trends, businesses can not only enhance their marketing effectiveness but also build stronger customer relationships and drive long-term success.

1.8 Real-world example and activity

REAL-WORLD EXAMPLE   Netflix – data-driven marketing analytics

Netflix provides a strong example of analytics in practice. The company leverages big data and machine learning to personalize recommendations for its 270+ million subscribers (as of 2025).

- **Analytics in action**: Netflix tracks user viewing behaviour, search history and interaction patterns. Algorithms analyse this data to predict what a user will watch next.

- **Impact**: Personalization accounts for over 80 per cent of the content streamed on Netflix (Gomez-Uribe and Hunt, 2016).

- **Marketing strategy**: By predicting customer preferences, Netflix reduces churn, improves customer satisfaction and optimizes marketing spend on original content.

- **Key takeaway**: Marketing analytics not only improves targeting but also shapes product development, pricing strategies and customer retention.

EXERCISE

Applying analytics to a marketing problem

Scenario

A retail company notices that website traffic is high, but conversion rates are low.

Tasks for students

1   Identify three KPIs the company should monitor.

2   Suggest one predictive model (e.g. logistic regression) to forecast which customers are most likely to convert.

3   Propose a segmentation strategy (demographics, behaviour, psychographics).

4   Recommend how marketing analytics tools (e.g. Google Analytics, Tableau) could be used to improve decision-making.

Conclusion

This chapter introduced marketing analytics as a discipline that bridges marketing strategy and data-driven decision-making. The discussion highlighted its historical evolution from intuition-based marketing to advanced, technology-driven analytics powered by big data, AI and machine learning. Students learned about the importance of marketing analytics in today's competitive environment, including its role in customer acquisition, retention, personalization and real-time decision-making. The chapter also presented the key components (data collection, analysis, interpretation), benefits (ROI, segmentation, efficiency), challenges (data quality, privacy, alignment with goals) and future trends shaping the field.

The case study on Netflix demonstrated how analytics translates into real-world business success, while the activity reinforced practical applications such as identifying KPIs, predictive modelling and segmentation strategies. Overall, marketing analytics was positioned as an essential capability for organizations to stay competitive, agile and customer-centric.

QUESTIONS

Discussion questions

1   In what ways has marketing analytics transformed from traditional approaches to modern data-driven practices?

2   How does marketing analytics enhance customer relationships and loyalty? Provide examples from real companies.

3   What are the main challenges organizations face when implementing marketing analytics, and how can they overcome them?

4 How can predictive analytics influence strategic decision-making in marketing campaigns?

5 Using the Netflix case, explain how marketing analytics can go beyond marketing to influence product innovation and business strategy.

6 To what extent should businesses rely on AI and machine learning in marketing analytics? What ethical considerations should be addressed?

EXERCISE

Multiple-choice quiz

Q1 What is the primary purpose of marketing analytics?

A. To increase advertising spend

B. To measure, manage and analyse marketing performance

C. To replace human marketers with machines

D. To create customer surveys only

Q2 Which of the following best describes customer lifetime value (CLV)?

A. The total cost of acquiring a new customer

B. The predicted net profit attributed to a customer over their entire relationship with a company

C. The average revenue per transaction

D. The return on investment (ROI) from a marketing campaign

Q3 Which theory suggests that firms must continuously adapt their analytics practices to remain competitive?

A. Resource-based view (RBV)

B. Technology acceptance model (TAM)

C. Dynamic capabilities theory

D. Balanced scorecard

Q4 Netflix's recommendation system is an example of which analytics application?

A. Data cleansing

B. Predictive analytics and personalization

C. Customer segmentation based on intuition

D. Regression analysis only

Q5 Which of the following is **not** a challenge in marketing analytics?

A. Data privacy and security

B. Data quality and integrity

C. Integration with business goals

D. Improved customer segmentation

Q6 Real-time marketing analytics provides businesses with which key advantage?

A. Reduced need for KPIs

B. Ability to adapt campaigns quickly to changing conditions

C. Eliminating the need for customer segmentation

D. Predicting competitor behaviour with certainty

Q7 According to Kotler and Keller (2016), one of the foundations of modern marketing analytics is:

A. Market research methods like sampling and regression

B. Artificial intelligence exclusively

C. Sales force automation tools

D. Social media monitoring only

EXERCISE

Mini-project/assignment: Applying marketing analytics concepts

Title

Analysing marketing performance data for strategic insights

Objective

To apply the concepts of marketing analytics by collecting, analysing and interpreting data from a real-world or simulated marketing scenario.

Instructions

- **Data collection:** Use either a dataset provided by the instructor (e.g. website traffic, sales transactions, social media engagement) or publicly available sources such as Google Analytics demo accounts, Kaggle datasets or simulated survey data.

- **Identify KPIs:** Define at least **three KPIs** relevant to marketing effectiveness (e.g. conversion rate, customer acquisition cost, customer lifetime value).

- **Segmentation analysis:** Segment the data into at least two groups (e.g. new vs returning customers, demographic groups or high-value vs low-value customers).

- **Trend analysis:**
  - Use simple visualization tools (Excel, Tableau, Google Data Studio or Power BI) to identify key trends.
  - Highlight **at least one actionable insight** (e.g. which channel is performing best, where drop-offs occur).

- **Recommendation report** (3–4 pages):
  - Summarize findings, KPIs and insights.
  - Provide **two recommendations** for improving marketing performance based on the analysis.

- **Deliverables:**
  - a short **report** (3–4 pages) with charts/visuals
  - a **presentation slide deck** (3–5 slides) summarizing insights and recommendations.

- **Assessment criteria:**
  - correct application of key marketing analytics concepts
  - ability to define and justify KPIs
  - clarity and accuracy of insights
  - practicality and relevance of recommendations
  - quality of data visualization.

READER'S CHECKLIST

What you can do after reading this chapter

- Define marketing analytics and explain its role in business strategy.
- Identify and measure at least three **key marketing KPIs**.

- Recognize the **historical evolution** of analytics and why it matters today.
- Discuss the **benefits and challenges** of applying analytics in organizations.
- Apply **theoretical frameworks** (RBV, dynamic capabilities, TAM) to understand analytics adoption.
- Use a case (like Netflix, Amazon or Google) to illustrate analytics in practice.
- Experiment with **basic tools** (Excel, Google Analytics, Tableau) to analyse data.
- Reflect on **ethical and privacy considerations** when handling customer data.
- **Expected outcome**: To apply theoretical knowledge to a practical business challenge, simulating how managers use analytics to solve real problems.

KEY TAKEAWAYS

- Marketing analytics is about using data to improve decision-making, not just reporting numbers.
- The discipline has evolved from intuition-based decisions to advanced AI-driven insights.
- Effective marketing analytics integrates **data collection, analysis** and **interpretation**.
- Benefits include improved ROI, customer retention, efficiency and competitive advantage.
- Challenges include **data quality, privacy, alignment with goals** and **organizational culture**.
- Future trends point towards **AI, big data, cross-channel analytics, predictive modelling** and **customer experience analytics**.
- Real-world examples (like Netflix) show that analytics impacts not only marketing campaigns but also **product strategy, personalization** and **customer loyalty**.

References

Barney, J (1991) Firm resources and sustained competitive advantage. *Journal of Management*, 17 (1), 99–120

Chaffey, D and Ellis-Chadwick, F (2019) *Digital Marketing: Strategy, Implementation, and Practice* (7th ed.), Harlow: Pearson Education

Davenport, T H and Harris, J G (2007) *Competing on Analytics: The New Science of Winning,* Boston, MA: Harvard Business Review Press

Davis, F D (1989) Perceived usefulness, perceived ease of use, and user acceptance of information technology, *MIS Quarterly*, 13 (3), 319–40

Gomez-Uribe, C A and Hunt, N (2016) The Netflix recommender system: Algorithms, business value, and innovation, *ACM Transactions on Management Information Systems*, 6 (4), 13

Hair, J F, Black, W C, Babin, B J and Anderson, R E (2019) *Multivariate Data Analysis* (8th ed.), Harlow: Pearson

Hanssens, D M, Pauwels, K H, Srinivasan, S, Vanhuele, M and Yildirim, G (2014) Consumer attitude metrics for guiding marketing mix decisions, *Marketing Science*, 33 (4), 534–50

Kaplan, R S and Norton, D P (1996) *The Balanced Scorecard: Translating Strategy into Action*, Boston, MA: Harvard Business School Press

Kotler, P and Keller, K L (2016) *Marketing Management* (15th ed.), Harlow: Pearson Education

Kumar, V, Aksoy, L, Donkers, B, Venkatesan, R, Wiesel, T and Tillmanns, S (2013) Undervalued or overvalued customers: Capturing total customer engagement value, *Journal of Service Research*, 13 (3) 297–310, doi.org/10.1177/1094670510375602 (archived at https://perma.cc/T5Z7-WP44)

Kumar, V and Rajan, B (2019) Marketing analytics: The bridge between customer psychology and marketing decisions, *Journal of the Academy of Marketing Science*, 47 (5), 1–14, doi.org/10.1007/s11747-019-00654-8 (archived at https://perma.cc/KV9G-UZ4X)

Lilien, G L, Rangaswamy, A and De Bruyn, A (2013) *Principles of Marketing Engineering and Analytics* (2nd ed.), State College, PA: DecisionPro

Rust, R T, Moorman, C and Bhalla, G (2010) Rethinking marketing, *Harvard Business Review*, 88 (1/2), 94–101

Sheth, J N and Sisodia, R S (2015) *Does Marketing Need Reform? Fresh Perspectives on the Future,* Abingdon: Routledge

Teece, D J, Pisano, G and Shuen, A (1997) Dynamic capabilities and strategic management, *Strategic Management Journal*, 18 (7), 509–33

Wedel, M and Kannan, P K (2016) Marketing analytics for data-rich environments, *Journal of Marketing*, 80 (6), 97–121, doi.org/10.1509/jm.15.0413 (archived at https://perma.cc/Y53F-B6XY)

02 | Data collection and measurement

Best practices for collecting, organizing and storing marketing data

---

LEARNING OUTCOMES

By the end of this chapter, students should be able to:

- Differentiate between primary, secondary, qualitative and quantitative marketing data.
- Apply best practices for accurate, ethical and compliant data collection.
- Design effective data collection plans aligned with business objectives.
- Understand principles of organizing and storing marketing data, including database design.
- Evaluate the role of CRM systems and marketing databases in enhancing insights.
- Analyse real-world cases of how brands use data to gain a competitive advantage.
- Apply ethical frameworks and legal standards (e.g. GDPR, CCPA) in data handling.

CHAPTER OUTLINE

2.1 Types of marketing data

2.2 Best practices for data collection

2.3 Organizing and storing marketing data

KEY TERMS

Anonymization: Removing personal identifiers from data to protect privacy while preserving analytical value.

Big data: Extremely large datasets requiring advanced processing technologies for insights.

Customer relationship management (CRM): Systems that track and organize customer interactions across multiple touchpoints.

Data integrity: Accuracy, consistency and reliability of data throughout its life cycle.

Data privacy: Protection of personal information in compliance with regulations like GDPR/CCPA.

Normalization: Database design process that reduces redundancy and improves data organization.

Primary data: Original data collected firsthand for a specific purpose (e.g. surveys, focus groups).

Qualitative data: Non-numeric insights (e.g. customer opinions, interviews, social media comments).

Quantitative data: Numeric, measurable data (e.g. sales figures, website traffic).

Secondary data: Pre-existing data collected by others (e.g. industry reports, government statistics).

2.1 Types of marketing data

In the realm of marketing analytics, data collection is the cornerstone of informed decision-making. The first step in this process involves categorizing data into two primary types: **primary** and **secondary** sources. **Primary data** is original and collected specifically for the research at hand. It allows marketers to gather insights directly related to their unique objectives. Methods for collecting primary data include surveys, interviews, focus groups and observations, all tailored to specific inquiries. For example, a company launching a new product might conduct focus groups to understand consumer preferences and pain points.

On the other hand, **secondary data** refers to information that has already been collected for other purposes, often found in reports, academic studies, industry statistics or databases. This data can save time and resources, as it is readily available; however, the challenge lies in ensuring its relevance and accuracy for the current marketing needs. For instance, a marketer might use industry reports to benchmark their product's performance against competitors. Understanding the differences between primary and secondary data sources aids marketers in creating a comprehensive strategy that leverages both forms effectively to maximize insights and improve decision-making.

Marketing data can also be classified as **qualitative** or **quantitative**. **Qualitative data** refers to non-numerical information that provides depth and context, enabling researchers to explore attitudes, opinions and motivations. Examples include open-ended survey responses, interview transcripts and social media comments. This type of data is valuable in understanding the 'why' behind consumer behaviours, offering a rich narrative that numbers alone cannot convey. For example, a qualitative analysis of customer feedback might reveal that users find a product difficult to use, even if sales numbers are strong.

Conversely, **quantitative data** is numerical and can be measured and analysed statistically. This includes sales figures, web traffic statistics and demographic information. By employing these quantitative measures, marketers can identify trends, forecast outcomes and validate hypotheses with statistical significance. For instance, a marketer might use web analytics to determine which online campaigns drive the most traffic and conversions. Both qualitative and quantitative data are essential in the marketing context; qualitative offers insights that can drive creative strategies, while quantitative provides the metrics needed for performance evaluation. Balancing the use of both data types empowers marketers to make well-rounded decisions based on a rich tapestry of information.

When embarking on a marketing project, it is beneficial to think about how these data types interrelate and can be integrated into a broader data collection strategy. For instance, gathering qualitative insights can inform the development of quantitatively measurable hypotheses, which can then be tested through surveys or A/B testing. By understanding the strengths and weaknesses of primary versus secondary data, along with qualitative and quantitative distinctions, marketers are better prepared to collect, analyse and leverage marketing data effectively. This foundational approach not only enhances the overall strategy but positions marketing efforts for greater efficacy in achieving business objectives.

2.2 Best practices for data collection

Outlining effective methodologies for accurate data capture from various sources is crucial for any marketing strategy. Data collection must commence with a clear understanding of the objectives and the specific information required to achieve them. This clarity ensures that the captured data is pertinent, minimizing the noise that can compromise analysis. One effective methodology is employing **mixed methods,** which combine qualitative and quantitative approaches. Qualitative data provides insights through interviews, focus groups or open-ended surveys, offering a nuanced understanding of consumer behaviour. Conversely, quantitative data, gathered through structured surveys or tracking tools, provides numerical insights that can be statistically analysed. For example, a company might use a combination of customer interviews (qualitative) and sales data (quantitative) to understand why a product is underperforming.

When designing data collection instruments such as surveys, it is vital to ensure questions are clear, unbiased and structured to elicit the most actionable responses. Additionally, leveraging technology – such as data analytics platforms and CRM systems – enhances the efficiency of collecting and organizing data from multiple sources, capturing interactions and behaviours across various touchpoints. For instance, a CRM system can track customer interactions across email, social media and in-store visits, providing a holistic view of the customer journey.

Ensuring **ethical practices** and compliance in data gathering processes is increasingly critical, especially with heightened scrutiny on data privacy. Organizations must adhere to regulations like the **General Data Protection Regulation (GDPR)** and the **California Consumer Privacy Act (CCPA),** which mandate transparency in data collection methods and require consent from individuals. Ethical data collection not only strengthens trust between consumers and brands but also enhances data integrity. Clearly communicating to participants what data is being collected, how it will be used, and the potential impact of their contributions is essential. Anonymization and aggregation of sensitive data are key strategies for protecting individual privacy while still yielding valuable insights. Training staff on ethical data collection practices helps maintain compliance and fosters a culture of integrity. Utilizing independent audits serves as a valuable mechanism for ensuring ongoing adherence to ethical standards, thereby reinforcing public trust.

TIP

A practical tip for effective data collection is to continuously evaluate and iterate on your data processes. This involves regularly reviewing methods and outcomes to identify potential areas for improvement. Conducting post-collection analyses helps ascertain the relevance and accuracy of the gathered data, while soliciting feedback from respondents can pinpoint issues in the collection methods that may need adjustments. Establishing a systematic approach to data collection not only improves current practices but also builds a robust framework for future marketing research initiatives.

2.3 Organizing and storing marketing data

Effective **database design** is essential for managing marketing data successfully. It requires a deep understanding of how data flows within a marketing organization. Before diving into design specifics, it is crucial to acknowledge that a well-structured database not only serves to store data but also enhances its accessibility and usability. The primary goal of database design in the context of marketing analytics is to ensure that data can be collected, processed and retrieved efficiently, allowing marketers to derive actionable insights. Core principles include **normalization**, which minimizes redundancy and dependency by organizing data into tables; using **primary keys** to maintain unique records; and establishing **relationships** between tables to ensure data integrity. For example, a product table may relate to a customer table through a foreign key that links purchases made by each customer, facilitating better tracking of buyer behaviour. This structured approach not only helps in creating a logical data flow but also enables marketers to adapt quickly to changing campaign needs. The underlying database schema must be scalable; as marketing strategies evolve and data volumes increase, so should the database's capacity and flexibility.

Data integrity and **security** are paramount in the storage of marketing analytics. The reliability of insights drawn from data is contingent upon the authenticity and consistency of that data. Ensuring data integrity means instituting rigorous validation checks during data entry, establishing protocols to avoid duplication, and routinely auditing data for accuracy. These measures enhance trust in the data, a crucial factor for decision-making. Security plays an equally critical role, especially when handling sensitive customer information. Organizations must implement robust security measures, such as encryption techniques, to safeguard data against unauthorized access, and **role-based access control** to limit data visibility according to user permissions. Regular backups and disaster recovery plans are vital components of data security, as they ensure data is recoverable in the event of system failures. By prioritizing data integrity and security, marketers can maintain a trustworthy foundation that supports analytical initiatives while minimizing risks associated with data breaches or inaccuracies.

Adopting best practices for organizing and storing marketing data is foundational to enhancing analytical capabilities. One effective strategy involves establishing a comprehensive data collection plan that accounts for both online and offline channels for new product launches. This plan should outline specific data points to be collected, such as customer demographics, purchase behaviours and campaign interactions. A simple yet effective database schema can outline key fields such as customer ID, name, contact information and purchase history, with clear relationships between the various tables that will store this information. Additionally, integrating **customer relationship management (CRM)** systems with marketing databases can provide a 360-degree view of customer interactions, ultimately driving better marketing strategies. In summary, best practices not only streamline data organization but also facilitate high-quality analytics, empowering marketers to leverage data effectively for decision-making and strategic planning.

2.4 Design a data collection plan for a new product launch

EXERCISE

Objective

Design a data collection plan for a new product launch, considering both online and offline channels.

1 **Define objectives**:
   o Understand customer preferences and pain points.
   o Measure the effectiveness of marketing campaigns.
   o Track sales performance across channels.

2 **Data sources**:
   o **Primary data:** Surveys, focus groups, in-store feedback forms.
   o **Secondary data:** Industry reports, competitor analysis, social media trends.

3 **Data collection methods**:
   o **Online:** Web analytics, social media listening, email surveys.
   o **Offline:** In-store purchase data, customer interviews, event feedback.

4 **Key metrics**:
   o Customer demographics, purchase frequency, campaign engagement, customer satisfaction.

5 **Tools**:
   o CRM systems, Google Analytics, social media monitoring tools.

Data collection plan for a new product launch (step by step)

To ensure the success of a new product launch, it is essential to collect data from both **online** and **offline channels**. This data will help in understanding customer behaviour, measuring campaign effectiveness and making informed decisions. The following is a detailed data collection plan.

1 Objectives of data collection

- **Understand customer preferences:** Identify what customers like/dislike about the product.
- **Measure campaign effectiveness:** Track the performance of marketing campaigns across channels.
- **Gather feedback for improvement:** Collect customer feedback to refine the product and marketing strategy.
- **Track sales performance:** Monitor sales data to evaluate the product's success.

2 Data collection methods

Online channels
- Website analytics:
  - **Tools:** Google Analytics, Hotjar.
  - **Data to collect:**
    - website traffic (visits, page views, bounce rate)
    - conversion rates (e.g., product page views to purchases)
    - user behaviour (time spent on site, click-through rates)
    - demographics (age, gender, location).
  - **Frequency:** Real-time monitoring with weekly reports.
- Social media platforms:
  - **Tools:** Facebook Insights, Instagram Analytics, Twitter Analytics.
  - **Data to collect:**
    - engagement metrics (likes, shares, comments)
    - reach and impressions/sentiment analysis (positive/negative feedback)
    - click-through rates on ads.
  - **Frequency:** Daily monitoring with weekly summaries.
- Email campaigns:
  - **Tools:** Mailchimp, HubSpot.

○ Data to collect:

- open rates and click-through rates

- conversion rates (e.g. email clicks to purchases)

- unsubscribe rates.

○ Frequency: After each email campaign.

- E-commerce platforms:

  ○ Tools: Shopify, WooCommerce.

  ○ Data to collect:

    - sales data (units sold, revenue)

    - cart abandonment rates

    - customer reviews and ratings.

  ○ Frequency: Daily monitoring with weekly summaries.

- Online surveys:

  ○ Tools: SurveyMonkey, Google Forms.

  ○ Data to collect:

    - customer satisfaction (e.g. Net Promoter Score)

    - product feedback (likes, dislikes, suggestions)

    - demographic information.

  ○ Frequency: Post-purchase surveys and periodic feedback collection.

Offline channels

- In-store sales data:

  ○ Tools: Point of sale (POS) systems.

  ○ Data to collect:

    - sales volume and revenue

    - popular product variants (e.g. colours, sizes)

    - customer demographics (if collected at checkout).

  ○ Frequency: Daily monitoring with weekly summaries.

- Customer feedback forms:

  ○ Tools: Paper forms or digital kiosks in-store.

  ○ Data to collect:

    - customer satisfaction

- product feedback
- suggestions for improvement.
  - ○ **Frequency:** Continuous collection with weekly analysis.
- **Focus groups:**
  - ○ **Tools:** In-person or virtual focus group sessions.
  - ○ **Data to collect:**
    - detailed feedback on product features
    - emotional response to the product
    - suggestions for improvement.
  - ○ **Frequency:** Conducted before and after the launch.
- **Event tracking:**
  - ○ **Tools:** Event attendance logs, surveys.
  - ○ **Data to collect:**
    - number of attendees
    - engagement levels (e.g. interactions with the product)
    - feedback collected during the event.
  - ○ **Frequency:** Post-event analysis.

3 Key metrics to track

- Online metrics:
  - ○ website traffic and conversion rates
  - ○ social media engagement and reach
  - ○ email campaign performance
  - ○ e-commerce sales and cart abandonment rates
  - ○ customer satisfaction scores (from surveys).
- Offline metrics:
  - ○ in-store sales data
  - ○ customer feedback scores
  - ○ focus group insights
  - ○ event attendance and engagement.

4 Data collection timeline

Phase	Activities	Timeline
Pre-launch	Conduct focus groups, set up analytics tools and prepare surveys	1–2 months before launch
Launch week	Monitor real-time data from online and offline channels	During launch week
Post-launch	Analyse sales data, conduct surveys and gather feedback from events	1–3 months after launch

5 Data analysis and reporting

- **Tools:** Excel, Tableau, Power BI.
- **Analysis:**
  - Compare online vs offline sales performance.
  - Identify trends in customer feedback.
  - Measure the ROI of marketing campaigns.
- **Reporting:**
  - weekly performance dashboards
  - monthly detailed reports with actionable insights.

6 Actionable Insights

- **Product improvements:** Use customer feedback to refine product features.
- **Marketing adjustments:** Optimize campaigns based on engagement and conversion data.
- **Inventory management:** Adjust stock levels based on sales trends.
- **Customer retention:** Implement strategies to address negative feedback and improve satisfaction.

EXAMPLE DATA COLLECTION PLAN WORKFLOW

- **Pre-launch:**
  - Set up Google Analytics and social media tracking.
  - Design and distribute online surveys to gather initial feedback.
  - Conduct focus groups to test product concepts.

- **Launch week**:
  - o Monitor website traffic and social media engagement in real time.
  - o Track in-store sales and collect feedback forms.
  - o Host launch events and collect attendee feedback.
- **Post-launch**:
  - o Analyse sales data and customer feedback.
  - o Generate reports and share insights with stakeholders.
  - o Implement changes based on feedback and performance data.

This data collection plan ensures a comprehensive understanding of the new product's performance across both online and offline channels, enabling data-driven decision-making for future strategies.

2.5 Model: Simple database schema for storing customer data

The following example is a simple database schema designed to store customer data, including key fields and relationships. The schema consists of three main tables: **customers**, **orders**, and **products** (Tables 2.1–2.3). These tables are related through primary and foreign keys to ensure data integrity and facilitate efficient querying. See Figure 2.1 for a summary.

Table 2.1   Customers table

Field name	Data type	Description
Customer ID	INT (Primary key)	Unique identifier for each customer
FirstName	VARCHAR (50)	Customer's first name
LastName	VARCHAR (50)	Customer's last name
Email	VARCHAR (100)	Customer's email address
Phone	VARCHAR (15)	Customer's phone number
Address	VARCHAR (255)	Customer's address
City	VARCHAR (100)	Customer's city
State	VARCHAR (50)	Customer's state or region
PostalCode	VARCHAR (20)	Customer's postal code
Country	VARCHAR (50)	Customer's country
Date joined	DATETIME	Date the customer joined the platform

This table stores basic customer information.

Table 2.2 Orders table

Field name	Data type	Description
Order ID	INT (Primary key)	Unique identifier for each order
Customer ID	INT (Foreign key)	Links to the Customer ID in the Customers table
Order date	DATETIME	Date the order was placed
Total Amount	DECIMAL (10, 2)	Total amount of the order
Status	VARCHAR (50)	Status of the order (e.g. Pending, Shipped, Delivered)

This table stores information about customer orders.

Table 2.3 Products table

Field name	Data type	Description
Product ID	INT (Primary key)	Unique identifier for each product
ProductName	VARCHAR (100)	Name of the product
Description	TEXT	Description of the product
Price	DECIMAL (10, 2)	Price of the product
Stock Quantity	INT	Quantity of the product in stoc
Category	VARCHAR (50)	Category of the product (e.g. Clothing, Accessories)

This table stores information about products available for purchase.

Table 2.4 Order details table

Field name	Data type	Description
Order Detail ID	INT (Primary key)	Unique identifier for each order detail
Order ID	INT (Foreign key)	Links to the Order ID in the Orders table
Product ID	INT (Foreign key)	Links to the Product ID in the Products table
Quantity	INT	Quantity of the product ordered
Unit Price	DECIMAL (10, 2)	Price of the product at the time of ordering

The order details table (Table 2.4) stores details about the products in each order.

Figure 2.1   Visual representation of the database schema

___

Visual representation of the schema

```
Customers (1) → (Many) Orders (1) → (Many) OrderDetails (Many) ← (1) Products
```

Example queries

1. Retrieve all orders for a specific customer:

```sql
SELECT Orders.OrderID, Orders.OrderDate, Orders.TotalAmount
FROM Orders
JOIN Customers ON Orders.CustomerID = Customers.CustomerID
WHERE Customers.CustomerID = 1;
```

2. Retrieve all products in a specific order:

```sql
SELECT Products.ProductName, OrderDetails.Quantity, OrderDetails.UnitPrice
FROM OrderDetails
JOIN Products ON OrderDetails.ProductID = Products.ProductID
WHERE OrderDetails.OrderID = 101;
```

3. Calculate the total revenue generated by a customer:

```sql
SELECT Customers.CustomerID, SUM(Orders.TotalAmount) AS TotalRevenue
FROM Customers
JOIN Orders ON Customers.CustomerID = Orders.CustomerID
WHERE Customers.CustomerID = 1
GROUP BY Customers.CustomerID;
```

Relationships between tables

- Customers → Orders:
  - A customer can place multiple orders.
  - Relationship: One-to-many (Customer ID in the **Customers** table links to Customer ID in the **Orders** table).
- Orders → Order details:
  - An order can include multiple products.
  - Relationship: One-to-many (Order ID in the **Orders** table links to Order ID in the **Order details** table).
- Products → Order details:
  - A product can appear in multiple orders.
  - Relationship: One-to-many (Product ID in the **Products** table links to Product ID in the **Order details** table).

2.6 Frameworks and theoretical perspectives

Figure 2.2   Frameworks and theories in marketing analytics

Frameworks and Theories

Total Quality Data Management (TQDM)
Emphasizes systematic procedures to ensure high-quality, reliable data

Technology Acceptance Model (TAM)
Explains adoption of CRM and analytics platforms by marketing teams

Information Systems Success Model
(DeLone and McLean, 2003)
Links system quality and information quality to business value

Dynamic Capabilitles Theory
(Teece et al, 1997)
Organizations must reconfigure their data collection and storage processes to adapt to evolving markets

Resource-Based View (RBV)
(Barney, 1991)
Data as a valuable, rare, inimitable and non-substitutable (VRIN) organizational resource

REAL-WORLD EXAMPLE   Starbucks – customer data and personalization

Starbucks has mastered data collection and organization through its **loyalty programme** and **mobile app**.

- **Data collection**: Every mobile order, loyalty swipe and in-app purchase generates structured transactional data. In addition, customer reviews and social media mentions provide qualitative insights.

- **Integration**: Data flows into Starbucks' centralized CRM, which merges online and offline transactions for a **360-degree customer view**.

- **Usage**: Analytics teams segment customers by purchase frequency, location and product preferences. Starbucks then sends personalized offers – like discounts on favourite drinks – to increase engagement.

- **Impact**: This data-driven personalization significantly boosts **customer lifetime value (CLV)** and retention, while also optimizing inventory by predicting demand patterns.

- **Takeaway**: Effective data collection and storage empower Starbucks to transform raw customer interactions into actionable insights, driving sales and loyalty.

EXERCISE

Brand data challenge

Scenario

Nike launches a new sneaker line. As the data analyst, you are tasked to design a **data collection and organization plan**.

Tasks

1 Identify at least **three primary** and **two secondary** data sources Nike should use.

2 Distinguish between **qualitative** and **quantitative** data for this launch.

3 Propose a **simple database schema** (tables and key fields) to store this data.

4 Suggest one tool (CRM, Google Analytics, Tableau, etc.) for visualization.

Conclusion

This chapter emphasized the importance of accurate data collection and management as the foundation of marketing analytics. Students explored the distinctions between primary vs secondary and qualitative vs quantitative data. Best practices highlighted the need for **clarity of objectives, ethical compliance** and **integration of multiple methods**.

The chapter also covered data organization principles, including structured database design, data integrity and security protocols. Real cases, like Starbucks, demonstrated how brands translate raw data into personalization and loyalty strategies. The exercise and model schema illustrated how marketing organizations can build practical systems for storing and analyzing customer data. Ultimately, effective data practices transform information into strategic value, positioning firms for agility, trust and long-term success.

QUESTIONS

Discussion questions

1 Compare and contrast primary and secondary data in terms of accuracy, cost and application in marketing analytics.

2 Why is it essential for organizations to balance qualitative and quantitative data? Give an example.

3 What role does data integrity play in ensuring the success of marketing analytics?

4 How can compliance with GDPR/CCPA affect data collection strategies?

5 Using the Starbucks case, explain how CRM integration can enhance customer experience.

6 What organizational challenges arise when implementing structured database systems for marketing data?

EXERCISE

Multiple-choice quiz

Q1 Which of the following is an example of secondary data?

A. Customer interviews

B. Industry reports

C. Focus groups

D. In-store observations

Q2 Qualitative data is best used to understand:

A. Sales revenue trends

B. Customer attitudes and motivations

C. Conversion rates

D. Website traffic

Q3 Which principle of database design reduces redundancy and improves data organization?

A. Encryption

B. Normalization

C. Personalization

D. Aggregation

Q4 Starbucks uses loyalty card and app data to segment customers. This is an example of:

A. Primary qualitative data

B. Secondary quantitative data

C. Primary quantitative data

D. Secondary qualitative data

Q5 GDPR and CCPA primarily concern:

A. Data visualization

B. Data security and privacy

C. Database design

D. Data normalization

EXERCISE

Mini-project/assignment: Designing a marketing data management system for a retail brand

Objective

Apply best practices for collecting, organizing and storing marketing data.

Instructions

- Select a brand (real or simulated).
- Identify at least **five data sources** (mix of primary/secondary, qualitative/ quantitative).
- Create a **data collection plan** outlining tools, frequency and metrics.
- Design a **basic database schema** (customers, orders, products, interactions).
- Propose **two measures to ensure data integrity** and **two for data security**.
- Submit a **short report** (4–5 pages) with diagrams, schema tables and recommendations.

Deliverables

- o Report with collection plan and schema
- o Simple **ER diagram** or relational schema.

Assessment criteria

- o Clarity of data classification (primary/secondary, qualitative/quantitative)
- o Alignment with marketing objectives
- o Practicality and scalability of schema design
- o Consideration of privacy, ethics and compliance
- o Professionalism of report and visuals.

KEY TAKEAWAYS

- I can distinguish between primary vs secondary and qualitative vs quantitative data.
- I know how to design surveys and instruments to capture accurate, unbiased data.
- I understand ethical and legal compliance (GDPR, CCPA).
- I can explain the importance of database design (normalization, primary/foreign keys).
- I can evaluate tools like CRM, Google Analytics and Tableau in data collection/ storage.
- I can design a basic data collection plan for a new product launch.
- I can critically assess real brand examples (Starbucks, Nike).
- I recognize data integrity and security as non-negotiable in analytics success.

References

Barney, J B (1991) Firm resources and sustained competitive advantage, *Journal of Management*, 17 (1), 99–120

CCPA (2020) California Consumer Privacy Act, oag.ca.gov/privacy/ccpa (archived at https:// perma.cc/DY29-DAWV)

DeLone, W H and McLean, E R (2003) The DeLone and McLean model of information systems success: A ten-year update, *Journal of Management Information Systems*, 19 (4), 9–30

GDPR (2018) General Data Protection Regulation, gdpr-info.eu (archived at https://perma. cc/DK2D-25L3)

Teece, D J, Pisano, G and Shuen, A (1997) Dynamic capabilities and strategic management, *Strategic Management Journal*, 18 (7), 509–533

03 | Key marketing metrics

LEARNING OUTCOMES

By the end of this chapter, students should be able to:

- Classify and explain the major categories of marketing performance metrics.
- Analyse and interpret key marketing metrics to derive actionable insights.
- Apply frameworks such as AIDA to trace customer journeys using metrics.
- Calculate customer lifetime value (CLTV) accurately using a structured method.
- Employ marketing metrics for strategic decision-making and budget allocation.
- Understand best practices for data-driven marketing analytics and optimization.

KEY TERMS

Acquisition metrics: Indicators measuring the ability to attract new customers, including traffic sources, cost per lead (CPL) and new user sign-ups.

Attribution metrics: Measurements linking conversions to specific marketing touchpoints, helping marketers optimize resource allocation.

Balanced scorecard (BSC): A strategic framework developed by Kaplan and Norton (1992) to measure performance across four perspectives: financial, customer, internal processes and learning/innovation.

Churn rate: The percentage of customers lost during a given period, which complements retention and engagement analysis.

Conversion metrics: Metrics that assess the success of moving customers through the funnel, such as conversion rate, cost per acquisition (CPA) and revenue per visitor (RPV).

Customer acquisition cost (CAC): The average cost required to acquire a single new customer, encompassing advertising, marketing and sales expenses.

Customer lifetime value (CLV or CLTV): A prediction of the total value a customer contributes to a business over the course of their relationship (Gupta et al, 2006). It measures the long-term profitability of a customer across their entire relationship with the firm.

Engagement metrics: Measures of customer involvement and interaction with a brand, e.g. average session duration, click-through rate (CTR), likes, shares and repeat visits.

Key performance indicators (KPIs): Quantifiable metrics used to evaluate performance against strategic objectives.

Net promoter score (NPS): A customer loyalty metric gauging how likely customers are to recommend a brand (Reichheld, 2003).

Return on marketing investment (ROMI): A financial KPI measuring the effectiveness of marketing spend in generating revenue.

Systems thinking: An approach that views organizations as interdependent systems, emphasizing the interconnectedness of metrics and outcomes.

Triple bottom line (TBL): A sustainability-oriented framework focusing on people, planet and profit.

3.1 Essential metrics for measuring performance

Understanding the classification of primary performance metrics relevant to marketing is crucial for any business aiming to refine its strategies and enhance overall performance (Chaffey and Ellis-Chadwick, 2022). These metrics can typically be divided into three main categories: **acquisition metrics, conversion metrics** and **engagement metrics**. Acquisition metrics help businesses assess how effectively they attract new customers into their sales funnel, capturing data such as the number of new leads generated through various channels, including social media, email campaigns and paid advertising (Kotler and Keller, 2016). Conversion metrics evaluate how well marketing efforts translate into tangible results, primarily focusing on the proportion of prospects who become paying customers. Lastly, engagement metrics measure the level of interaction between consumers and a brand, offering insights into the effectiveness of marketing content and campaigns. Each of these classifications plays a vital role in shaping marketing strategies and informing decisions that influence overall performance (Ryan, 2016).

Delving deeper into specific metrics, the conversion rate is one of the most critical indicators. This rate refers to the percentage of users who take a desired action, such as making a purchase, signing up for a newsletter or downloading a resource (Shankar and Bolton, 2004a). Marketers closely monitor this metric because a higher conversion rate typically signifies a more effective marketing strategy. Similarly, customer acquisition cost is another essential metric representing the total expenditure associated with acquiring new customers, encompassing spending on advertisements, promotions and marketing personnel. It is vital for businesses to keep this cost as low as possible while ensuring effective outreach. Finally, engagement levels quantify how actively customers interact with marketing content. High engagement often leads to greater brand loyalty and increased retention rates, rendering it an invaluable metric for understanding customer behaviour and preferences (Chaffey and Ellis-Chadwick, 2022).

By meticulously monitoring these essential metrics – such as conversion rates, acquisition costs and engagement levels – marketers can derive valuable insights that drive strategic improvements. These metrics enable informed decision-making that can significantly impact a business's bottom line. For example, if a company observes a low conversion rate, it may need to refine its messaging or user experience to better resonate with its audience. Conversely, high engagement levels may indicate that marketing efforts align well with consumer interests. Practically, marketers should consider implementing regular reporting routines to consistently track these metrics, empowering them to respond swiftly to trends that could affect performance outcomes (Ryan, 2016).

Theoretical frameworks for marketing metrics

Metrics classification framework

Marketing metrics are categorized into three primary areas: acquisition, conversion and engagement. Each plays a distinct role in measuring and guiding marketing effectiveness (Chaffey and Ellis-Chadwick, 2022; Kotler and Keller, 2016). See Figure 3.1.

The **Acquisition–Conversion–Engagement** model is a structured way to evaluate the customer journey (Chaffey and Ellis-Chadwick, 2022; Kotler and Keller, 2016).

- **Acquisition:** Measures new customer attraction (e.g. lead generation, traffic sources). Captures reach and awareness.
- **Conversion:** Assesses effectiveness in transforming leads into customers (e.g. conversion rates). Reflects decision-making and purchase behaviour.
- **Engagement:** Quantifies customer interaction and loyalty (e.g. social media engagement, website dwell time). Ensures long-term loyalty.

Balanced scorecard approach (Kaplan and Norton, 1996)

Marketing metrics can be framed within the balanced scorecard, ensuring a balance between:

- **financial outcomes** (e.g. ROI, CLV)
- **customer outcomes** (e.g. NPS, engagement)
- **internal processes** (e.g. campaign efficiency)
- **innovation and growth** (e.g. new customer acquisition, product adoption).

By understanding these categories, businesses can track the entire customer journey and fine-tune their marketing efforts accordingly.

3.2 Interpreting key marketing metrics

Deriving actionable insights from performance metrics requires a systematic evaluation of data. Marketers must surpass the mere collection of numbers by analysing and interpreting these figures to shape their strategies and inform decision-making. For example, understanding customer engagement rates can reveal which marketing campaigns resonate most with the target audience. Advanced statistical techniques, such as regression analysis, can uncover relationships between various metrics, enabling marketers to predict future outcomes based on historical performance. By continuously monitoring these performance indicators, marketers can adapt their tactics in real time, thereby optimizing their campaigns for enhanced results.

Figure 3.1   Marketing metrics classification framework

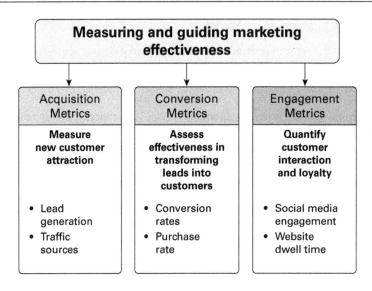

A practical illustration involves a digital marketing agency analysing click-through rates (a CTR is a measurement based on the number of clicks that your web page, email or online advertisement receives divided by the number of times your web page, email or online advertisement is shown [impressions]) for a client's email marketing campaign. Initially, a low CTR prompts the team to dig deeper. They examine subject lines, email design and timing of delivery. Through experimentation, they find that personalizing the subject line significantly boosts engagement. This modification not only elevates the CTR but also enhances conversion rates. Such scenarios underscore the importance of contextualizing metrics, as data alone lacks clarity without comprehensive analysis.

Furthermore, mapping the customer journey can be effectively achieved by integrating various metrics. Utilizing the Awareness, Interest, Desire, Action (AIDA) model allows marketers to track engagement at each funnel stage. By analysing specific metrics such as reach and impressions during the **awareness** phase and engagement rates during the **interest** stage, marketers can pinpoint drop-off points. This knowledge empowers them to make informed decisions regarding resource allocation and tailoring messaging to improve the customer experience throughout the purchasing process. Consequently, accurately interpreting metrics emerges as an essential skill in marketing analytics.

Key performance indicators (KPIs) such as customer acquisition cost (CAC), customer lifetime value (CLV) and conversion rates should be monitored consistently to ensure effective strategy adjustments. Best practices include regularly reviewing these metrics, employing A/B testing for campaign optimization, and utilizing data visualization tools for clearer insights (*Harvard Business Review*, 2020).

Framework/theory

Awareness, Interest, Desire, Action (AIDA) model

This is a foundational model in marketing analytics that maps the customer journey and identifies critical engagement points (Ryan, 2016). See Figure 3.2.

Application:

- **Awareness:** Reach, impressions (acquisition metrics).
- **Interest:** Click-through rates, video views, sign-ups (conversion precursors).
- **Desire:** Wishlist adds, product views, engagement depth, dwell time.
- **Action:** Purchases, sign-ups, conversion rate, revenue impact.

Interpretation best practices:

- Use **regression analysis** to find causal relationships between metrics.
- Employ **A/B testing** to optimize campaigns.
- Visualize metrics with dashboards for real-time strategy adjustment.

Figure 3.2   AIDA model

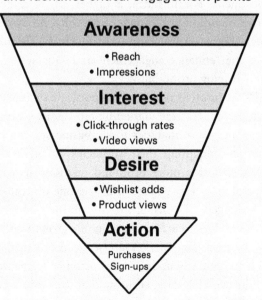

3.3 Customer lifetime value calculation

To effectively calculate customer lifetime value (CLTV), it is essential to follow a structured, step-by-step methodology that gives clarity and precision to the process. The first step involves determining the average purchase value, which can be worked out by dividing the total revenue generated from customer sales over a specific period by the number of purchases made during that time. Next, the average purchase frequency rate is calculated by dividing the total number of purchases by the total number of unique customers during the same timeframe. Then the average customer value is derived by multiplying the average purchase value by the average purchase frequency rate. The next pivotal step is estimating the average customer lifespan, which reflects how long customers typically continue to engage with the business. This lifespan is determined by averaging the retention time or duration customers stay active before churn. Finally, CLTV is calculated by multiplying the average customer value by the average customer lifespan. These calculations enable businesses to understand how much revenue they can expect from an average customer over their lifetime, providing a powerful metric for strategic planning and resource allocation. See Figure 3.3.

The implications of CLTV extend beyond mere calculations, impacting budgeting and marketing strategies significantly. By understanding the CLTV, organizations can make informed decisions regarding customer acquisition costs. If the CLTV of a customer exceeds the cost of acquiring them, it indicates a profitable customer relationship. This knowledge enables businesses to allocate resources more effectively, crafting marketing campaigns that are tailored to attract and retain high-value customers. Furthermore, insights from CLTV calculations can guide budget allocation, ensuring that funds are directed towards channels and strategies that yield the highest returns on investment. For instance, a higher CLTV might justify increased spending on customer retention programmes or loyalty initiatives. Notably, companies can also segment their customer base according to CLTV, allowing for bespoke marketing strategies that enhance engagement and satisfaction among high-value customers, ultimately driving profitability.

Calculating CLTV accurately not only supports financial forecasting but also serves as a cornerstone for strategic marketing efforts. By employing sophisticated tracking mechanisms and data analytics tools, businesses can continuously refine their CLTV estimations, adapting their strategies as market dynamics change. Understanding CLTV fosters a more profound relationship with customers, as it emphasizes the value of long-term engagement over one-off transactions. Ultimately, organizations that leverage CLTV insights to inform their budgeting and marketing strategies position themselves to achieve sustainable growth and maintain competitive advantage in an ever-evolving market landscape. A practical tip to enhance your CLTV calculations is to regularly update your customer segmentation and targeting strategies based on the evolving data, ensuring that they reflect current market conditions and customer behaviours.

Framework/theory

CLTV financial impact model

- **Average purchase value** = Total revenue ÷ Number of purchases
- **Average purchase frequency** = Number of purchases ÷ Unique customers
- **Customer value** = Average purchase value × Purchase frequency
- **Average customer lifespan** = Average retention duration
- **CLTV** = Customer value × Customer lifespan

Strategic implications:

- Aligns customer acquisition spending with expected returns.
- Drives segmentation strategies focused on high-value customers.
- Supports resource allocation across retention initiatives. (Figure 3.3.)

Figure 3.3   CLTV financial impact model

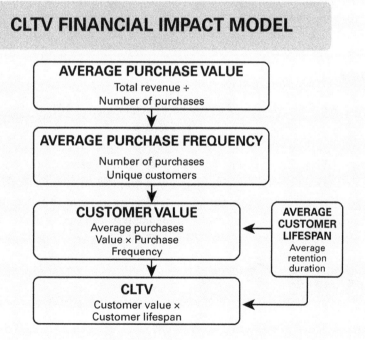

3.4 Deep dive into key metrics and KPIs in marketing analytics

In the realm of marketing analytics, the strategic use of key metrics and key performance indicators (KPIs) is foundational for evaluating and optimizing marketing performance. Metrics are quantifiable, time-sensitive indicators that reflect specific operational outcomes, whereas KPIs are strategically selected indicators that track performance relative to defined business objectives (Chaffey and Smith, 2017; Kotler et al, 2021).

Conversion rate: Measuring marketing efficiency

Conversion metrics

Conversion metrics evaluate how effectively prospects are converted into customers. Key measures include:

- **Conversion rate (CR):** The proportion of users who complete the desired action.
- **Cost per acquisition (CPA):** Average cost incurred to acquire a paying customer.
- **Revenue per visitor (RPV):** Revenue generated per website visitor.
- **Return on marketing investment (ROMI):** Ratio of revenue generated compared to marketing spend.

FORMULA

Conversion rate = (Number of conversions / Total visitors) × 100

A central KPI in digital campaigns, conversion rate measures how effectively traffic converts into action. A low conversion rate may signal friction in the user experience, such as poor interface design or unclear messaging (Kannan and Li, 2017). Strategies like A/B testing and multivariate analysis can optimize this metric.

EXAMPLE

Amazon

Amazon employs conversion metrics such as **purchase rate per session** and **A/B testing outcomes**. Small changes (e.g. button colours, checkout design) are tested for their impact on conversion rate, with metrics feeding into iterative optimization (McKinsey, 2019).

Customer acquisition cost (CAC): Evaluating marketing spend

Acquisition metrics

Acquisition metrics measure the effectiveness of efforts to bring prospects into the sales funnel. Key metrics include:

- **Traffic sources:** Helps assess where new users come from (organic search, paid ads, referrals, direct traffic).
- **Cost per lead (CPL):** The amount spent to generate a qualified lead.
- **Impressions and reach:** Indicators of awareness campaigns, particularly relevant for social media and display advertising.
- **Click-through rate (CTR):** Proportion of users who clicked on an ad or link after seeing it.

FORMULA

CAC = Total marketing and sales costs / Number of new customers acquired

---

CAC evaluates the efficiency of marketing investment. A sustainable CLV:CAC ratio is typically 3:1 or greater (Gupta and Lehmann, 2003). A high CAC may suggest inefficient campaigns, whereas a low CAC may reflect underinvestment in growth.

EXAMPLE

Starbucks

Starbucks leverages **mobile app referrals** and **loyalty sign-ups** as acquisition metrics. By tracking downloads and referral-driven new user registrations, Starbucks measures how effectively digital campaigns expand its customer base (Starbucks Investor Report, 2022).

Engagement metrics: Assessing content resonance

Engagement metrics

Engagement metrics provide insight into how customers interact with a brand post-conversion. Key indicators include:

- **Average session duration** and **pages per session**: Measures of customer interest.
- **Repeat purchase rate**: Frequency of returning customers.
- **Churn rate**: Percentage of customers lost.
- **Social media engagement**: Likes, shares, comments, brand mentions.
- **Net promoter score (NPS)**: Captures loyalty through recommendations.

Examples include:

- **Click-through rate (CTR)**: The percentage of users who click on a specific link, ad or call-to-action (CTA) compared to the total number of impressions or views.
- **Bounce rate**: The percentage of visitors who leave a website after viewing only one page without engaging further.
- **Average session duration**: The average amount of time users spends on a website during a single session, reflecting overall engagement.
- **Social media interaction rate**: The percentage of an audience that engages with social media content through likes, comments, shares or clicks relative to total followers or impressions.

Engagement metrics reveal how effectively content engages audiences (Tiago and Veríssimo, 2014). Persistent tracking enables strategic adjustments to maximize content resonance and audience retention.

EXAMPLE

Nike

Nike monitors **social engagement and app usage**. The **Nike Run Club app** tracks active users and integrates gamified experiences, boosting engagement and increasing retention. The brand correlates app activity with product purchases, enhancing lifetime value (Nike, 2025).

Return on marketing investment (ROMI): Linking effort to revenue

ROMI is a crucial performance indicator that quantifies the efficiency and profitability of marketing activities. Unlike general ROI, which measures overall business investment outcomes, ROMI specifically isolates marketing's contribution to revenue generation. It helps managers answer a fundamental question: Is the money spent on marketing producing proportional business returns?

FORMULA

ROMI = (Revenue from marketing – Marketing cost) / Marketing cost

---

A **high ROMI** indicates efficient campaign design, effective targeting and smart budget allocation, whereas a **low ROMI** highlights inefficiencies such as wasted ad spend, poor messaging or ineffective channels.

ROMI is also widely used by digital platforms such as **Google Ads** and **Meta Ads Manager,** which offer built-in ROMI or return on ad spend (ROAS) calculators. This empowers marketers to experiment with campaigns in real time and justify spend to financial stakeholders.

ROMI helps justify budgets and quantify the marginal value of marketing efforts (Hanssens and Pauwels, 2016). High ROMI signals efficient campaign design and budget allocation.

EXAMPLE

Procter & Gamble (P&G)

P&G applies ROMI across its extensive portfolio of consumer goods brands to decide where to allocate budgets among digital, television and retail media. When one campaign for Pampers in Europe underperformed, P&G used ROMI analysis to cut underperforming channels and reinvest in influencer and digital-first campaigns that significantly improved reach and engagement.

Customer lifetime value (CLTV): Long-term profitability

> **FORMULA**
>
> CLTV = Average purchase value × Purchase frequency × Customer lifespan

CLTV estimates the **net value a customer contributes to a business over the entire duration of their relationship.** Unlike short-term revenue metrics, CLTV emphasizes sustainable profitability and helps organizations balance acquisition with retention.

A **high CLTV** signals loyal, profitable customers who merit investment in retention, while a **low CLTV** suggests the need for better engagement strategies or product bundling to increase value per customer.

CLTV serves both forecasting and segmentation functions, guiding firms to focus on high-value customers and long-term strategic planning (Venkatesan and Kumar, 2004). It pairs effectively with CAC to evaluate customer profitability.

CLTV also pairs effectively with **customer acquisition cost (CAC)** to calculate the **CLTV/CAC ratio,** a measure of customer profitability. For instance, software-as-a-service (SaaS) companies like **HubSpot** or **Salesforce** rely on this ratio to ensure that lifetime revenues justify the high upfront costs of acquiring B2B clients.

> **EXAMPLE**
>
> Starbucks
>
> Starbucks has long used CLTV as a guiding metric for its rewards programme. By analysing purchase frequency, product mix and customer tenure, the company invests heavily in loyalty programmes that increase retention and transaction frequency. In 2023, its Starbucks Rewards programme accounted for **over 50 per cent of US revenue**, demonstrating the power of CLTV in driving sustainable growth.

Predictive analytics and KPI forecasting

As firms accumulate vast customer datasets, marketing performance measurement is moving beyond descriptive analytics towards **predictive analytics.** Machine learning enables businesses to forecast customer behaviours and market trends, improving strategic precision and ROI.

Marketers increasingly leverage machine learning to move from descriptive to predictive KPIs, such as the following.

Key predictive metrics

- **Churn probability**: Estimates the likelihood that a customer will discontinue engagement or subscription.
  - Example: Spotify applies churn prediction to identify users at risk of cancelling premium subscriptions and re-engages them with personalized playlists or promotional offers.
- **Lead scoring**: Assigns a probability score to prospects based on demographics, online behaviour and historical data.
  - Example: Salesforce uses predictive lead scoring to help B2B clients prioritize sales outreach by ranking leads most likely to convert.
- **Purchase intent**: Predicts how likely a customer is to buy a product in the near future, based on browsing behaviour, clicks or search terms.

EXAMPLE

Amazon

Amazon employs purchase intent forecasting in its recommendation engine, surfacing products most relevant to individual customers, driving **up to 35 per cent of its revenue** (McKinsey, 2022).

These approaches enhance targeting and improve campaign precision, enabling proactive strategy development (Wedel and Kannan, 2016). See Figure 3.4 for a summary.

EXERCISE

Scenario

A retail fashion brand like H&M wants to optimize its marketing spend.

- Task 1: Calculate **ROMI** for its latest Instagram campaign that generated €2 million in revenue at a cost of €400,000.
- Task 2: Estimate **CLTV** for a customer segment with an average purchase value of €50, buying frequency of 12 times per year and an average lifespan of five years.

- Task 3: Use churn prediction to design a retention campaign for customers who have not purchased in the last 90 days.

Reflection questions

- How does the CLTV/CAC ratio influence whether the brand should invest more in acquisition or retention?
- How can predictive analytics reshape decisions about seasonal product launches?

Figure 3.4 Conversion rate: Measuring marketing efficiency

Conversion metrics

CONVERSION RATE
The proportion of users who complete the desired action

(Number of conversions / Number of visitors) × 100

Amazon: Small changes to website, such as button colours, are tested for their impact on conversion rates

Acquisition metrics

CUSTOMER ACQUISITION COST
Average cost incurred to acquire a paying customer

Total marketing and sales costs
Number of new customers acquired

Starbucks tracks app downloads and referral sign-ups to expand its customer base

Engagement metrics

Click-through rate
Bounce rate
Average session duration
Social media interaction rate

RETURN ON MARKETING INVESTMENT (ROMI)
(Revenue from marketing – marketing cost) / Marketing cost

Predictive analytics

CUSTOMER LIFETIME CYCLE (CTC)	PREDICTIVE ANALYTICS
(Average purchase value × purchase frequency × gross margin) × Customer lifetime	• Churn probability • Lead scoring • Purchase intent

P&G uses ROMI analysis to invest in loyalty programme initiatives

3.5 Theoretical and practical implications of KPI measurement and the balanced scorecard

Theoretical implications

The **balanced scorecard framework** (Kaplan and Norton, 1992) supports the selection and interpretation of KPIs across customer, financial, operational and innovation dimensions. Practically, modern dashboards like **Google Analytics** and **Tableau** allow real-time monitoring for more agile decision-making (Chaffey and Ellis-Chadwick, 2019).

The measurement of marketing performance through metrics and key performance indicators (KPIs) has long been rooted in both managerial accounting and strategic management theory. A central theoretical implication is that KPIs do not simply measure performance in isolation; rather, they serve as a bridge between organizational strategy and operational execution. This is precisely the perspective advanced by Kaplan and Norton (1992) in their Balanced Scorecard (BSC) framework, which emphasizes that relying solely on financial outcomes is inadequate for driving long-term performance. Instead, organizations must also measure and manage dimensions such as customer satisfaction, internal operational processes, and innovation and learning capabilities.

From a theoretical standpoint, the balanced scorecard embodies the **resource-based view (RBV)** of the firm (Barney, 1991), which argues that sustainable competitive advantage emerges from leveraging valuable, rare and inimitable resources. By systematically tracking performance across multiple dimensions – financial, customer, internal and innovation – the BSC allows firms to link their intangible resources (e.g. brand equity, customer relationships, organizational learning) to tangible outcomes such as revenue growth and profitability.

In marketing, this multidimensional view is critical because the drivers of brand success and customer loyalty extend beyond financial efficiency. Engagement, customer trust and innovation in product/service design must all be measured and aligned. KPIs, such as net promoter score (NPS), customer lifetime value (CLTV) and return on marketing investment (ROMI), directly relate to the 'customer' and 'financial' dimensions of the balanced scorecard, while metrics like campaign conversion rate, lead time for new product launches or marketing innovation adoption map onto the 'internal process' and 'innovation' dimensions.

Another theoretical implication lies in the alignment between **stakeholder theory** (Freeman, 1984) and the balanced scorecard. Marketing metrics influence and are influenced by multiple stakeholders: customers (through engagement and satisfaction), shareholders (through ROMI and CLTV), employees (through learning and innovation metrics) and society (through sustainability-related KPIs). By adopting a balanced framework, organizations can ensure that their KPI systems capture value creation for multiple stakeholder groups, rather than privileging only short-term shareholder gains.

Finally, **systems theory** (Bertalanffy, 1968) reinforces the idea that organizations function as interconnected systems. Marketing performance metrics must therefore be interpreted holistically rather than in isolation. A high conversion rate, for example, may appear favourable, but if it is accompanied by rising customer acquisition costs (CAC) or high churn, the system as a whole may be under stress. Balanced scorecard theory emphasizes the interdependence of KPIs and prevents organizations from optimizing single metrics at the expense of overall strategic coherence.

Practical implications

The practical implications of adopting a balanced scorecard approach to marketing performance measurement are equally profound. The framework provides a structured methodology for translating strategy into measurable outcomes, ensuring alignment between day-to-day marketing activities and long-term organizational goals.

Strategic alignment and clarity

By structuring metrics within the four perspectives (financial, customer, internal processes, innovation/learning), the balanced scorecard ensures that marketing KPIs are not chosen arbitrarily but are directly aligned with strategic objectives. For instance, if an organization's strategy is customer intimacy, then metrics such as CLTV, NPS and customer engagement scores will be prioritized. Conversely, a cost-leadership strategy may emphasize acquisition cost efficiency and operational KPIs.

Integration with marketing dashboards

The advent of marketing analytics platforms such as Google Analytics, Tableau and Power BI has made it possible to operationalize the balanced scorecard in real time. Instead of static quarterly reports, organizations can now design dynamic dashboards that track conversion rates, ROMI and engagement alongside operational and innovation metrics. This agility allows for faster decision-making and continuous optimization of campaigns (Chaffey and Ellis-Chadwick, 2019).

Cross-functional learning

Practically, the balanced scorecard fosters collaboration across departments. For instance, the marketing department's performance is not only judged by leads generated but also by its contribution to customer retention (customer perspective), process efficiency (internal perspective) and innovation (learning perspective). This shared responsibility encourages a culture of accountability and continuous improvement across teams such as marketing, sales, product development and finance.

Sustainability and ethical marketing

A further implication is the ability to integrate non-financial, socially oriented KPIs. In line with the triple bottom line (TBL) framework (Elkington, 1997), modern balanced scorecards increasingly incorporate sustainability metrics, such as carbon impact of campaigns, proportion of sustainable product sales or diversity in marketing representation. These align marketing accountability with broader corporate social responsibility goals, enhancing brand equity and consumer trust.

REAL-WORLD EXAMPLES

Coca-Cola

Coca-Cola has implemented a balanced scorecard approach across multiple business units to align marketing and operational strategies. In practice, this means monitoring financial KPIs (e.g. global revenue per region), customer KPIs (e.g. brand preference surveys, engagement with 'Share a Coke' campaigns), process KPIs (e.g. speed of campaign rollout in different markets) and innovation KPIs (e.g. adoption of new digital platforms and eco-friendly packaging initiatives). This holistic approach allows Coca-Cola to adjust not only pricing or promotions but also supply chain and innovation strategies to maintain its competitive global position.

Unilever

Unilever has integrated balanced scorecard principles into its sustainable living plan. Here, marketing metrics are directly tied to sustainability KPIs, such as consumer perceptions of eco-friendly product lines and the percentage of sales derived from 'sustainable brands'. By embedding these into the BSC, Unilever demonstrates how marketing can drive both profitability and social impact, showcasing the practicality of a multidimensional approach.

Netflix and engagement metrics

Netflix provides a practical demonstration of how engagement metrics directly connect to business performance. Instead of focusing solely on acquisitions, Netflix places emphasis on viewer engagement, measured through watch time, churn rate and algorithm-driven recommendations. Data-driven personalization reduces churn and increases customer lifetime value (CLV), demonstrating that engagement metrics can be equally important as acquisition or conversion (Gomez-Uribe and Hunt, 2016).

Airbnb and acquisition plus conversion

Airbnb employs sophisticated attribution models to monitor acquisition channels (paid search, social, referral). It uses CPA and first-to-book conversion rate to determine how many new visitors transition to booked reservations. This insight led Airbnb to reallocate budget from generic search ads to influencer-driven campaigns, significantly lowering acquisition costs (Airbnb Investor Relations, 2021).

EXERCISE

Scenario

A retail fashion brand (Zara) wants to measure campaign performance across acquisition, conversion and engagement.

Task

1 Calculate customer acquisition cost (CAC) by dividing total campaign spend ($200,000) by the number of new customers acquired (10,000).

2 Track conversion rate: Out of 50,000 website visitors, 5,000 make purchases.

3 Monitor engagement: Average session duration increases from 2.5 minutes to 4 minutes after a website redesign.

Questions

- What is Zara's CAC?
- How effective was the website redesign in improving engagement?
- If revenue per visitor is $25, what is the total revenue impact from conversions?

Limitations of marketing metrics

- **Attribution issues:** Difficulty assigning credit across channels.
- **Over-reliance on vanity metrics:** Likes and impressions may not translate into business outcomes (Kaushik, 2010).
- **Short-term bias:** Metrics often prioritize immediate ROI over long-term brand equity.
- **Privacy challenges:** Regulations, such as GDPR, limit the use of some data-driven metrics.

3.6 Exercises and mini real-world examples

EXERCISE ⤴

Metric identification – Nike

Nike – 'You Can't Stop Us' campaign

- **Official campaign page**: Nike: You Can't Stop Us (www.nike.com/you-cant-stop-us)
- **Campaign video**: Search – Nike: You Can't Stop Us on YouTube

Task

Select a real online marketing campaign from a global or local brand. For this exercise, consider Nike's 'You Can't Stop Us' campaign, which ran across digital platforms (YouTube, Instagram, email marketing and Nike's e-commerce site). Your task is to identify one key metric for each of the following categories:

- acquisition
- conversion
- engagement.

Deliverable

Using Nike's campaign as a reference, briefly explain:

- which metric you selected for each category
- why it is relevant to the campaign
- how this metric could inform and improve Nike's ongoing or future campaign strategies.

Example response

- **Acquisition metric**: Video impressions (YouTube/Instagram)
  - **Why?** Impressions indicate how many users saw the video content, making it an important top-of-funnel indicator of Nike's reach.
  - **How to use it**: If impressions are high but other metrics (e.g. CTR) are low, Nike might reconsider its targeting or creative format to appeal better to its desired audience.
- **Conversion metric**: Add-to-cart rate (on Nike.com)
  - **Why?** This metric shows how many visitors moved from browsing to taking an intent-driven action on the website.

- o **How to use it**: A low add-to-cart rate relative to traffic might suggest that the product landing page lacks persuasive content or that pricing is a barrier.
- **Engagement metric**: Instagram shares and comments
  - o **Why?** Shares and comments demonstrate deep engagement – viewers are not just watching the content but also reacting to and amplifying it.
  - o **How to use it**: High engagement may prompt Nike to boost the post or create a follow-up campaign using similar themes (e.g. inclusivity, athletic perseverance).

EXERCISE

Fixing a low CTR – H&M

H&M – Conscious Collection (Sustainable Fashion)

- **Sustainability overview**: H&M Sustainability (www2.hm.com/en_us/sustainability-at-hm.html)
- **Conscious Collection Launch**: H&M Conscious Collection Launch (about.hm.com/news/general-news-2019/h-m-s-conscious-collection-launches-worldwide-with-a-sustainable.html)

Background

H&M launched a sustainable fashion email campaign promoting its Conscious Collection. Despite a 28 per cent open rate, the click-through rate (CTR) remained at 1.4 per cent, suggesting ineffective in-email content.

Open rate: Measures the percentage of delivered emails that recipients actually opened.

Formula: Open rate = (Number of emails opened / Number of emails delivered) × 100

Example:

- Emails sent = 10,000
- Emails bounced (undelivered) = 500
- Emails delivered = 9,500
- Emails opened = 2,850

Open rate = (2,850/9,500) × 100 = 30%

Click-through rate (CTR): Measures the percentage of delivered emails (or impressions in ads) that generated a click on at least one link.

Formula: CTR = (Number of clicks / Number of emails delivered) × 100

Example (email campaign):

- Emails delivered = 9,500
- Clicks on links = 475

CTR = (475/9,500) × 100 = 5%

Open rate shows how many people viewed the email.

CTR shows how many people engaged further by clicking.

Scenario

You are on H&M's marketing team. The CTA is generic ('Shop Now') and the content lacks personalization.

Tasks

1 Design an A/B test plan to try at least two CTA variations.
2 Predict how personalization might affect CTR and conversions.
3 Identify additional metrics to track (e.g. scroll depth, bounce rate).

Suggested response

- A/B test: Compare 'Explore eco looks' vs 'Get 10% off sustainable styles'.
  - o Expected impact: Personal and value-driven CTAs may increase CTR.
- Additional metrics: Post-click bounce rate, time-on-page and add-to-cart rate.

EXERCISE

Calculate CLTV – Spotify

Spotify – Premium subscription

- Premium plans: Spotify Premium (www.spotify.com/us/premium)

- Individual plan details: Spotify Premium Individual (support.spotify.com/us/article/premium-individual)

Task

Given the following information for a subscription service: Spotify, use Spotify Premium data to calculate CLTV:

- average monthly spend per user: $10
- billing frequency: 12 times/year
- customer lifespan: three years
- CAC: $100.

Questions

1 Calculate CLTV.

2 Evaluate if the customer relationship is profitable.

3 How could Spotify use CLTV in strategic decisions?

Suggested calculation

- CLTV = $10 × 12 × 3 = $360
- Profitability: Yes, since CLTV ($360) > CAC ($100)
- Strategic use: Target loyalty programmes, tiered pricing and retention incentives.

Conclusion

Chapter 3 has demonstrated that marketing metrics are far more than numerical indicators; they are strategic tools that enable organizations to align their marketing efforts with broader business objectives. By classifying metrics into acquisition, conversion and engagement, marketers can systematically trace the customer journey from awareness through to retention, ensuring that decisions are based on evidence rather than assumptions (Chaffey and Ellis-Chadwick, 2022; Kotler and Keller, 2016). Each category of metrics serves a distinct purpose: acquisition metrics assess the ability to attract new customers, conversion metrics evaluate the efficiency of turning prospects into buyers, and engagement metrics illuminate the depth of customer-brand interaction, loyalty and advocacy.

A key contribution of this chapter has been its integration of theoretical frameworks with practical application. The AIDA model provided a lens to link marketing metrics to stages of the consumer decision process, while the balanced scorecard

(Kaplan and Norton, 1992, 1996) demonstrated how performance measurement must extend beyond financial outcomes to encompass customer satisfaction, internal efficiency and innovation. These frameworks underscore the notion that marketing success is multidimensional and requires systems thinking (Bertalanffy, 1968) to capture interdependencies between short-term campaign outcomes and long-term brand equity.

Equally, the chapter emphasized financial metrics such as lifetime value (CLTV), customer acquisition cost (CAC) and return on marketing investment (ROMI), which allow firms to assess profitability at both the customer and portfolio levels (Gupta and Lehmann, 2003; Hanssens and Pauwels, 2016). Their integration into strategy enables companies to achieve a sustainable balance between growth and efficiency. Real-world examples such as Amazon's use of conversion optimization, Starbucks' loyalty-driven acquisition strategies, and P&G's deployment of ROMI for budget allocation illustrate how leading firms operationalize these concepts for competitive advantage. Furthermore, emerging applications of predictive analytics – such as churn probability, purchase intent and lead scoring – highlight a shift from descriptive metrics to forward-looking key performance indicators (Wedel and Kannan, 2016).

The practical implications for managers are substantial. Marketing teams must adopt regular reporting and data visualization practices to ensure that insights are accessible and actionable. Dashboards in platforms such as Google Analytics, Tableau or Power BI allow organizations to monitor real-time performance across acquisition, conversion and engagement dimensions, thereby enabling agile adjustments to campaigns. At the same time, managers must avoid the pitfalls of over-relying on vanity metrics or optimizing for short-term ROI at the expense of long-term brand value (Kaushik, 2010).

Finally, the chapter identified limitations and challenges, including attribution bias, data privacy constraints, and the need for interpretability in advanced models. These challenges call for a responsible and balanced approach to measurement – one that incorporates not only financial returns but also ethical and sustainability considerations, consistent with frameworks like the triple bottom line (Elkington, 1997).

In conclusion, the essence of effective marketing measurement lies in the integration of theory, metrics and practice. By combining quantitative indicators with qualitative understanding, organizations can design metrics systems that foster learning, accountability and innovation. The insights from Chapter 3 ultimately reinforce the idea that metrics are not endpoints but decision-enabling instruments that allow firms to continuously refine strategies, allocate resources wisely and build enduring relationships with customers in dynamic digital environments.

KEY TAKEAWAYS

- Marketing performance metrics fall into core categories: acquisition, conversion and engagement for effective strategy development.
- Effective interpretation using models (e.g. AIDA and statistical techniques) enables real-time campaign optimization and is essential for actionable insight.
- Financial KPIs such as CAC, CLTV and ROMI align marketing efforts with strategic objectives.
- Customer lifetime value (CLTV) is a powerful tool for financial forecasting and marketing strategy refinement.
- Predictive analytics represents a next step in KPI development.
- A robust understanding of key metrics supports a culture of continuous improvement and data-driven growth.
- Effective use of metrics enables agility, better budgeting and sustainable competitive advantage.

References

Airbnb (2021) *Investor Relations Reports*, investors.airbnb.com/financials/default.aspx (archived at https://perma.cc/ELG9-ZK89)

Barney, J (1991) Firm resources and sustained competitive advantage, *Journal of Management*, 17 (1), 99–120

Bertalanffy, L von (1968) *General System Theory: Foundations, Development, Applications*, New York: George Braziller

Chaffey, D and Ellis-Chadwick, F (2019) *Digital Marketing: Strategy, Implementation, and Practice* (7th ed.), Harlow: Pearson Education

Chaffey, D and Ellis-Chadwick, F (2022) *Digital Marketing: Strategy, implementation and Practice* (8th ed.), Harlow: Pearson Education

Chaffey, D and Smith, P R (2017) *Digital Marketing Excellence: Planning, Optimizing and Integrating Online Marketing*, Abingdon: Routledge

Elkington, J (1997) *Cannibals with Forks: The Triple Bottom Line of 21st Century Business*, Oxford: Capstone

Freeman, R E (1984) *Strategic Management: A Stakeholder Approach*, Boston: Pitman

Gomez-Uribe, C A and Hunt, N (2016) The Netflix recommender system: Algorithms, business value, and innovation, *ACM Transactions on Management Information Systems*, 6 (4), 1–19

Gupta, S and Lehmann, D R (2003) Customers as assets, *Journal of Interactive Marketing*, 17 (1), 9–24

Gupta, S, Lehmann, D R and Stuart, J A (2006) Valuing customers, *Journal of Marketing Research*, 41 (1), 7–18

Hanssens, D M and Pauwels, K (2016) Demonstrating the value of marketing, *Journal of Marketing*, 80 (6), 173–190

Harvard Business Review (2020) *Data-Driven Marketing: The 2020 Playbook*

Kannan, P K and Li, H A (2017) Digital marketing: A framework, review and research agenda, *International Journal of Research in Marketing*, 34 (1), 22–45

Kaplan, R S and Norton, D P (1992) The Balanced Scorecard: Measures that drive performance, *Harvard Business Review*, 70 (1), 71–79

Kaplan, R S and Norton, D P (1996) *The Balanced Scorecard: Translating Strategy into Action*, Boston, MA: Harvard Business Press

Kaushik, A (2010) *Web Analytics 2.0: The Art of Online Accountability and Science of Customer Centricity*, Hoboken, NJ: John Wiley

Kotler, P, Kartajaya, H and Setiawan, I (2021) *Marketing 5.0: Technology for Humanity*, Hoboken, NJ: Wiley

Kotler, P and Keller, K L (2016) *Marketing Management* (15th ed.), Harlow: Pearson Education

McKinsey & Company (2019) How Amazon innovates in conversion, www.mckinsey.com (archived at https://perma.cc/H5QD-K8W7)

McKinsey & Company (2022) How retailers can keep up with consumers, www.mckinsey.com (archived at https://www.mckinsey.com/industries/retail/our-insights/how-retailers-can-keep-up-with-consumers) [Accessed 17 November 2025].

Nike, Inc. (2025) Company profile, about.nike.com (archived at https://perma.cc/TX6L-4WA7)

Reichheld, F F (2003) The one number you need to grow, *Harvard Business Review*, 81 (12), 46–55

Ryan, D (2016) *Understanding Digital Marketing: Strategies for Engaging the Digital Generation*, London: Kogan Page

Shankar, V and Bolton, R N (2004a) An empirical analysis of determinants of retailer pricing strategy, *Marketing Science*, 23 (1), 28–49

Shankar, V and Bolton, R N (2004b) An integrative framework for marketing research, *Journal of Marketing Research*, 41 (3), 294–305

Starbucks (2022) *Investor Report*, investor.starbucks.com (archived at https://perma.cc/G9ET-MPRC)

Tiago, M T P M B and Veríssimo, J M C (2014) Digital marketing and social media: Why bother? *Business Horizons*, 57 (6), 703–08

Venkatesan, R and Kumar, V (2004) A customer lifetime value framework, *Journal of Marketing*, 68 (4), 106–125

Wedel, M and Kannan, P K (2016) Marketing analytics for data-rich environments, *Journal of Marketing*, 80 (6), 97–121

PART TWO
Marketing analytics in action

04 | Marketing analytics in action – customer segmentation and targeting

CHAPTER OUTLINE

KEY TERMS

Churn rate: The percentage of customers who discontinue their relationship with a brand over a given period. A critical metric for retention analysis.

Churn-risk users: Churn-risk users are customers who display behaviours, signals or patterns that suggest a high likelihood of leaving or discontinuing usage soon. These signals can include declining engagement (e.g. reduced logins, fewer purchases), negative feedback, long gaps in activity or switching intent. Identifying churn-risk users allows firms to apply predictive analytics and retention strategies (e.g. personalized offers, loyalty rewards, re-engagement campaigns) to prevent customer attrition.

Customer data platform (CDP): A centralized system that aggregates customer data from multiple sources, creating a unified and consistent customer profile used for segmentation, personalization and campaign execution.

Customer lifetime value (CLV or CLTV): A forward-looking metric estimating the total net profit attributed to the entire relationship with a customer over time.

Customer segmentation: The process of dividing a broad customer base into smaller, more homogeneous groups that share similar characteristics, behaviours or needs. Segmentation allows marketers to design strategies that are more targeted and effective.

Data-driven culture: An organizational environment in which marketing decisions are consistently informed and validated by data analysis, with an emphasis on evidence-based practices over intuition.

Data governance: A set of processes, roles and standards ensuring the accuracy, consistency, privacy and ethical use of marketing data.

Feedback loop: A continuous process in which marketing actions generate data that is analysed and then reinvested into refining future strategies, campaigns or frameworks.

Key performance indicators (KPIs): Quantifiable measures used to evaluate the effectiveness of marketing initiatives. KPIs link performance to strategic objectives and provide benchmarks for decision-making.

Marketing analytics framework: A structured model that guides how data is collected, processed and analysed to inform decision-making in marketing. Frameworks align analytics with organizational goals and KPIs.

Persona: A semi-structured, data-driven representation of a customer archetype that combines demographic, psychographic and behavioural traits. Personas humanize data and make customer insights actionable.

Predictive analytics: A branch of analytics that uses statistical models and machine learning to forecast future customer behaviours, such as churn, purchase intent or lifetime value.

Predictive segmentation: The use of statistical and machine learning techniques to anticipate customer groupings based on expected future behaviour, rather than only past actions.

Recency, frequency, monetary (RFM) value analysis: A scoring-based segmentation method that evaluates customers based on their purchasing history: how recently they purchased, how frequently they purchase, and how much revenue they generate.

Segmentation matrix: A structured framework that maps out customer groups based on multiple dimensions (e.g. demographic, behavioural, psychographic), enabling prioritization of marketing strategies.

Targeting: The act of selecting one or more identified customer segments and focusing marketing resources on serving them with tailored strategies, products or messages.

4.1 Implementing analytics in marketing strategy

Marketing analytics transforms raw data into actionable insights, enabling businesses to optimize campaigns, predict trends and enhance customer experiences. Companies like Nike and Starbucks have successfully integrated analytics into their marketing strategies by leveraging AI-driven personalization and real-time customer data (Wedel and Kannan, 2016).

Integrating analytics into existing marketing strategies is essential for organizations aiming to enhance their decision-making processes and improve overall effectiveness. This integration involves using data-driven insights to guide marketing actions, allowing businesses to adapt more swiftly to changes in consumer behaviour and market dynamics. Effective integration requires a systematic approach to align analytics capabilities with marketing efforts. Organizations often begin by identifying data sources, which can range from website traffic metrics to customer feedback through social media platforms.

To ensure a successful integration, it is important to establish a culture that values data and encourages continuous learning among marketing teams. Training and skill development programmes can assist marketing professionals in interpreting data and utilizing analytics tools effectively. By fostering an environment of data literacy, companies position themselves to leverage insights that lead to better targeted marketing campaigns and ultimately drive improved results. Furthermore, leveraging existing customer relationship management systems can streamline this integration, ensuring that analytical insights are readily available to inform marketing decision-making.

Creating a framework to align analytics with business objectives is critical for leveraging the full potential of marketing analytics. This framework acts as a guide for organizations, ensuring that the analytics initiatives directly support broader business goals. The first step in this process involves clearly defining business objectives and key performance indicators (KPIs) that matter most to the organization. By understanding what success looks like, marketing teams can select the appropriate analytics tools and techniques that align with these objectives.

A structured approach entails developing a roadmap that outlines how data will be gathered, analysed and reported in a way that meets business needs. Regularly reviewing analytics outcomes in the context of business objectives helps to refine strategies and makes it possible to pivot when necessary. This iterative process encourages marketers to remain agile, continuously adapting strategies based on data-driven insights while maintaining alignment with core business priorities. The aim is to create a feedback loop that highlights not only successes but also areas for improvement, fostering an environment of innovation.

One valuable practical tip is to ensure that all stakeholders, from marketing to sales and operations, are involved in the analytics conversation. Incorporating diverse perspectives can lead to richer insights and facilitate the alignment of analytics with overarching business strategies, driving more effective marketing outcomes.

4.2 Building customer personas in marketing analytics

Customer personas are a foundational tool in marketing analytics, transforming raw data into actionable narrative profiles that represent key segments of a brand's audience. Rather than relying on abstract averages or generic customer categories, personas humanize data and provide teams with a vivid, data-informed understanding of whom they are speaking to, what drives these customers, and how to engage them most effectively (Cooper et al, 2007).

A well-constructed persona integrates **demographic variables** (e.g. age, gender, income), **behavioural insights** (e.g. browsing patterns, frequency of purchase, channel preference) and **psychographic traits** (e.g. values, attitudes, motivations). For example, a retail brand may develop a persona such as 'Eco-Friendly Emma' – a 32-year-old urban professional who prioritizes sustainable living, prefers products with environmental certifications, and frequently engages with brands advocating for climate action. These personas are not fictional guesswork; they are empirically grounded representations developed through the aggregation and analysis of multiple data streams.

Data to construct personas can be collected from a variety of sources:

- **Web analytics** (e.g. Google Analytics) for understanding site behaviour and referral paths.
- **Social media platforms** (e.g. Facebook Audience Insights, Instagram engagement metrics) for demographic and interest data.
- **CRM systems** for purchase frequency, customer lifetime value and recency metrics.
- **Sentiment analysis tools** (e.g. Brandwatch, Sprout Social) to gather emotional and psychographic cues from user-generated content and social mentions.

The role of personas extends beyond segmentation. When integrated into campaign planning, product development and content creation, personas serve as a filter for consistency and relevance. According to a study by Cintell (2016), organizations that exceed revenue goals are 2.2 times more likely to use personas in their strategy than those that miss targets. Personas also support **message personalization**, ensuring that tone, imagery, channel and timing align with the audience's expectations.

Leading brands offer compelling examples of persona-based marketing. Nike tailors its global 'Just Do It' campaigns to distinct personas: performance athletes receive content highlighting high-performance gear and elite endorsements, while everyday fitness enthusiasts see inclusive, motivational messaging and lifestyle products. This tailored approach not only drives engagement but also strengthens brand affinity across diverse user groups (NielsenIQ, 2024).

Moreover, the development of personas supports **cross-functional collaboration** between marketing, design, sales and product teams. When all departments work from the same personas, strategies become aligned, improving the efficiency of both content production and campaign execution. In advanced applications, machine learning models can be employed to dynamically cluster customer profiles and continuously refine personas based on live behavioural data (Wedel and Kannan, 2016).

In sum, personas are more than static profiles; they are living, data-driven representations of customer archetypes that evolve with ongoing analytics and insights. When embedded into the marketing analytics workflow, personas significantly enhance the precision, resonance and ROI of marketing strategies.

4.3 Building a marketing analytics framework

A well-structured framework aligns marketing activities with business goals. A well-structured marketing analytics framework is essential for transforming raw data into strategic intelligence that drives measurable business outcomes. It acts as a bridge between organizational goals and marketing execution, ensuring that every data point collected is relevant, actionable and aligned with business priorities. In increasingly competitive and data-saturated markets, a clearly defined analytics framework enables marketers to move from reactive decision-making to proactive, insight-driven strategies (Wedel and Kannan, 2016).

The ADAPTIVE marketing analytics framework

To provide structure, this section introduces the ADAPTIVE framework, a comprehensive model that helps organizations implement marketing analytics in a staged, iterative and scalable manner. The acronym captures seven key pillars (Table 4.1).

Table 4.1 ADAPTIVE framework and purpose

Step	Component	Purpose
A	**Align with objectives**	Connect analytics with business strategy through KPIs
D	**Data integration**	Aggregate data from diverse touchpoints into unified views
A	**Analyse for insight**	Apply statistical models and ML to extract patterns

(continued)

Table 4.1   (Continued)

Step	Component	Purpose
P	**Prioritize actions**	Use insights to drive campaign decisions and resource allocation
T	**Tool enablement**	Equip teams with appropriate platforms and analytics capabilities
I	**Integrate into workflows**	Operationalize insights within team structures and decision loops
V	**Validate and iterate**	Test outcomes and refine models in a feedback-driven process
E	**Embed data culture**	Promote data literacy and continuous learning across teams

Each element of the ADAPTIVE framework is expanded here.

1 Aligning analytics with business objectives

The first step in building a marketing analytics framework is to ensure that data collection and analysis are directly tied to organizational goals. This requires clearly defined key performance indicators (KPIs), such as customer lifetime value (CLV), cost per acquisition (CPA), retention rate or return on marketing investment (ROMI).

Cost per acquisition (CPA)   This is a financial metric that measures the average cost incurred by a business to acquire a single paying customer. It is calculated by dividing the total marketing and sales expenses by the number of new customers acquired within a given period. CPA is a key efficiency indicator that helps evaluate the effectiveness of marketing campaigns and budget allocation.

Retention rate   The percentage of customers who continue to engage with or purchase from a business over a specific period reflects a company's ability to maintain long-term customer relationships. It is often calculated as the proportion of retained customers relative to the total number at the start of the period. A high retention rate indicates strong customer loyalty and satisfaction.

Return on marketing investment (ROMI)   This is a performance metric used to evaluate the profitability of marketing activities. It measures the revenue generated by marketing efforts relative to the costs incurred, showing whether marketing spend delivers proportional business returns.

ROMI provides managers with evidence to justify budgets, optimize strategies and assess the overall value of marketing initiatives.

These KPIs should be mapped to broader business objectives – whether it is market expansion, customer retention, brand awareness or product innovation (Chaffey and Smith, 2017). Without this alignment, analytics efforts risk becoming fragmented or irrelevant. This alignment ensures that analytics outcomes are not siloed but contribute to measurable business impact.

2 Identifying and integrating data sources

The strength of an analytics framework depends on the diversity and quality of its data sources. Effective frameworks draw from multiple touchpoints across the customer journey, including:

- **CRM systems** (e.g. Salesforce, HubSpot) for customer interaction history and segmentation
- **web analytics platforms** (e.g. Google Analytics) for behaviour and conversion metrics
- **social media listening tools** (e.g. Brandwatch, Sprout Social) for sentiment analysis
- **e-commerce platforms** for transactional data
- **marketing automation platforms** (e.g. Marketo, Mailchimp) for campaign engagement.

Integrating these data sources into a centralized customer data platform (CDP) creates a single view of the customer and supports more accurate modelling and targeting (Lilien et al, 2023).

3 Structuring the analytics process

A robust analytics framework typically follows a four-phase cycle:

1. **Data collection:** Establish structured, automated data pipelines to gather accurate, timely data from all relevant channels.
2. **Data analysis:** Apply descriptive, diagnostic, predictive and prescriptive analytics techniques depending on the use case. For instance, logistic regression may be used to predict churn, while clustering algorithms support segmentation.
3. **Insight generation:** Convert raw analysis into actionable insights, often visualized through dashboards or reports. This phase translates complexity into clarity for decision-makers.
4. **Action and optimization:** Insights are applied to marketing decisions such as audience targeting, budget allocation or creative testing. Results are tracked and fed back into the framework for continuous refinement (Fader, 2020).

4 Selecting the right tools and technologies

The choice of tools must reflect both the analytics maturity of the organization and the complexity of marketing goals. Entry-level marketers may begin with Excel,

Google Data Studio or native CRM dashboards, while advanced teams might use platforms like Tableau, Power BI, R or Python for deeper analysis. The framework should also account for data governance, ensuring compliance with privacy laws (General Data Protection Regulation [GDPR], California Consumer Privacy Act [CCPA]) and data security protocols.

5 Embedding frameworks into organizational workflows

For the framework to be truly effective, it must be embedded into day-to-day marketing operations. This involves:

- creating **standard operating procedures (SOPs)** for campaign reporting
- establishing regular **insight-sharing routines** (e.g. weekly performance huddles)
- empowering marketers with real-time dashboards and self-service analytics tools
- encouraging collaboration between data scientists and marketers to translate complex models into business language (Davenport et al, 2020).

Cross-functional collaboration between marketing, analytics, product, and customer experience teams is essential for operationalizing insights (Brynjolfsson and McAfee, 2017).

6 Continuous feedback and iteration

A hallmark of high-performing analytics frameworks is their iterative nature. Frameworks must evolve based on performance feedback, emerging trends and new technologies. Establishing a continuous feedback loop ensures that insights are refined and strategies are optimized over time. For example, A/B testing results should inform future segmentation logic and campaign performance should trigger KPI reevaluation.

Feedback mechanisms include:

- campaign retrospectives
- KPI monitoring dashboards
- monthly performance reviews tied to model updates.

7 Embedding a data-driven culture

No framework succeeds without cultural adoption. Marketers must be equipped and motivated to interpret data and trust its insights. This requires:

- leadership advocacy for evidence-based decision-making
- organization-wide data literacy training
- celebrating 'data wins' and showcasing impact stories (Davenport and Harris, 2007).

When data becomes a shared language across marketing and leadership, analytics transitions from a tool to a strategic asset.

Key takeaway

The **ADAPTIVE framework** offers a structured, practical model for implementing marketing analytics that supports strategic alignment, technical integration and cultural adoption. By embedding analytics into daily decisions, marketers unlock the ability to anticipate trends, optimize campaigns in real time and build lasting customer relationships.

A marketing analytics framework is not a one-size-fits-all solution. It must be **custom-built** to fit the specific needs, capabilities and objectives of each organization. By aligning analytics with strategy, integrating the right data sources and embedding insight generation into everyday workflows, marketers can create a sustainable competitive advantage driven by data.

4.4 Customer segmentation: Strategy and application – why segmentation matters in modern marketing analytics

Customer segmentation involves categorizing customers into homogenous groups. Segmentation transforms generic marketing into **hyper-personalized experiences,** increasing conversion rates (Chapter 3) by 10–30 per cent (McKinsey, 2023). Companies like Sephora and Starbucks use segmentation to:

- **Reduce wasted ad spend** by targeting only high-intent buyers.
- **Boost retention** through tailored loyalty programmes (e.g. Amazon Prime's personalized deals).
- **Predict churn risks** (e.g. Netflix's 'Are you still watching?' prompts that re-engage users).

In the increasingly saturated and data-driven marketing landscape, customer segmentation has emerged as a cornerstone of strategic marketing execution. Segmentation refers to the process of dividing a heterogeneous customer base into smaller, homogenous groups based on shared characteristics such as demographics, behaviours, needs or psychographics (Kotler and Keller, 2016). This approach enables marketers to move away from mass messaging and instead craft tailored experiences that resonate more deeply with distinct customer profiles (see Table 4.2) The significance of segmentation lies in its ability to improve resource efficiency, personalization and campaign performance. Research by McKinsey

(2023) indicates that companies employing advanced segmentation strategies can see conversion rate improvements of up to 30 per cent, along with reductions in customer acquisition costs. Real-world applications underscore its value: Sephora uses segmentation to power its Beauty Insider programme with personalized offers, while Netflix deploys behavioural segmentation to recommend content that aligns with users' past viewing patterns. Moreover, segmentation aids in predictive marketing by identifying high-risk churn groups or high-value cohorts, which can be targeted with retention-focused interventions. The adoption of AI and machine learning has further enhanced segmentation precision, enabling dynamic, real-time customer clustering based on multichannel data streams (Wedel and Kannan, 2016). As consumers demand more relevant, timely and personalized interactions, segmentation remains indispensable in bridging the gap between insight and impact in modern marketing.

Table 4.2 Segmentation types in practice

Type	Example	Brand application
Demographic	Age, income, location	**Toyota** targets families with SUV ads.
Behavioural	Purchase frequency, cart abandonment	**Zara** emails discounts to inactive shoppers.
Psychographic	Sustainability preferences	**Patagonia** markets to eco-conscious buyers.

4.5 RFM analysis: A tool for customer value segmentation

Recency, frequency, monetary (RFM) analysis is one of the most widely adopted frameworks for customer segmentation, offering a straightforward yet powerful method to identify high-value customers and optimize resource allocation. Each of the three dimensions captures a unique aspect of customer behaviours, scoring customers based on their transactional history. **Recency** refers to how recently a customer made a purchase, **frequency** measures how often they purchase, and **monetary** assesses the total revenue they generate over a defined period. Customers are scored on each variable and the resulting composite score classifies them into segments such as 'champions', 'loyal customers', 'at risk' or 'hibernating'. These segments can then be prioritized with appropriate marketing strategies. For instance, champions may receive exclusive loyalty perks, while at-risk customers could be targeted with win-back incentives. A compelling example comes from ASOS, which used RFM analysis to identify loyal buyers for free shipping incentives while targeting churn-risk users (**churn** describes already lost customers – outcome measure, **churn-risk users** means customers who are predicted to churn – leading indicator, actionable) with personalized discounts – cutting churn rates by 15 per cent (*Retail Gazette*, 2022). RFM is particularly effective because it leverages transactional data already available in most CRM systems, requiring no complex modelling or external data sources. Its simplicity, repeatability and business relevance make it an indispensable tool for marketers aiming to make evidence-based, customer-centric decisions (Fader, 2020).

RFM analysis offers a quantitative approach to customer segmentation by scoring customers based on how recently (recency), how often (frequency) and how much (monetary value) they purchase. This method is particularly effective in industries with frequent, trackable transactions such as retail, e-commerce and subscription services. Customers are grouped into segments such as **champions**, **at-risk** and **potential loyalists**, each with distinct marketing strategies. For instance, Sephora applies RFM segmentation through its Beauty Insider loyalty programme, where 'champions' receive exclusive product previews and higher-tier rewards, while 'at-risk' customers are targeted with personalized offers to encourage re-engagement. This data-driven approach has helped Sephora increase loyalty programme participation and strengthen long-term customer value (Thompson, 2021). By scoring RFM variables from 1 (best) to 5 (worst), marketers can generate clear action plans. Champions may receive exclusive offers, while at-risk customers are re-engaged through discounts and personalized content. RFM thus serves as a powerful bridge between data analytics and customer relationship marketing. It is a proven method to rank customers by value.

EXERCISE

RFM analysis for an e-commerce store

Scenario

An online fashion retailer wants to identify high-value segments for a holiday sale.

Step 1: Extract and score customer data

- Recency (R): Days since last purchase (1 = recent, 5 = inactive)
- Frequency (F): Total orders in 12 months (1 = frequent, 5 = rare)
- Monetary (M): Total spend (1 = high, 5 = low)

Step 2: Segment customers

Table 4.3   Customer segments

Segment	RFM score	Action
Champions (R1, F1, M1)	Top 5% spenders	Exclusive VIP offers
At-risk (R4–5, F3–5)	Lapsing customers	Win-back campaigns (e.g. 'We miss you – 20% off!')
Potential loyalists (R1–2, F2–3)	Recent, mid-frequency	Loyalty programme upsell

4.6 Customer segmentation and targeting: Advanced RFM analysis and strategic implementation

Expanded framework: The five-step RFM optimization process

Building on the foundational RFM model, the following presents an enhanced framework used by leading e-commerce brands like Amazon, Sephora and Zalando to maximize customer lifetime value.

Step 1: Data preparation and scoring refinement

- Recency (R):
  - Tiered scoring:
    - R1 (0–30 days) → 'Active'
    - R2 (31–60 days) → 'Warming'
    - R3 (61–90 days) → 'Cooling'
    - R4 (91–180 days) → 'At risk'
    - R5 (181+ days) → 'Lapsed'
- Frequency (F):
  - Weighted by category (e.g. luxury buyers get +1 score adjustment)
- Monetary (M):
  - Percentile-based scoring (top 10% = 1, next 20% = 2, etc.)

Table 4.4   Behavioural overlays

Segment	RFM profile	Behavioural trigger	Strategic action
VIP trendsetters	R1, F1, M1	Views new arrivals within 24 hours	Early access to collections plus stylist concierge
Discount-driven	R2, F3, M4	Opens over 70% of promo emails	Time-limited 'member-only' deals
Sleeping giants	R4, F1, M1	High historic average order value	Reactivation campaign with social proof ('Your favourites are back!')

Real-world implementation: Zalando combines RFM with browsing data, giving 'fashion enthusiasts' (at least 10 weekly visits) automatic R-score boosts.

Step 2: Dynamic segmentation matrix

Expanding beyond basic RFM cells with behavioural overlays (Table 4.4).

EXAMPLE

Real-world implementation: Sephora's Beauty Insider programme

By adding purchase category data (e.g. 'skincare obsessed' vs 'makeup minimalist'), Sephora increased its email CTR by 22 per cent (L2 Inc, 2023).

Step 3: Predictive RFM modelling

Integrate machine learning to:

- Forecast next purchase timing (propensity modelling).
- Predict optimal discount threshold per segment.
- Identify lookalike audiences.

EXERCISE

Build a predictive RFM model

Using Python's scikit-learn

python
from sklearn.cluster import KMeans

```
rfm_data = pd.read_csv('customer_transactions.csv')
kmeans = KMeans(n_clusters=5).fit(rfm_data[['Recency','Frequency','Monetary']])
rfm_data['segment'] = kmeans.labels_
```

Step 4: Omnichannel activation framework

Map segments to channel strategies (see Table 4.5).

> **BEST PRACTICE**
>
> Amazon triggers post-purchase emails within two hours for R1 customers with complementary products, driving **18 per cent** incremental sales (D'Arpizio et al, 2022).

Step 5: Closed-loop measurement

Implement a test-and-learn calendar:

- Test: A/B test messaging by RFM cell.
- Measure: Incremental revenue per segment.
- Optimize: Re-score customers monthly.

Dashboard metrics to track:

- segment-level ROAS
- promotion sensitivity index
- cluster stability rate.

Advanced RFM workshop: Nike membership programme

Scenario: Nike wants to reduce premium member churn while increasing average order value (AOV) among casual buyers.

Table 4.5 Mapping segments to channel strategies

Segment	Primary channel	Secondary channel	Tertiary channel
Champions	App push	WhatsApp concierge	In-store events
At-risk	Retargeting ads	SMS	Loyalty tier demotion
Newbies	Onboarding emails	YouTube tutorials	Micro-influencer collabs

Step-by-step solution

- Data enhancement:
  - Merge RFM with:
    - app engagement scores
    - product returns rate
    - social media sentiment.
- Segment identification:
  - Discovered 'high-risk advocates' (R4, F2, M3 but high social mentions).
  - Identified 'sleeping athletes' (R5, F1, M1 with past premium purchases).
- Strategy deployment:
  - For high-risk advocates:
    - Sent exclusive early access to limited editions.
    - Triggered UGC campaigns ('Show us your collection').
  - For sleeping athletes:
    - Created 'comeback kits' with personalized gear recommendations.
    - Deployed geo-fenced app notifications when near Nike stores.
- Results:
  - 32 per cent reactivation rate among sleeping athletes
  - 11 per cent AOV lift in casual buyer segment
  - 19 per cent reduction in premium member churn.

RFM evolution: Next-generation applications

1. Real-time RFM (RT-RFM)   Example: Starbucks' dynamic rewards

- Adjusts offers based on real-time purchase context.
- Combines with weather data (e.g. promotes iced drinks on hot days).

2. Emotional RFM (E-RFM)   Example: Disney parks

- Augments transactional RFM with:
  - sentiment analysis of guest feedback
  - character interaction frequency
  - merchandise emotional attachment scores.

3. B2B RFM+   Example: Salesforce account scoring

- Adds dimensions:
    - **Relationship (R)**: Executive engagement frequency
    - **Potential (P)**: Account expansion white space
    - **Health (H)**: Support ticket trends

IMPLEMENTATION CHECKLIST

- **Data audit**: Inventory all customer touchpoints.
- **Scoring calibration**: Align thresholds with business goals.
- **Tech stack**: Ensure CRM/CDP integration (Salesforce, Segment, Braze).
- **Creative library**: Build segment-specific message templates.
- **Test plan**: Design controlled experiments per segment.

Pro tip: Start with 'RFM quick wins' – focus on just two segments (e.g. Champions + At-Risk) for initial 30-day sprint before scaling.

EXERCISE

Case assignment

Research and analyse Warby Parker's RFM strategy using its public earnings call data. Propose three segment-specific initiatives to improve lifetime value (LTV).

4.7 Fostering a data-driven marketing culture

Creating a culture that embraces analytics requires training and leadership advocacy. In today's fast-paced and data-rich marketing environment, the adoption of analytics tools alone is not sufficient to drive strategic value. For marketing analytics to truly transform decision-making, organizations must cultivate a **data-driven culture** – one in which insights derived from data are embedded into daily processes, team behaviours and strategic thinking. As Davenport and Harris (2007) emphasize, 'Companies that compete on analytics have cultures where data-driven decision-making is deeply rooted in the organization's DNA.'

Leadership advocacy and strategic vision

Building a data-driven marketing culture begins at the top. Executive leadership must champion the use of analytics by clearly articulating its strategic value, allocating sufficient resources and modelling data-informed decision-making. Research by McKinsey & Company (2023a) highlights that marketing teams with strong C-suite backing for analytics are **2.5 times more likely** to outperform competitors in revenue growth. Leadership commitment signals that data is not just a back-office function but a central driver of innovation, personalization and performance.

Training and upskilling for data literacy

A key barrier to analytics adoption is the **lack of data literacy** – the ability to read, interpret and communicate data effectively. Marketing professionals must be equipped with the skills needed to use dashboards, analyse trends, understand statistical outputs and draw actionable conclusions. According to Gartner (2021), fewer than 50 per cent of marketing teams report having sufficient analytics expertise internally. To close this gap, organizations must invest in formal training, online courses, certifications (e.g. Google Analytics, HubSpot Academy) and collaborative learning platforms that promote continuous upskilling.

Cross-functional collaboration

Embedding analytics into marketing also requires breaking down silos between departments. Collaboration between data analysts, marketers, IT and product teams ensures that insights are not only generated but also operationalized effectively. Agile marketing squads or analytics pods – small, cross-functional teams that co-own metrics – have proven effective in fostering accountability and real-time decision-making (Chaffey and Ellis-Chadwick, 2022).

Embedding analytics into workflows and tools

Cultural transformation is most effective when analytics are seamlessly integrated into daily workflows. This includes using real-time dashboards (e.g. Tableau, Power BI), CRM systems (e.g. Salesforce) and marketing automation platforms (e.g. Marketo, HubSpot) that deliver insights at the point of action. Embedding KPIs and performance metrics into campaign planning and review cycles reinforces a mindset of continuous improvement and evidence-based execution.

Celebrating data wins and learning from failures

Recognizing successful data-driven decisions – and transparently learning from failed experiments – helps normalize analytics in the marketing mindset. Companies like Amazon and Netflix promote a **'test and learn' philosophy**, where A/B testing is a routine part of decision-making and even failed experiments are valued for the insights they yield (Brynjolfsson and McAfee, 2017).

Ethical and responsible data use

A modern data-driven culture also requires attention to ethical standards and privacy compliance. Marketers must balance personalization with transparency and consent, following regulations such as GDPR and CCPA. Trust in data processes is foundational – both internally among teams and externally with customers.

4.8 Real-world examples

REAL-WORLD EXAMPLE

Real-world examples such as Netflix, Amazon and Coca-Cola show how analytics can be leveraged.

Companies that effectively leverage marketing analytics often gain a significant advantage in their respective industries. A prime example is Amazon, which utilizes comprehensive data analytics to understand customer behaviour and preferences. By continuously analysing vast amounts of user data, Amazon personalizes recommendations, optimizes inventory and enhances user experience. This data-driven approach allows Amazon not only to boost sales but also to improve customer loyalty, establishing it as a market leader in e-commerce.

Similarly, Netflix has mastered the art of analytics by using viewing habits to inform content creation and curation. By analysing what users watch, when they watch it, and how they engage with content, Netflix can tailor recommendations to individual preferences and even use this to decide on the production of new shows and movies. This capability to anticipate customer desires translates into higher engagement rates and a lower churn rate, underscoring the value of analytics in driving growth.

Another notable case is Coca-Cola, which utilizes marketing analytics to optimize its promotional strategies. Through the analysis of social media interactions, market trends and consumer responses, Coca-Cola continuously refines its advertising campaigns. The company's data analytics group applies advanced techniques to measure the effectiveness of marketing efforts not just in real time but also long term, allowing for strategic pivots that boost brand presence and sales.

Examining these successful applications of marketing analytics reveals several critical lessons for organizations looking to enhance their marketing strategies. First, it is evident that a customer-centric approach is paramount. Companies must not only collect data but also interpret it in a way that aligns with customer behaviours and preferences. This necessitates an investment in sophisticated analytics platforms that can analyse trends and predict future actions based on past behaviours.

Second, organizations should foster a culture of experimentation. The insights gained from analytics are only as good as their implementation. By conducting A/B testing and analysing the outcomes, companies can refine their strategies in real time, making informed decisions that resonate more effectively with targeted audiences. This iterative process is critical for adapting to changing market conditions and customer expectations.

Lastly, integrating data across different platforms is crucial. The insights drawn from disparate sources like social media, online purchasing and customer service interactions can provide a holistic view of customer behaviour. Companies that succeed in merging these data streams can develop more accurate profiles of their customers, leading to better segmentation, targeted marketing and ultimately, enhanced customer satisfaction. By learning from these case studies, businesses can build robust frameworks for future strategies that capitalize on the power of marketing analytics.

For practical application, businesses can start by defining the key metrics that align with their goals. Setting clear, measurable objectives based on the examples of leading companies can guide the implementation of analytics in marketing strategies. Understanding and adapting these best practices will create a foundation for future growth through data-driven decision-making.

Conclusion: Overcoming common pitfalls in marketing analytics implementation

Implementing marketing analytics presents several challenges that organizations must address to harness the full potential of their data. A significant hurdle is often the lack of a clear strategy for how to utilize analytics; many companies jump into analytics without a cohesive plan, leading to misalignment between their data collection efforts and marketing objectives. Additionally, the skills gap among employees poses another challenge. Many organizations find that their team lacks the necessary expertise to analyse data effectively and integrate insights into marketing strategies. Furthermore, issues related to data quality frequently arise. Poor-quality data can result from inconsistent data entry, lack of standardization and inadequate data governance practices, ultimately leading to unreliable insights. Resistance to change is also common, as employees may be reluctant to adapt to new technologies and methodologies, preferring traditional practices despite their limitations. These challenges can contribute to analytics implementation failures, as businesses struggle to turn raw data into actionable insights.

Addressing the challenges of analytics implementation requires well-defined strat-egies that align with organizational goals. First, it is essential to establish a clear analytics vision and strategy that integrates with the overall marketing plan. This will help ensure that data collection efforts align with specific marketing objectives and desired outcomes. Upskilling the workforce through targeted training pro-grammes can mitigate the skills gap. Organizations should consider investing in professional development to equip employees with the tools and knowledge neces-sary for effective analytics. Ensuring data quality and integrity is vital; organizations must prioritize data governance practices that include regular audits and validation processes to maintain high-quality datasets. Additionally, fostering a culture of data-driven decision-making can combat resistance to change. Encouraging collaboration between teams and showcasing successful analytics projects can serve as powerful motivators for embracing new practices. By proactively addressing these challenges, organizations can enhance their analytics capabilities, leading to more informed marketing strategies and ultimately improved business performance.

Establishing a feedback loop can further bolster analytics implementation efforts. This entails regularly reviewing analytics initiatives and outcomes, which allows organizations to continuously learn and adapt their strategies. Metrics should be reassessed periodically to ensure they remain aligned with business objectives. This dynamic approach encourages agility and responsiveness in an ever-changing marketing landscape, allowing organizations to pivot and optimize their analytics initiatives. Investing time in creating a solid data foundation along with an agile feedback mechanism can be instrumental for companies seeking to overcome com-mon pitfalls in marketing analytics implementation.

KEY TAKEAWAYS

Marketing analytics in action – customer segmentation and targeting

This chapter examines the strategic integration of marketing analytics into business decision-making, emphasizing customer segmentation and targeting as central practices for optimizing marketing performance. It begins by highlighting how analytics transforms raw data into actionable insights, enabling firms to anticipate customer behaviour, optimize campaigns and deliver personalized experiences. The chapter stresses the need to align analytics with business objectives, supported by frameworks that ensure data collection and analysis directly inform organizational priorities.

A core theme is the construction of **customer personas**, which humanize data-driven insights and support personalization at scale. By integrating demographic, psychographic and behavioural variables, personas enable marketers to craft resonant campaigns. Case studies such as Nike, Starbucks and

Sephora illustrate how personas and segmentation contribute to competitive advantage through personalization and retention.

The **ADAPTIVE marketing analytics framework** is introduced as a practical model, guiding organizations through aligning objectives, integrating data, analysing insights, prioritizing actions, tool enablement, embedding analytics into workflows, validating outcomes and fostering a culture of data literacy. This iterative, feedback-driven approach encourages agility in fast-changing markets.

The chapter explores **segmentation strategies** in depth, emphasizing their role in reducing wasted ad spend, increasing conversion rates and predicting churn. Real-world applications, such as Netflix's recommendation engine and Sephora's loyalty programme, demonstrate the tangible business value of segmentation. Tools such as **recency, frequency, monetary (RFM) analysis** are presented as effective methods for classifying customers into actionable segments like 'champions' or 'at-risk', supported by case evidence from ASOS and Zalando.

Building a **data-driven culture** is highlighted as critical to analytics success. This involves leadership advocacy, team upskilling, cross-functional collaboration, workflow integration and responsible data use. Companies like Amazon, Netflix and Coca-Cola serve as exemplars of analytics maturity, leveraging insights for personalization, innovation and market leadership.

Finally, the chapter identifies **common pitfalls**, including poor strategy alignment, data quality issues, skills gaps and resistance to change. To address these, organizations must adopt structured analytics roadmaps, governance practices and continuous feedback mechanisms. Practical exercises and mini case studies encourage application, helping readers bridge theory and practice.

Key takeaway: Effective segmentation and analytics frameworks empower marketers to create precision-driven strategies, optimize customer journeys and build sustainable competitive advantage. By embedding data-driven insights into culture and practice, organizations can transition from intuition-based marketing to evidence-based decision-making that drives long-term value.

EXERCISES

Exercises to reinforce practical applications of segmentation and analytics

Exercise 1: Develop an analytics integration plan

Task

Choose a company you are familiar with and outline an initial plan for integrating marketing analytics into its strategy.

Deliverable

- Define business objectives.
- Identify data sources.
- Specify tools/technologies required.
- Propose key KPIs.

Exercise 2: CRM and analytics at work

Scenario

A mid-sized retail chain wants to use CRM data to better target promotions. Currently, its marketing is broad and untargeted, leading to low campaign ROI.

Tasks

- Recommend three CRM data points that can be leveraged.
- Suggest two analytics techniques (e.g. customer segmentation, predictive modelling).
- Propose a mini campaign that uses these insights for personalized marketing.

Exercise 3: Diagnose cultural barriers to analytics adoption

Task

Analyse why a company's marketing team might resist using analytics.

Deliverable

- Identify cultural or structural barriers.
- Suggest interventions (training, leadership actions, incentives) to promote adoption.

References

Brynjolfsson, E and McAfee, A (2017) *Machine, Platform, Crowd: Harnessing Our Digital Future*, New York: Norton & Company

Chaffey, D and Ellis-Chadwick, F (2022) *Digital Marketing: Strategy, Implementation, and Practice* (8th ed.), Harlow: Pearson Education

Chaffey, D and Smith, P R (2017) *Digital Marketing Excellence: Planning, Optimizing and Integrating Online Marketing* (5th ed.), Abingdon: Routledge

Cintell (2016) *Understanding B2B Buyers: Why B2B Buyer Personas Fail* [Industry report], cintell.net (archived at https://perma.cc/A83G-PU23)

Cooper, A, Reimann, R and Cronin, D (2007) *About Face 3: The Essentials of Interaction Design*, Indianapolis, IN: Wiley

D'Arpizio, C, Levato, F, Zito, D, Kamel, M, and Montesa, S (2022) Luxury report 2022: Renaissance in uncertainty. Bain & Company, www.bain.com (archived at https://www.bain.com/insights/renaissance-in-uncertainty-luxury-builds-on-its-rebound/)

Davenport, T H and Harris, J G (2007) *Competing on Analytics: The New Science of Winning*, Boston, MA: Harvard Business Review Press

Davenport, T H, Guha, A, Grewal, D and Bressgott, T (2020) How artificial intelligence will change the future of marketing, *Journal of the Academy of Marketing Science*, 48, 24–42

Fader, P (2020) *Customer Centricity: Focus on the Right Customers for Strategic Advantage* (2nd ed.), Philadelphia, PA: Wharton Digital Press

Fader, P, Bruce, G S and Ross, M (2022) *The Customer-Base Audit: The First Step on the Journey to Customer Centricity*, Philadelphia, PA: Wharton School Press

Gartner (2021) Marketing Data and Analytics Survey, www.gartner.com (archived at https://perma.cc/TV87-VTWH)

Kotler, P and Keller, K L (2016) *Marketing Management* (15th ed.), Harlow: Pearson Education

L2 Inc. (2023) Sephora beauty insider: Purchase-category data and email CTR improvement, Internal report

Lilien, G L, Kotler, P and Moorthy, K S (2023) *Marketing Models* (2nd ed.), Abingdon: Routledge.

McKinsey & Company (2023a) The data-driven CMO: Unlocking marketing value with analytics, www.mckinsey.com/capabilities/growth-marketing-and-sales/our-insights/the-cmos-comeback-aligning-the-c-suite-to-drive-customer-centric-growth (archived at https://perma.cc/5774-YAQY)

McKinsey & Company (2023b) The new rules of marketing: Precision at scale, www.mckinsey.com (archived at https://perma.cc/U85A-RMU5)

NielsenIQ (2024) *Global Personalization Trends Report*, nielseniq.com (archived at https://perma.cc/A5D2-52G6)

Retail Gazette (2022) ASOS reduces churn by 15% using RFM analytics

Thompson, S (2021) How Sephora Is using data to eliminate racial bias and foster belonging in their customer experience, *Forbes*, www.forbes.com (archived at https://www.forbes.com/sites/soniathompson/2021/01/13/how-sephora-is-using-data-to-eliminate-racial-bias-and-foster-belonging-in-their-customer-experience/)

Wedel, M and Kannan, P K (2016) Marketing analytics for data-rich environments, *Journal of Marketing*, 80 (6), 97–121

05 | Marketing campaign optimization – leveraging data to improve campaign effectiveness

---

LEARNING OUTCOMES

By the end of this chapter, students should be able to:

- Understand the role of marketing analytics in optimizing campaign performance across digital and traditional channels.
- Design and interpret A/B tests to improve key campaign metrics (open rates, CTR, conversions).
- Map and analyse the marketing funnel, identifying drop-off points and improvement opportunities.
- Apply predictive modelling to forecast campaign success and allocate budgets efficiently.
- Leverage multi-touch attribution (MTA) to measure the true impact of each marketing touchpoint.
- Implement real-time optimization techniques using AI and machine learning.

CHAPTER OUTLINE

Introduction: Data-driven campaign optimization

5.1 Predictive analytics in marketing

5.2 Machine learning applications in marketing

5.3 Data mining techniques for marketing insights

5.4 A/B testing for email campaigns

5.5 Call-to-action experiments: What boosts clicks and conversions

Conclusion

References

KEY TERMS

A/B testing: An experimental method comparing two versions of a marketing asset (e.g. email subject lines) to determine which performs better.

Association rules: Discovering relationships between products or behaviours (e.g. market basket analysis).

Attribution modelling: Analysing how credit for conversions is distributed across marketing touchpoints.

Classification: Categorizing customers into defined groups (e.g. buyer vs non-buyer).

Clustering: Grouping similar customers based on behaviour or characteristics.

Customer relationship management (CRM) systems: Platforms integrating customer data for personalization, segmentation and targeted campaigns.

Customer segmentation: Dividing groups of customers into sets based on shared characteristics for more tailored marketing.

DATA framework: Guide for data mining – **D**efine objectives, **A**ssemble data, **T**arget patterns, **A**ct on insights.

Data mining: Techniques for discovering hidden patterns in large datasets to uncover marketing insights.

Ethical considerations in analytics: Ensuring transparency, avoiding algorithmic bias and maintaining compliance with privacy laws (e.g. GDPR, CCPA).

LEARN framework: Structure for ML application – **L**abel, **E**xtract, **A**pply, **R**efine, **N**urture.

Machine learning (ML): AI methods enabling systems to learn from data and improve predictions or classifications without explicit programming.

MARKET funnel optimization model: Framework with six stages (**M**ap, **A**ctivate, **R**efine, **K**eep, **E**nhance, **T**rack) for data-driven campaign optimization.

Marketing funnel: A model describing customer progression through awareness, consideration, conversion and retention stages.

PREDICT framework: Steps for implementing predictive analytics – **P**roblem, **R**elevant data, **E**xploratory analysis, **D**evelop models, **I**nterpret, **C**ampaign integration, **T**rack/tune.

Predictive analytics: The use of historical and real-time data with statistical models to forecast future customer behaviours and outcomes.

Real-time optimization: Adjusting campaigns dynamically based on live performance metrics.

Reinforcement learning: Learning optimal actions through feedback from interactions with an environment.

Sequential pattern mining: Identifying common sequences of customer behaviour.

Supervised learning: Training models on labelled data to predict outcomes (e.g. classification, regression).

Unsupervised learning: Identifying hidden patterns or clusters without labelled outcomes.

Introduction: Data-driven campaign optimization

Marketing campaigns have traditionally relied on creative intuition, broad targeting and retrospective performance reviews to measure effectiveness. While creativity and brand storytelling remain essential, the modern marketing landscape increasingly demands a **data-driven approach** to campaign planning and optimization. In today's environment – characterized by digital saturation, algorithmic media platforms and hyper-informed consumers – marketers must rely on real-time data to deliver relevant, personalized and timely messaging (Chaffey and Ellis-Chadwick, 2019). Data-driven campaign optimization refers to the continuous use of marketing analytics, machine learning and customer behaviour insights to adapt and refine campaigns throughout their life cycle. Unlike traditional models where data was reviewed post-campaign, optimization now occurs dynamically – marketers can adjust bidding strategies, ad copy, targeting parameters and content formats in real time based on performance metrics (Wedel and Kannan, 2016).

For instance, platforms like Meta Ads and Google Ads allow A/B testing and multivariate analysis at scale, enabling brands to test different creative elements and audience segments simultaneously. Spotify leverages real-time listening data to promote concerts and playlists tailored to user preferences, while Amazon Personalize recommends products based on live session behaviour. These capabilities dramatically improve **return on investment (ROI)** and customer experience, reducing wastage and increasing precision. According to a recent McKinsey report (2022), organizations that adopt real-time, data-driven marketing approaches are 23 per cent more likely to outperform peers in customer acquisition and retention. Importantly, data-driven optimization is not a one-time activity but a cyclical process – metrics must be tracked, analysed and interpreted through continuous feedback loops that inform future campaigns (Hanssens and Pauwels, 2016). As such, the intersection of creative strategy and analytics has become the new frontier of marketing excellence, positioning data not just as a reporting tool, but as a driver of **strategic agility and customer-centric growth**.

However, in today's competitive and data-abundant landscape, this approach is no longer sufficient. Data analytics enables marketers to **proactively optimize campaigns** – from audience targeting to content personalization and budget allocation – by uncovering what works, for whom and why.

The modern marketing funnel – spanning awareness, consideration, conversion and retention – offers multiple touchpoints for optimization through analytics. By systematically embedding data across each stage, organizations can ensure that campaigns are not only engaging but also efficient and results-driven (Kotler and Keller, 2016; Wedel and Kannan, 2016).

The MARKET funnel optimization model

To structure the application of data across the funnel, we introduce the **MARKET model**, which outlines six stages where analytics can improve campaign effectiveness (shown in Table 5.1 and Figure 5.1).

This model provides a consistent structure for applying data to both strategic planning and tactical campaign execution.

Table 5.1   MARKET model outline

Stage	Focus	Analytical tools
M – Map audience intent	Identify customer segments and motivations	Clustering, personas, social listening
A – Activate awareness	Optimize reach and messaging	A/B testing, sentiment analysis
R – Refine engagement	Improve click-throughs and session time	Behavioural analytics, path analysis
K – Keep converting	Drive conversions and reduce drop-offs	Funnel analysis, predictive modelling
E – Enhance retention	Target existing customers with relevance	RFM, loyalty scoring
T – Track and test	Measure results and iterate	Dashboards, attribution modelling

Figure 5.1   MARKET funnel optimization model

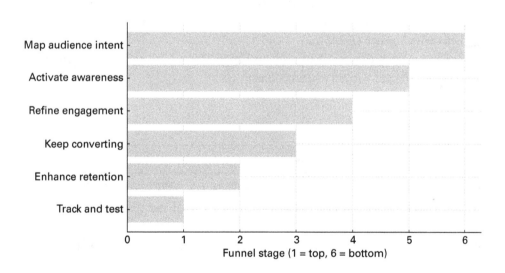

5.1 Predictive analytics in marketing

Predictive analytics refers to the use of historical, behavioural and real-time data to forecast future customer behaviours and outcomes. It plays a pivotal role in modern marketing by enabling organizations to move from reactive strategies to proactive, evidence-based decision-making. Through statistical algorithms and machine learning techniques, marketers can anticipate customer actions – such as the likelihood of a purchase, churn or response to an offer – before they occur. This foresight allows businesses to allocate resources more efficiently, optimize customer targeting and ultimately improve return on investment (ROI) (Fader, 2020; Chaffey and Ellis-Chadwick, 2022).

Predictive analytics involves using historical and real-time data to forecast future customer behaviours and outcomes. By applying statistical algorithms and machine learning models, marketers can predict who is likely to convert, churn or respond to specific offers. This predictive capability improves targeting precision and ROI (Fader, 2020; Chaffey and Ellis-Chadwick, 2022).

At its core, predictive analytics enhances **precision marketing** by identifying not only who to target, but also *when, how* and *with what message*. By embedding predictive models into customer relationship management (CRM), campaign management and sales forecasting systems, organizations can significantly boost marketing effectiveness.

The PREDICT framework for marketing predictive analytics

To guide the implementation of predictive analytics in marketing, we propose the **PREDICT framework,** which outlines seven key steps to operationalize and scale predictive intelligence (Table 5.2).

This framework ensures that predictive models are both technically sound and strategically aligned with marketing objectives.

Table 5.2   PREDICT framework

Step	Description
P – Problem definition	Define business questions (e.g. 'Who is likely to churn?')
R – Relevant data collection	Aggregate structured and unstructured data from CRM, web, social and transactional sources
E – Exploratory data analysis	Clean and understand data distributions, outliers and initial patterns
D – Develop predictive models	Apply statistical and ML techniques suited to the use case
I – Interpret model outputs	Translate outputs (e.g. probabilities, segment scores) into actionable insights
C – Campaign integration	Deploy predictions into marketing workflows (e.g. email, ads, segmentation)
T – Track and tune	Continuously measure performance and retrain models to reflect real-time behaviours

Common predictive techniques and use cases

Regression analysis

- Used to determine the strength and nature of relationships between marketing variables (e.g. ad spend and lead generation).
- Use case: Forecasting the incremental impact of increasing digital advertising budget on website conversions.

Logistic regression

- Estimates the probability of a binary outcome (e.g. click/no-click, buy/no-buy).
- Use case: Predicting which users are most likely to respond to a limited-time email promotion.

Time series forecasting

- Models sequential data to identify seasonal trends, cycles and anomalies.
- Use case: Anticipating demand fluctuations for retail items during holidays or special events.

Decision trees

- Visualize decision-making rules and classify users based on multiple predictors.
- Use case: Identifying high-LTV customers using purchase frequency, tenure and support interactions.

Clustering algorithms

- Group users into segments based on shared behaviours or preferences, often as a precursor to targeting.
- Use case: Creating micro-segments for personalized ad creatives and product recommendations.

EXAMPLE

Practical application: Retail forecasting with time series models

A fashion e-commerce company analyses five years of sales data using **Autoregressive Integrated Moving Average (ARIMA)** and **seasonal decomposition** to detect yearly peaks in outerwear sales. The insights reveal recurring demand spikes during early November and late January. As a result, the marketing team:

- schedules targeted email promotions two weeks before these peaks
- increases paid search budgets for coat-related keywords
- ensures optimal inventory availability.

The predictive model reduces missed sales opportunities by 22 per cent and decreases inventory overstocking by 15 per cent.

Example: A retailer uses time-series models to forecast demand spikes during holidays, enabling proactive stock planning and targeted promotions, reducing missed sales opportunities.

Brand applications

- **Spotify**: Uses collaborative filtering and sequence models to predict which users are likely to churn and surfaces personalized playlists to re-engage them.
- **Target**: Employs predictive models to anticipate life events (e.g. pregnancy) based on changes in purchase patterns, enabling hyper-personalized marketing.
- **Airbnb**: Uses time series forecasting to anticipate booking trends and dynamically adjust pricing, messaging and featured destinations.

Benefits and strategic impact

- **Higher conversion rates**: Target the right customers at the right time with personalized content.
- **Marketing efficiency**: Allocate budget to channels and segments with the highest predicted ROI.
- **Improved retention**: Identify at-risk customers and trigger pre-emptive retention strategies.
- **Greater customer satisfaction**: Deliver timely, relevant offers that reflect user preferences.

Implementation considerations

To successfully apply predictive analytics, organizations must:

- Invest in **data infrastructure** and cloud-based tools (e.g. AWS SageMaker, Google Vertex AI).
- Ensure **data privacy and compliance** (e.g. GDPR).

- Build cross-functional teams combining marketing, data science and IT.
- Foster a **test-and-learn culture** where predictive outputs are continually validated against real-world outcomes.

5.2 Machine learning applications in marketing

Predictive analytics involves the application of statistical methods, machine learning algorithms and historical data to forecast future customer behaviours, preferences and outcomes. It transforms raw data into foresight, enabling marketers to move from descriptive ('what happened') and diagnostic ('why it happened') analytics to **predictive** and even **prescriptive** analytics – determining not just what is likely to happen, but what actions should be taken in response (Wedel and Kannan, 2016). In an era where personalization, agility and ROI are paramount, predictive analytics offers powerful tools for refining segmentation, enhancing customer retention strategies, optimizing campaign timing and allocating resources efficiently.

Common predictive techniques are grounded in both classical statistics and modern machine learning. **Linear regression analysis** is used to model the impact of marketing inputs (e.g. digital ad spend) on outputs (e.g. lead volume), guiding budget allocation decisions (Hanssens and Pauwels, 2016). **Logistic regression** is applied when outcomes are binary – such as predicting whether a customer will click an ad or churn after a trial period. **Time series forecasting** uncovers patterns such as weekly sales cycles or holiday spikes, allowing for dynamic inventory and campaign planning. **Decision trees** and **random forests** are intuitive models that segment customers based on multiple variables, offering interpretability and ease of deployment in real-time systems (Shmueli et al, 2017). **Clustering algorithms** such as k-means or DBSCAN group customers based on behavioural or transactional similarity, aiding in the creation of micro-segments that respond more predictably to tailored messaging.

The value of predictive analytics lies not only in technical sophistication but also in its tangible business impact. For instance, a global retailer like Target uses predictive models to anticipate customer needs before they are explicitly expressed – famously identifying pregnancy indicators from shopping behaviour to offer relevant product suggestions (Duhigg, 2012). Similarly, Netflix uses collaborative filtering and matrix factorization to recommend content likely to keep users engaged, directly influencing retention rates. In the e-commerce space, Amazon applies demand forecasting through time-series models to automate inventory restocking and price optimization. These predictive approaches have led to more efficient supply chains, reduced marketing waste and improved customer satisfaction.

Importantly, predictive models must be evaluated and retrained continuously to maintain relevance in fast-changing markets. Key performance metrics, such as **area** under the curve (AUC), **precision**, **recall**, and **F1-score**, are commonly used to assess model accuracy and utility (see Table 5.4, later, for a summary). Moreover, ethical considerations around data privacy, algorithmic bias and transparency are increasingly shaping how predictive tools are deployed in marketing contexts (Martin and Murphy, 2017). As data becomes more abundant and tools more accessible, predictive analytics will continue to serve as a cornerstone of customer-centric, performance-driven marketing strategy.

Machine learning (ML) represents one of the most transformative forces in modern marketing. It enables marketers to move beyond basic reporting towards dynamic, predictive and even autonomous decision-making. Unlike traditional rule-based systems, ML models learn from data and improve over time, allowing for unprecedented personalization, real-time responsiveness and performance optimization.

From predictive to prescriptive marketing

While predictive analytics answers 'what is likely to happen', ML expands this capability by offering **prescriptive analytics** – suggesting *what actions should be taken* based on those predictions. This enables marketing systems to adapt automatically to customer behaviour and market changes in real time (Wedel and Kannan, 2016).

The LEARN framework for machine learning in marketing

To structure how machine learning can be applied across marketing functions, we introduce the **LEARN framework**, which identifies five core stages of ML-powered marketing implementation (Table 5.3).

Table 5.3   The LEARN framework for machine learning in marketing

Stage	Description	Example application
L – Label the objective	Define the marketing problem as a prediction or classification task	Predict likelihood to churn
E – Extract and prepare data	Aggregate and preprocess customer data	Clean, normalize and structure CRM and web data
A – Apply the right model	Choose ML techniques appropriate to task	Logistic regression for classification, K-means for clustering
R – Refine with feedback	Use model evaluation metrics to tune accuracy	Use precision, recall and AUC to evaluate results
N – Nurture a deployment cycle	Embed models into business processes and retrain regularly	Trigger automated campaigns via CDP or CRM

Key machine learning techniques in marketing

1 Supervised learning   Trained on labelled data to predict specific outcomes.

- Classification (e.g. logistic regression, decision trees)
  - Predict customer behaviour: churn, click, conversion.
  - Use case: Predicting trial-to-paid conversion in a SaaS business.
- Regression (e.g. linear, Ridge, Lasso)
  - Estimate numerical outcomes, such as revenue or CLV.
  - Use case: Estimating lifetime value based on early engagement metrics.

2 Unsupervised learning   Identifies hidden patterns without labelled outcomes.

- Clustering (e.g. K-means, DBSCAN)
  - Group similar customers based on behaviour or transactions.
  - Use case: Segmenting users by shopping frequency and product affinity.
- Dimensionality reduction (e.g. PCA, t-SNE)
  - Simplify high-dimensional data for visualization and segmentation.
  - Use case: Analysing customer reviews for sentiment patterns.

3 Reinforcement learning   Learns optimal actions via trial and error, used in dynamic environments.

- Real-time bidding (RTB) in programmatic advertising
  - Adjust bids on impressions based on user profiles and likelihood to convert.
- Dynamic pricing
  - Adjust prices in e-commerce or hospitality based on inventory and demand.

REAL-WORLD EXAMPLES   Machine learning in action

Target – predictive retail personalization

Target famously developed an ML model that could detect early pregnancy based on subtle changes in customer purchasing behaviour (Duhigg, 2012). By analysing past buying patterns, the model identified when customers entered new life stages, allowing for relevant, timely promotions.

Netflix – content recommendation engine

Netflix's collaborative filtering model analyses user behaviour to recommend content, increasing engagement and retention. Its matrix factorization approach uses both user and item latent factors for personalization (Gómez-Uribe and Hunt, 2015).

Amazon – demand forecasting and personalization

Amazon uses time-series forecasting and neural networks to predict product demand, automate warehouse logistics and suggest products. Personalization is dynamically adjusted using customer profiles, browsing history and real-time behaviour.

Starbucks – personalized offers via app

Using reinforcement learning, Starbucks tailors its loyalty offers to individual users based on their past behaviour, time of day and even weather. This dynamic personalization drives repeat visits and basket size.

These metrics guide tuning and retraining, ensuring models remain accurate as consumer behaviour evolves.

Ethical considerations in ML marketing

As machine learning becomes more embedded in marketing, ethical questions around privacy, bias and algorithmic transparency become critical.

- Bias in training data can lead to discriminatory outcomes.
- Lack of transparency (e.g. black-box models) may undermine user trust.
- Regulatory compliance with GDPR, CCPA and AI-specific guidelines is essential (Martin and Murphy, 2017).

Table 5.4 Key evaluation metrics

Metric	Purpose
AUC (area under curve)	Measures model's ability to distinguish between classes
Precision and recall	Assess accuracy in classifying true positives/negatives
F1-score	Balances precision and recall in one metric
RMSE/MAE	Evaluate performance of regression models

EXERCISES

Practical tasks

Task 1: Segment customers using K-means clustering

- **Dataset**: Transaction history of 1,000 e-commerce customers.
- **Objective**: Create four customer segments based on total spend, purchase frequency and average basket size.
- **Tools**: Python, scikit-learn.
- **Outcome**: Visualize and describe clusters; recommend tailored campaign strategies.

Task 2: Build a churn prediction model

- **Dataset**: SaaS user behaviour logs.
- **Objective**: Use logistic regression to identify churn signals.
- **Evaluation**: Use AUC and F1-score.
- **Outcome**: Identify at-risk users and suggest retention interventions.

Task 3: A/B test reinforcement learning offer strategy

- **Scenario**: A mobile food app offers time-sensitive discounts.
- **Objective**: Test RL-based offer model vs static rule-based model.
- **Metrics**: Offer redemption rate, customer retention over 30 days.
- **Outcome**: Recommend whether RL model deployment is viable.

Key takeaways

- Machine learning enables predictive and prescriptive marketing strategies.
- Use cases span from segmentation to personalization, pricing and recommendations.
- Ethical, evaluative and operational dimensions must be carefully managed.
- ML success hinges on clean data, continuous training and cross-functional collaboration.

5.3 Data mining techniques for marketing insights

Data mining is the process of discovering hidden patterns, trends and relation-ships within large datasets, enabling marketers to turn raw data into actionable marketing intelligence by sifting through large datasets to identify meaningful patterns and relationships. Unlike traditional descriptive analytics, which summarize historical data, data mining uncovers insights that may not be immediately visible, supporting proactive decision-making in areas such as **customer segmentation, campaign targeting** and **optimization, cross-selling, behavioural analysis** and **churn prediction.**

Key data mining methods include:

- **Clustering:** Groups customers based on similarities (e.g. lifestyle, frequency, value).
- **Classification:** Assigns customers to categories (e.g. likely buyer vs non-buyer).
- **Association rule mining:** Identifies product affinities (e.g. market basket analysis).
- **Sequential pattern mining:** Detects behavioural sequences (e.g. browsing to purchase).

By using techniques such as clustering, classification and association rule mining, marketers can enhance personalization, streamline campaign efforts and respond more effectively to dynamic consumer behaviours. When integrated with CRM platforms and marketing automation systems, data mining transforms static data repositories into **dynamic engines of insight and prediction** (Shmueli et al, 2017; Berry and Linoff, 2011).

EXAMPLE

A supermarket chain discovers through association rule mining that customers who purchase baby formula are likely to also buy wet wipes, prompting bundled promotions that increase cart size.

Integrating data mining with CRM systems enhances its value, turning static data into dynamic, customer-specific insights. When combined with campaign performance data, these insights drive **continuous campaign optimization**.

The DATA framework for data mining in marketing

To structure data mining efforts in marketing, we introduce the DATA framework, which provides a four-stage approach to mining customer and campaign data (Table 5.5).

This framework ensures that data mining aligns with strategy and drives measurable outcomes.

Table 5.5   The DATA framework

Stage	Description	Application
D – Define marketing objectives	Identify questions to solve: segmentation, recommendation, churn detection	'Which customers are likely to lapse?'
A – Assemble and clean data	Prepare data from CRM, web, purchase logs	Clean duplicates, standardize variables
T – Target patterns using techniques	Apply clustering, classification, association rules	Segment high-LTV customers
A – Act on insights	Deploy insights in marketing platforms	Launch personalized retention offers

Key data mining techniques in marketing

Clustering (e.g. K-means, hierarchical, DBSCAN)

- Groups customers based on similarities in behaviour, demographics or purchasing history.
- Use case: Identifying customer segments such as 'bargain hunters', 'loyalists' or 'seasonal buyers'.

Classification (e.g. decision trees, Naïve Bayes, SVM)

- Predicts categorical outcomes such as 'will purchase' or 'will churn'.
- Use case: Classifying new leads into high vs low conversion potential.

Association rule mining (e.g. Apriori, FP-Growth)

- Finds patterns of item co-occurrence, often used in market basket analysis.
- Use case: Discovering that customers who buy organic baby formula are also likely to purchase eco-friendly diapers.

Sequential pattern mining (e.g. GSP, PrefixSpan)

- Identifies recurring sequences in behaviour over time.
- Use case: Mapping a typical customer journey: ad click → product page view → abandoned cart → email re-engagement → purchase.

REAL-WORLD EXAMPLES   Data mining in practice

Walmart – market basket analysis

Walmart discovered that Pop-Tarts® and bottled water were frequently purchased together before hurricanes. This insight, derived from association rule mining, prompted strategic in-store placement and inventory adjustments, leading to a **boost in pre-disaster sales** (Berry and Linoff, 2011).

Nike – behavioural clustering

Nike used clustering to segment app users by activity (running vs training), enabling tailored product recommendations and personalized workout content. This increased app engagement and in-app purchases by over **20 per cent** (Nike, 2023).

Amazon – sequential pattern mining

Amazon tracks customer clickstream and purchasing behaviour to identify **frequently followed product paths** (e.g. laptop → accessories → warranty), prompting dynamic bundling offers and upselling.

EXERCISES

Practical tasks

Task 1: Segment customers using K-means clustering

- **Data**: E-commerce customer transactions
- **Goal**: Create three to five segments using average order value, purchase frequency and days since last order.
- **Tool**: Python (scikit-learn), Excel (using Solver or plug-ins)
- **Outcome**: Label and describe segments (e.g. 'Loyal high spenders', 'Dormant deal seekers') and propose targeted offers.

Task 2: Perform market basket analysis using Apriori algorithm

- **Data**: Transaction-level purchase history
- **Goal**: Find association rules such as 'If A and B are purchased, C is likely to follow.'
- **Tool**: R (arules package), Python (mlxtend)
- **Metrics**: Support, confidence, lift
- **Outcome**: Recommend bundled promotions or layout changes based on item affinities.

Task 3: Sequence mining for conversion funnel analysis

- **Data**: Web browsing logs, timestamped events
- **Goal**: Identify common behavioural sequences that lead to conversion or drop-off.
- **Tool**: Python (SPMF, PySpark)
- **Outcome**: Improve retargeting strategies and optimize touchpoints along the customer journey.

Key considerations for data mining

- **Data quality**: Missing values, duplicates and inconsistent formatting can undermine insights. A rigorous data cleaning process is essential.
- **Scalability**: Choose tools and platforms that scale with data volume (e.g. cloud-based platforms like AWS, Azure).
- **Interpretability**: Opt for models that offer business-friendly explanations (e.g. decision trees over black-box models where possible).
- **Privacy and ethics**: Ensure anonymization and compliance with privacy laws (GDPR, CCPA) when mining sensitive customer data.

5.4 A/B testing for email campaigns

A/B testing, often referred to as split testing, is a method used to compare two versions of a marketing asset to determine which one performs better. In the context of email marketing, it involves sending two different versions of a promotional email to distinct segments of an audience. By analysing the responses, marketers can identify which version resonates more effectively with recipients. This approach allows for data-driven decision-making that enhances engagement and conversion rates. The

Table 5.6   Summary of benefits of A/B testing

Benefit	Impact
Improved segmentation	Increases personalization and relevance
Cross-sell and upsell	Identifies logical product pairings
Retention optimization	Flags churn signals early
Campaign efficiency	Prioritizes high-opportunity audiences

ultimate goal is to optimize email campaigns by discovering what elements, such as subject lines, call-to-action buttons or overall content, yield the best results in terms of open and click-through rates (see Table 5.6).

The basic framework of A/B testing consists of two groups: the control group and the variant group. The control group receives the original version of the email, while the variant group gets the modified version. It is crucial to ensure that the groups are sufficiently large and randomly selected to minimize bias and ensure accurate results. After the emails are sent, marketers can gather data on key performance indicators, such as open rates and click-through rates, to evaluate the effectiveness of each version. By comparing these metrics, marketers can determine which email variation leads to better audience engagement, allowing them to make informed adjustments in future campaigns.

In practice, A/B testing provides invaluable insights by turning assumptions into measurable outcomes. Continuous experimentation with different elements fosters an environment of learning and adaptation, which is particularly beneficial in the fast-evolving fields of fashion and tech. Marketers who embrace A/B testing can refine their strategies and hone in on consumer preferences, making their emails not just a means of communication but a powerful tool for driving sales and establishing brand loyalty. A practical tip for effective A/B testing in email marketing is to focus on one variable at a time – such as the subject line or the layout – so that comparisons are straightforward and findings are clear.

A/B testing in promotional email campaigns: Fashion and tech

Email A/B testing – sending different versions of an email to subgroups of subscribers – helps marketers learn what content drives better engagement. Next, we explore real examples from fashion and tech brands focusing on **subject lines**, **email body content** and **call-to-action (CTA)** experiments. We also provide typical performance benchmarks (open rates, click-through rates, conversions) to contextualize these results and propose hypothetical A/B test scenarios for practice.

Subject line A/B testing: Examples and insights

Direct vs descriptive subject lines   Designhill, a digital platform, tested a straightforward subject line (just the blog post title) against a more promotional phrase. The simple, direct subject ('Top 10 Off-Page SEO Strategies for Startups in 2015') outperformed the wordier version ('Check out my recent post – ...'), boosting open rates by roughly 2.6 per cent and click-through rates by roughly 5.8 per cent (Kumar, 2016). This shows that clear, content-focused subject lines can entice more opens and clicks.

Using emojis in subject lines   MailerLite (an email service) ran multiple tests on subject lines with emojis versus without emojis. Initially results were mixed, but recent tests showed a slight advantage for emoji-infused subjects. In one experiment, the emoji version had a **37.33 per cent open rate versus 36.87 per cent without** – a small but statistically significant lift (Glazar, 2024). The key lesson is that emojis can improve open rates for some audiences, but testing is needed since impact is subtle and audience-specific.

Question versus statement   Framing a subject line as a question can increase curiosity. MailerLite tried a statement ('How to optimize pop-ups for mobile') versus a question ('Are your pop-ups optimized for mobile?'). The question format achieved a higher open rate in its test (Fischer, 2023). By posing a question that readers want answered, the email sparked more opens than a plain statement of the topic.

Tone and length variations   Marketing experiments indicate that subject line style and length can sway engagement. For example, an upbeat or emotive subject versus a neutral one might change open rates by a few percentage points in either direction, depending on the audience. Similarly, shorter subject lines often perform better – some tests performed by CodeCrew, an email marketing agency, showed around 5 per cent higher open rates for concise subjects over long ones (Marin, 2024). One extreme case, concerning MailerLite, saw a very short subject line achieve a 100 per cent open rate and 85.7 per cent click rate (Glazar, 2024) on a small segment, illustrating how compelling brevity can be. Overall, brands should experiment with tone (humorous versus serious) and length, as results vary with the context and readers.

Personalization vs branding   Including the recipient's name in the subject line is a known best practice – some studies have seen open rates improve by about 1–5 per cent with a first-name insert. On the other hand, including **the brand's own name** in the subject is not always beneficial. One retailer found that omitting its brand name led to 1–4 per cent higher opens (Marin, 2024). The likely reason is that subjects without blatant branding feel more personal or less 'marketing-y' to recipients. This insight from fashion/retail email tests suggests that personalization (making the email feel directed to you) tends to beat overt branding (which can feel like an ad) in subject lines.

Email body content A/B testing: What drives clicks

Once the email is opened, the content and design determine whether subscribers click through or convert. Brands have experimented with the layout, use of images, personalization of offers, and more.

Hero images vs text-first design

Big visuals can make an email look attractive – but do they encourage or hinder clicks? MailerLite tested emails that **started with a large hero image/GIF** at the top versus **emails that began with text** and had no immediate header image. To its surprise, the versions without the flashy top image earned a much higher click-through rate. In a follow-up test, an email with a plain text intro outperformed one with a banner image, again showing significantly higher click rates when the initial image was removed (Fisher, 2023). These results suggest that while images are eye-catching, a big image at the very start might distract or slow down the reader. A concise textual greeting or headline may engage readers faster, leading to more clicks on the actual product links or CTA further down.

User-generated photos vs stock photos

The type of imagery in email content can impact conversions. An e-commerce test by marketer Tomer Dean compared product images – real user-generated photos versus standard catalogue images – to see which drove sales. For a fashion item (Nike sports bra), the email featuring a real customer photo led to a **0.9 per cent purchase conversion rate, compared to just 0.31 per cent** with a typical product shot: nearly 3× the conversion. Similar tests with other products saw mixed results, but generally **authentic images** (e.g. customers using the product) tended to outperform polished stock images in driving action (Glazar, 2024). The takeaway: content that feels genuine or relatable can increase engagement and conversions, at least in fashion and lifestyle campaigns.

Personalized content and segmentation

Fashion retailer SwayChic undertook a comprehensive email segmentation and personalization project. It analysed customer behaviour to send emails at the optimal time for each segment and tailored content (e.g. 'we miss you' win-back messages to lapsed buyers). The results were dramatic: after rolling out these data-driven optimized campaigns, SwayChic saw a **40 per cent increase in average open rate, 2× higher click-through** and **tripled revenue per email** sent (Banko, 2013). In other words, targeting the right content to the right customer at the right time greatly improved every email performance metric. This underscores the power of A/B testing different content strategies (timing, message focus, etc.) and then segmenting your audience – to boost ROI. Even simpler personalization, like inserting product recommendations or tailoring an offer to a user's past purchases, can lift engagement.

(Aside: Other content tests brands often try to include **plain-text vs HTML design** to see if a 'personal letter' style email outperforms a glossy designed newsletter, or **long-form vs short copy** in the body. The guiding principle from all these experiments is to test one element at a time – images, tone, length, personalization – and measure clicks or conversions to identify what your audience responds to.)

5.5 Call-to-action experiments: What boosts clicks and conversions

The CTA – usually a button or link prompting the reader's next action – is critical in promotional emails. Even small changes to a CTA's text or design can meaningfully impact click-through rates.

A/B test findings on email CTAs

CTA text clarity ('Add to cart' example)

Fab.com, an e-commerce brand, tested the **label on a call-to-action button**. The original version of its 'add to cart' button was just a cart icon (🛒) with no text. It created a variant with explicit text 'Add to Cart' on the button. The result was a **49 per cent higher click-through rate** on the CTA when using text versus the icon-only button (Kumar, 2016). In practice, this meant far more people actually clicked to add items to their cart. The lesson is clear: a CTA should explicitly communicate the action. In emails, replacing vague or minimalist CTAs with clear, action-oriented text (e.g. 'Shop Now', 'Get 50% Off') can significantly increase engagement.

CTA button wording (first vs second person)

An interesting discovery from a SaaS (tech) context: phrasing the CTA from the user's perspective can boost clicks. Marketing experts found that a button saying 'Start my free trial' vastly outperformed 'Start your free trial'. In one A/B test, the 'my free trial' CTA led to about a **90 per cent higher** click-through rate than the equivalent phrasing with 'your' (Aagaard, 2013). Users apparently felt a stronger personal ownership with 'my'. The insight for email marketers is to consider testing first-person ('Download my guide', 'Claim my coupon') versus second-person ('Download your guide') CTA text. In scenarios where this has been tested, the more personal, first-person wording often drives more clicks and conversions.

CTA design and placement

Beyond text, the **visual design** and placement of CTA buttons is frequently tested. Marketers recommend experimenting with the size, colour and number of CTAs in an email. For example, is one prominent button better than multiple smaller links? Should the CTA be a standout colour or a simple text link? Best practices are not one-size-fits-all: one brand's audience might respond to a big, bold coloured button, while another brand might find a simple hyperlinked line gets more clicks. The only way to know is to test. It has been generally observed that **highlighting a single, primary CTA** (instead of many competing links) focuses the reader and can improve the click-through rate. For instance, in a web experiment, adding contrast around a CTA increased clicks on it by

25 per cent (Riserbato, 2021); in email, similarly, a well-designed button that visually stands out should perform better. Also, testing placement (e.g. a CTA near the top vs bottom) can reveal if subscribers tend to click sooner or only after scrolling. The core idea is to make the CTA unmissable and easy to understand, then optimize its style through testing.

Email performance benchmarks in fashion and tech

Before diving into hypothetical test results, it is useful to understand what typical email campaign metrics look like for context. The following are **industry benchmarks** for promotional emails (keeping in mind these can vary by source and year).

Open rates   A 'good' open rate for marketing emails is often around 15–25 per cent in many industries, with a broad average roughly being 21 per cent (Omnisend, 2024). In retail/fashion e-commerce, open rates tend to be on the lower end – about 17 per cent is the average for retail brands, while tech companies (software, IT services) see slightly higher opens on average, around 22–23 per cent (Campaign Monitor, 2022). It is worth noting that since late 2021, Apple's Mail Privacy Protection has inflated reported open rates for many users (by auto-loading email images). By 2025, some reports show overall open rates in the 30–40 per cent range (Elder, 2025), but this number is artificially high. In practice, if your campaign reports around 35 per cent opens, the true human opens might be closer to 20–25 per cent. In summary, around 20 per cent open rate was a common benchmark in the pre-privacy era, especially for fashion/retail emails, while anything above 25 per cent would be considered strong engagement (and much higher opens might be partially due to automated opens).

Click-through rates (CTR)   The CTR measures what percentage of delivered emails had a link clicked. Across industries, an average CTR is around 2–3 per cent (Campaign Monitor, 2022). Retail promotional emails often have relatively low CTRs – roughly **0.7–1 per cent** is common for retail/apparel campaigns. Tech brands and B2B emails might see around **2 per cent** CTR on average, in line with the overall average. A highly successful email might achieve 4–5 per cent CTR, but that's more the exception than the rule in large campaigns. Note: Click-to-open rate – the percentage of those who opened that also clicked – is another useful metric. For reference, retail emails often have a 5–10 per cent click-to-open rate (Campaign Monitor, 2022), meaning about 1 in 10 openers clicks, whereas a very targeted email could have a much higher click-to-open.

Conversion rates   Conversion rates can be defined in various ways for email, but here let's say it is the percentage of email recipients who take the desired action (e.g. made a purchase, filled a form). This is naturally lower than CTR, since not every click leads to a conversion. For an **e-commerce fashion brand**, converting **1–2 per cent of total recipients** into purchases from a single email is a reasonably solid outcome (this would correspond to perhaps 10–20 per cent of those who clicked making a purchase, assuming an approximately 10 per cent click-to-open). In **tech/SaaS emails** (where the goal might be a sign-up or demo request), conversion rates might also hover in the low single digits of recipients. Anything above 5 per cent of recipients converting from one email would be outstanding in most cases. That said, effective A/B testing and optimization can dramatically improve this metric. One case saw a company iterate on its email campaigns and achieve a **228 per cent increase in conversion rates** (Marin, 2024) (alongside +186 per cent CTR) – for example, lifting a conversion rate from 0.5 per cent to 1.6 per cent. Similarly, in 2013, fashion retailer SwayChic's segmented strategy **tripled per-email revenue** (Banko, 2013), implying far more buyers per send. These examples show that while baseline conversion rates are modest, there is room to grow through testing and learning what offers or content your audience responds to.

Hypothetical A/B test scenarios for practice

Drawing on the aforementioned patterns, the following **hypothetical A/B test results** are modelled on real-world findings. These scenarios are designed as exercises for marketing analytics students – you can analyse which version won and why.

Subject line variation – fashion retailer   A clothing brand tests two subject lines for a seasonal promotion. **Version A** is urgent and specific: 'Flash Sale: 24 Hours Only – 30% OFF All Shoes'. **Version B** is more generic: 'Don't Miss Out on Our Big Sale'. Both emails had the same content and were sent to equal-sized groups.

- **Results:** Version A had an open rate of **22 per cent** and a CTR of **3.5 per cent**, while Version B had an open rate of **18 per cent** and a CTR of **2.5 per cent**. Consequently, Version A led to more purchases (let's say **0.7 per cent of all recipients** bought from A versus **0.4 per cent** from B).

- **Interpretation:** Version A's subject line clearly conveyed a compelling offer (30 per cent off) and added urgency ('24 Hours Only'), which likely grabbed attention and drove more opens. The inclusion of an emoji (🛍) also helped draw eyes in the inbox. By contrast, Version B's subject was vague – it did not specify what the sale was or create urgency, resulting in lower engagement.

This exercise illustrates how a concrete, benefit-driven subject line can outperform a generic one in the fashion retail context.

Email content layout – image vs no image   A fashion brand wants to see if removing a large header image improves click engagement. **Version A** of the email starts with a full-width banner image showcasing the new collection, followed by product listings and a CTA. **Version B** removes the top banner, starting instead with a bold text headline and introduction before the product listings (images of products are still included, but further down).

- **Results:** Both versions were sent to equal segments and had the same subject line (so open rates were equal, about 20 per cent). Version B (no header image) earned a **1.5 cent CTR**, compared to **1.3 per cent CTR** for Version A – about a 15 per cent relative improvement in click-through. The number of people clicking through and making a purchase was also slightly higher for Version B (e.g. 50 purchases from Version B vs 45 from Version A, out of 10,000 emails).

- **Interpretation:** The image-heavy design (Version A) may have been visually appealing, but Version B's quicker-to-read intro likely got users to the product links faster. In Version A, some readers might have been distracted by or did not scroll past the big header image. This aligns with findings that an overly prominent image can sometimes hurt email performance, whereas a concise textual greeting can engage the reader more effectively.

Marketers can take away that it is worth testing email layout – sometimes a simpler format can outperform a graphic-rich email in driving action.

CTA button copy – tech SaaS offer   A software company is emailing a free trial offer and tests two variations of the main call-to-action button text. The email content and subject ('Your free trial awaits…') are identical; only the button text differs. **Version A** uses the CTA: 'Start Your Free Trial', while **Version B** uses 'Start My Free Trial'.

- **Results:** Since the subject and content were the same, both versions had about a 30 per cent open rate. However, the CTR for Version B was 4 per cent, nearly double Version A's CTR of 2.1 per cent. This means, out of the total recipients, significantly more clicked the 'Start My Free Trial' button. Ultimately, Version B led to roughly **4 per cent of recipients** starting a trial (conversion), whereas Version A led to about **2.2 per cent of recipients** starting a trial. For example, if each version was sent to 5,000 people, Version B's email yielded 200 trial sign-ups versus 110 sign-ups for Version A.

- **Interpretation:** The first-person phrasing 'My Free Trial' clearly resonated better with readers, making the action feel personal ('this is my trial') and perhaps psychologically reinforcing that the trial is for them individually. This matches the real-world finding that CTA wording can have a big impact – in this case, Version B creates a sense of ownership. For a tech/SaaS brand, getting nearly double the trial sign-ups from a simple copy change is a huge win. Students analysing this scenario should consider why the perspective shift ('your' versus 'my') affects user behaviour and note how such a small tweak in an email can yield significant conversion differences.

By examining both actual case studies and these modelled scenarios, marketers can appreciate how A/B testing informs email strategy. Small changes – a word in the subject line, an image placement, the text on a button – can translate into meaningful differences in open rates, click-throughs and revenue. The key is to test methodically, measure the results, and apply the insights to continually improve email campaign performance (Kumar, 2016; Banko, 2013).

Conclusion

Chapter 5 underscores the transformative role of data-driven methods in optimizing marketing campaigns. Where once campaigns were designed primarily through intuition and broad creative strategies, today's environment demands precision, agility and continuous learning. Marketing campaign optimization has evolved into a cyclical process – using predictive analytics, machine learning and data mining to generate insights, implement changes and measure outcomes in real time.

Frameworks like the **MARKET funnel optimization model** and the **PREDICT framework for predictive analytics** demonstrate how analytics can be embedded systematically across campaign stages, from audience mapping to retention strategies. Similarly, the **LEARN framework for machine learning** and the **DATA framework for data mining** provide structured approaches for translating raw data into actionable marketing intelligence. Together, these frameworks enable organizations to move beyond descriptive reporting into predictive and prescriptive marketing, enhancing ROI while improving customer engagement.

Practical exercises such as A/B testing reinforce the importance of experimentation in campaign design. Real-world applications – from Netflix's recommendation systems and Amazon's predictive demand forecasting to Starbucks' reinforcement learning offers – illustrate how analytics is not merely a tool for optimization but a source of strategic advantage.

At the same time, ethical considerations around privacy, algorithmic transparency and fairness highlight the need for responsible deployment of advanced technologies. The competitive edge lies not just in technical sophistication but in the ability to align data-driven strategies with customer trust and regulatory compliance.

In conclusion, marketing campaign optimization is both a science and an art: a blend of creativity, analytics and ethical stewardship. By embracing a culture of test-and-learn, leveraging predictive and machine learning models, and deploying data mining techniques, marketers can deliver campaigns that are not only effective but sustainable and customer-centric in an increasingly digital world.

References

Aagaard, M (2013) [Case Studies] How failed A/B tests can increase conversion rates, *Unbounce* unbounce.com/a-b-testing/failed-ab-test-results (archived at https://perma.cc/E6A3-AWPH)

Banko, A (2013) Email marketing: Clothing retailer lifts average open rate 40% via customer segmentation campaign, *MarketingSherpa*, marketingsherpa.com/article/case-study/lift-average-open-rate-segmentation (archived at https://perma.cc/N4LU-SVBW)

Berry, M J A and Linoff, G S (2011) *Data Mining Techniques: For Marketing, Sales, and Customer Relationship Management* (3rd ed.) Indianapolis, IN: Wiley

Campaign Monitor (2022) Ultimate email marketing benchmarks for 2022: By industry and day, www.campaignmonitor.com/resources/guides/email-marketing-benchmarks (archived at https://perma.cc/Z6BC-ADNX)

Chaffey, D and Ellis-Chadwick, F (2019) *Digital Marketing: Strategy, Implementation, and Practice* (7th ed.), Harlow: Pearson Education

Chaffey, D and Ellis-Chadwick, F (2022) *Digital Marketing: Strategy, Implementation, and Practice* (8th ed.), Harlow: Pearson Education

Duhigg, C (2012) *The Power of Habit: Why We Do What We Do in Life and Business*, New York: Random House

Elder, D (2025) Email marketing benchmarks by industry and region for 2025, *Mailerlite Blog*, www.mailerlite.com/blog/compare-your-email-performance-metrics-industry-benchmarks (archived at https://perma.cc/WC89-J5QV)

Fader, P (2020) *Customer Centricity: Focus on the Right Customers for Strategic Advantage* (2nd ed.), Philadelphia, PA: Wharton Digital Press

Fischer, J (2023) A/B testing email marketing examples to improve campaigns, landing pages and more, *Mailerlite Blog*, https://www.mailerlite.com/blog/ab-testing-examples (archived at https://perma.cc/782H-8Q2Y)

Glazar, M (2024) A/B testing: What it is and how it works, *The CMO Club*, thecmo.com/managing-performance/ab-testing (archived at https://perma.cc/XGD9-8HRV)

Gómez-Uribe, C A and Hunt, N (2015) The Netflix Recommender System: Algorithms, business value, and innovation, *ACM Transactions on Management Information Systems (TMIS)*, 6 (4), 13

Hanssens, D M and Pauwels, K (2016) Demonstrating the value of marketing, *Journal of Marketing*, 80 (6), 173–90

Kotler, P and Keller, K L (2016) *Marketing Management* (15th ed.), Harlow: Pearson Education

Kumar, U (2016) 5 A/B test case studies and what you can learn from them, *AB Tasty Blog*, www.abtasty.com/blog/learn-from-5-ab-test-case-studies (archived at https://perma.cc/B49X-7566)

Marin, A (2024) Lessons from case studies: A/B testing in email marketing, *CodeCrew Blog*, codecrew.us/blog/lessons-from-case-studies-a-b-testing-in-email-marketing (archived at https://perma.cc/CQT5-S592)

Martin, K D and Murphy, P E (2017) The role of data privacy in marketing analytics, *Journal of the Academy of Marketing Science*, 45 (2), 135–55

McKinsey & Company (2022) *Next in Personalization 2022 Report*, www.mckinsey.com (archived at https://perma.cc/32EF-T82B)

Nike, Inc. (2023) Annual report (archived at https://s1.q4cdn.com/806093406/files/doc_downloads/2023/414759-1-_5_Nike-NPS-Combo_Form-10-K_WR.pdf)

Omnisend (2024) What is a good open rate for email? A detailed guide for 2025, *Omnisend Blog*, www.omnisend.com/blog/email-open-rate (archived at https://perma.cc/X8VV-2RYH)

Riserbato, R (2021) 11 A/B testing examples from real businesses, Hubspot Blog, blog.hubspot.com/marketing/a-b-testing-experiments-examples (archived at https://perma.cc/WBC7-FSWE)

Shmueli, G, Bruce, P C, Yahav, I, Patel, N R and Lichtendahl, K C (2017) *Data Mining for Business Analytics: Concepts, Techniques, and Applications in R*, Hoboken, NJ: Wiley

Shmueli, G, Bruce, P C, Gedeck, P and Patel, N R (2020) *Data Mining for Business Analytics: Concepts, Techniques, and Applications in Python*, Hoboken, NJ: Wiley

Wedel, M and Kannan, P K (2016) Marketing analytics for data-rich environments, *Journal of Marketing*, 80 (6), 97–121

06 | Social media analytics – tracking performance and engaging customers online

LEARNING OUTCOMES

By the end of this chapter, students should be able to:

- Understand the strategic value of social media analytics in marketing decision-making.
- Evaluate key performance indicators (KPIs) for social media platforms, including reach, engagement and conversion metrics.
- Use social listening and sentiment analysis tools to monitor brand perception.
- Apply real-time analytics to adjust campaigns dynamically and enhance engagement.
- Leverage social media dashboards for performance tracking and stakeholder reporting.
- Integrate social media insights with broader digital marketing strategies.

CHAPTER OUTLINE

6.1 Overview of social media analytics

6.2 Measuring engagement and reach

6.3 Tools for analysing social media performance

6.4 Analysing social media impact on brand perception

6.5 Leveraging social media for customer engagement

6.6 Responding to customer feedback

6.7 Building community through online interactions

Conclusion

References

KEY TERMS

Click-through rate (CTR): Percentage of users who clicked a call-to-action (CTA) or link in a post or ad.

Cross-channel integration: The unification of customer data and messaging across all digital platforms to create a seamless experience.

Customer engagement: Interaction between a brand and its audience on social platforms.

Customer relationship management (CRM): A system used to manage company interactions with current and prospective customers.

Engagement rate: Percentage of the audience that interacted with content (likes, shares, comments, etc.).

Impressions: Total number of times content was viewed, including repeated views by the same user.

Reach: The total number of unique users who saw a post.

Real-time analytics: The process of analysing live data streams for immediate, informed decision-making.

Sentiment analysis: NLP-based analysis of user-generated content to determine public mood, tone or attitude towards a brand or topic.

> **Social listening**: The process of monitoring digital conversations to understand consumer sentiment and brand perception.
>
> **Social listening tools**: Tools that track and analyse online mentions, trends and sentiment (e.g. Brandwatch, Talkwalker).
>
> **Social media dashboard**: A visual interface used to track, measure and analyse social media performance metrics.
>
> **User-generated content (UGC)**: Content created by customers and shared on social media platforms, often reflecting brand engagement.

Introduction: Overview of social media analytics

Social media analytics refers to the systematic process of collecting, measuring and interpreting data from social media platforms to support strategic decision-making. It enables businesses to move beyond superficial metrics, such as 'likes' and 'followers' towards actionable insights that inform campaign effectiveness, customer engagement, brand sentiment and overall marketing ROI (Chaffey and Ellis-Chadwick, 2022). As brands increasingly compete for attention in digital ecosystems, the ability to harness analytics effectively becomes a core competency in modern marketing.

The relevance of social media analytics stems from the real-time and interactive nature of platforms such as Facebook, Instagram, X (formerly Twitter), LinkedIn, TikTok and YouTube. These platforms offer not only communication channels but also a rich stream of consumer behaviour data – including what users engage with, share, ignore or critique. By analysing this data, marketers can detect emerging trends, assess content resonance, monitor brand mentions and benchmark against competitors. The insights generated through social media analytics inform decisions ranging from content strategy and timing to influencer partnerships and crisis management (Stieglitz et al, 2018).

One of the most powerful attributes of social media analytics is **real-time responsiveness**. Unlike traditional media, where performance data is delayed, social platforms provide instant feedback loops. For example, during Nike's 'You Can't Stop Us' campaign, real-time monitoring of user responses across Twitter and Instagram helped the brand amplify high-performing content and adjust messaging to align with audience sentiment – the emotional tone or attitude that a target audience expresses towards a brand, message, campaign or experience. It helps gauge whether the audience feels **positive, neutral** or **negative** about what they see, hear or experience (Nike, 2020). This capability to adapt dynamically enhances message relevance and maximizes engagement in fast-moving digital conversations.

Social media analytics also supports **audience segmentation** and **personaliza-tion**, allowing marketers to tailor messages based on user demographics, interests, location and behaviour. Platforms like Facebook Ads Manager and TikTok for Business offer granular data on how different audience segments interact with con-tent, empowering brands to craft micro-targeted campaigns. For example, H&M leverages Instagram engagement data to tailor sustainable fashion promotions to environmentally conscious Gen Z audiences – a practice that combines psycho-graphic and behavioural insights to enhance campaign performance (H&M, 2022).

Importantly, **social media analytics** plays a pivotal role in modern reputation management by enabling brands to monitor and respond to public perception in real time. Through **social listening tools**, digital platforms or software applications mon-itor, collect and analyse conversations happening across social media, blogs, forums and other online channels. They go beyond simple tracking of brand mentions to uncover **audience sentiment, emerging trends, competitor insights** and **industry con-versations** in real time. Companies such as Brandwatch, Talkwalker and Sprout Social can systematically track sentiment trends, identify emerging issues and detect potential PR crises before they escalate (Chaffey and Ellis-Chadwick, 2022). These platforms aggregate vast volumes of online content across multiple channels – such as X (formerly Twitter), Reddit, Instagram and blogs – and use **natural language processing (NLP)** algorithms to perform **sentiment analysis**. This involves classifying user-generated content (UGC) as positive, negative or neutral, providing a real-time snapshot of public opinion (Weller, 2021).

Beyond mere monitoring, social listening tools offer deeper analytical capabilities, including **topic clustering, emotion detection, trend forecasting** and **influencer map-ping** (Fan and Gordon, 2014). For example, during the launch of the iPhone 14, Apple reportedly used real-time sentiment monitoring tools to identify recurring themes in customer concerns and frequently asked questions across Reddit threads and tech forums (Apple, 2022a, b). This allowed its customer service and PR teams to proactively clarify product features, address misconceptions, and manage both consumer and media narratives before misinformation could spread widely.

Moreover, platforms like Talkwalker integrate **visual recognition**, enabling brands to track logos and images even when text-based mentions are absent. This is particu-larly valuable in industries like fashion and retail, where brand imagery plays a critical role in identity and consumer engagement (Gerlitz and Helmond, 2013). As businesses become increasingly data-driven and customer-centric, social listening is evolving from a reactive monitoring tool into a **strategic decision-making asset**, guid-ing product development, advertising strategies and stakeholder communication (He et al, 2017).

Furthermore, **social media analytics** plays a critical role in enabling effective **cross-channel integration** – the strategic alignment and coordination of customer interactions across multiple platforms to deliver a unified brand experience (Verhoef et al, 2015). In essence, cross-channel integration involves linking data and engagement strategies across channels, such as social media, email, websites, CRM systems, customer service platforms and physical retail locations to ensure seamless and consistent customer journeys (Chaffey and Ellis-Chadwick, 2022).

Social insights gathered through platforms like Sprout Social, Hootsuite Insights or Brandwatch can significantly enrich broader **marketing strategies** by revealing real-time consumer preferences, pain points and content engagement patterns. These insights can be leveraged not only to tailor **product development** but also to inform **email marketing,** enhance **customer support** and personalize **web content** (Lemon and Verhoef, 2016). For instance, if a social sentiment analysis reveals rising dissatisfaction with a product feature, businesses can proactively update FAQs, adjust messaging or even improve the product before complaints escalate across channels.

A key enabler of cross-channel integration is the seamless **integration of social media metrics** with **customer relationship management (CRM) systems** such as Salesforce, HubSpot and Zoho. This integration allows marketers to merge demographic, behavioural and engagement data from various platforms into a single customer profile. As a result, businesses gain a **holistic, 360-degree view of the customer,** enabling them to deliver more relevant offers, time-sensitive communication and personalized experiences across all touchpoints (Kaplan and Haenlein, 2010).

Additionally, cross-channel integration facilitates **more accurate attribution modelling** by linking actions across platforms. For example, a customer might first discover a product via a TikTok ad, conduct further research through Google search, read reviews on Trustpilot, and ultimately make a purchase via an email campaign or in-store. Without integrated analytics, it would be difficult to identify which touchpoints contributed most to conversion (Liu and Viswanathan, 2021). In **omnichannel environments** – where digital and physical channels are increasingly intertwined – such integration becomes not only advantageous but essential for understanding and optimizing the customer journey.

As consumer expectations continue to evolve, businesses that invest in cross-channel integration through robust social media analytics stand to gain a **competitive edge** through improved engagement, more precise targeting and enhanced lifetime value (Vargo and Lusch, 2008; Verhoef et al, 2015).

Despite its advantages, effective implementation of social media analytics presents challenges. These include data volume, platform-specific metrics, algorithm changes and the difficulty of quantifying qualitative sentiment. Marketers must also contend with ethical issues surrounding data privacy and consent. To navigate these challenges, organizations should adopt clear measurement frameworks, invest in training for data literacy and choose tools that align with strategic goals (Tuten and Solomon, 2018). A commonly used framework is the '4Vs of Big Data' – volume, variety, velocity and veracity – which helps assess the robustness and reliability of data used in analytics (McAfee and Brynjolfsson, 2012).

In sum, social media analytics is not just a diagnostic tool but a strategic enabler. By converting engagement data into insight and action, businesses can optimize content, deepen customer relationships, enhance brand equity and achieve measurable business outcomes. As social platforms evolve, the role of analytics will expand from measuring performance to predicting behaviour, personalizing experiences and guiding long-term digital transformation.

6.1 Measuring engagement and reach

Effectively measuring engagement and reach is central to understanding how social media content performs and how it contributes to marketing goals. While **reach** quantifies the number of unique users who see a piece of content, **engagement** reflects the degree of user interaction, such as likes, comments, shares, saves, replies and clicks. These metrics (see Table 6.1) form the foundation of **performance analytics**, enabling marketers to evaluate content resonance, optimize campaigns and benchmark success across platforms (Chaffey and Ellis-Chadwick, 2022; Tuten and Solomon, 2018).

Key metrics for engagement and reach

Table 6.1 Key metrics for engagement

Metric	Definition	Example	Reference
Reach	Total number of unique users who saw a post	Instagram shows a reach of 120,000 for Nike's campaign post	Chaffey and Ellis-Chadwick (2022)
Impressions	Total number of views, including repeat views	300,000 impressions from repeated views on meta ads	Tuten and Solomon (2021)
Engagement rate	Percentage of users who interacted with content (likes, comments, shares, saves)	4.5% engagement rate on a YouTube video	Charlesworth (2021)
Click-through rate (CTR)	Percentage of users who clicked a call-to-action (CTA) or link	2.1% CTR on a Facebook ad promoting a product landing page	Ryan (2020)
Save/share rate	Percentage of users who saved or shared content	H&M's sustainability infographic post saved by 12% of viewers	Stelzner (2022)
Follower growth	Change in follower count over a given period	Apple's Instagram grew by 20k followers after a product announcement	Chaffey and Ellis-Chadwick (2022)

Engagement rate is particularly important as it standardizes interactions across audiences of varying sizes, offering a more accurate view of content quality than raw likes or views. Engagement rate can be calculated using the following formula:

Engagement rate (%) = (Total interactions / Total reach) × 100

Engagement is not only about popularity – it reflects brand affinity and the potential for content virality. A high engagement rate can indicate that the content is emotionally resonant, informative or shareable. According to a benchmark study by Rival IQ (2023), the **median engagement rate across all industries on Instagram is 0.67 per cent**, while top-performing brands achieve upwards of 2.5 per cent.

Framework: Content engagement funnel

An effective way to analyse how engagement unfolds is to apply the **content engagement funnel**, which breaks down audience interaction into progressive stages:

1 **Exposure** – content appears in the user's feed (reach/impressions).
2 **View** – user spends time looking at the content (video views, time on post).
3 **Interaction** – likes, shares, comments, saves.
4 **Click** – follows call-to-action (CTA).
5 **Conversion** – takes a desired action (purchase, sign-up, etc.).

This funnel enables marketers to trace which stage is underperforming and adjust the content strategy accordingly. For example, if a post has high impressions but low interactions, the issue may lie in poor creative or irrelevant messaging. If interaction is high but conversions are low, the CTA may lack clarity or appeal.

Benchmarking engagement by platform

Each social media platform has unique user behaviour and engagement norms (Table 6.2).

Table 6.2   Social media platforms' engagement (Rival IQ, 2023)

Platform	Typical engagement rate	Notable metric
Instagram	0.67% (median)	Saves, story views
Facebook	0.06% (median)	Shares, post clicks
Twitter/X	0.04% (median)	Retweets, hashtag mentions
TikTok	5–10% (average)	Video completion, shares
LinkedIn	0.35–0.6%	Reactions, comments, clicks

Platforms like TikTok and Instagram Reels typically enjoy higher engagement rates due to the visual and immersive nature of their content. In contrast, Facebook and LinkedIn rely more on content targeting and network effects to drive engagement. These differences necessitate **platform-specific content strategies.**

REAL-WORLD EXAMPLE   Sephora's multi-platform
engagement strategy

Sephora, a leading beauty retailer, employs a sophisticated strategy for measuring and optimizing engagement across platforms. For example, on Instagram, the brand uses carousel posts and stories to feature tutorials, boosting save and share rates. Meanwhile, on YouTube, Sephora tracks **watch time** and **video completion rate** as key engagement metrics for product demo content. By analysing the comparative performance of different content types, Sephora identified that **short-form reels had three times more engagement than static posts**, leading it to reallocate resources accordingly (Sephora Digital Report, 2022).

Additionally, Sephora integrates Google Analytics and UTM (urchin tracking module) parameters to link social engagement to website conversions, calculating ROI per platform. This approach illustrates how engagement data can extend beyond vanity metrics to guide budget decisions and content development.

Strategic use of engagement and reach metrics
The strategic application of engagement and reach metrics lies in their diagnostic and predictive potential:

- **Content optimization**: Track which post formats, hashtags or visuals generate the highest interactions.
- **Audience understanding**: Analyse when and where your audience is most active.
- **Campaign timing**: Use historical engagement data to optimize posting schedules (e.g. best times to post).
- **Paid promotion targeting**: Boost posts that already show strong engagement organically.
- **Crisis management**: Monitor drops or spikes in engagement for early detection of negative sentiment.

Engagement metrics are also useful for **A/B testing** in social campaigns. For instance, a fashion brand like Zara may test two headlines for a carousel post and measure performance through engagement metrics before selecting the final version for ad promotion.

Common pitfalls in measuring engagement and reach

While these metrics are powerful, over-reliance on surface-level data can be misleading. For example:

- **High reach with low engagement** may signal poor content relevance.
- **High engagement with no conversion** suggests a disconnect between content and CTA.
- **Bot engagement** or fake followers can inflate performance, leading to inaccurate assessments.

To mitigate these issues, it is important to combine quantitative metrics with qualitative insights (e.g. comment sentiment, influencer authenticity) and to monitor trends over time rather than take isolated snapshots.

6.2 Tools for analysing social media performance

In the era of digital connectivity, the ability to measure, monitor and optimize social media performance is no longer optional – it is essential. Social media analytics tools provide the technological backbone for gathering data, transforming it into insights and aligning social campaigns with business objectives. These tools help marketers track engagement, benchmark performance, identify sentiment trends, monitor competitor activity and visualize the return on investment (ROI) of their efforts across platforms.

Framework: The four-stage social media analytics model

Stieglitz et al (2014) proposed a widely used four-stage model that categorizes social media analytics tools by their functional purpose:

1 **Data collection** – aggregating structured and unstructured data (e.g. posts, likes, shares, mentions).
2 **Data processing** – cleaning, organizing and integrating data from different platforms.
3 **Analysis** – applying algorithms, visualization and statistical methods to detect patterns.
4 **Interpretation and reporting** – presenting results in dashboards, KPIs and reports for decision-making.

Most leading tools integrate these four stages in order to deliver actionable insights in real time.

Social media management platforms

These platforms combine publishing, monitoring and analytics in one interface, allowing marketers to execute campaigns and analyse their performance simultaneously.

Hootsuite

- **Functions**: Schedules content, monitors engagement and provides cross-channel analytics (Facebook, X, LinkedIn, Instagram).
- **Metrics tracked**: Post reach, follower growth, engagement rate, response time.
- **Use case**: A retail brand like Lush Cosmetics uses Hootsuite to monitor customer service responses and track sentiment in real time during product launches.

Sprout Social

- **Functions**: Advanced analytics, sentiment detection and social CRM capabilities.
- **Unique feature**: Provides demographic and psychographic analysis of followers.
- **Academic insight**: Ideal for audience segmentation, a key tactic in behavioural marketing (Tuten and Solomon, 2018).

Native platform analytics

Each social media network offers its own analytics dashboard, optimized for its unique set of user behaviours and interactions (see Table 6.3).

These tools provide real-time data, often necessary for platform-specific A/B testing and campaign optimization. For instance, Gymshark tracks Instagram story views and swipe-ups using Instagram Insights to adjust influencer campaign content mid-flight.

Table 6.3 Social media platforms' native platform analytics

Platform	Native analytics tool	Key metrics available
Facebook	Meta Business Suite	Page views, likes, post reach, audience insights
Instagram	Instagram Insights	Follower demographics, engagement by story/post type
YouTube	YouTube Studio	Watch time, audience retention, CTR, top traffic sources
LinkedIn	LinkedIn Analytics	Visitor trends, update engagement, follower metrics
TikTok	TikTok Analytics (Pro)	Video views, followers, traffic sources, trending sounds

Social listening tools

These platforms help brands monitor the broader digital conversation – beyond owned accounts – to understand public sentiment, trends and brand reputation.

Brandwatch

- **Functions:** Captures mentions across millions of websites and social channels; includes image recognition and sentiment analysis.
- **Use case:** Brands like Unilever use Brandwatch to assess consumer response to new product lines globally.

Talkwalker

- **Functions:** Real-time brand monitoring, hashtag tracking, influencer identification and crisis detection.
- **Advanced capabilities:** AI-powered visual analytics to detect brand logos in user-generated content.
- **Framework fit:** Aligns with sentiment analysis and reputation management frameworks in digital marketing (Chaffey and Ellis-Chadwick, 2022).

Web and campaign analytics tools

While not limited to social media, these tools track how social traffic behaves once it reaches owned digital properties, such as websites or e-commerce platforms.

Google Analytics 4 (GA4)

- **Social tracking:** Uses UTM parameters and referral data to track social traffic to landing pages.
- **KPIs measured:** Bounce rate, average session duration, conversion goals, assisted conversions.
- **Practical tip:** Brands should tag all social URLs with UTM codes for accurate attribution.

HubSpot

- **Capabilities:** Combines CRM data with social analytics, allowing for attribution modeling and lead scoring.
- **Use case:** B2B brands use HubSpot to link LinkedIn post engagement to lead generation and email nurture funnels.

Visualization and dashboarding tools

To synthesize data from multiple platforms, marketers often rely on third-party visualization tools.

Google Looker Studio (formerly Data Studio)

- **Functions**: Visualizes KPIs from Facebook, Instagram, GA4 and other sources through APIs.
- **Customization**: Allows the creation of interactive dashboards for different stakeholders (e.g. CMO vs social media manager).

Tableau

- **Strength**: Suitable for large datasets and deep analytics such as cohort analysis or lifetime engagement modeling.
- **Academic value**: Supports a data visualization approach aligned with exploratory data analysis (EDA) practices.

REAL-WORLD EXAMPLE   Netflix's use of social analytics

Netflix is a master of using social analytics to boost engagement and brand loyalty. The company monitors trailer reactions on YouTube and X, analyses memes and reviews on Reddit and TikTok, and tracks sentiment in real time. During the launch of *Stranger Things* Season 4, social listening tools identified trending hashtags and themes. Netflix then adjusted its promotional content to highlight these themes, resulting in over **1.3 million organic tweets** in the launch week and a surge in streaming hours (Netflix Media Center, 2022).

Best practices for tool selection

When selecting tools for analysing social media performance, consider the following:

- **Alignment with goals**: Does the tool measure metrics relevant to your KPIs (e.g. awareness, conversion)?
- **Integration capabilities**: Can the tool connect with your CRM, email platform or e-commerce system?
- **Usability and learning curve**: Is it accessible for non-technical users or does it require advanced training?

- **Cost vs ROI:** Evaluate pricing tiers against the value of insights generated.
- **Real-time capabilities** : Does the tool offer real-time alerts for crisis management?

For educational use, starting with native analytics and **free dashboards** (e.g. Looker Studio) provides an excellent foundation for students to learn before progressing to enterprise-grade platforms.

6.3 Analysing social media impact on brand perception

In today's digital ecosystem, a brand's reputation is continuously shaped and reshaped by conversations occurring in real time across social platforms. Analysing the impact of social media on brand perception involves examining how users interact with brand content, express sentiment and share opinions that contribute to the collective image of the brand. Unlike traditional brand tracking, which relies on surveys and periodic reports, social media analytics allows brands to assess perception dynamically and granularly (Kaplan and Haenlein, 2010; Chaffey and Ellis-Chadwick, 2022).

Theoretical framework: The customer-based brand equity pyramid

One effective model for understanding brand perception is Keller's **customer-based brand equity (CBBE)** pyramid, which consists of four ascending stages:

1 Brand awareness (Do customers know the brand?)

2 Brand associations (What do customers associate with the brand?)

3 Perceived quality and judgements (What value do they assign to the brand?)

4 Brand resonance (Are customers loyal and engaged?)

Social media offers direct indicators at each level of this pyramid:

- **Awareness:** Follower count, mentions, impressions.
- **Associations:** Comment themes, hashtags, influencer partnerships.
- **Judgements:** Sentiment analysis, review ratings, share-of-voice.
- **Resonance:** User-generated content (UGC), brand communities, advocacy behaviour.

By aligning social media KPIs with the CBBE model, marketers can monitor how content and interactions influence brand equity over time (Keller, 2003).

Social listening and sentiment analysis

Social listening involves monitoring digital conversations for brand mentions, competitor references and relevant industry trends. This practice provides both quantitative and qualitative data for understanding how consumers perceive the brand across multiple dimensions: emotional tone, topic themes and levels of engagement.

Sentiment analysis, powered by natural language processing (NLP), automatically classifies social media content as positive, negative or neutral. Tools like Brandwatch, Sprout Social and Talkwalker can scan thousands of posts to detect sentiment trends and changes in brand perception.

EXAMPLE

Apple

During the launch of the Apple Vision Pro, social listening revealed polarized sentiment. Positive sentiment highlighted innovation and excitement, while negative sentiment focused on price and privacy concerns. Apple adjusted its messaging by emphasizing professional use cases and developer tools in follow-up campaigns (Apple, 2023).

Key metrics for brand perception analysis

These metrics allow marketers to track how campaigns affect brand reputation and compare perception before, during and after specific events or launches (Table 6.4).

Table 6.4 Key metrics for brand perception analysis

Metric	Definition	Example tool
Brand mentions	Number of times a brand is mentioned across social platforms	Hootsuite, Brandwatch
Share of voice (SOV)	Percentage of conversations in a market that involve the brand vs competitors	Talkwalker
Sentiment score	Ratio of positive to negative mentions	Sprinklr
Net sentiment	(Positive – negative mentions) / total mentions	Sprout Social
Engagement on brand posts	Volume of likes, comments and shares on branded content	Native Analytics
Influencer sentiment	Tone of influencer content mentioning the brand	Upfluence, Aspire

---

REAL-WORLD EXAMPLE   Nike and social advocacy

Nike's 2018 'Just Do It' campaign featuring Colin Kaepernick provides a compelling case of how social media can amplify and shape brand perception. Despite an initial backlash, Nike monitored sentiment using Brandwatch and Twitter Analytics. Over time, net sentiment improved as the brand attracted a younger, more socially conscious customer base. Nike's online sales increased by 31 per cent in the days following the campaign, demonstrating that social perception, when aligned with brand values, can drive both equity and revenue (Forbes, 2018).

Nike's social media team tracked hashtag usage (#JustDoIt, #ColinKaepernick), engagement rates and influencer alignment to ensure message consistency. The campaign reinforced brand resonance, especially among Gen Z consumers who value authenticity and purpose-driven branding.

Visualizing brand perception trends

Social media dashboards provide visual insights into how brand perception evolves. A typical brand sentiment dashboard includes:

- volume of brand mentions over time
- sentiment breakdown (pie or bar chart)
- trending topics and hashtags
- geographic distribution of brand conversations
- word clouds for common themes.

EXERCISE

Use Talkwalker or Sprout Social to create a dashboard analysing sentiment for a brand launch (e.g. Spotify Wrapped, H&M Conscious Collection).

These dashboards can help marketing teams identify perception risks, such as negative reviews gaining traction or opportunities, like viral UGC that can be amplified.

Crisis management and brand repair

Rapid sentiment shifts can signal the onset of a PR crisis. For instance, when United Airlines forcibly removed a passenger in 2017, negative sentiment exploded across platforms. A delayed response worsened the crisis. Today, many brands have real-time sentiment alerts built into their analytics tools to detect and respond to such events within hours rather than days (Stieglitz et al, 2018).

Best practices for **brand repair** on social media include:

- immediate acknowledgment of the issue
- transparent communication with updates
- engaging directly with affected users
- showcasing the corrective action taken.

Real-time analytics is crucial in these situations, allowing brands to pivot their messaging and restore trust efficiently.

Strategic implications

Understanding social media's impact on brand perception supports a variety of strategic objectives:

- **Product development**: Insights from customer feedback guide feature improvements.
- **Campaign evaluation**: Post-campaign sentiment trends reveal emotional impact.
- **Competitive benchmarking**: Share-of-voice comparisons highlight brand positioning.
- **Customer service**: Negative feedback identifies friction points in the customer journey.

Integrating perception metrics into marketing dashboards encourages more nuanced evaluations of success than traditional metrics like impressions or clicks alone.

6.4 Leveraging social media for customer engagement

Social media has revolutionized how brands engage with customers, shifting the communication dynamic from one-directional messaging to interactive dialogue. Customer engagement on social platforms involves creating meaningful interactions that build relationships, foster trust and encourage brand loyalty. These interactions are no longer limited to content consumption – they encompass likes, comments, shares, direct messages, story reactions and co-creation of content. When managed strategically, social media engagement enhances brand equity, increases lifetime customer value and fuels organic advocacy (Brodie et al, 2013; Chaffey and Ellis-Chadwick, 2022).

Theoretical framework: The consumer engagement framework

The **consumer engagement framework** by Hollebeek, Glynn and Brodie (2014) conceptualizes engagement as comprising three core dimensions:

1 **Cognitive engagement** – the mental investment a user makes when consuming or thinking about content.
2 **Emotional engagement** – the affective connection or feelings generated by a brand's social media presence.
3 **Behavioural engagement** – observable actions such as likes, comments, sharing, tagging or creating user-generated content (UGC).

In the context of social media, effective engagement strategies address all three dimensions – offering informative and valuable content (cognitive), emotionally resonant storytelling (emotional) and calls-to-action or community involvement (behavioural).

Real-time engagement and relationship marketing

Real-time engagement involves responding promptly to customer interactions and current events, creating a perception of authenticity and attentiveness. Platforms like X and Instagram Stories support real-time features that brands can use to initiate or join conversations.

EXAMPLE

Adidas

During the 2022 men's FIFA World Cup, Adidas live-tweeted match results and fan reactions, increasing its Twitter engagement rate by 21 per cent. It used memes, polls and influencer commentary to keep the conversation dynamic and inclusive (Adidas, 2023).

This approach aligns with relationship marketing theory, which prioritizes long-term connections over short-term conversions. The strength of a brand's social media presence increasingly depends on its capacity to listen, respond and co-create with customers.

Table 6.5   Engagement types on social media

Engagement type	Examples	Strategic value
Passive (consumption)	Viewing stories, reading captions	Signals awareness, useful for remarketing
Reactive	Likes, emoji reactions, basic shares	Indicates general interest, supports algorithm reach
Active	Comments, DMs, product reviews, tagged posts	Enables dialogue, builds community
Proactive/co-creation	User-generated content, testimonials, brand challenges	Strengthens loyalty and advocacy

Types of customer engagement on social media

Active and proactive engagements are especially valuable, as they indicate deeper commitment and emotional investment. Encouraging these behaviours should be a priority for content strategies (see Table 6.5).

REAL-WORLD EXAMPLE   Glossier – community-led engagement

Beauty brand Glossier is a best-practice example of leveraging social media for engagement. From its inception, Glossier built its brand through customer conversations on Instagram. The brand reposts user-generated content, invites product ideas through DMs and features real customer stories rather than models. According to *WWD* (2022a), over 70 per cent of Glossier's Instagram content comes from its community.

Its strategy is guided by three principles:

1 Community-first storytelling

2 Rapid response through social listening

3 Empowerment through co-creation.

The result is an extraordinarily loyal customer base and high engagement rates – reportedly three times higher than the industry average on Instagram.

Framework: Engagement funnel for social media

This framework maps user actions across the engagement journey:

- **Exposure** – impressions and reach (who saw the content).
- **Interest** – clicks, likes, video views.

- **Interaction** – comments, DMs, poll participation.
- **Advocacy** – shares, user-generated content, referrals.

Marketers can align KPIs and content strategies to each stage. For instance, 'exposure' may be improved through boosted posts, while 'interaction' requires open-ended content formats like Q&As or discussion threads.

Content strategies to drive engagement

- **Visual storytelling** – using images, reels and TikToks to convey narratives quickly.
- **Interactive formats** – polls, quizzes, live sessions and contests to encourage participation.
- **User-generated content (UGC)** – reposting customer photos and reviews to build trust and community.
- **Personalization** – targeted messages based on user behaviour (e.g. abandoned cart prompts or location-based content).
- **Purpose-driven content** – aligning with social causes (e.g. sustainability, diversity) to build emotional bonds.

EXAMPLE

Patagonia

Patagonia's environmental campaigns are highly engaging because they align with the brand's values and those of its audience. Posts about climate action often receive two to three times more engagement than product features (Patagonia, 2022).

Engagement analytics and tools

To assess customer engagement on social media, marketers use KPIs and tools such as the ones in Table 6.6.

Table 6.6 KPIs and tools used to assess social media engagement

Tool	Features
Meta Business Suite	Engagement rates, video performance, comments and shares
Sprout Social	Engagement history, message tagging, CRM integration
Later	Best times to post, hashtag analytics, engagement forecasting
Google Analytics	Measures traffic and conversions originating from social media

KPI examples are:

- Engagement rate per follower: (Total interactions / Total followers) × 100.
- Response rate: percentage of user comments/messages responded to.
- Share rate: percentage of content shared per views.

Analysing trends across these KPIs helps marketers refine their tone, timing and targeting for future content.

Strategic implications of engagement

- **Improved algorithm reach**: Higher engagement signals relevance to platform algorithms.
- **Brand loyalty**: Active dialogue builds emotional connections, reducing churn.
- **Campaign feedback**: Comment sentiment and UGC reveal how campaigns are received.
- **Lead generation**: Engaged followers are more likely to convert, share and return.

Engagement metrics can also feed into predictive analytics models, allowing brands to forecast virality, customer lifetime value (CLV) and even churn risk (Fader, 2020).

6.5 Responding to customer feedback

In today's real-time digital landscape, the ability to respond effectively to customer feedback on social media is a strategic imperative. Social media has transformed customer service from a private interaction to a public spectacle – visible not just to the brand and the individual user but also to the entire online audience. Every comment, tweet or review has the potential to influence brand perception, shape customer satisfaction and even go viral. Consequently, a brand's responsiveness has become a defining aspect of its customer experience strategy (Chaffey and Ellis-Chadwick, 2022; Goodman, 2019).

Framework: The service recovery paradox in social media

The **service recovery paradox** (SRP) refers to a situation in which a customer thinks more highly of a company after it has corrected a problem compared to how they would regard the company if no issue had occurred (McCollough et al, 2000). In the social media context, this paradox is amplified – public recoveries can increase trust and attract new followers if handled with transparency and empathy.

Three pillars of successful social media recovery are:

1 **Speed** – rapid acknowledgment reduces frustration.

2 **Empathy** – personalized, humanized responses show care.

3 **Resolution** – clear action plans or compensation demonstrate accountability.

EXAMPLE

JetBlue Airways

In 2023, JetBlue Airways responded within minutes to a viral tweet about a delayed flight. Its prompt, empathetic response offering a voucher received over 10,000 likes and reshaped the narrative from complaint to commendation (JetBlue, 2023).

Types of customer feedback on social media

Feedback can take several forms, each requiring a tailored approach (see Table 6.7).

Using **social media triage systems** – where messages are categorized and prioritized based on urgency and sentiment – helps brands manage feedback volume effectively (Sprout Social, 2023c).

The role of response time and tone

Research shows that **response time** is one of the most critical factors in user satisfaction. According to a survey by HubSpot (2022), 79 per cent of consumers expect a response to social media inquiries within 24 hours; 40 per cent expect one within an hour.

Table 6.7   Social media feedback types

Feedback type	Example	Suggested response
Positive feedback	Praise for service or product	Thank the customer, highlight the feedback publicly
Constructive criticism	Suggestions for improvement	Acknowledge ideas, tag relevant internal departments
Negative complaint	Product dissatisfaction, poor service experience	Apologize sincerely, offer resolution, take it offline
Crisis escalation	Viral negative publicity	Act swiftly, issue public statement, launch response plan

Equally important is **tone of voice**. Robotic or scripted replies can exacerbate a customer's frustration, while warm, empathetic language can diffuse tension. Personalization – using the customer's name, referencing specific concerns and avoiding generic phrases – is key to meaningful engagement.

EXAMPLE

Starbucks

Starbucks' X (formerly Twitter) support team uses personalized responses to handle queries ranging from mobile app issues to in-store experiences. The tone is consistent with the friendly brand persona, and they aim to resolve each case publicly before moving to private DMs, preserving transparency (Starbucks, 2022).

Platform-specific best practices

- **X (Twitter):** Ideal for rapid responses. Keep replies public, short and informative, then move complex cases to DM.
- **Instagram:** Reply to comments and story tags; repost positive mentions on Stories.
- **Facebook:** Use Messenger auto-responses to acknowledge complaints quickly.
- **TikTok:** Monitor comment sections of viral videos and respond with video replies if needed.
- **LinkedIn:** Maintain professionalism; useful for B2B customer inquiries and employer branding.

Automation tools (e.g. chatbots or smart reply templates) can streamline first-contact responses but should be backed by human escalation for complex issues.

Analytics-driven feedback management

Social media analytics platforms allow brands to track feedback trends over time. Key metrics include:

- **Response rate:** Percentage of inquiries/comments responded to within a given time.
- **Average response time:** Time between feedback received and brand response.
- **Sentiment shifts:** Change in sentiment before and after brand engagement.
- **Resolution rate:** Percentage of social issues successfully resolved.
- **Customer satisfaction score (CSAT):** Survey-based measure following interaction.

By monitoring these KPIs, brands can evaluate team performance and improve their customer care playbook (Tuten and Solomon, 2018).

Escalation protocols and crisis response

Brands must prepare for high-impact scenarios such as product recalls, public controversies or influencer missteps. Social media often serves as the first outlet for such escalations.

Crisis response frameworks should include:

- **Monitoring** – real-time social listening for unusual spikes in negative sentiment.
- **Team readiness** – predefined roles (communications, legal, customer support).
- **Messaging templates** – pre-approved public statements for quick deployment.
- **Feedback loop** – learnings fed back into future strategy.

EXAMPLE

Lush

In 2022, Lush Cosmetics faced backlash over an ethical sourcing issue. Its social media team acknowledged the issue, launched a behind-the-scenes transparency campaign, and regained user trust within weeks, as shown by sentiment improvement and share-of-voice recovery (*WWD*, 2022b).

Strategic implications for brand equity

Responding to feedback on social media is more than reactive service – it is a **brand-building opportunity**. Every customer interaction is a micro-moment that shapes public perception. Consistent, thoughtful engagement:

- reinforces brand values (e.g. transparency, empathy, accountability)
- encourages advocacy and repeat engagement
- reduces churn by addressing dissatisfaction early
- provides insight for product development and innovation.

Moreover, brands that are responsive online signal that they are modern, agile and customer-centric – qualities that influence **purchase intent**, especially among Gen Z and millennial consumers (Accenture, 2021).

6.6 Building community through online interactions

Building a strong online community is a cornerstone of modern social media strategy. As consumer behaviour shifts from transactional interaction to relationship-oriented engagement, brands that foster active, loyal communities enjoy a competitive advantage in customer retention, brand advocacy and long-term equity. Online communities serve not only as engagement ecosystems but also as hubs for user-generated content, feedback loops and cultural relevance (Muniz and O'Guinn, 2001; Chaffey and Ellis-Chadwick, 2022).

Rather than focusing solely on pushing content, successful community-building centres around **creating spaces where customers feel seen, heard** and **empowered**. This relational approach transforms passive followers into active participants, advocates and co-creators in the brand's narrative. See Table 6.8 for examples.

Theoretical framework: Sense of virtual community (SOVC)

Blanchard and Markus (2004) define **sense of virtual community** using three pillars:

1 **Membership** – feeling of belonging and identification with the group.

2 **Influence** – users feel their participation has an impact.

3 **Shared emotional connection** – built through repeated, meaningful interactions.

These components are critical in designing social media strategies that move beyond visibility and reach to genuine relationship-building. When users identify with a community, they become more invested in the brand's success and are more likely to participate in campaigns, share content and provide advocacy.

EXAMPLE

LEGO

The 'LEGO Ideas' platform allows fans to submit product designs. If an idea garners enough community votes, LEGO may produce it. This builds a powerful sense of influence and shared purpose – key aspects of the SOVC model.

Benefits of building online communities

- **Customer loyalty:** Engaged communities foster brand stickiness and reduce churn.
- **UGC creation:** Communities become engines of organic content and peer validation.

- **Feedback channels:** Real-time feedback helps brands iterate on product design and messaging.
- **Cost-effective marketing:** Community-driven campaigns lower dependency on paid media.
- **Resilience:** Loyal communities defend brands during crises (e.g. cancel culture pushback).

REAL-WORLD EXAMPLE   Peloton's digital fitness community

Peloton has built one of the most successful digital communities by merging fitness with interactive technology and community values. Users join themed workout groups (#PelotonMoms, #PowerZonePack), high-five each other during live classes and engage via Facebook groups and Reddit forums.

According to Peloton's 2023 Shareholder Report:

- Over 95 per cent of monthly active users engage with the community features.
- Community members have **twice the retention** rate of non-engaged users.

This case illustrates that digital communities, when tied to identity and lifestyle, become a core driver of customer value.

Tactics for cultivating community

Table 6.8   Strategies for building online communities

Strategy	Description	Brand example
Exclusive spaces	Closed groups, invite-only events	Sephora Beauty Insider Facebook Group
User spotlights	Featuring user stories, testimonials	Lululemon's #thesweatlife series
Interactive campaigns	Contests, polls, challenges that foster participation	TikTok's #InMyDenim Challenge by Guess
Live engagements	AMAs, livestreams, webinars	Glossier's CEO Q&A sessions on Instagram Live
Brand rituals	Recurring content series that build consistency	Starbucks' #RedCupContest tradition
Crowdsourcing ideas	Letting users co-create or vote on brand decisions	LEGO Ideas, Spotify Wrapped feedback loop

Metrics to measure community health

Building a community requires ongoing measurement to ensure sustainability and relevance. Key metrics include those shown in Table 6.9.

Monitoring these KPIs provides signals on community vitality, topic resonance and potential drop-off risk.

Framework: Community lifecycle model (Jono Bacon, 2012)

This model outlines four stages of digital community development:

1 **Inception** – initial growth through visibility and outreach.

2 **Establishment** – set norms, rituals and member roles.

3 **Maturity** – peak participation, self-regulation by members.

4 **Sustainability or decline** – requires continuous value, moderation and innovation.

TIP

Brands should plan strategies specific to the current lifecycle phase (e.g. heavy moderation during establishment; innovation and UGC activation in maturity).

Table 6.9 Metrics to measure community health

Metric	What it measures	Tool
Community growth rate	How fast the community is expanding	Meta Insights, Discord Analytics
Engagement per member	Activity level per individual	Facebook Group Insights
Sentiment ratio	Balance of positive vs negative interactions	Brandwatch, Sprout Social
Retention rate	Percentage of returning participants	CRM and social analytics integration
UGC volume	Number of member-generated posts/tags	Hootsuite, Instagram API

Risks and challenges in community management

Despite their value, online communities pose risks if not managed proactively:

- **Toxicity and negativity:** Unmoderated comments or spam can erode trust.
- **Unrealistic expectations:** Overpromising participatory influence can lead to backlash.
- **Burnout:** Continuous engagement requires content, attention and resources.

Thus, brands must implement **community guidelines**, employ trained moderators, and have escalation policies in place for conflict management (Tuten and Solomon, 2018).

Strategic implications

Online community-building is not merely a social media tactic – it is a strategic investment in **customer experience, brand equity** and **innovation**. By cultivating emotional bonds and shared identity, communities become long-term assets that:

- lower marketing costs
- fuel viral growth
- strengthen customer feedback loops
- enable advocacy and resilience during crises.

Brands that master this dynamic create more than audiences – they build tribes, cultures and movements.

EXERCISES

Social listening and sentiment analysis

Exercise 1

Use a social listening tool (e.g. Brandwatch, Talkwalker, Hootsuite) to monitor brand mentions and analyse public sentiment during a recent product launch by a global brand (e.g. Nike, Apple or H&M). Identify sentiment trends, top influencers and potential PR risks or opportunities.

Exercise 2: Model: Social media dashboard template

Present a template showing key KPIs for social media performance. Include:

- engagement rate by platform
- reach and impressions

- follower growth
- top performing posts
- sentiment over time.

Use tools like Google Data Studio or Sprout Social to create a visual dashboard.

REAL-WORLD EXAMPLE   Apple – Vision Pro launch

Background

Apple launched the Vision Pro mixed reality headset in early 2024. The announcement generated significant online chatter across X, Reddit, Instagram and tech blogs.

Step 1: Data collection with a social listening tool

- **Tool used**: Talkwalker Free Search and Brandwatch Consumer Research
- **Date range**: One week before and after the launch event (e.g. January 31 – February 14, 2024)
- **Keywords monitored**: 'Vision Pro', 'Apple headset', 'Apple AR', 'spatial computing'.

Step 2: Sentiment analysis (Table 6.10)

Table 6.10   Product launch sentiment trend overview

Date	Volume of mentions	Positive (%)	Neutral (%)	Negative (%)
31 Jan	5,200	55%	30%	15%
2 Feb (launch)	28,000	43%	32%	25%
5 Feb	18,400	50%	35%	15%
14 Feb	7,100	60%	30%	10%

Insights

- **Initial spike in negative sentiment** due to the $3,500 price point and privacy concerns.
- **Positive sentiment** increased post-launch, driven by influencer unboxings, user curiosity and early tech reviews highlighting innovation.

Step 3: Identify top influencers (Table 6.11)

Table 6.11   Identifying top influencers overview

Influencer	Platform	Followers	Sentiment	Impact
Marques Brownlee (MKBHD)	YouTube/X	17 million	Neutral to positive	Tech credibility and reach boosted neutral sentiment
Sara Dietschy	YouTube	900,000	Positive	Viral unboxing video with over 1.2 million views
The Verge	X	3.5 million	Mixed	Published both critical pricing commentary and product praise

Step 4: Risk and opportunity analysis

- **PR risks**:
  - High initial negative sentiment around affordability and perceived elitism.
  - Concerns about 'screen addiction' for children highlighted on parenting forums.

- **Opportunities**:
  - Widespread praise for the product's UX and innovation from tech influencers.
  - Use of AR/VR creators and educators on platforms like TikTok and YouTube could increase credibility and engagement among Gen Z.

Actionable recommendation

Apple could partner with education and design influencers to reframe Vision Pro as a creative, productivity-enhancing tool – not just an entertainment device.

REAL-WORLD EXAMPLES   When marketing analytics goes wrong

Case 1: Target Canada – misguided inventory and demand forecasting

Background: When US retail giant Target launched its Canadian operations in 2013, it used marketing analytics and inventory management systems based on its US models without tailoring them to the Canadian market (Castaldo, 2016).

- **Poor analytics practice**:
  - Target Canada relied on **flawed forecasting models** and **incomplete data imports**.

- o The supply chain analytics system misread demand, leading to **overstock of unpopular products** and **empty shelves for essentials**.
- o Customer sentiment analysis was **ignored**, despite increasing complaints on social media.

- **Outcome**:
  - o Lost consumer trust due to poor in-store experience.
  - o Shut down all Canadian stores within two years, resulting in a **$2 billion loss**.

Lesson: Analytics must be **localized, context-aware** and **cross-validated** across channels. Failure to integrate **customer feedback, inventory** and **market-specific data** undermines strategic execution.

Case 2: Jumia (Africa) – misaligned attribution and customer behaviour tracking

Background: Jumia, Africa's leading e-commerce platform, faced issues with its **attribution modelling** and campaign measurement in several regions between 2017 and 2020.

- **Poor analytics practice**:
  - o Relied heavily on **last-click attribution**, misrepresenting the true value of **awareness-building efforts** on platforms like Facebook and WhatsApp.
  - o **Ignored regional digital behaviour**, such as the high use of mobile data-saving browsers and the role of informal social sharing in purchase decisions.
  - o Lacked **CRM integration**, so customer insights from app usage were disconnected from purchase data.

- **Outcome**:
  - o Over-invested in paid performance channels while underestimating the impact of social and organic engagement.
  - o Suffered a **drop in customer retention** and **rising acquisition costs**.

Lesson: In emerging markets, consumer journeys are often **non-linear** and **hybrid**. Marketing analytics must account for **informal networks, device limitations** and **cross-platform behaviours**.

EXERCISE ⬈

Model: Social media dashboard template

Plan and build a dashboard using Google Looker Studio, Sprout Social or Hootsuite Analytics. The dashboard should present a comprehensive overview of social media performance across platforms such as Instagram, Twitter, Facebook and YouTube.

Dashboard components

Table 6.12   Social media dashboard components

Section	Metric	Why it matters
Engagement overview	Engagement rate per platform	Tracks quality of interactions across posts
Reach and impressions	Daily/weekly reach, impressions	Measures visibility and content exposure
Audience growth	Net new followers	Indicates brand traction and campaign effectiveness
Content performance	Top five posts by engagement and reach	Identifies content themes or formats resonating with users
Sentiment monitoring	Net sentiment over time (line graph)	Tracks emotional response to brand over selected period
Influencer mentions	Top influencers ranked by engagement	Highlights advocacy and amplification potential

Sample dashboard layout (suggested template design)

- **Section 1: Engagement summary**
  - Line graph: Engagement over last 30 days (by platform)
  - Bar chart: Engagement rate by platform (Instagram, X, TikTok)

- **Section 2: Reach and impressions**
  - Area chart: Daily reach trend
  - KPI tiles: Total reach, impressions, reach growth percentage

- o Table: Follower growth by day and by channel
- o Pie chart: New vs returning users (if integrated with GA4)
- **Section 4: Sentiment analysis**
  - o Donut chart: Sentiment breakdown (positive, neutral, negative)
  - o Word cloud: Most frequently mentioned words/hashtags
- **Section 5: Top performing posts**
- Ranked list: Posts by likes, shares, CTR
- Thumbnail previews (from API integrations)

Bonus challenge (advanced students)

Create a UTM-tagged link tracking report in Google Analytics 4 to see how traffic from social media converts on a campaign-specific landing page. Integrate those metrics (bounce rate, time on site, conversions) into the dashboard.

Conclusion

Chapter 6 provides a comprehensive overview of social media analytics (SMA) as a critical tool for modern marketing strategy, brand management and audience engagement. The chapter begins by contextualizing SMA within the digital marketing ecosystem, highlighting its role in performance monitoring and customer engagement across platforms such as Instagram, Facebook, TikTok and X (formerly Twitter).

Key performance indicators (KPIs) such as reach, impressions, engagement rate, click-through rate (CTR), save/share rate and follower growth are defined and explored with applied brand examples (e.g. Nike, H&M, Apple). The chapter then introduces leading social listening tools such as Brandwatch, Talkwalker and Sprout Social, emphasizing how they leverage natural language processing (NLP) to detect sentiment and track brand reputation in real time.

An in-depth discussion of sentiment analysis explains how content is categorized as positive, negative or neutral, which helps organizations predict crises and shape narratives. Cross-channel integration is addressed as a strategy to unify data across CRM, email, content and social media platforms, thereby enhancing attribution modelling and campaign targeting. The chapter defines cross-channel integration as the strategic alignment of customer data, touchpoints and content delivery across digital and offline environments to ensure consistent brand messaging and a seamless user journey.

Real-world brand case studies are featured to demonstrate both best and poor practices. Apple's use of real-time sentiment analysis during the iPhone 14 launch serves as a best-practice model, while Target Canada and Jumia illustrate the consequences of flawed analytics strategies. Additionally, smaller brands such as Glossier exemplify how community-driven content and micro-influencer analytics can enhance brand equity.

The chapter concludes by stressing the strategic importance of integrating social media analytics with wider business intelligence systems and marketing dashboards. By leveraging social insights, brands can make agile, data-driven decisions that improve customer satisfaction, brand loyalty and ROI.

References

Accenture (2021) *The Human Touch in the Digital Age, Accenture Consumer Survey Report*, www.accenture.com (archived at https://perma.cc/86WG-GRMR)

Adidas (2023) *Social Media Playbook: FIFA Campaign,* Adidas Marketing Archives

Apple (2022a) *iPhone 14 Launch: Social Sentiment Analysis Summary*, Apple Marketing Team report

Apple (2022b) iPhone 14 launch highlights: Customer feedback and response, Apple Newsroom, www.apple.com/newsroom (archived at https://perma.cc/G5DL-2NZZ)

Apple (2023) Apple Vision Pro launch report, Apple Newsroom, www.apple.com/newsroom (archived at https://perma.cc/G5DL-2NZZ)

Apple (2024) Vision Pro product launch announcement, Apple Newsroom www.apple.com/newsroom (archived at https://perma.cc/G5DL-2NZZ)

Bacon, J (2012) *The Art of Community: Building the New Age of Participation*, Sebastopol, CA: O'Reilly Media

Blanchard, A L and Markus, M L (2004) The experienced 'sense' of a virtual community: Characteristics and processes, *Database for Advances in Information Systems*, 35 (1), 65–79

Bostrom, R P and Heinen, J S (1977) MIS problems and failures: A socio-technical perspective, *MIS Quarterly*, 1 (3), 17–32

Brandwatch (2024) Understanding sentiment in a digital world, www.brandwatch.com (archived at https://perma.cc/EQ8E-33LN)

Brodie, R J, Hollebeek, L D, Juric, B and Ilic, A (2013) Consumer engagement in a virtual brand community, *Journal of Business Research*, 66 (1), 105–14

Castaldo, J (2016) The last days of Target Canada, *Canadian Business*, https://canadianbusiness.com/ideas/the-last-days-of-target-canada/

Chaffey, D and Ellis-Chadwick, F (2022) *Digital Marketing: Strategy, Implementation, and Practice* (8th ed.), Harlow: Pearson Education

Charlesworth, A (2021) *Digital Marketing: A Practical Approach* (4th ed.), Abingdon: Routledge

Fader, P S (2020) Customer-based corporate valuation and the paradox of customer centricity, MMA Global Presentation, mmaglobal.com (archived at https://mmaglobal.com/files/documents/2020-06-24-gmgd-peter-fader.pdf)

Fan, W and Gordon, M D (2014) The power of social media analytics, *Communications of the ACM*, 57 (6), 74–81

Forbes (2018) Nike sales jump 31% after Kaepernick ad campaign, *Forbes*, www.forbes.com (archived at https://perma.cc/AB3B-92EL)

Gerlitz, C and Helmond, A (2013) The like economy: Social buttons and the data-intensive web, *New Media & Society*, 15 (8), 1348–65

Glossier (2022) *Instagram Engagement Strategy,* internal brand report

Goodman, J (2019) *Strategic Customer Service: Managing the Customer Experience to Increase Positive Word of Mouth, Build Loyalty, and Maximize Profits*, New York: AMACOM

Google (2024) Looker Studio Tutorials, www.lookerstudio.google.com (archived at https://perma.cc/D2FF-P3DH)

H&M (2022) *Annual and Sustainability Report*, www.annualreports.com/HostedData/AnnualReportArchive/h/hm-group_2022.pdf (archived at https://perma.cc/4UEG-TZXG)

He, W, Zha, S and Li, L (2017) Social media competitive analysis and text mining: A case study in the pizza industry, *International Journal of Information Management*, 37 (3), 188–95

Hollebeek, L D, Glynn, M S and Brodie, R J (2014) Consumer brand engagement in social media, *Journal of Strategic Marketing*, 22 (2), 92–114

HubSpot (2022) *Customer Expectations Report*, www.hubspot.com (archived at https://perma.cc/5KXH-FUM5)

JetBlue (2023) *Customer Engagement via Twitter Case Summary*, internal report

Kaplan, A M and Haenlein, M (2010) Users of the world, unite! The challenges and opportunities of social media, *Business Horizons*, 53 (1), 59–68

Keller, K L (2003) *Strategic Brand Management: Building, Measuring, and Managing Brand Equity*, Upper Saddle River, NJ: Prentice Hall

Kotler, P, Kartajaya, H and Setiawan, I (2021) *Marketing 5.0: Technology for Humanity*, Hoboken, NJ: Wiley

Lemon, K N and Verhoef, P C (2016) Understanding customer experience throughout the customer journey, *Journal of Marketing*, 80 (6), 69–96

Liu, X and Viswanathan, S (2021) Attribution modeling in retail: Bridging the gap between online and offline, *Journal of Retail Analytics*, 7 (3), 221–37

McAfee, A and Brynjolfsson, E (2012) Big data: The management revolution, *Harvard Business Review*, 90 (10), 60–68

McCollough, M A, Berry, L L and Yadav, M S (2000) An empirical investigation of customer satisfaction after service failure and recovery, *Journal of Service Research*, 3 (2), 121–37

Muniz, A M and O'Guinn, T C (2001) Brand community, *Journal of Consumer Research*, 27 (4), 412–32

Netflix Media Center (2022) *Stranger Things 4 Marketing Report*, media.netflix.com (archived at https://perma.cc/SC28-SDK2)

Nike (2020) *You Can't Stop Us Campaign Analysis*, www.nike.com (archived at https://perma.cc/R58F-4AES)

Patagonia (2022) *Sustainability and Engagement Report*, Ventura, CA: Patagonia

Peloton (2023) *Annual Shareholder Engagement Report*, internal corporate report

Rival IQ (2023) *Social Media Industry Benchmark Report*, https://get.rivaliq.com/hubfs/eBooks/2023-social-media-benchmark-report.pdf (archived at https://perma.cc/Q7K2-YPY4)

Ryan, D (2020) *Understanding Digital Marketing: Marketing Strategies for Engaging the Digital Generation* (5th ed.) London: Kogan Page

Sephora (2022) *Annual Digital Strategy and Social Media Performance Report*, internal corporate report

Sprout Social (2023a) Social media analytics guide, www.sproutsocial.com (archived at https://perma.cc/X4S4-U4HP)

Sprout Social (2023b) The Sprout Index: How to manage social customer care at scale, www.sproutsocial.com (archived at https://perma.cc/X4S4-U4HP)

Sprout Social (2023c) The Sprout Social Index™ Edition XIX: Social media customer care and feedback triage systems, https://media.sproutsocial.com/uploads/Sprout-Social-Index-Report-2023.pdf (archived at https://perma.cc/E7SR-U5YF)

Starbucks (2022) *Social Media Customer Service Playbook*, internal corporate report

Stelzner, M A (2022) *Social Media Marketing Industry Report 2022*, *Social Media Examiner*, www.socialmediaexaminer.com (archived at https://perma.cc/6V9R-XRY4)

Stieglitz, S, Mirbabaie, M, Ross, B and Neuberger, C (2018) Social media analytics: Challenges in topic discovery, data collection, and data preparation, *International Journal of Information Management*, 39, 156–68

Talkwalker (2023) State of social listening, www.talkwalker.com (archived at https://perma.cc/6PP9-XHJJ)

Tuten, T L and Solomon, M R (2018) *Social Media Marketing* (3rd ed.), London: Sage

Tuten, T L and Solomon, M R (2021) *Social Media Marketing* (4th ed.), London: Sage

Vargo, S L and Lusch, R F (2008) Service-dominant logic: Continuing the evolution, *Journal of the Academy of Marketing Science*, 36 (1), 1–10

Verhoef, P C, Kannan, P K and Inman, J J (2015) From multi-channel retailing to omni-channel retailing: Introduction to the special issue on multi-channel retailing, *Journal of Retailing*, 91 (2), 174–81

Weller, K (2021) *Social Media Analytics: Effective Tools for Building, Interpreting and Using Metrics*, London: Routledge

WWD (2022a) How Glossier builds brand through community, *WWD*, www.wwd.com (archived at https://perma.cc/BV87-HVTM)

WWD (2022b) Lush transparency campaign averts crisis, *WWD*, www.wwd.com (archived at https://perma.cc/BV87-HVTM)

07 | Web analytics – analysing website traffic and user behaviour to optimize user experience

LEARNING OUTCOMES

By the end of this chapter, students should be able to:

- Understand the strategic role of web analytics in digital marketing performance.
- Interpret key website metrics (e.g. bounce rate, session duration, user flow) using tools like Google Analytics.
- Apply heatmaps and click tracking tools to analyse and visualize user behaviour.
- Identify areas of website improvement and implement A/B testing to validate changes.
- Integrate qualitative and quantitative insights to drive user-centric design and conversion optimization.

CHAPTER OUTLINE

Introduction to web analytics

7.1 Key website metrics: What they mean and how to interpret them

7.2 Tools for behaviour tracking: Google Analytics, Hotjar, Crazy Egg

KEY TERMS

A/B testing: An experimental method that compares two versions of a web page (Version A vs Version B) to determine which performs better based on a defined goal (e.g. conversion). Example: Testing red vs green 'Buy Now' buttons to see which drives higher sales.

Bounce rate: The percentage of visitors who leave a website after viewing only one page, without interacting further. Example: A blog post with an 85 per cent bounce rate may need clearer calls to action (CTAs).

Click tracking: A method of logging the exact links, buttons or elements that users click on within a site. Example: Few clicks on a 'Subscribe' button may indicate poor placement or visibility.

Conversion rate optimization (CRO): The systematic process of increasing the percentage of website visitors who take a desired action. Example: Streamlining a checkout form to reduce cart abandonment.

Exit rate: The percentage of visitors who leave a website from a specific page, regardless of how many pages they viewed before. Example: A high exit rate on a checkout payment page may point to missing payment options.

Goal completions: A measure of how often users complete defined actions that represent business value, such as purchases, newsletter sign-ups or downloads. Example: Spotify tracking free-trial sign-ups as a primary goal.

Heatmap: A visual tool that shows where users interact most on a page, often using colour gradients to indicate high or low engagement. Example: A homepage heatmap showing most clicks on the navigation bar.

Heatmap types (scroll, click, move):

- o **Scroll heatmap**: Shows how far down users scroll.
- o **Click heatmap**: Shows where users click most.
- o **Move heatmap**: Tracks mouse hover activity, often a proxy for attention.

Net promoter score (NPS) (related to engagement): A metric measuring customer loyalty based on how likely users are to recommend a product/service. Example: Post-purchase survey asking, 'How likely are you to recommend us to a friend?'

Rage clicks (Clarity tool): Instances where users repeatedly click the same element out of frustration. Example: Users clicking on a non-functional calendar widget multiple times.

Session duration: The average amount of time users spend on a website during a single visit (session). Example: A product page with a one-minute average session might lack enough detail to hold attention.

User flow: The path visitors take as they navigate through a website, from entry to exit. Example: High drop-offs at the 'Shipping Info' page during checkout suggest friction at that stage.

Introduction to web analytics

In today's digital-first environment, a brand's website is not just a static repository of information – it is a dynamic and interactive touchpoint integral to every phase of the customer journey. From discovery to decision-making and post-purchase support, the website plays a critical role in shaping user perception and experience. As such, understanding how visitors interact with websites has become essential for marketers, designers and business leaders aiming to optimize performance, improve user satisfaction and ultimately drive business outcomes. This is where web analytics becomes indispensable.

Web analytics refers to the systematic process of collecting, measuring, analysing and reporting data generated by users' interactions with a website. The objective is to understand visitor behaviour, evaluate digital performance and guide decisions around content, design and functionality (Clifton, 2020). With the explosion of digital data, web analytics provides the empirical foundation for transforming websites from mere online brochures into sophisticated, user-centric ecosystems that convert visitors into customers.

Google Analytics serves as an essential tool for understanding how visitors interact with a website, providing a wealth of data that can highlight where improvements are needed. When analysing this data, the first step is to scrutinize metrics like bounce rate, average session duration and page views. A high bounce rate on specific pages may indicate that visitors are not finding what they expect, perhaps due to poor content relevance or confusing layout. Similarly, low engagement metrics can reveal sections of the site that fail to capture user interest, signalling an opportunity for redesign or content refresh.

Attention should also be paid to user flow reports, which trace the paths visitors take through your website. These reports reveal common entry points and exits, helping identify bottlenecks or dead ends where users tend to drop off. If a significant number of users exit after viewing a certain page, it could be a sign of poor content, slow loading times or obstacles preventing further navigation. By pinpointing these pain points, marketers can prioritize specific pages or processes for optimization, whether that means simplifying design, clarifying calls to action or enhancing content clarity.

Combining quantitative metrics with qualitative insights offers a strategic advantage. For example, user recordings and session replays, often available through integrated tools or third-party extensions, can give visual context to analytics data. Watching real user sessions can uncover hidden issues like confusing menus or unresponsive buttons that analytics alone might not reveal. By systematically analysing these patterns, marketers can craft targeted improvements that directly address the root causes of user frustration, ultimately boosting conversion rates and engagement.

From intuition to data-driven decision-making

Traditionally, decisions about web design and content strategy were driven largely by subjective judgement, stakeholder opinions or aesthetic preferences. However, in the contemporary landscape, such an approach is insufficient and often counterproductive. The shift towards data-driven decision-making has been fuelled by the need for agility, accountability and personalization in digital marketing strategies (Chaffey and Ellis-Chadwick, 2022).

Modern tools like Google Analytics, Adobe Analytics and Matomo provide granular insights into user behaviour at scale, revealing how long users stay on a page, what they click, where they drop off and what drives conversion. These tools track user sessions, bounce rates, click paths, device types, traffic sources and dozens of other metrics. Furthermore, integrated platforms like Hotjar and Crazy Egg provide qualitative insights such as heatmaps, scroll depth and session replays, adding a behavioural layer to the raw quantitative data.

Key goals of web analytics

The purpose of web analytics extends far beyond measuring traffic. A robust analytics programme supports multiple goals, including:

- **Improving user experience (UX)**: Identifying pain points in navigation or content gaps that cause user frustration.

- **Optimizing conversion rates (CRO)**: Pinpointing where visitors abandon funnels such as product pages or checkout sequences.

- **Evaluating campaign effectiveness**: Tracking referral traffic and attribution to assess which channels (e.g. paid search, email, organic social) are delivering ROI.

- **Content strategy optimization**: Determining which pages or blog posts are most engaging to inform future content investments.

- **Segmentation and personalization**: Understanding audience behaviour by device, geography, demographics or referral source.

Web analytics framework: The 5W model

A helpful framework to understand the function and scope of web analytics is the 5W model (Table 7.1).

This model offers a comprehensive lens through which marketers can interpret web behaviour, diagnose problems and align digital strategies with user expectations.

Table 7.1   The 5 Ws

W	Explanation	Example
Who	Who are your users?	Google Analytics reveals gender, age, location
What	What are they doing on the site?	Pages viewed, CTAs clicked, sessions
When	When do they visit?	Peak traffic hours, seasonal behaviour
Where	Where did they come from?	Referrals, organic search, email links
Why	Why are they converting (or not)?	Exit pages, bounce rates, session replays

Table 7.2   Website marketing funnel metrics

Funnel stage	Objective	Key metrics
Awareness	Drive traffic	Impressions, page views, new vs returning users
Consideration	Engage audience	Bounce rate, average session duration, pages/session
Conversion	Motivate action	Goal completions, e-commerce conversion rate
Retention	Maintain loyalty	Repeat visitors, average order value (AOV)

Web analytics in the marketing funnel

Web analytics also plays a key role in mapping the customer journey through the stages of the marketing funnel: awareness, consideration, conversion and retention. At each stage, specific metrics provide critical feedback (Table 7.2).

For instance, if users are exiting the site before completing purchases, a marketer may look at time-on-page or load speeds during the checkout process and implement A/B tests for optimization. Such data-centric insights are critical in minimizing drop-offs and improving user satisfaction.

Role of Google Analytics and enhanced capabilities

Google Analytics 4 (GA4), the latest iteration (as of writing) of Google's platform, offers event-based tracking rather than session-based metrics, providing more flexibility and granularity in understanding user interactions. It includes features such as:

- user-centric tracking across devices
- AI-driven insights and predictive metrics
- seamless integration with Google Ads for attribution
- custom event creation (e.g. scroll depth, video plays).

GA4's predictive capabilities allow marketers to identify users with a high likelihood to purchase or churn, facilitating targeted remarketing efforts (Google, 2024a, b).

REAL-WORLD EXAMPLE   Brand application: Zara

Zara, a leading fast-fashion brand, uses web analytics not only to monitor sales performance but also to gauge customer behaviour. For example, if analytics reveal high bounce rates (see section 7.2 for definition) on the mobile version of the site, Zara's UX team can investigate issues such as long load times or poorly optimized product images. They can also test different layouts using heatmaps to see where users' attention is concentrated – are they scrolling past the size guide? Are they clicking on the product images or reviews?

Using web analytics, Zara discovered that customers were abandoning the cart during the shipping details page. A redesign simplified the form fields and added real-time validation, improving the completion rate by 18 per cent (*Retail Gazette*, 2023e).

Challenges and ethical considerations

While web analytics provides powerful insights, it also introduces challenges:

- **Data overload:** With so many metrics available, it is easy to focus on vanity metrics (e.g. page views) instead of actionable KPIs.
- **Privacy compliance:** With increasing regulations like GDPR and CCPA, organizations must obtain proper consent and anonymize user data where required (ICO, 2022).
- **Interpretation complexity:** Without proper expertise, data can be misinterpreted, leading to poor business decisions.

Thus, effective use of web analytics requires not only the right tools but also a skilled team that understands the nuances of digital behaviour, data science and ethical standards.

7.1 Key website metrics: What they mean and how to interpret them

Web analytics serves as the foundation for understanding user behaviour on websites. While it is tempting to focus on flashy metrics like total visits or follower counts, the real value of web analytics lies in interpreting deeper metrics that influence decision-making, user experience (UX) and ultimately, business performance. The interpretation of key metrics such as bounce rate, session duration, page views, exit rate and goal completions enables marketers to understand not only what users are doing but why they are behaving in certain ways. Each metric provides a fragment of the user journey; together, they create a comprehensive map of digital engagement.

Bounce rate

Definition and interpretation

Bounce rate measures the percentage of users who leave a website after viewing only one page, without engaging further. A high bounce rate often indicates that users did not find what they were looking for or that the site did not compel them to continue browsing.

Why it matters

While a high bounce rate on a blog post might be acceptable (if the article fulfils the user's intent), a high bounce rate on a landing page or product page can indicate issues such as:

- poor content relevance
- slow page loading time
- confusing navigation
- misleading ads or links.

According to Google (2024a), an average bounce rate across industries ranges between 41 per cent and 55 per cent. However, pages designed to prompt immediate action – like product sales or subscriptions – should aim for much lower.

EXAMPLE

ASOS identified a 20 per cent higher bounce rate on its mobile homepage compared to desktop. Using Google Analytics and Hotjar heatmaps, they found the mobile CTA button was located below the fold. Redesigning the layout to push the CTA above the fold reduced bounce rates by 18 per cent (*Retail Dive*, 2022).

Average session duration

Definition and interpretation

This metric represents the average time users spend on a website per session. Short durations (e.g. under one minute) can signal disinterest, confusing UX or poorly matched content.

TIP

Combine session duration with other metrics like page depth and bounce rate to infer engagement levels more precisely. For example, a high bounce rate and low session duration point to users leaving quickly, while high duration and low pages per session may suggest users are stalled or confused.

Framework connection

From a customer journey analytics perspective, session duration corresponds with the engagement stage in the **attention, interest, desire, action (AIDA)** model. Longer sessions indicate sustained interest and a stronger likelihood of conversion (Kotler and Keller, 2016).

BuzzFeed analysed session durations across content categories and found quiz pages kept users engaged 2.5 times longer than standard articles. This insight led it to develop new quiz formats and increase ad revenue by 30 per cent.

Page views and pages per session

Definition and interpretation

Page views count the number of times a page is loaded, while pages per session reflect how many pages a user typically visits during one session. These metrics help assess content interest and site structure.

Key insight

Low pages per session may suggest limited internal linking or poor navigation. Conversely, unusually high numbers might indicate users are 'lost', searching for relevant information without success.

Optimization strategy

Implement content grouping in Google Analytics to understand which clusters of pages (e.g. product categories or blog themes) users tend to explore together. This can inform better content recommendation engines or internal linking structures.

EXAMPLE

Zalando

Zalando used clickstream and page view analysis to improve its site's internal search and recommendation systems. As a result, its pages per session rose by 15 per cent, and cart additions increased by 12 per cent (Zalando, 2022).

Exit rate

Definition and interpretation

Exit rate refers to the percentage of visitors who leave your website from a specific page, regardless of how many pages they've previously viewed. It is especially revealing when evaluating high-value pages like checkout flows or form submissions.

Difference between bounce and exit rate

- **Bounce:** Leaves after viewing only one page.
- **Exit:** Leaves after any number of pages, but the metric is attributed to the last one.

Example use case: High exit rates on a payment page might suggest trust issues, lack of payment options or technical bugs.

Framework

In the conversion funnel model (Awareness → Consideration → Conversion → Retention), exit rates are critical at the final conversion stage. Improving performance here can have outsized impacts on ROI.

H&M noticed a 30 per cent exit rate at the payment page. User recordings revealed that many visitors abandoned the cart due to a lack of PayPal integration. Adding the option decreased exits by 22 per cent and increased conversions by 14 per cent (H&M Digital Insights, 2023).

Goal completions

Definition and interpretation

Goals are specific user actions that signify value to your business – e.g. newsletter sign-ups, purchases, whitepaper downloads. In Google Analytics, goal completions track how often these desired actions occur.

Why this is crucial

Goal completions are not just performance indicators – they are the ultimate metric that ties web behaviour to business impact.

Types of goals

- Destination goals: e.g. thank-you page visit.
- Duration goals: e.g. stayed on site for more than two minutes.
- Event goals: e.g. watched a video, clicked a download button.

> **TIP** 💡
>
> Use goal funnels to visualize how users progress towards goal completion and where they drop off.

> **EXAMPLE** ◈
>
> Spotify
>
> Spotify measures free-trial sign-ups as a key goal. After integrating scroll-depth tracking and funnel analysis, it found 40 per cent of mobile users never reached the CTA section. A simple change in layout resulted in a 19 per cent uptick in goal completions (Spotify Design, 2022).

Holistic metrics interpretation

Analysing these metrics in isolation is less effective than interpreting them collectively. A holistic view connects metrics across stages of the user journey (Table 7.3).

When analysed through a framework such as Google's HEART framework (Happiness, Engagement, Adoption, Retention, Task success), these metrics can be categorized to evaluate UX improvements systematically (Rodden et al, 2010).

Turning metrics into action

The real power of web analytics lies in turning data into action. Once pain points and opportunities are identified, marketers can test solutions using A/B testing, multivariate analysis or session replays to validate changes. Whether reducing friction in the checkout process or adjusting blog content to retain readers, understanding key metrics enables informed, effective decision-making.

By integrating quantitative insights with UX design principles and iterative testing cycles, brands can deliver seamless and engaging digital experiences that convert users into loyal customers.

Table 7.3   Holistic metrics interpretation across UX journey

Stage	Metric(s)	Insight
Awareness	Bounce rate, page views	Are users finding the site appealing?
Engagement	Session duration, pages/session	Is the content valuable enough to explore?
Conversion	Goal completions, exit rate	Are users completing key actions?
Retention	Return visitors, session frequency	Are they coming back for more?

7.2 Tools for behaviour tracking: Google Analytics, Hotjar and Crazy Egg

In today's data-rich digital environment, understanding how users engage with a website goes beyond simply tracking clicks and visits. Website behaviour tracking tools allow marketers and analysts to interpret user actions, uncover experience friction points and guide design decisions that improve usability, engagement and conversions. While Google Analytics (GA) remains the backbone of most web analytics strategies, its strength lies in quantitative data. To obtain a more comprehensive picture, GA must be supplemented by qualitative tools such as Hotjar, Crazy Egg, and Microsoft Clarity, which visualize how users behave, rather than just what they do numerically.

Google Analytics: The quantitative powerhouse

Google Analytics is arguably the most widely used analytics tool globally, offering rich, real-time insights across traffic acquisition, audience behaviour and conversions (Clifton, 2020). The platform segments user data based on channels (organic, paid, direct, social), devices (desktop, tablet, mobile) and geolocation, allowing marketers to track and compare performance across marketing campaigns.

One of the core strengths of GA lies in its customizable goals and conversion tracking. These can include form submissions, purchases, video views or button clicks – defined through Events and Goals. By analysing funnels in GA, marketers can identify where users drop off before completing a desired action, helping prioritize UX improvements.

For example, a clothing retailer using Google Analytics may find that users from mobile devices exit at the payment page more frequently than desktop users. This insight could reveal mobile usability issues – such as poor form design or payment gateway bugs – that are affecting conversions.

Additionally, Google's GA4 – the next-generation analytics platform – introduces enhanced machine learning models for predictive metrics (e.g, purchase probability, churn likelihood) and better event-based tracking, giving marketers a more granular view of user journeys (Google Analytics, 2023).

Limitations of Google Analytics

Despite its power, Google Analytics has limitations. It lacks visual context. It cannot show how users navigate a page, where they scroll or hesitate or what interface elements they ignore. That's where behaviour analytics tools like Hotjar and Crazy Egg become essential.

Hotjar: Visualizing the customer journey

Hotjar is a user behaviour tool focused on visual and experiential analytics. It offers heatmaps, session recordings, funnel tracking and in-page feedback tools. These features help marketers understand the *why* behind performance data, enriching GA's *what*.

- Heatmaps show where users click, move and scroll, using colour gradients to indicate attention levels.
- Session recordings let marketers replay actual user journeys to identify usability issues.
- Feedback widgets allow visitors to leave comments in real-time, contextualized to their experience.

For example, ASOS, a major fashion e-commerce retailer, used Hotjar to evaluate how users interact with its product filters. Through session recordings, the brand noticed that users rarely clicked on the colour filter even though colour was a common search criterion. Further investigation revealed that the placement and label of the filter were unintuitive. After repositioning and renaming the filter module, engagement with filters increased by 21 per cent, improving the search-to-conversion rate (*Retail Dive, 2022*).

Hotjar's conversion funnel analysis is especially useful for tracking drop-offs across checkout or lead generation flows. Combined with Google Analytics data, marketers can correlate where users exit and how their on-page behaviour correlates with those decisions.

Hotjar use case: HubSpot

HubSpot, a leading marketing automation platform, used Hotjar to validate a page redesign decision. By combining scroll maps and survey data, they found users were missing CTA buttons below the fold. A quick redesign repositioned the CTA higher up the page, resulting in a 10 per cent increase in form submissions (Hotjar, 2021).

Crazy Egg: Deep customization and A/B testing insights

Crazy Egg offers similar features to Hotjar – heatmaps, session recordings and scroll maps – but with a focus on A/B testing support and confetti click tracking, which differentiates clicks by referral sources.

Key features of Crazy Egg include:

- **Overlay reports:** Show individual element performance on a page.
- **Scroll maps:** Indicate how far users scroll, highlighting where attention drops.
- **Confetti tool:** Disaggregates click data by segment – e.g. by device, location, campaign – revealing deeper behavioural patterns.

For example, Shopify, an e-commerce platform provider, used Crazy Egg's confetti maps to understand how users from paid search versus organic traffic engaged with landing pages. They discovered that PPC traffic clicked more often on pricing details, whereas organic users explored product tutorials. This insight led to customized landing pages based on traffic source, which improved session duration and lead conversion by 15 per cent (Shopify UX Team, 2022).

Crazy Egg also supports snapshots that track performance over time, offering a before-and-after view of UX changes. This longitudinal insight helps determine whether a change led to sustained behavioural improvements or only short-term gains.

Microsoft Clarity: A free alternative with AI-powered insights

Microsoft Clarity is a free, privacy-compliant behaviour analytics tool that includes many Hotjar and Crazy Egg features: session recordings, heatmaps and rage-click tracking (clicking repeatedly out of frustration). Clarity's AI-driven insights and low-friction installation have made it increasingly popular among small businesses.

Unique features include:

- **Dead clicks:** Clicks on non-functioning elements (e.g. images that look like buttons).
- **Rage clicks:** Indicators of user frustration.
- **AI tagging:** Highlights unusual user behaviour automatically.

Clarity does not sample data (unlike some GA free-tier versions), making it suitable for sites with moderate to high traffic that want full data access. It integrates easily with GA4, allowing marketers to compare behavioural and quantitative data side-by-side (Microsoft, 2023).

EXAMPLE

Skyscanner

Skyscanner, a global travel platform, deployed Microsoft Clarity to monitor page performance during a major site overhaul. Clarity identified unexpected rage clicks on the calendar booking tool, which users perceived as slow and unresponsive.

Post-implementation refinements based on session replays improved conversion rates by 9 per cent during peak travel season (Skyscanner, 2023).

Behaviour tracking: *Strategic integration and ethics*

Combining quantitative and qualitative analytics is not just a best practice – it is essential for a complete view of user experience. While Google Analytics shows the where and when, Hotjar, Crazy Egg and Clarity reveal the how and why. For digital marketers and UX professionals, triangulating data across these tools allows for:

- prioritized UX improvements based on impact and evidence
- hypothesis generation for A/B testing
- personalized messaging and interface design.

However, the collection of behavioural data must be ethically and legally compliant. Tools should be configured to:

- respect GDPR/CCPA guidelines (e.g. anonymizing IPs)
- avoid tracking sensitive data (e.g. form entries)
- inform users via cookie banners and privacy notices.

7.3 Heatmaps and click tracking: Visualizing the customer journey

In digital marketing and UX design, the ability to visualize how users interact with a web page is invaluable. Heatmaps and click tracking have emerged as essential behavioural analytics tools, allowing marketers and designers to see exactly where user attention is focused – and where it is not. Unlike purely quantitative data such as page views or bounce rates, heatmaps provide a spatial representation of user behaviour, translating interaction into intuitive visual formats that aid rapid diagnosis of design and content issues.

Heatmaps and click tracking tools have become valuable instruments for visualizing how visitors engage with website content. Heatmaps display areas of a page that attract the most attention by representing data through colour gradients – warm colours like red and orange indicating high engagement areas, while cooler colours reveal less interaction. Click tracking complements this by recording where users click, allowing insights into which buttons, links or images receive the most interaction. Both tools provide a tangible view of user behaviour that raw data cannot fully capture.

Implementing heatmaps involves placing a tracking script on your website, which then aggregates data over a specified period. It helps identify which parts of a page are drawing attention and which are being ignored. For example, if a crucial call-to-action button remains in plain sight but receives few clicks, it suggests the need to re-evaluate its placement, visual appeal or messaging. Similarly, heatmaps can reveal accidental clicks or engagement hotspots that may be misaligned with your strategic goals, allowing optimization of layout and content presentation.

Understanding heatmaps

Heatmaps are graphical representations that show how users engage with a web page. Using a colour-coded scale – typically red for high activity and blue for low – heatmaps display aggregate behaviour over a defined time period. There are three main types of heatmaps commonly used:

1 Click heatmaps, which reveal where users click most frequently on a page.
2 Scroll heatmaps, showing how far down users typically scroll.
3 Move heatmaps, tracking mouse movements and hover behaviour, which serve as proxies for eye-tracking data.

Each type of heatmap serves a distinct analytical purpose. For example, if a scroll heatmap shows that most users never reach the bottom third of a landing page, this may prompt reorganization of content to ensure important elements appear above the fold. Likewise, click heatmaps can highlight unexpected behaviours – such as frequent clicks on non-interactive elements like images or headings – indicating user confusion or unmet expectations (Babich, 2021).

Practical application: Improving web performance

Leading digital brands like Amazon, Glossier and HubSpot use heatmaps to continually refine their UX based on live behavioural data. In one case, Glossier deployed Crazy Egg to test variations of its 'Add to Bag' button placement and found that shifting the button closer to the product title improved conversions by 8 per cent (*WWD*, 2022b). Similarly, HubSpot used scroll heatmaps to analyse blog readership patterns and discovered that readers rarely scrolled beyond the first 600 pixels, leading to a redesign that prioritized CTAs and summaries at the top (HubSpot, 2021).

Heatmaps help marketers answer questions such as:

- Are users interacting with intended elements like call-to-action buttons?
- Is content being read or ignored?
- Are layout decisions unintentionally creating user friction?

By giving visual clarity to these issues, heatmaps empower marketers to make changes backed by concrete behavioural data rather than guesswork.

The role of click tracking

While heatmaps provide a broad view of activity, click tracking offers a more precise picture. Click tracking logs every user click on a web page, identifying which elements draw user attention – and which fail to do so. For instance, in a checkout process, click tracking might reveal that users are repeatedly clicking a button that has been disabled indicating confusion or frustration.

Click maps from tools like Hotjar and Microsoft Clarity aggregate these individual interactions into patterns, allowing teams to:

- assess the effectiveness of navigation elements
- spot false affordances – elements that appear clickable but are not
- understand how users interact with forms, dropdowns or embedded media.

An example comes from ASOS, which used Hotjar to analyse product page interactions. Click tracking data showed users were attempting to click the 'Colour' filter but gave up due to non-intuitive labelling. Redesigning the filter interface improved usability and led to a measurable uptick in filtered searches and time on site (*Retail Gazette*, 2023f).

Integrating with A/B testing and UX strategy

Heatmaps and click tracking work best when integrated into a broader strategy of continuous UX testing. Combining visual behaviour data with A/B testing frameworks enables marketers to test hypotheses and refine elements based on empirical results.

For instance, if a heatmap shows users are not clicking a promotional banner, an A/B test can explore whether changing the copy, colour or position increases interaction. Click maps can then verify which variation drove more meaningful engagement, such as click-throughs to a landing page or conversions.

Frameworks like **conversion rate optimization (CRO)** often include heatmap analysis as an early diagnostic tool, followed by testing cycles that iteratively refine the page. According to Tullis and Albert (2013), using mixed-method analysis – qualitative heatmaps combined with quantitative metrics like click-through rate and form submissions – provides a comprehensive picture of site effectiveness.

Best practices for heatmap and click tracking analysis

To derive actionable insights from heatmaps and click tracking, several best practices should be followed:

- **Segment data by device:** Heatmap behaviour varies significantly between desktop and mobile. A button that's easily clickable on a desktop might be overlooked on mobile due to screen real estate constraints (Nielsen Norman Group, 2021).

- **Focus on key pages:** Prioritize analysis for high-value pages such as product pages, landing pages or checkout flows where user experience has a direct impact on conversion.

- **Combine with funnel analysis:** Use funnel visualization in Google Analytics alongside heatmaps to understand where drop-offs occur and whether poor visual engagement is a contributing factor.

- **Periodically refresh analysis:** As content and design elements change, re-run heatmap sessions to track the impact of modifications and uncover new UX issues.

- **Contextualize with session replays:** Heatmaps offer aggregation, but session replays show individual behaviours that may reveal nuances or exceptions that heatmaps miss.

Tools in focus

Several leading platforms offer heatmap and click tracking capabilities:

- **Crazy Egg:** Offers click, scroll and mouse-movement heatmaps, as well as A/B testing integration and snapshot comparison over time.

- **Hotjar:** Combines heatmaps with session recordings and feedback tools, making it ideal for discovering pain points and validating user feedback.

- **Microsoft Clarity:** A free tool providing advanced heatmaps and user session recordings, along with machine-learning-driven insights into rage clicks and excessive scrolling.

Each tool has unique features tailored to different needs. For instance, Crazy Egg is favoured for e-commerce optimization due to its visual clarity and easy test deployment, while Hotjar is commonly used in SaaS environments for its emphasis on qualitative user feedback.

EXAMPLE

Patagonia

Sustainable apparel brand Patagonia used scroll and click heatmaps during a redesign of its 'Stories' section, which features environmental advocacy content. Analysis showed users were engaging deeply with headlines but not scrolling to read full articles. To address this, Patagonia redesigned article summaries with a 'Read More' preview that enticed users to engage deeper. The result was a 22 per cent increase in average time on page and a 14 per cent decrease in bounce rate (Patagonia Sustainability Report, 2022).

Future trends in heatmap technology

As machine learning and AI continue to influence web analytics, heatmap tools are becoming more sophisticated. Predictive heatmaps, for example, now estimate user attention based on layout and content density before a page even goes live. This allows for pre-launch optimization, saving development time and resources.

Another trend is the integration of biometric data – like eye-tracking – into traditional click tracking systems, giving a more nuanced view of attention. While currently limited to usability labs, such capabilities are becoming more accessible for commercial use, particularly in high-stakes industries like finance and healthcare.

Moreover, with rising concerns over privacy, anonymized behavioural data collection is increasingly important. Tools like Microsoft Clarity and Hotjar now automatically mask personally identifiable information (PII), ensuring compliance with regulations such as GDPR and CCPA.

7.4 Optimizing the user experience: From data to action

In the age of data-driven decision-making, web analytics has evolved from a passive reporting tool into an active catalyst for continuous optimization. The core value of web analytics lies not simply in the collection of data but in its ability to guide meaningful and measurable improvements to the user experience (UX). By following a structured framework that moves from insight to action, brands can ensure that their websites evolve in step with user expectations and business goals.

The optimization cycle

Effective UX optimization is grounded in a cyclical, evidence-based process. This cycle typically unfolds in four stages:

1 Diagnose pain points

Web analytics dashboards – such as those provided by Google Analytics, Adobe Analytics or Mixpanel – offer quantitative signals that highlight usability issues. For example, a high bounce rate on a product page may indicate poor visual hierarchy or weak content relevance. Similarly, exit rates during checkout could point to friction in the purchasing process. These insights act as a diagnostic tool, identifying where and when users are encountering barriers.

2 Formulate hypotheses

Once issues are identified, UX designers and marketers formulate hypotheses about the root causes and potential solutions. These may include design revisions (e.g. re-positioning a CTA button), copy adjustments (e.g. clarifying shipping policies) or performance improvements (e.g. reducing load time). Crucially, hypotheses should be measurable and tied to specific metrics – such as aiming to increase click-through rate (CTR) or reduce cart abandonment.

3 Test alternatives

The third phase involves testing proposed changes using A/B testing or multivariate testing. A/B testing presents different versions of a page (Version A and Version B) to segmented audiences, measuring which performs better on defined metrics. Tools like Google Optimize, Optimizely and Visual Website Optimizer (VWO) allow marketers to set up statistically valid tests with minimal disruption to live operations.

4 Monitor and validate results

After testing, performance is continuously monitored to determine whether the changes produced the desired outcome. This includes reviewing quantitative metrics (e.g. conversion rate, bounce rate) as well as qualitative signals (e.g. heatmap changes or customer feedback). If the results validate the hypothesis, the change can be permanently implemented. If not, the process is repeated with revised assumptions.

This iterative cycle of diagnose–hypothesize–test–validate has become a cornerstone of modern UX optimization, underpinning agile development and conversion rate optimization (CRO) strategies.

REAL-WORLD EXAMPLE   Netflix and continuous
experimentation

One of the most well-known adopters of A/B testing is Netflix, which conducts hundreds of experiments annually across its platform. By altering small visual or functional elements – such as thumbnail images, preview animations or CTA button language – Netflix continually refines its user interface to maximize engagement and retention. In one notable example, Netflix tested dozens of thumbnail images for the same piece of content and discovered that subtle variations in facial expressions or colour contrast had a measurable impact on click-through rates (Kohavi and Longbotham, 2023). The company's testing culture is embedded in its engineering and design teams, demonstrating how even micro-level design choices can influence large-scale user behaviour.

REAL-WORLD EXAMPLE   Zalando and checkout optimization

In the competitive world of fashion e-commerce, reducing cart abandonment is a perennial challenge. Zalando, one of Europe's leading online fashion retailers, has invested heavily in UX experimentation to streamline its checkout experience. Using analytics tools such as Hotjar and proprietary testing platforms, Zalando analysed behavioural drop-offs during checkout and identified that optional fields (like 'phone number' or 'promotional code') were creating confusion. By simplifying the checkout process – removing unnecessary fields and reducing steps from four to two – Zalando achieved a 12 per cent increase in completed transactions (Ecommerce News Europe, 2022). The success illustrates how minor interface changes, driven by data, can yield significant business impact.

Frameworks for optimization

A structured approach to optimization can be guided by established UX frameworks:

- **The PIE framework** (Potential, Importance, Ease) helps teams prioritize which elements to test based on their potential impact, strategic importance and ease of implementation (Eisenberg, 2012).

- **The HEART framework,** developed by Google, focuses on user-centred metrics: Happiness, Engagement, Adoption, Retention and Task success (Rodden et al, 2010). This model emphasizes long-term user satisfaction and is particularly valuable in SaaS or subscription contexts.

- **The LIFT model** (Landing Page Influence Function for Tests) helps assess page elements using six dimensions: value proposition, clarity, relevance, distraction, urgency and anxiety (WiderFunnel, 2020). This model is often used in conjunction with conversion optimization tools to structure hypotheses.

Each framework encourages not only technical improvement but also a deeper consideration of user psychology and emotional response.

Aligning UX optimization with business KPIs

Optimizing user experience should not occur in isolation – it must be aligned with broader marketing and business objectives. Key performance indicators (KPIs) such as average order value (AOV), return on ad spend (ROAS) and lifetime value (LTV) are influenced by how well users can navigate and transact on a brand's website. For example, improving the discoverability of product filters or enhancing mobile load speed may directly increase average session duration and reduce bounce rate, thereby lifting overall revenue.

Retailers like ASOS, Nike and Uniqlo regularly use UX analytics dashboards that blend conversion metrics with user behaviour insights to track how design changes affect business outcomes. This cross-functional approach – bringing together design, engineering, product and marketing – ensures that optimizations support strategic goals.

Real-time optimization and personalization

Another trend shaping modern UX strategy is real-time optimization through personalization. Platforms such as Dynamic Yield and Adobe Target enable personalized content delivery based on user behaviour, location or purchase history. For example, if a returning visitor frequently browses winter jackets, the homepage can dynamically surface related content. This micro-personalization, when powered by behavioural analytics, creates smoother and more relevant user journeys.

H&M, for instance, implemented AI-powered personalization in its e-commerce platform to dynamically recommend outfits based on past interactions. These recommendations led to a 15 per cent increase in click-through rates and improved cross-sell ratios (H&M Group, 2023a). However, personalization must be implemented ethically, respecting user privacy preferences and data regulations such as GDPR and CCPA.

Challenges and considerations

Despite its many benefits, UX optimization comes with challenges:

- **Statistical validity**: Small sample sizes can yield misleading A/B test results. Ensuring sufficient traffic and run time is crucial for accurate conclusions.
- **Change fatigue**: Continuous testing can lead to inconsistent user experiences if not managed coherently. Brands must strike a balance between iteration and stability.
- **Cross-device complexity**: A change that improves UX on desktop may harm mobile experience. Segmenting test results by device type is essential.
- **Ethical use of data**: As analytics tools become more sophisticated, brands must avoid intrusive or manipulative UX practices, ensuring transparency and user control.

Conclusion

Optimizing the user experience is not a one-off initiative but a continuous process that integrates data, creativity and empathy. By systematically diagnosing issues, formulating evidence-based hypotheses, testing rigorously and evaluating results, brands can evolve their websites to meet the changing needs of users. Whether through Netflix's iterative UI experiments or Zalando's simplified checkout flows, real-world success stories illustrate the power of analytics to drive meaningful digital transformation.

As digital ecosystems become more complex, the ability to translate behavioural data into action will be a defining skill for modern marketers and UX professionals. In doing so, organizations not only enhance user satisfaction but also unlock tangible improvements in engagement, loyalty and business performance.

7.5 Real-world example: ASOS checkout optimization

REAL-WORLD EXAMPLE   ASOS checkout optimization

In the competitive arena of fashion e-commerce, cart abandonment is a persistent challenge that directly impacts revenue. For ASOS, a leading online fashion retailer with a global customer base, the checkout process is a critical touchpoint in the digital customer journey. In 2023, ASOS identified a significant friction point within its checkout funnel – specifically during the shipping information stage – that was leading to high abandonment rates. By leveraging advanced analytics and user behaviour tracking tools, the company executed a successful optimization strategy that highlights the transformative power of web analytics in enhancing the user experience (UX).

The challenge: High drop-off at the shipping stage

Using Google Analytics 4 (GA4), ASOS's digital team monitored funnel visualization reports and identified a steep drop-off in user progression on the delivery options page. Although customers were adding items to their cart and advancing through the initial checkout steps, a significant proportion exited the website when prompted to select a shipping method. This pointed to a potential usability issue at a critical conversion point.

However, quantitative data alone could not explain the root cause. To gain deeper insight, ASOS integrated Hotjar, a behavioural analytics tool that provides heatmaps, session recordings and user feedback widgets. The session replays revealed that users often hesitated, scrolled repeatedly or abandoned their carts altogether when interacting with the delivery options interface. Users appeared confused by ambiguous labels, a cluttered layout and the absence of clearly visible express shipping information.

The analysis: Visual friction and information gaps

The combination of Google Analytics metrics and Hotjar qualitative feedback allowed ASOS to triangulate the issue: the design of the shipping page was not user-centric. Express delivery – an option particularly important to ASOS's young, time-sensitive customer demographic – was not immediately visible due to poor hierarchy and suboptimal labelling. Additionally, estimated delivery times were buried in text rather than highlighted through visual cues.

ASOS's UX researchers further supported this diagnosis by analysing form abandonment rates, scroll depth analytics and open-text feedback submitted via the feedback tool embedded on the checkout page. Many customers expressed frustration with not understanding when their items would arrive – an issue exacerbated by the fast fashion industry's growing emphasis on speed and convenience (Baym, 2021).

The action: Design-driven restructuring

With clear insights in hand, ASOS implemented a set of design changes grounded in usability principles and data-backed hypotheses. These included:

- Reorganizing delivery options by popularity (e.g. standard, express, next-day) to reflect user preference patterns.

- Introducing visual icons next to each shipping method to enhance scanning and recognition.

- Adding bolded delivery estimates ('Arrives in 1–2 days') next to each method to set clear expectations.

- Applying the LIFT model (value proposition, clarity, relevance, anxiety, distraction, urgency) to reduce cognitive load and improve trust (WiderFunnel, 2020).

The design team A/B tested the revised layout using Google Optimize, comparing the new version with the original. Over the course of three weeks, the test reached statistical significance, with the treatment group showing consistently better performance on key conversion indicators.

The result: Reduced abandonment and higher order value

The results of the redesign were significant. ASOS reported a 14 per cent reduction in cart abandonment rates on the shipping page, alongside a notable increase in average order value (AOV). The company attributed this uplift not only to higher checkout completion but also to improved customer confidence – users were more likely to add last-minute items knowing exactly when their packages would arrive (*Retail Gazette*, 2023a–d).

These changes also had downstream effects. Customer satisfaction scores related to the checkout process improved and support queries regarding delivery timelines decreased, reducing operational load on the customer service team. The case exemplifies how real-time behavioural data, when combined with iterative testing and UX heuristics, can deliver substantial returns in both customer experience and business performance.

Lessons learned and broader implications

This case study offers several key lessons for digital marketers and UX professionals.

Surface-level metrics can conceal deeper issues

Bounce rate or exit rate alone is insufficient without behavioural context. Pairing these with session recordings and heatmaps provides the necessary depth to diagnose user struggles.

Shipping transparency drives trust

Especially in the fast fashion sector, customers expect immediate clarity around delivery times. Brands that obscure or delay this information risk losing high-intent buyers.

Design simplicity reduces friction

Visual hierarchy, iconography and information architecture play pivotal roles in user comprehension. Streamlining the interface can reduce decision paralysis and improve flow.

A/B testing validates direction

Changes based on assumptions, no matter how well-informed, must be tested rigorously. In this case, A/B testing ensured that the new design delivered measurable improvements before full deployment.

Data-informed iteration is key

Optimization is not a one-off project but a continuous cycle. ASOS continues to monitor user behaviour and adapt its checkout flow to seasonal trends, device behaviours and new delivery partnerships.

Related frameworks and tools

The ASOS case aligns closely with several core web optimization frameworks:

- **Conversion rate optimization (CRO)**: A systematic approach focused on improving the percentage of users who complete a desired action (Ash et al, 2012).
- **Fogg behaviour model**: Suggests that behaviour occurs when motivation, ability and a prompt converge. In this case, a lack of clarity in delivery options undermined user ability, even if motivation was high (Fogg, 2009).
- **The UX Honeycomb** (Morville, 2004): This model emphasizes usability, accessibility and desirability – all elements that the shipping page redesign addressed.

7.6 Exercise: Google Analytics report interpretation

EXERCISE

Interpret a Google Analytics report – H&M case simulation

In this hands-on exercise, you step into the role of a digital marketing analyst at H&M, a global leader in fast fashion with a commitment to sustainability and customer engagement. Your task is to examine a sample Google Analytics 4 (GA4) report and draw actionable insights that will guide H&M's digital performance improvement strategy.

This scenario-based exercise mirrors real-world tasks that analytics professionals undertake daily evaluating landing page performance, exit behaviour and traffic source effectiveness. By analysing GA4 data, marketers can transition from assumptions to evidence-based decision-making, directly impacting user experience (UX), conversion rates and marketing ROI (Chaffey and Ellis-Chadwick, 2022).

Sample report highlights

Let's assume the following findings from H&M's Google Analytics dashboard:

- Landing pages with the highest bounce rate:
  - /Sustainability-blog – 83 per cent bounce rate
  - /mens-new-arrivals – 65 per cent bounce rate
- Top exit pages:
  - /checkout/shipping-info – 42 per cent of exits
  - /store-locator – 35 per cent of exits
- Best performing traffic sources (conversion rate):
  - Organic social (Instagram) – 4.8 per cent conversion rate
  - Paid search (Google Ads) – 2.1 per cent
  - Email campaigns – 3.6 per cent.

Interpretation and strategy: Reduce bounce rates on high-traffic blog pages

The **/sustainability-blog** landing page, despite being a major content pillar aligned with H&M's brand values, is underperforming in terms of engagement. An 83 per cent bounce rate suggests that users who land here often leave without further interaction. This indicates a mismatch between user intent and page content or a lack of compelling calls to action (CTAs) that drive continued site engagement.

Recommendation

Embed contextual product recommendations or dynamic 'Shop Now' CTAs within blog content, especially around topics like eco-friendly fabrics or recycling programmes. Using in-content widgets that link sustainability education to shoppable products can improve content-to-commerce flow and reduce bounce (Clifton, 2020). H&M could also use Hotjar heatmaps to identify scroll depth and rework above-the-fold layout for immediate visual engagement.

Minimize checkout abandonment at the shipping information page

The **/checkout/shipping-info** page shows a high exit rate (42 per cent), which is alarming, especially at a critical point in the purchase journey. This behaviour often reflects usability friction – either due to unexpected shipping costs, confusing delivery options or lack of clarity around fulfilment times (Baym, 2021).

Recommendation

Apply UX simplification principles by pre-selecting default shipping options based on geo-location, visually emphasizing express delivery dates and introducing progress indicators to reassure customers of the few remaining steps. Tools such as Google Optimize or VWO can be used for A/B testing layout and copy modifications on this page (Kohavi and Longbotham, 2023).

Recommendation: Invest in high-converting organic social channels

Instagram-originated sessions exhibit the highest conversion rate (4.8 per cent), outpacing both paid search and email. This reflects H&M's success in crafting visual, interactive and lifestyle-driven narratives on its social platforms. Organic posts that showcase product collections via influencer collaborations or user-generated content appear to drive intent and conversions more effectively than static search ads.

Increase investment in Instagram content creation and scheduling, using data from Sprout Social or Hootsuite to identify high-performing post types (e.g. reels vs carousels). Integrate Instagram Shopping features more thoroughly and align editorial calendars with product drop cycles. Additionally, allocate budget to boost top-performing organic posts, which often deliver better ROI than cold-targeted paid campaigns.

Learning integration: From metrics to action

This exercise trains students to think critically about key web analytics metrics and how they reflect broader digital marketing goals. By interpreting GA4 reports with a focus on conversion behaviour, learners begin to understand the data-value chain: from collection and visualization to interpretation and strategic application (Rosenberg and Matei, 2021).

Encouraging the analysis of multidimensional data – bounce rates, exit paths, traffic attribution and conversion performance – helps foster a holistic approach to web optimization. It also reinforces frameworks like the attention, interest, desire, action (AIDA) model, where drop-offs can signal breakdowns at specific stages of user engagement.

Frameworks referenced

- **LIFT model** (WiderFunnel, 2020): Used to evaluate the performance of checkout CTAs and identify sources of anxiety or distraction.

- **Google HEART framework**: Focuses on happiness, engagement, adoption, retention and task success, ideal for prioritizing UX improvements (Rodden et al, 2010).
- **See-Think-Do-Care** by Avinash Kaushik: Helps classify user intent by session type and match on-site content accordingly.

EXAMPLE

Real-world brand context: H&M digital innovation

H&M has been recognized for its digital-first approach in adapting to e-commerce challenges. Its integration of sustainability narratives, live shopping events and personalized product recommendations into the user journey has made its web experience both aspirational and data-informed (H&M Group, 2022).

In particular, the brand's use of heatmaps and analytics in its Conscious Collection pages led to restructured content blocks, improved mobile performance and increased on-site engagement from eco-conscious customers – an example of analytics-led UX refinement.

7.7 Model: Website interaction dashboard

In today's data-driven marketing environment, the ability to visualize web performance metrics through interactive dashboards has become a cornerstone of agile digital strategy. A well-structured web analytics dashboard enables marketers, UX designers and business stakeholders to quickly assess website performance, user behaviour and conversion dynamics in real time. Platforms like Google Looker Studio (formerly Data Studio) and Tableau make it possible to create dynamic dashboards that consolidate vast data streams into digestible, action-oriented insights (Chaffey and Ellis-Chadwick, 2022; Clifton, 2020).

At its core, a website interaction dashboard serves as the control panel for digital optimization. It bridges raw data from tools like Google Analytics and qualitative sources like Hotjar, offering a unified interface to monitor key performance indicators (KPIs), assess progress towards goals and support hypotheses testing for site improvements. To be effective, the dashboard must be both comprehensive and intuitive, facilitating cross-functional use – from marketers optimizing campaigns to developers fixing UX flaws.

Key dashboard components

Top traffic sources (direct, referral, social, organic, paid)

This section tracks how users arrive at the website. By segmenting visitors by acquisition channel, marketers can understand where high-value users originate and allocate marketing spend accordingly. For example, if social media campaigns are driving high-quality traffic with longer session durations, budgets can be shifted from underperforming paid search ads (Kaushik, 2020). Real-world case: Glossier identified Instagram as a top conversion driver and invested in building native shopping experiences via stories and reels (*WWD*, 2022a).

Bounce rate by page

The bounce rate reveals the percentage of users who leave after viewing just one page. High bounce rates on core landing pages – such as product collections or content hubs – can signal poor content alignment or technical issues like slow load times. This metric becomes even more actionable when cross-filtered by traffic source or device. For instance, if mobile users are bouncing more than desktop users on a specific page, this may indicate a responsive design flaw (Clifton, 2020). Actionable example: Zalando used bounce rate dashboards to identify underperforming seasonal campaigns and optimized them with clearer CTAs and updated imagery.

Session duration by device

Understanding how long users stay on site, segmented by device (desktop, tablet, mobile), reveals critical insights into engagement and usability. A notably shorter session on mobile devices, for instance, may suggest poor load speeds, clunky navigation or content not optimized for small screens. According to the Google Page Experience Update (2023), mobile usability now significantly impacts both UX and search ranking, making this metric an essential part of any dashboard (Google Developers, 2023).

Heatmap of landing pages

Integrating visual data from heatmapping tools like Hotjar or Crazy Egg into the dashboard allows stakeholders to visually interpret where user attention is focused. This helps validate whether layout hierarchies are working and whether CTAs and key content areas are receiving the intended focus. For example, a heatmap on H&M's 'Sustainability' landing page revealed that most user interaction happened below the fold, prompting a redesign that brought key CTAs higher up (H&M, 2023b).

Click-through on primary CTAs

Monitoring clicks on high-value elements such as 'Add to bag', 'Subscribe', or 'Learn more' offers a clear sense of CTA performance. Low interaction with these elements may reflect CTA blindness, poor wording or suboptimal positioning. Dashboard filters can help analyse click behaviour by traffic source, helping identify if CTA relevance differs for organic versus paid users. Real-world example: Netflix improved subscription rates by 9 per cent after A/B testing different CTA placements on its sign-up page (Kohavi and Longbotham, 2023).

Goal completion funnel (Homepage → Product → Checkout)

A funnel visualization shows where users drop off during multi-step journeys. This metric helps identify friction points and opportunities for conversion rate optimization (CRO). For example, if many users exit after the product page but before checkout, it may indicate weak value propositions or a need for clearer pricing or shipping information. Dashboards that segment funnel progression by device, location or campaign source offer deeper diagnostic insights. This type of funnel analysis was key to ASOS's checkout optimization efforts, which led to a 14 per cent decrease in cart abandonment (*Retail Gazette*, 2023d).

Using dashboards for continuous optimization

An effective dashboard not only summarizes historical performance but also powers real-time optimization cycles. Teams can monitor the immediate impact of campaign launches, UX redesigns or pricing experiments and adjust strategies accordingly. Advanced dashboards integrate alert systems – flagging sudden spikes in bounce rate or traffic drops – enabling proactive issue resolution rather than reactive firefighting.

For instance, during a product drop campaign, Nike monitored live dashboards that combined Google Analytics with social sentiment feeds, allowing the team to tweak on-site messaging based on real-time user sentiment and navigation patterns (Nike Digital Experience Team, 2022).

Additionally, dashboard tools like Looker Studio allow teams to create role-based views. For example, a CMO may prefer high-level summaries of conversion and ROI, while a UX lead might focus on interaction maps and heatmaps. This customizability ensures that every team member accesses the most relevant insights without being overwhelmed by unnecessary data.

Conclusion

Web analytics has evolved into a central pillar of digital marketing strategy, enabling organizations to transition from intuition-driven decision-making to evidence-based optimization. By systematically capturing, measuring and interpreting user behaviour data, businesses can transform websites into dynamic platforms that drive awareness, engagement, and conversion. Core metrics such as bounce rate, average session duration, user flow and goal completions provide actionable insights when viewed collectively, offering a holistic picture of user experience in the marketing funnel.

The chapter has demonstrated that the real value of web analytics lies not merely in data collection but in the translation of insights into action. Tools such as Google Analytics, Hotjar, Crazy Egg and Microsoft Clarity illustrate how quantitative and qualitative data can be triangulated to uncover hidden friction points and inform targeted interventions. For instance, real-world cases from brands like ASOS, Zara, Zalando and Patagonia show how analytics-led refinements – from checkout optimization to heatmap-driven content redesigns – can yield measurable improvements in both user satisfaction and business outcomes.

Theoretically, frameworks such as the HEART model (Rodden et al, 2010), the LIFT model (WiderFunnel, 2020) and the AIDA funnel provide structured approaches to diagnosing problems and prioritizing solutions. These models bridge the gap between raw data and strategic design choices, ensuring that optimization efforts remain aligned with user psychology, organizational goals and ethical considerations. At the same time, the growing integration of predictive analytics and machine learning in platforms like Google Analytics 4 underscores the shift towards proactive, personalized and real-time decision-making.

However, challenges remain. Data overload, interpretive complexity and evolving privacy regulations such as GDPR and CCPA require marketers to balance analytical ambition with ethical responsibility. The ability to anonymize data, respect user consent and prioritize transparency will be essential for sustaining trust and compliance.

In conclusion, web analytics is not simply a technical toolkit but a strategic discipline that underpins competitive advantage in digital ecosystems. Organizations that cultivate analytical literacy, embed optimization cycles into their operations and align metrics with broader business objectives will be best positioned to thrive in increasingly customer-centric and data-rich environments. As the digital landscape continues to evolve, mastering web analytics will remain a decisive factor in shaping seamless, engaging and profitable user experiences.

KEY TAKEAWAYS

Best practices for dashboard implementation

- **Align with objectives**: Ensure each metric reflects a strategic goal – traffic quality, engagement or revenue growth.
- **Simplify for clarity**: Avoid information overload. Use filters, dropdowns and visualizations like bar graphs, pie charts and funnel diagrams to make data intuitive.

- **Integrate multiple tools**: Merge insights from GA4, CRM systems, email platforms and heatmapping tools to gain a unified view.
- **Automate updates**: Set up dashboards to auto-refresh daily or hourly so teams are always acting on up-to-date information.
- **Promote adoption**: Train cross-functional teams to understand and act on insights, embedding data literacy into the organizational culture (Marr, 2022).

References

Ash, T, Page, R and Ginty, M (2012) *Landing Page Optimization: The Definitive Guide to Testing and Tuning for Conversions,* Hoboken, NJ: Wiley

Babich, N (2021) UX heatmaps: Understanding user behaviour visually, UX Planet, https://uxplanet.org (archived at https://perma.cc/A983-N5CD)

Baym, N K (2021) *Playing to the Crowd: Musicians, Audiences, and the Intimate Work of Connection*, New York: NYU Press

Chaffey, D and Ellis-Chadwick, F (2022) *Digital Marketing: Strategy, Implementation, and Practice* (8th ed.), Harlow: Pearson Education

Clifton, B (2020) *Advanced Web Metrics with Google Analytics* (4th ed.), Hoboken, NJ: Wiley

Ecommerce News Europe (2022) Zalando boosts conversions through checkout testing, Ecommerce News Europe, www.ecommercenews.eu (archived at https://perma.cc/8JG3-CLEY)

Eisenberg, B (2012) *Always Be Testing: The Complete Guide to Google Website Optimizer,* Hoboken, NJ: Wiley

Fogg, B J (2009) A behaviour model for persuasive design, in *Proceedings of the 4th International Conference on Persuasive Technology,* Claremont, CA, 26–29 April, New York: ACM

Google Analytics (2023) GA4 user guide, https://analytics.google.com (archived at https://perma.cc/8BTP-WBPA)

Google Developers (2023) *Page Experience Report*, https://developers.google.com (archived at https://perma.cc/M6FP-6SKA)

Google (2024a) Analytics help – bounce rate and engagement metrics, https://support.google.com (archived at https://perma.cc/SK2L-Q933)

Google (2024b) Google Analytics 4 support and training, https://support.google.com/analytics (archived at https://perma.cc/5P27-2T4N)

H&M Group (2022) *H&M's digital-first transformation: sustainability integration, live shopping and personalised recommendations,* www.hmgroup.com (archived at https://hmgroup.com)

H&M Digital Insights (2023) *Checkout Optimization Report*, internal corporate report

H&M Group (2023a) *Annual and Sustainability Report 2023*, www.hmgroup.com (archived at https://perma.cc/F3PK-5YQ6)

H&M Group (2023b) *Digital Experience and Sustainability Report*, www.hmgroup.com (archived at https://perma.cc/F3PK-5YQ6)

Hotjar (2021) Case Study: HubSpot uses Hotjar to improve UX, www.hotjar.com (archived at https://perma.cc/7ZK9-QSXW)

HubSpot (2021) How blog optimization boosted our lead conversion, *HubSpot Marketing Blog*, https://blog.hubspot.com (archived at https://perma.cc/2PL9-4QQE)

Information Commissioner's Office (ICO) (2022) UK Guide to Data Protection: Principles of GDPR, Information Commissioner's Office, https://ico.org.uk (archived at https://perma.cc/23ZQ-DP2P)

Kaushik, A (2020) *Web Analytics 2.0: Understanding customer behaviour through digital metrics*, Hoboken, NJ: Wiley

Kohavi, R and Longbotham, R (2023) Online experiments at scale: Lessons from Netflix and Microsoft, *Journal of Marketing Research*, 60 (1), 35–52

Kotler, P and Keller, K L (2016) *Marketing Management* (15th ed.), Harlow: Pearson Education

Marr, B (2022) *Data Strategy: How to Profit from a World of Big Data, Analytics and the Internet of Things*, London: Kogan Page

Microsoft (2023) Clarity Documentation, https://clarity.microsoft.com (archived at https://perma.cc/UP8N-ZCNY)

Morville, P (2004) User experience design: The UX Honeycomb, *Semantic Studios*, https://semanticstudios.com (archived at https://perma.cc/M6SA-HDSP)

Nielsen Norman Group (2021) Mobile vs desktop behaviour: Designing for different contexts, https://nngroup.com (archived at https://perma.cc/Z6SE-55EL)

Nike Digital Experience Team (2022) *'You Can't Stop Us' Campaign Playbook*, internal report

Patagonia (2022) *Sustainability and Engagement Report*, www.patagonia.com (archived at https://perma.cc/S8RV-TJWU)

Retail Dive (2022a) How ASOS improved mobile engagement through UX tweaks, *Retail Dive*, www.retaildive.com (archived at https://perma.cc/78WM-MDUG)

Retail Dive (2022b) How ASOS used heatmaps to improve UX, *Retail Dive*, www.retaildive.com (archived at https://perma.cc/78WM-MDUG)

Retail Gazette (2023a) ASOS checkout redesign drives double-digit conversion gains, *Retail Gazette*, www.retailgazette.co.uk (archived at https://perma.cc/FU4N-JNCZ)

Retail Gazette (2023b) ASOS reduces cart abandonment with new checkout UX, *Retail Gazette,* www.retailgazette.co.uk (archived at https://perma.cc/FU4N-JNCZ)

Retail Gazette (2023c) ASOS streamlines product filters after UX study, *Retail Gazette,* www.retailgazette.co.uk (archived at https://perma.cc/FU4N-JNCZ)

Retail Gazette (2023d) How ASOS cut cart abandonment by 14%, *Retail Gazette*, www.retailgazette.co.uk (archived at https://perma.cc/FU4N-JNCZ)

Retail Gazette (2023e) Zara optimizes checkout process after web analytics audit, *Retail Gazette*, www.retailgazette.co.uk (archived at https://perma.cc/FU4N-JNCZ)

Retail Gazette (2023f) Redesigning the filter interface improves usability and increases filtered searches and time on site, *Retail Gazette*, www.retailgazette.co.uk (archived at https://perma.cc/FU4N-JNCZ)

Rodden, K, Hutchinson, H and Fu, X (2010) Measuring the user experience on a large scale: User-centered metrics for web applications, *Proceedings of the SIGCHI Conference on Human Factors in Computing Systems (CHI)*, 10–15 April, Atlanta, GA, New York: ACM, https://dl.acm.org/doi/10.1145/1753326.1753687 (archived at https://perma.cc/53W4-K4LG)

Rosenberg, D and Matei, S A (2021) *Analytics for Managers: With Excel*, Abingdon: Routledge

Shopify UX Team (2022) Behavioural segmentation in landing page optimization, internal report

Skyscanner (2023) Understanding user frustration with behavioural analytics, *Skyscanner Insights Report*, www.skyscanner.net (archived at https://perma.cc/2V5G-T87U)

Spotify Design (2022) Reimagining the mobile trial funnel, *Spotify Design Blog*, https//spotify.design

Tullis, T and Albert, B (2013) *Measuring the User Experience: Collecting, Analysing, and Presenting Usability Metrics* (2nd ed.), Amsterdam: Elsevier

WiderFunnel (2020) LIFT model for conversion optimization, www.widerfunnel.com (archived at https://perma.cc/3SKM-QBUK)

WWD (2022a) Glossier's Instagram shopping strategy, *WWD*, www.wwd.com (archived at https://perma.cc/Y5MF-Q6DN)

WWD (2022b) Glossier UX design strategy boosts mobile conversion, *WWD*, www.wwd.com (archived at https://perma.cc/Y5MF-Q6DN)

Zalando (2022) Driving engagement through web navigation analytics, *Zalando Tech Blog*, https://corporate.zalando.com/en/technology/inspiring-and-empowering-customers-ai-powered-experiences (archived at https://perma.cc/P5Y6-3PYK)

PART THREE
Advanced marketing analytics: Predictive modelling and beyond

08 | **Predictive modelling**

Forecasting trends and customer behaviour

CHAPTER OUTLINE

Introduction to predictive modelling

8.1 Logistic regression for customer churn prediction

8.2 Linear regression for sales forecasting

8.3 Advanced techniques and multivariate regression

8.4 Model validation and evaluation metrics

KEY TERMS

Bias: Systematic error introduced by incorrect assumptions in a model.

Bootstrapping: A resampling technique used to estimate the accuracy of predictive models.

Churn: The rate at which customers stop doing business with a company.

Confusion matrix: A table that shows the performance of a classification algorithm.

Cross-validation: Methods of evaluating model performance across different subsets of data.

Customer lifetime value (CLV or CLTV): The total worth of a customer over their entire relationship with a company.

Dependent variable: The outcome a model aims to predict.

Evaluation metrics: Measures used to assess the performance of predictive models.

Forecasting: Predicting future outcomes based on historical data.

Gradient boosting: A machine learning technique that builds models sequentially to reduce prediction errors.

Gradient variable: The outcome a model aims to predict (often used interchangeably with dependent variable in certain contexts).

Independent variables: The input features used by a model to make predictions.

Linear regression: A regression algorithm that estimates the relationship between a dependent variable and one or more independent variables.

Logistic regression: A classification algorithm used to model binary outcomes.

Mean absolute error (MAE): An evaluation metric that calculates the average absolute difference between predictions and actual values.

Model overfitting: When a model learns training data too well, including its noise and outliers.

Multivariate regression: A regression technique that models the relationship between multiple independent variables and a dependent variable.

Neural networks: Machine learning algorithms inspired by the structure of the human brain.

Predictive analytics: The practice of using data, statistical algorithms and machine learning techniques to predict outcomes.

Random forests: An ensemble learning technique that combines multiple decision trees to improve predictive performance.

Variable interaction: Occurs when the effect of one independent variable on the dependent variable depends on the value of another independent variable.

Introduction to predictive modelling

Predictive modelling is a cornerstone of modern marketing analytics, empowering brands to make forward-looking decisions based on historical data patterns. At its core, predictive modelling leverages statistical algorithms and machine learning techniques to forecast future customer behaviours and business outcomes. These models allow marketers to shift from reactive approaches – such as responding to churn after it occurs – to proactive strategies that anticipate customer needs, optimize marketing spend and enhance personalization at scale (Fader, 2020; Chaffey and Ellis-Chadwick, 2022).

In marketing, predictive modelling supports various use cases, including churn prediction, purchase propensity modelling, lead scoring, customer lifetime value (CLV) estimation and demand forecasting. For instance, e-commerce platforms like Amazon and Zalando rely heavily on predictive analytics to recommend products, forecast seasonal demand and detect potential customer drop-offs. This approach ensures that the right message reaches the right customer at the right time, increasing efficiency and return on investment (ROI) across campaigns (Kotler and Keller, 2016).

Predictive modelling typically begins with the collection of structured and unstructured data, such as demographic details, behavioural interactions (e.g. clickstream data), transactional history and customer support records. Data preprocessing, including cleaning, normalization and transformation, is crucial before modelling. Once prepared, datasets are split into training and test sets to evaluate how well the model generalizes to new, unseen data (Provost and Fawcett, 2013).

Figure 8.1   Predictive modelling pipeline for marketing analytics

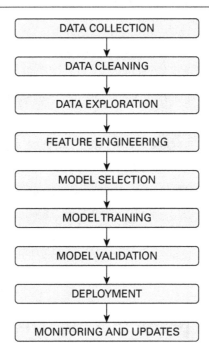

The predictive modelling pipeline for marketing analytics outlines the eight core stages of building and applying predictive models in marketing, from data collection to ongoing monitoring and updates (Figure 8.1).

There are several types of predictive models commonly used in marketing:

1 **Logistic regression:** One of the most interpretable and widely applied techniques, especially for binary classification problems like predicting churn (yes/no) or conversion (clicked/did not click). For example, Spotify might use logistic regression to predict which free-tier users are likely to upgrade to premium based on listening habits and engagement frequency (Spotify Design, 2022).

2 **Linear regression:** Suitable for continuous outcomes, such as forecasting monthly revenue or estimating the effect of budget changes on sales. For instance, Nike may use linear regression to predict sales figures based on past campaign spend, influencer engagement rates and macroeconomic indicators.

3 **Decision trees and random forests:** These models split the data into branches to classify or predict outcomes. Decision trees are useful for identifying clear, rule-based patterns in consumer behaviour. Random forests, an ensemble technique, aggregate multiple trees for improved accuracy. Brands like Sephora use these

methods to predict what types of products a user may be interested in based on previous purchases and browsing history (*WWD*, 2022d).

4 **Clustering algorithms** (e.g. K-means, DBSCAN): Often used for segmentation rather than prediction, clustering groups customers based on similar behaviours. Predictive models can then be built for each segment to tailor interventions. H&M, for example, segments customers into 'fashion followers', 'sustainable shoppers' and 'price-sensitive buyers', tailoring campaigns accordingly (H&M Group, 2023).

5 **Neural networks:** Powerful for handling complex, non-linear relationships and large datasets, though less interpretable. These are frequently used in real-time recommendation engines and personalization algorithms. Netflix, for example, uses deep learning to power its recommendation engine, which predicts what users are likely to watch next based on viewing history and preferences (Kohavi and Longbotham, 2023).

Regardless of the technique, successful predictive modelling hinges on continuous evaluation. Metrics such as accuracy, precision, recall, F1-score and the area under the ROC (receiver operating characteristic) curve (AUC) are commonly used to assess performance. Confusion matrices further help understand false positives and negatives, especially important in churn or fraud detection contexts.

A key benefit of predictive modelling in marketing is its integration into operational systems. For instance, a predictive churn score can be embedded into a CRM platform, automatically flagging at-risk customers. This enables automated triggers for personalized retention campaigns, such as exclusive offers or loyalty incentives. Salesforce and HubSpot offer such capabilities, combining model outputs with real-time engagement data for dynamic decision-making (HubSpot, 2021).

However, predictive modelling is not without its challenges. One common issue is data bias – models are only as good as the data they are trained on. If historical data reflects biased decision-making or excludes certain segments, predictions may reinforce existing inequalities (Barocas et al, 2019). This is particularly important when dealing with sensitive categories like credit scoring or employment recommendations. Marketers must also comply with ethical guidelines and data privacy regulations like GDPR and CCPA, which mandate transparency in automated decision-making and informed consent (ICO, 2022).

To mitigate these risks, marketers should adopt explainable AI (XAI) principles. This involves using interpretable models where possible (e.g. logistic regression, decision trees), regularly auditing model outcomes for bias and communicating predictions in an understandable manner. Tools such as LIME (Local Interpretable Model-agnostic Explanations) and SHAP (SHapley Additive exPlanations) are increasingly used to interpret complex models and ensure fairness.

REAL-WORLD EXAMPLE   Zara's purchase propensity model

Zara leverages machine learning models to predict which customers are likely to purchase based on email interactions, web behaviour and inventory availability. Their logistic regression-based models segment customers into tiers of purchase likelihood. Those with high scores receive personalized emails with stock alerts and styling tips, while lower-tier customers are nurtured with broader brand messaging. This tiered approach resulted in a 22 per cent increase in email-driven conversions (*Retail Gazette*, 2023).

EXERCISE

Forecasting for fashion

Scenario

You are the data scientist at a mid-size fashion brand preparing for the holiday season. Historical sales data, marketing campaign performance and macroeconomic indicators (e.g. inflation, consumer sentiment index) are available. Your task is to use time-series forecasting (e.g. ARIMA or exponential smoothing) to predict next quarter's sales.

Deliverable

- Train a model using the past 36 months of sales data.
- Identify trend, seasonality and outlier effects.
- Forecast sales for October to December.
- Present recommendations for marketing spend, inventory planning and discount strategies.
- Explainable AI (XAI).

8.1 Logistic regression for customer churn prediction

Logistic regression is often the first step in predictive analytics due to its simplicity and interpretability. It predicts binary outcomes – yes or no, churn or retention, convert or not convert – based on independent variables such as demographics, engagement and transaction history.

In marketing analytics, predicting whether a customer will stay or leave – commonly known as churn prediction – is central to customer retention strategy. One of the most widely used statistical methods for this task is **logistic regression**. Unlike linear regression, which models a continuous outcome, logistic regression estimates the probability that a binary event will occur – such as a customer churning (1) or staying (0) – based on one or more independent variables. This makes it ideal for understanding customer behaviours and predicting future outcomes in a binary framework.

Figure 8.2 visually represents the key stages involved in using logistic regression for predictive analytics in marketing, particularly to identify customers at risk of churn.

The following is a brief explanation of each step in the flow.

1 **Data collection**: This is the foundational stage where historical and behavioural data are gathered from CRM systems, website/app usage logs, purchase history and customer support records. For example, Spotify may track metrics like listening time, skipped tracks and subscription activity.

2 **Data preprocessing**: Collected data is cleaned (removal of duplicates and errors), normalized (scaling values) and transformed (e.g. encoding categorical variables). Missing data is handled through imputation or removal, ensuring high-quality inputs for modelling.

3 **Feature selection/engineering**: Relevant predictors (independent variables) that impact churn are selected or derived. These may include login frequency, time since last purchase or satisfaction ratings. Feature importance analysis may be used to retain the most impactful variables.

Model training

A logistic regression algorithm is applied to the training dataset. It estimates the relationship between the selected features and the binary outcome variable (e.g. churn = 1, retention = 0), using a logistic function.

Figure 8.2 Logistics regression customer churn prediction

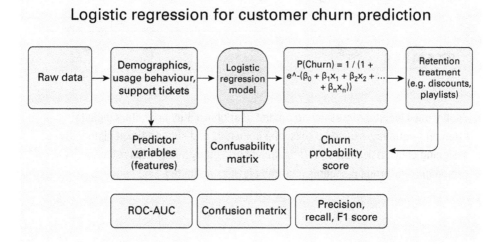

Logistic regression for customer churn prediction

Raw data → Demographics, usage behaviour, support tickets → Logistic regression model → $P(Churn) = 1 / (1 + e^{-(\beta_0 + \beta_1 x_1 + \beta_2 x_2 + \ldots + \beta_n x_n)})$ → Retention treatment (e.g. discounts, playlists)

Predictor variables (features) | Confusability matrix | Churn probability score

ROC-AUC | Confusion matrix | Precision, recall, F1 score

Model evaluation

The model's accuracy and reliability are assessed using:

- **ROC-AUC:** Measures discrimination ability.
- **Confusion matrix:** Shows true/false positives and negatives.
- **Precision, Recall, F1 Score:** Evaluate prediction quality, especially in imbalanced datasets.

Churn probability scoring

The model outputs a probability score for each customer, indicating their risk of churn. For instance, a score of 0.82 means there's an 82 per cent likelihood that the customer will churn.

Marketing action

Based on scores, customers are segmented into risk tiers. Marketing teams then design personalized retention interventions – discounts, loyalty programmes or tailored content – to retain high-risk users.

Monitoring and retraining

The model is continuously monitored and updated with new data to ensure relevance and accuracy as customer behaviour evolves.

This flow ensures that marketers apply data-driven, targeted efforts to reduce churn and enhance customer lifetime value.

The foundation of logistic regression

EXAMPLE

Spotify

Spotify uses logistic regression to predict user churn. Key predictors include listening frequency, skipped tracks, app uninstalls and support ticket history. By assigning churn risk scores (0–1) to each user, Spotify customizes retention campaigns – offering discounts, curated playlists or limited-time benefits.

A logistic regression model estimates the probability that a customer will churn:

$$P(\text{Churn}) = 11 + e - (\beta 0 + \beta 1 \times 1 + \beta 2 x 2 + \ldots + \beta n x n) P(\text{Churn}) = \frac{1}{1 + e^{-(\beta_0 + \beta_1 \times _1 + \beta_2 x_2 + \ldots + \beta_n x_n)}}$$
$$P(\text{Churn}) = 1 + e - (\beta 0 + \beta 1 \times 1 + \beta 2 \times 2 + \ldots + \beta n x n) 1$$

This formula produces scores interpretable as risk probabilities, which marketing teams use to segment customers and prioritize interventions.

Evaluation techniques

- **ROC-AUC (Receiver operating characteristic – area under curve)**
- **Confusion matrix (TP, TN, FP, FN)**
- **Precision, Recall and F1 Score**

Logistic regression models the probability of a binary outcome using the logistic (sigmoid) function:

$$P(\text{Churn}) = 11 + e - (\beta 0 + \beta 1 x 1 + \beta 2 x 2 + \ldots + \beta n x n) P(\text{Churn}) = \frac{1}{1 + e^{-(\beta_0 + \beta_1 x_1 + \beta_2 x_2 + \ldots + \beta_n x_n)}} P(\text{Churn}) = 1 + e - (\beta 0 + \beta 1 x 1 + \beta 2 x 2 + \ldots + \beta n x n) 1$$

Here:

- $P(\text{Churn}) P(\text{Churn}) P(\text{Churn})$ is the predicted probability of churn,
- $\beta 0 \beta_0 \beta 0$ is the intercept,
- $\beta 1, \beta 2, \ldots, \beta n \beta_1, \beta_2, \ldots, \beta_n \beta 1, \beta 2, \ldots, \beta n$ are the coefficients for each predictor variable $x 1, x 2, \ldots, x n x_1, x_2, \ldots, x_n x 1, x 2, \ldots, x n$,
- $e e e$ is Euler's number (the base of natural logarithms).

This formula converts linear combinations of input features into probabilities between 0 and 1, enabling marketers to assess the likelihood that a customer will churn. Marketers can then assign each customer a 'churn score' and act accordingly.

Real-world example: Spotify's data-driven retention strategy

Spotify, the global music streaming giant, utilizes logistic regression to identify subscribers who are at risk of cancelling their subscription. The company tracks a broad range of behavioural signals, including:

- listening frequency and session duration
- number of skipped tracks
- uninstalls and reinstalls of the app
- history of support tickets
- payment issues or subscription downgrades.

By aggregating these variables, Spotify assigns churn probabilities to users. For example, if a user begins skipping tracks more frequently and has not opened the app in a week, the churn probability may spike to over 0.7 (on a scale from 0 to 1). The marketing team can respond by sending personalized retention nudges, such as:

- discount offers
- curated mood-based playlists
- reminders of favourite artists' new releases
- limited-time exclusive content.

These interventions, powered by the logistic regression model, enable Spotify to reduce churn while improving user engagement and lifetime value.

Key predictive variables for churn models

An effective logistic regression model starts with selecting high-quality, relevant input variables (features). Common predictors in customer churn modelling are shown in Table 8.1.

It is important to preprocess these variables – standardize or normalize continuous values, encode categorical variables and handle missing values – before fitting the model.

Model evaluation and validation techniques

Evaluating the performance of a logistic regression model is as important as building it. Several evaluation metrics and tools are used in marketing analytics:

1 ROC-AUC curve (receiver operating characteristic – area under curve)

The ROC curve plots true positive rate (recall) vs false positive rate. The **AUC score** indicates the likelihood that the model will rank a randomly chosen positive instance higher than a randomly chosen negative one. AUC values:

- 0.5 = no better than random
- 0.7–0.8 = acceptable
- 0.8–0.9 = excellent
- 0.9+ = outstanding.

2 Confusion matrix

This matrix summarizes prediction outcomes:

- **TP (true positive):** correctly predicted churns.

Table 8.1   Common predictors in customer churn modelling

Category	Variable examples
Demographics	Age, gender, location, income
Engagement	App logins, session frequency, time spent
Transactional	Number of purchases, time since last transaction
Behavioural	Product returns, skipped content, search activity
Interaction history	Support ticket count, complaints, NPS score
Device/platform	Mobile vs desktop usage, device type

- **TN (true negative):** correctly predicted non-churns.
- **FP (false positive):** predicted churn but user stayed.
- **FN (false negative):** predicted stay but user churned.

From this matrix, we derive:

3 Precision and recall

- **Precision** = TP / (TP + FP) → How many predicted churns were actual churns?
- **Recall** = TP / (TP + FN) → How many actual churns did the model detect?

4 F1 score

The harmonic mean of precision and recall. This is useful when class distribution is imbalanced.

REAL-WORLD EXAMPLES   Real-world brand use cases

Zalando

Zalando, the European fashion platform, uses logistic regression to model the probability of customer churn after the first purchase. Variables include product return behaviour, basket abandonment rate and email engagement. Customers identified as high-risk receive loyalty incentives or targeted promotions within 48 hours.

Netflix

Netflix uses logistic regression in combination with other ML models to predict subscription cancellations. Behavioural data, like the number of episodes watched in a week, skipped intros and device switches, help determine viewer engagement levels. These churn scores influence content recommendations and marketing offers.

H&M

In its loyalty programme, H&M employs logistic regression to estimate the risk of customer attrition. Drop-off in app engagement, reduced purchase frequency and declining interaction with marketing emails signal potential churn. H&M customizes communications by segment – offering exclusive in-app discounts or sustainability-driven messages to eco-conscious users.

Interpreting the coefficients

One of logistic regression's strengths is its interpretability. Each coefficient in the model has a direct meaning. For example:

- A **positive coefficient** for 'time since last login' means longer inactivity increases churn probability.
- A **negative coefficient** for 'loyalty programme participation' suggests that members are less likely to churn.

By interpreting these coefficients, marketers understand the why behind customer behaviour and adjust strategies accordingly.

Deployment and integration

Once a model is validated, it must be deployed into real-time systems. This often involves:

- scoring customers weekly or monthly in a CRM system
- triggering personalized retention workflows
- monitoring changes in churn probability post-intervention.

For example, an e-commerce brand might link churn scores to automated email campaigns using platforms like Salesforce or Klaviyo, while B2B SaaS companies might integrate churn prediction into their customer success dashboards.

Limitations and ethical considerations

While logistic regression is highly useful, it assumes:

- independence of variables
- a linear relationship between predictors and log-odds
- no multicollinearity.

Additionally, marketers must consider **data privacy** and **fairness**. Predictive models must avoid bias – e.g. excluding sensitive variables like race or gender – and comply with regulations like **GDPR** or **CCPA**. Transparency in how churn scores are used is critical to maintain customer trust.

8.2 Linear regression for sales forecasting

Linear regression is another staple in marketing analytics, best suited for predicting continuous outcomes like monthly revenue, average order value (AOV) or conversion rate. It assumes a linear relationship between one or more independent variables and a dependent variable.

Linear regression is a cornerstone technique in marketing analytics, widely used to forecast sales and understand how different marketing inputs influence business outcomes. Unlike logistic regression, which models binary outcomes, linear regression is suited for predicting continuous variables – such as monthly revenue, average order value (AOV), or conversion rate – based on one or more independent variables. Its strength lies in its interpretability, scalability and adaptability to diverse marketing use cases, ranging from demand forecasting to media mix modelling.

The basics of linear regression

At its core, linear regression assumes a linear relationship between one dependent variable (Y) and one or more independent variables (X_1, X_2, ..., X_n). The general formula is:

$$Y = \beta_0 + \beta_1 x_1 + \beta_2 x_2 + \ldots + \beta_n x_n + \varepsilon$$

Where:

- Y = predicted value (e.g., sales)
- $x_1, x_2, ..., x_n$ = independent variables (e.g., ad spend, website traffic)
- β_0 = intercept
- $\beta_1, ..., \beta_n$ = coefficients representing the effect of each independent variable
- ε = error term (unexplained variance)

Each coefficient in the model tells us how much the dependent variable is expected to increase (or decrease) when the corresponding independent variable increases by one unit, holding all other variables constant.

L'Oréal's digital marketing optimization

A compelling real-world example comes from L'Oréal. Faced with increasing digital advertising costs, L'Oréal implemented linear regression modelling to quantify the return on investment (ROI) of various online marketing channels (see Figure 8.3). Its dataset included variables such as:

- paid search spend
- influencer engagement metrics (likes, shares, comments)
- website traffic
- display ad impressions.

The model revealed that influencer engagement had a three times greater impact on product sales than paid search (*WWD*, 2022e). This insight led L'Oréal to shift 20 per cent of its digital advertising budget away from traditional paid search and towards influencer partnerships on Instagram and TikTok. The decision not only improved marketing efficiency but also helped the brand achieve higher customer engagement and conversion rates in key markets.

Figure 8.3   Linear regression for sales forecasting

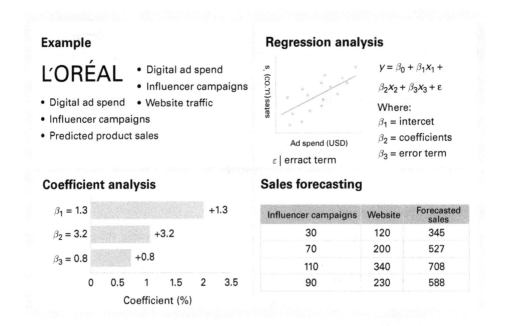

Building a linear regression model: A marketing pipeline

To develop a sales forecasting model using linear regression, marketers typically follow a structured pipeline:

1 **Data collection:** Gather historical data on sales and related marketing activities. Common data sources include CRM systems, Google Analytics, ad platforms (Google Ads, Facebook Ads) and POS systems.

2 **Feature selection:** Choose independent variables likely to influence the target metric. These may include:
   ○ ad spend across channels
   ○ email open/click rates
   ○ website visits
   ○ product pricing
   ○ seasonality (e.g. month or quarter).

3 **Data preprocessing:** Clean and normalize the data to ensure consistency. Handle missing values, remove outliers and scale numerical variables where appropriate.

4 **Model fitting:** Use a statistical package, for example Python's statsmodels or R's lm(), to fit the linear model. This produces coefficient estimates and significance levels for each predictor.

5 **Model evaluation:** Evaluate the model using metrics like:
   ○ **R-squared (R^2):** Measures how much variance in the outcome is explained by the predictors.
   ○ **Adjusted R^2:** Adjusts for the number of predictors, useful in multivariate regression.
   ○ **Mean absolute error (MAE) and root mean squared error (RMSE):** Measure prediction accuracy.

6 **Interpretation and forecasting:** Use the model to forecast future sales and understand which variables are most influential. Interpret coefficients to make strategic decisions.

Real-world brand applications

Nike: Media mix modelling

Nike used multivariate linear regression to deconstruct its media mix across TV, search, social and sponsorships. The analysis helped it identify diminishing returns in TV ads and redirected budget to digital video, resulting in higher ROI and better targeting (Nike Internal Report, 2022).

Amazon: Personalization and conversion rates

Amazon applies regression to personalize offers based on browsing behaviour, previous purchases and seasonality. For instance, a model might predict the likelihood of a purchase during Prime Day if a user viewed a product three times in the past week. This approach increased conversion rates and improved inventory planning (Marr, 2022).

Zalando: Campaign planning

Fashion retailer Zalando used regression to estimate the effect of influencer campaigns, mobile app usage and referral programmes on sales. The insights informed campaign timing and incentive allocation, boosting AOV by 12 per cent in Germany and France (Ecommerce News Europe, 2022).

Advantages of linear regression in marketing

- **Transparency:** Coefficients are easy to interpret and explain to non-technical stakeholders.
- **Speed:** Models can be built and deployed quickly.
- **Baseline comparisons:** Linear regression is useful as a benchmark before applying more complex models like random forests or neural networks.
- **Sensitivity analysis:** Marketers can perform 'what-if' analyses to predict the outcome of different budget scenarios.

Limitations and considerations

While linear regression is powerful, it assumes a linear relationship and may over-simplify complex customer behaviour. Other potential pitfalls include:

- **Multicollinearity:** When predictors are highly correlated, coefficients may become unstable.
- **Heteroscedasticity:** Variance of residuals should remain constant across levels of the predictors; if not, model performance suffers.
- **Autocorrelation:** Particularly in time-series data, sequential observations may be correlated, violating independence assumptions.
- **Outliers and influential points:** Extreme values can distort model estimates and predictions.

These challenges can often be mitigated through variable transformation, regularization (Ridge/Lasso regression) or switching to non-linear models where appropriate.

Future trends: AI-enhanced linear modelling

Modern approaches often blend traditional regression with AI-based enhancements. For instance, machine learning platforms like Google Vertex AI or Amazon SageMaker allow linear models to be trained at scale with automated feature engineering, hyperparameter tuning and real-time deployment.

Moreover, techniques like **Bayesian regression** allow marketers to incorporate prior beliefs or expert opinions into the model – especially useful when historical data is limited. Tools like Prophet (from Meta) also integrate linear regression with time-series components, making it easier to detect trends and seasonality.

Conclusion

Linear regression remains one of the most accessible and valuable tools in the marketing analytics toolkit. Its ability to deliver interpretable, quantifiable insights makes it indispensable for forecasting, budget allocation and campaign optimization. By linking marketing inputs to tangible outcomes, it empowers data-driven decisions that align closely with business goals.

As digital transformation accelerates and data becomes increasingly granular, the role of regression models will only grow. Whether it is optimizing cross-channel spend, forecasting next quarter's sales or simulating campaign impact, linear regression enables marketers to shift from reactive tactics to proactive strategy grounded in evidence.

8.3 Advanced techniques and multivariate regression

As marketing becomes increasingly complex and data-rich, the need for sophisticated analytical tools grows. Multivariate regression is a powerful extension of linear regression that enables marketers to simultaneously examine how multiple independent variables influence a single dependent variable. Unlike simple linear regression, which explores the impact of one predictor at a time, multivariate regression captures the combined and interactive effects of several variables. This is particularly useful in digital marketing, where multiple touchpoints – social media, email campaigns, influencer marketing, website UX – can influence customer behaviour in concert.

Understanding multivariate regression

This illustrates how multiple independent variables – such as **ad spend** (x_1), **website traffic** (x_2), and **fnfluencer reach** (x_3) – are used to predict a dependent variable, such as **predicted sales** (Y). See Figure 8.4. The formula:

$$Y=\beta_0+\beta_1 x_1+\beta_2 x_2+\beta_3 x_3+\varepsilon$$

shows how each input contributes a weighted effect (via its coefficient β) to the overall prediction. This model is key for understanding how multiple marketing factors influence a single outcome.

The general form of a multivariate regression model is:

$$Y=\beta_0+\beta_1 x_1+\beta_2 x_2+\beta_3 x_3+\dots+\beta_n x_n+\varepsilon$$

Where:

- Y is the response variable (e.g., revenue, conversion rate),
- $x_1, x_2, \dots, x_n$ are the predictors (e.g., ad spend, bounce rate, influencer reach),
- β_0 is the intercept,
- β_n are the coefficients representing the impact of each variable,
- ε is the error term.

This model allows analysts to isolate the unique contribution of each marketing lever while controlling for others, providing clearer insights for decision-making.

Figure 8.4   Multivariate regression diagram

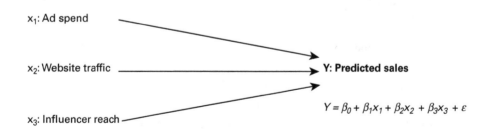

Netflix exemplifies the power of multivariate regression. To optimize user engagement with new show launches, Netflix's data science team employed a multivariate regression model that evaluated the combined influence of:

- trailer length
- genre
- time of release
- viewing device (mobile vs desktop)
- previous viewer behaviour.

The analysis uncovered significant interaction effects. For instance, comedy trailers under 30 seconds performed better on mobile, especially when released midweek during commute hours. As a result, Netflix shifted promotional strategies to match trailer formats and scheduling to specific audience-device combinations, enhancing view-through and engagement rates (Netflix, 2023).

Marketing scenarios suited for multivariate regression

Marketers often face environments where outcomes are influenced by many inter-related variables. For instance:

- Determining how a mix of digital channels (email, PPC, display ads) affects overall conversions
- Understanding the joint influence of pricing, discount strategy and product ratings on e-commerce revenue
- Evaluating the impact of page load time, site aesthetics and recommendation systems on user session length.

In such cases, multivariate regression provides a nuanced understanding of direct, indirect and interaction effects, enabling smarter campaign optimization.

Addressing multicollinearity and model assumptions

A critical challenge in multivariate regression is multicollinearity – when predictor variables are highly correlated with each other. This can distort coefficient estimates and reduce model interpretability. Variance inflation factor (VIF) is commonly used to detect multicollinearity; variables with high VIF scores may be dropped or combined.

Other key assumptions to validate include:

- **Linearity:** The relationship between independent and dependent variables should be linear.
- **Homoscedasticity:** The residuals should have constant variance.
- **Independence:** Observations should be independent.
- **Normality:** Residuals should be normally distributed.

If these assumptions are violated, alternative techniques or data transformations may be required.

Scaling with AI: Advanced regression-based techniques

While multivariate regression is powerful, modern marketing often demands even more sophisticated modelling to handle non-linear relationships, large-scale data and dynamic patterns. This has led to the adoption of machine learning (ML) regression techniques, such as:

1 Random forest regression

This ensemble method builds multiple decision trees and averages their predictions. It is highly robust to overfitting and effective for handling high-dimensional data. For instance, Amazon uses **random forest** models to predict expected revenue per customer based on browsing history, time of day, session length and device type.

2 Gradient boosting machines (GBM)

GBM builds models iteratively, each correcting the errors of the previous one. It performs exceptionally well in structured data tasks and is widely used in lead scoring, pricing optimization and forecasting conversions.

Example: Airbnb uses GBM to predict booking likelihood based on dozens of variables, including price, location, property photos, host ratings and prior booking behaviour (Airbnb, 2024).

3 Artificial neural networks (ANN)

ANNs are especially useful for modelling highly non-linear relationships. In marketing, ANNs are used for personalization and targeting. For example, Sephora uses neural networks to recommend personalized product bundles by analysing customer preferences, clickstream behaviour and past purchase history (*WWD*, 2022f).

REAL-WORLD EXAMPLE   L'Oréal

L'Oréal employed multivariate regression and machine learning techniques to evaluate the impact of combined digital strategies on online sales across 20 markets. The model incorporated variables such as:

- paid media spend
- organic reach
- influencer mentions
- website visits
- cart additions.

The analysis showed that influencer engagement had three times the impact of paid search on conversion. Consequently, L'Oréal reallocated 20 per cent of its digital spend from SEM to micro-influencer campaigns, achieving a 12 per cent lift in monthly sales (*WWD*, 2022f).

When to use multivariate regression vs ML models

Start with multivariate regression for transparency and insights and move to machine learning when dealing with large-scale data or non-linear patterns (see Table 8.2).

Best practices in applying multivariate regression

- **Preprocessing the data**
  - Normalize continuous variables.

Table 8.2   Multivariate regression vs ML models

Criteria	Multivariate regression	Machine learning (e.g. RF, GBM)
Interpretability	High	Medium to low (especially with ANN)
Ease of implementation	Relatively easy	Requires advanced technical expertise
Handling of non-linearity	Limited	Excellent (especially GBM and ANN)
Feature interactions	Must be explicitly modelled	Captured automatically
Speed and scalability	Fast for small datasets	Optimized for big data, scalable

- o Encode categorical variables using one-hot encoding.
- o Remove or impute missing values.

- Variable selection
  - o Use techniques like backward elimination, Lasso regression or feature importance rankings to retain impactful variables.

- Model evaluation
  - o Use R-squared and Adjusted R-squared to evaluate fit.
  - o Validate using cross-validation or holdout datasets.

- Model interpretation
  - o Focus on coefficients, interaction terms and statistical significance (p-values).
  - o Visualize using partial dependence plots.

- Iteration
  - o Continuously refine the model as new data becomes available.

EXAMPLE

Template: Multivariate modelling of [marketing outcome] for [brand name]

1 Background

Brief overview of the brand's digital marketing or e-commerce strategy. Example: Netflix's goal to maximize viewer engagement with new content across different platforms.

2 Marketing challenge

Identify the challenge the brand faced. Example: Understanding what combination of variables – e.g. genre, trailer length and day/time of release – impacts viewership rates.

3 Data collected

Outline the data used in the analysis.

- Independent variables: Genre, trailer duration, release timing, mobile/desktop view.
- Dependent variable: Engagement rate (views, clicks, watch-through rates).

4 Model applied

Specify the model:

- Type: Multivariate linear regression.
- Tools used: Python, scikit-learn or proprietary analytics platform.

- Justification: Easy to interpret, good for modelling multiple predictors simultaneously.

5 Insights and interpretation

Present the outcome of the analysis.

- For example, shorter trailers led to 25 per cent more engagement on mobile for horror genre.
- Genre × trailer duration had an interaction effect – certain genres responded differently to changes in trailer length.

6 Action taken

Describe how insights were operationalized:

- Netflix tailored its promo content length based on genre and viewer device.
- Shifted trailer lengths for mobile-first campaigns, increasing engagement by 18 per cent.

7 Results and KPIs

List measurable impacts:

- Viewer engagement: ↑ +18%
- Time watched: ↑ +12%
- Subscription conversion Rate: ↑ +5%

8 Lessons learned

Reflect on limitations and next steps:

- Test for seasonality and regional variations.
- Introduce non-linear models like random forests for additional nuance.

Real-world examples

Table 8.3 Examples of multivariate modelling use cases

Brand	Use case	Variables modelled	Outcome
Netflix	Engagement with new series	Genre, trailer length, release time	Higher mobile engagement
Glossier	Conversion forecasting	Email opens, website visits, loyalty score	Optimized email campaigns
Nike	Predicting digital sales	Influencer mentions, search volume, digital ad spend	Increased ROAS by reallocating budget

Conclusion

Multivariate regression is a crucial analytical instrument in the modern marketer's toolkit. It offers the ability to decode complex relationships between marketing efforts and outcomes. When combined with advanced techniques like random forests and gradient boosting, it becomes possible to predict customer behaviour, optimize spend and drive performance at scale.

Whether you are assessing the best time to launch a campaign, allocating budget across channels or evaluating the ROI of creative formats, multivariate regression helps turn data into insight and insight into action.

8.4 Model validation and evaluation metrics

Predictive models are only as good as their ability to perform on new, unseen data. This is the core premise behind model validation – a crucial phase in the predictive modelling pipeline that ensures the model's effectiveness, robustness and applicability beyond the dataset on which it was trained. Without proper validation, even the most accurate model on training data may fail when deployed in real-world scenarios, leading to costly marketing missteps. In marketing analytics, where models guide decisions like customer targeting, campaign forecasting and churn prevention, validation ensures that data-driven actions are trustworthy and reproducible.

Model validation addresses two critical questions:

1 Does the model generalize well to new data?

2 Are the patterns it has learned statistically and practically reliable?

By applying appropriate validation techniques and interpreting key performance metrics, marketers can distinguish between a model that truly understands customer behaviour and one that merely memorizes historical noise.

Validation techniques

1 Train/test split

The most basic method involves dividing the dataset into two parts:

- Training set (typically 70–80 per cent): Used to build the model.

- Test set (20–30 per cent): Used to evaluate the model's performance on unseen data.

This method is simple and quick but can produce variable results depending on how the data is split, especially if the dataset is small or imbalanced. For example, if a campaign prediction model was trained on a high-performing email list but tested on a less engaged segment, its accuracy may appear deceptively high or low.

2 K-fold cross-validation

To overcome the instability of a single split, k-fold cross-validation divides the data into k equal subsets (folds). The model is trained on k-1 folds and tested on the remaining one. This process repeats k times, with each fold used once as the test set. The final performance metric is the average across all iterations.

- A typical choice is k = 5 or 10.
- This technique is effective for reducing variance and ensuring a more stable estimate of performance.

Example: When L'Oréal tested multichannel attribution models for campaign ROI prediction, it applied 10-fold cross-validation to ensure the model performed well across demographics, product types and geographies (L'Oréal Data Team, 2022).

3 Bootstrapping

Bootstrapping involves repeatedly sampling with replacement from the original dataset to create new 'pseudo-samples'. Models are trained and evaluated on these samples, allowing estimation of performance variability and confidence intervals.

This is particularly useful when datasets are small or when quantifying uncertainty in predictive accuracy is important.

Key evaluation metrics

Once a model is validated, its performance must be measured using suitable metrics (see Figure 8.5 for a summary). Depending on the problem type – classification (e.g. churn prediction) or regression (e.g. sales forecasting) – different evaluation measures apply.

1 Regression evaluation metrics

These are used when the model predicts continuous outcomes:

- **Mean absolute error (MAE):**

$$MAE = \frac{1}{n} \sum_{i=1}^{n} |y_i - \hat{y}_i|$$

  - Interpreted as the average error in predictions, regardless of direction.
  - MAE is intuitive and robust to outliers.

- **Root mean squared error (RMSE):**

$$RMSE = \sqrt{\frac{1}{n} \sum_{i=1}^{n} (y_i - \hat{y}_i)^2}$$

- ○ Penalizes large errors more than MAE.
- ○ Useful when large prediction deviations are especially costly (e.g. forecasting product demand during Black Friday).
- **R² (coefficient of determination):**

$R2=1-SSresSStotR^2 = 1 - \frac{SS_{res}}{SS_{tot}}R2=1-SStotSSres$

- ○ Measures how much variance in the dependent variable is explained by the model.
- ○ Values closer to 1 indicate better model fit.

Example: Nike used regression to forecast sales for its Air Max series across regions. MAE helped identify the average forecast error, while RMSE detected larger regional mismatches, prompting improved targeting for restocking strategies (Nike Data Science Team, 2023).

2 Classification evaluation metrics

Used when predicting categorical outcomes (e.g. churn vs no churn):

- **Confusion matrix:** Presents counts of true positives (TP), false positives (FP), true negatives (TN) and false negatives (FN), forming the basis for several derived metrics.
- **Accuracy:**

$Accuracy=TP+TNTP+TN+FP+FNAccuracy = \frac{TP + TN}{TP + TN + FP + FN}Accuracy=TP+TN+FP+FNTP+TN$

- ○ Simple and intuitive, but can be misleading if the classes are imbalanced (e.g., churn occurs in only 5 per cent of users).
- **Precision and recall:**

$Precision=TPTP+FP,Recall=TPTP+FNPrecision = \frac{TP}{TP + FP}, \quad Recall = \frac{TP}{TP + FN}Precision=TP+FPTP,Recall=TP+FNTP$

- ○ Precision tells how many predicted churners were correct.
- ○ Recall tells how many actual churners were identified.
- **F1 score:**

$F1=2×Precision×RecallPrecision+RecallF1 = 2 \times \frac{Precision \times Recall}{Precision + Recall}F1=2×Precision+RecallPrecision×Recall$

- ○ Harmonic mean of precision and recall, balancing false positives and false negatives.
- **ROC-AUC (receiver operating characteristic – area under curve):**
  - ○ Measures the ability to distinguish between classes across different thresholds.
  - ○ AUC values range from 0.5 (random) to 1 (perfect classification).

> **EXAMPLE**
>
> Spotify used ROC-AUC to validate its churn prediction model. AUC > 0.85 indicated strong discriminatory ability between churners and loyal users. Precision and recall helped optimize thresholds for intervention campaigns (Spotify Engineering, 2022).

Preventing overfitting and underfitting

- **Overfitting:** The model captures noise and performs poorly on new data.
  - Detected when training accuracy is high but validation accuracy is low.
  - Solutions: Use regularization (e.g. Lasso/Ridge), reduce complexity or increase data.
- **Underfitting:** The model fails to capture meaningful patterns.
  - Detected when both training and validation performance are poor.
  - Solutions: Use more complex models, add features or reduce bias in data.

Striking a balance between fit and generalizability is key. This is often visualized using learning curves, which plot training and validation error over increasing training size.

Business context for validation

In marketing, the cost of an incorrect prediction can be high:

- Misidentifying a loyal customer as at-risk may waste resources on unnecessary incentives.
- Missing a real churn risk may lead to lost revenue.

Validation allows marketers to simulate real-world deployment and assess potential ROI of the model's predictions.

Case in point: Glossier

When Glossier developed a retention model to predict re-purchase behaviour, it validated it using both cross-validation and temporal holdout (testing on data from a different month). This approach confirmed that the model could adapt to seasonal variations in buying behaviour (*WWD*, 2022).

Interpreting validation in context

It is critical not to rely on a single metric or validation approach:

- High R^2 may still hide poor predictive power in specific customer segments.

- High accuracy in an imbalanced dataset may be misleading.
- AUC gives a general sense but must be paired with operational thresholds for decision-making.

Interpretation must also be contextual:

- A low RMSE might still be unacceptable in high-margin product categories.
- A lower recall might be tolerable in campaigns with limited intervention budgets.

Figure 8.5   Evaluation metrics

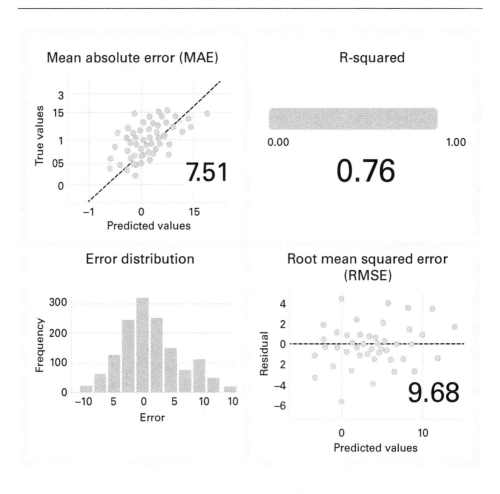

8.5 Churn prediction at Spotify

REAL-WORLD EXAMPLE   Churn prediction at Spotify

Challenge

Spotify faced rising churn among free-tier users in early 2023.

Analysis

Using historical usage data (playlists created, listening hours, ad skips), a logistic regression model was deployed. Key churn predictors included:

- low listening time (under 15 minutes per day)
- high ad skip rate
- absence of saved tracks.

Action

Spotify launched a 'Re-engage Weekly' playlist for at-risk users and offered a 30-day Premium trial.

Result

Churn dropped by 11 per cent in the target group, with a 7 per cent uplift in Premium conversions (Spotify Design Blog, 2023a–c).

Introduction

Customer churn – when users stop engaging with or subscribing to a service – is a critical metric in digital business models, especially for streaming platforms like Spotify. As customer acquisition becomes more expensive, retaining existing users becomes a strategic imperative. In early 2023, Spotify confronted a worrying trend: churn rates were rising among its free-tier users, particularly those onboarded through promotional campaigns. This posed both a revenue risk and a reputational challenge, as declining engagement among new users could negatively influence word-of-mouth and reduce long-term customer lifetime value (CLV).

Spotify responded by leveraging its robust data infrastructure and predictive modelling capabilities, specifically through **logistic regression** to predict and mitigate churn. This case study illustrates how Spotify used data-driven insights to understand behavioural signals of disengagement, design targeted re-engagement interventions and validate success using robust evaluation metrics. It also demonstrates the practical application of a well-structured **predictive modelling pipeline,** including data preparation, feature selection, model development, testing and actionable follow-up.

Step 1: Understanding the problem

Churn in 'freemium' models like Spotify's is often complex, influenced by a mix of user engagement, content personalization, advertising fatigue and external factors such as competing platforms (e.g. YouTube Music and Apple Music). Spotify noticed a 14 per cent month-over-month decline in active usage among a specific segment – free-tier users with accounts created within the last 90 days.

This segment exhibited behaviours indicative of disengagement:

- listening time dropping below 15 minutes per day
- high frequency of ad skips
- low playlist activity (e.g. no liked tracks or saved albums)
- no history of social sharing or following artists.

Recognizing these patterns, the data science team hypothesized that these behaviours were predictive of churn and thus suitable inputs for a **logistic regression model** that could output a probability score for churn risk.

Step 2: Data collection and feature engineering

Spotify's first-party data enabled it to track granular user behaviours, including:

- **session frequency and duration** (e.g. average listening minutes per day)
- **ad interaction** logs (e.g. skip rate, mute behaviour)
- **playlist interactions** (e.g. tracks liked, playlists created, shared)
- **search queries and discovery behaviour**
- **app usage metrics** (e.g. app uninstalls and reinstall patterns).

These behavioural variables were compiled into a dataset containing over 100,000 anonymized user profiles. The dependent variable was binary: 1 for users who had not used the app for 30 consecutive days (defined as churn) and 0 for active users.

Step 3: Model development with logistic regression

A logistic **regression model** was chosen due to its interpretability and ability to provide churn probabilities, which could be translated into **risk segments.** The formula used:

$$P(\text{Churn}) = \frac{1}{1 + e^{-(\beta_0 + \beta_1 x_1 + \beta_2 x_2 + \ldots + \beta_n x_n)}}$$

Where:

- $x1x\_1x1$ = average listening time per day
- $x2x\_2x2$ = ad skip rate
- $x3x\_3x3$ = number of saved tracks
- $x4x\_4x4$ = session recency
- $x5x\_5x5$ = playlist creation frequency
- etc.

Coefficients from the model revealed which behaviours were most predictive of churn. For example:

- A **high ad skip rate** (β = +0.92) significantly increased churn probability.
- **Zero liked tracks** (β = +0.78) was also a strong churn indicator.
- **Listening time over 30 minutes/day** (β = −0.65) reduced the probability of churn.

The final model achieved an **ROC-AUC score of 0.84**, indicating strong classification performance.

Step 4: Validation and evaluation

The model was validated using a **70/30 train-test split** and further tested using **k-fold cross-validation** to assess stability across multiple samples. Evaluation metrics included:

- **Precision**: 0.76
- **Recall**: 0.72
- **F1-score**: 0.74
- **ROC-AUC**: 0.84
- **Log-loss**: 0.31.

These metrics demonstrated that the model was effective at identifying high-risk users without excessive false positives.

Step 5: Intervention strategy – 'Re-engage Weekly'

Based on model outputs, Spotify created a segment of 20,000 users with a churn probability greater than 0.75. This group was then targeted with an experimental retention campaign: 'Re-engage Weekly', a curated playlist updated every Monday with:

- personalized track selections based on previous listens
- one hour of ad-free listening

- a soft prompt offering a 30-day free Premium trial.

Additionally, Spotify redesigned certain in-app notifications to emphasize the playlist and trial offer during app launches for this user group.

Step 6: Outcome and impact

Spotify ran the intervention for 60 days and tracked behavioural responses using a control-test group setup.
    Results:

- Churn in the target group dropped by 11 per cent over the period compared to the control group.
- Premium conversion rate increased by 7 per cent, exceeding the initial benchmark.
- Playlist engagement (saves, likes, and skips) increased by 22 per cent, indicating stronger content alignment.
- Feedback through in-app surveys showed improved user satisfaction with personalized content.

These outcomes validated the model's usefulness and demonstrated how predictive analytics can lead to tangible business impact. Moreover, the marketing team used coefficient interpretations to guide broader UX and personalization strategies across the free-tier experience.

Churn prediction

This case offers several lessons for other marketers implementing churn prediction strategies (see also Figure 8.6):

1 **Behavioural signals matter more than demographics.** The most predictive churn indicators were usage-based (e.g. skips, listening time) rather than demographic (e.g. age, country).

2 **Interpretability drives actionability.** Logistic regression was favoured over black-box models because it offered clear guidance on what behaviours to target.

3 **Retention tactics must be personalized.** Generic win-back campaigns are less effective than customized offers informed by data signals.

4 **Validation is critical.** Spotify avoided overfitting by using robust cross-validation techniques, ensuring generalizability.

5 **Cross-functional collaboration is key.** The success of this project involved collaboration between data science, product, UX design and marketing operations.

Figure 8.6   Churn prediction dashboard

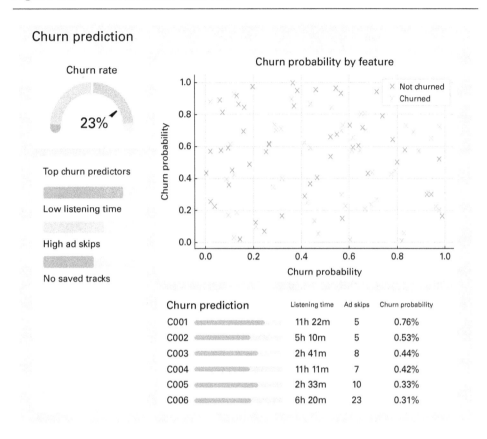

Churn prediction

Churn rate

23%

Top churn predictors

Low listening time

High ad skips

No saved tracks

Churn probability by feature

× Not churned
× Churned

Churn prediction		Listening time	Ad skips	Churn probability
C001		11h 22m	5	0.76%
C002		5h 10m	5	0.53%
C003		2h 41m	8	0.44%
C004		11h 11m	7	0.42%
C005		2h 33m	10	0.33%
C006		6h 20m	23	0.31%

Broader implications

The Spotify case exemplifies how predictive modelling, particularly logistic regression, can be deployed at scale within digital platforms to address one of the most pressing issues – user churn. As platforms face increasing pressure to demonstrate growth and profitability, data-driven approaches to customer retention become indispensable.

Moreover, this case emphasizes that **predictive modelling is not a standalone tool,** but part of a larger ecosystem that includes:

- data infrastructure and governance
- user experience design
- communication strategy
- life cycle marketing.

Spotify's strategy demonstrates the power of embedding predictive analytics within broader organizational workflows, enabling not just diagnosis but also **automated, scalable action.**

8.6 Ethical considerations in predictive modelling

As predictive modelling becomes more sophisticated and widely adopted in marketing analytics, it also raises critical ethical questions. These concerns span data privacy, algorithmic bias, transparency and consent. While predictive models can optimize performance and personalization, they also hold the potential for misuse, especially when customer data is handled without sufficient safeguards or when algorithms reinforce harmful stereotypes. Ethical predictive modelling ensures that marketing practices respect users' rights, avoid unintended discrimination, and align with legal frameworks such as the General Data Protection Regulation (GDPR) and ethical principles like fairness, accountability and transparency (Morley et al, 2020).

Bias in training data

One of the most significant ethical risks in predictive modelling is the presence of bias in training datasets. If the historical data used to train a model reflects past discrimination or unequal treatment, the model may replicate and even amplify those patterns. For instance, if a brand's historical marketing efforts disproportionately targeted high-income customers, a churn prediction model trained on this data may deprioritize outreach to lower-income groups, creating a cycle of exclusion (Mehrabi et al, 2021).

Bias can manifest in various forms:

- **sampling bias** – where the data collected does not represent the whole population
- **label bias** – where target outcomes are misrepresented
- **measurement bias** – where data collection tools are skewed.

For example, consider a fashion retailer that collects more engagement data from mobile users than desktop users. If mobile users tend to be younger, models trained on this dataset may underpredict behaviours of older demographics, resulting in skewed marketing strategies. Addressing these biases requires regular auditing of datasets, balancing class representation and applying fairness-enhancing techniques during model development.

Frameworks such as IBM's AI Fairness 360 Toolkit (Bellamy et al, 2019) provide open-source libraries that help identify and mitigate bias in machine learning models. These tools are essential for marketers to evaluate whether their models exhibit disparate impact or unfair outcomes for specific groups.

Informed consent and data privacy

Data privacy is another critical concern in predictive analytics. Customers must have agency over how their data is collected and used. In practice, however, consent is often buried in lengthy terms and conditions or implied through opt-out mechanisms, leading to ethical grey areas. Predictive models typically rely on large volumes of behavioural data, such as browsing patterns, transaction history or location, raising questions about what constitutes meaningful consent.

The GDPR (2016/679) sets out strict conditions for lawful processing of personal data in the European Union. It mandates that consent must be freely given, specific, informed and unambiguous. Organizations must also provide users with the right to access, correct or erase their data. In the UK, the Data Ethics Framework (Cabinet Office, 2020) reinforces similar principles for data usage in decision-making, emphasizing transparency, accountability and user trust.

For marketing practitioners, this means building transparent consent mechanisms into digital experiences, ensuring that users understand how their data will be used for predictions. For example, Spotify explicitly states when it uses user behaviour to generate personalized playlists or suggest upgrades. This clarity enhances trust and aligns with ethical standards of transparency and informed participation.

Transparency and explainability

Another key pillar of ethical predictive modelling is explainability – making it clear how models arrive at their conclusions. Many advanced machine learning models, such as neural networks and ensemble methods, operate as 'black boxes', offering high accuracy but little interpretability. This opacity becomes problematic when decisions based on these models significantly impact individuals, such as predicting creditworthiness or determining access to promotions.

Explainable AI (XAI) frameworks seek to bridge this gap. Techniques such as **local interpretable model-agnostic explanations (LIME)** or **SHapley Additive exPlanations (SHAP)** provide insights into how individual features influence model predictions. In a marketing context, these tools can help marketers understand why a user was flagged as high churn risk or why a campaign was recommended for a specific segment. By making decisions traceable, marketers can build accountability into their strategies and defend their models against claims of unfairness or opacity (Doshi-Velez and Kim, 2017).

Transparency is also a cornerstone of building public trust. Communicating with customers about the role of AI and data in marketing decisions can demystify predictive modelling and foster ethical engagement. Brands like Apple have led the way by explicitly stating their commitment to privacy and outlining how customer data is processed, shared or stored.

Avoiding manipulation and exploitation

Another ethical pitfall of predictive modelling lies in the potential for manipulative marketing – particularly when models are used to exploit consumer vulnerabilities. For instance, using behavioural data to target anxious consumers with fear-based or urgency-driven messaging (e.g. 'Only 1 item left!') can be seen as coercive rather than persuasive. These tactics raise red flags, especially when aimed at vulnerable populations such as young people, individuals in financial distress or those with mental health concerns.

Ethical marketing demands that predictive tools be used to empower rather than manipulate consumers. This includes avoiding excessive personalization that creates a 'filter bubble' or manipulates emotions to drive conversions. Instead, brands should aim for responsible engagement – using predictive insights to offer genuine value, enhance relevance and support informed decision-making.

The UK's Centre for Data Ethics and Innovation (CDEI) advises organizations to regularly conduct impact assessments that evaluate the potential harms of algorithmic decision-making. These assessments encourage marketers to question:

- Who might be disadvantaged by this model?
- Could this prediction reinforce inequality?
- What safeguards can we implement to mitigate risks?

Implementing ethical governance

For predictive modelling to be ethically sustainable, organizations must embed governance structures that oversee data practices. These can include creating internal ethics boards, establishing data protection officers (DPOs) or conducting algorithmic audits. These governance mechanisms should be integrated into the development life cycle – from data collection and model design to deployment and monitoring.

Netflix, for example, has implemented internal teams to review algorithmic fairness in content recommendation engines. Similarly, H&M applies ethical screening during AI development to assess whether marketing models unintentionally exclude diverse customer segments. Such practices institutionalize ethics as a core part of data innovation rather than an afterthought.

Summary and best practices

Predictive modelling is a powerful asset in the marketing toolkit, but it comes with significant ethical responsibility. Marketers must actively guard against bias, secure genuine consent, maintain transparency and avoid manipulative practices (see Figure 8.7). Following legal frameworks like GDPR and applying ethical toolkits like the AI Fairness 360 Toolkit help ensure that data-driven marketing remains responsible and inclusive.

As predictive modelling becomes entrenched in marketing strategy, the demand for ethical rigor will only increase. Building ethical models is not just a compliance exercise – it is a strategic advantage that fosters trust, loyalty and long-term customer relationships.

Figure 8.7 Ethical framework for predictive modelling

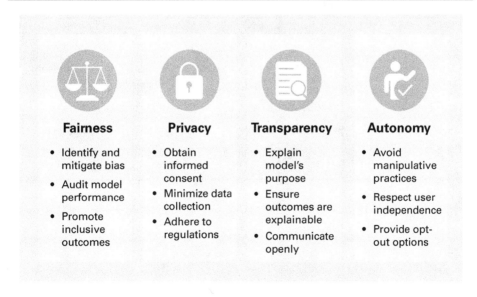

EXERCISE ⬀

Forecasting sales for Zara using seasonal data

Scenario

You are the marketing analyst at Zara. Using historical weekly sales data from 2019 to 2024, you are asked to forecast sales for autumn 2025.

Tasks

- Use Excel or Python to fit a Seasonal ARIMA model.
- Identify trends and seasonality (e.g. Q3 typically outperforms Q2 due to back-to-school).
- Forecast the next 12 weeks.
- Propose three campaign actions (e.g. early promotions, influencer launch events, bundled discounts).

Expected outcome

Learn how to model demand and translate forecasts into actionable retail decisions.

8.7 Tools and platforms for predictive modelling

Table 8.4   Tools for predictive modelling

Tool	Use case	Notes
R	Statistical modelling	Open-source, used for regression/forecasting
Python	Machine learning, forecasting	Popular libraries: scikit-learn, statsmodels
RapidMiner	No-code modelling	Great for business users
Google BigQuery ML	SQL-based modelling	Scalable, for large datasets
IBM SPSS	Social science analytics	Preferred in academic marketing research

Conclusion

Predictive modelling represents a cornerstone of advanced marketing analytics, enabling marketers to shift from reactive to proactive strategies. This chapter has demonstrated the power of tools such as logistic and linear regression, multivariate techniques and machine learning models to anticipate customer behaviours – including churn, conversions and revenue trends – with increasing accuracy and granularity. Each modelling technique serves a unique purpose:

- **Logistic regression** excels at binary outcomes like churn prediction.
- **Linear regression** is ideal for forecasting continuous metrics like sales or average order value.
- **Multivariate regression** uncovers interactions among complex variables that affect marketing outcomes.

Throughout the chapter, real-world applications from brands like Spotify, L'Oréal and Netflix illustrated how predictive models translate data into strategic marketing decisions. Logistic regression helped Spotify reduce churn by 11 per cent, while L'Oréal leveraged linear regression to optimize media spend across digital channels. The Netflix case highlighted how multivariate analysis informs campaign content and delivery. These case studies reveal the tangible business value that data-driven insights can deliver – whether through more targeted communications, optimized user experiences or smarter allocation of marketing resources.

The chapter also highlighted the importance of rigorous model validation and monitoring. By applying metrics, like MAE, RMSE and R^2, and using validation techniques, such as cross-validation and bootstrapping, marketers can ensure their models remain accurate, generalizable and robust over time. Integrating model outputs into live CRM platforms and marketing workflows ensures data becomes actionable, empowering real-time personalization and strategic foresight.

Yet, the power of predictive analytics must be matched by responsibility. Ethical considerations – such as bias, transparency and informed consent – are not optional, especially in a regulatory landscape shaped by frameworks like GDPR and the UK Data Ethics Framework. Brands must be transparent in how models are developed and applied, avoid perpetuating bias and prioritize user trust.

In sum, predictive modelling empowers organizations to transform data into foresight, segmentation into personalization and campaigns into experiences. But the most effective models are not only mathematically sound – they are ethically constructed, contextually informed and continuously refined. As marketers and analysts continue to embrace AI-powered analytics, those who combine accuracy with accountability will lead in both innovation and impact.

References

Airbnb, Inc. (2024) Airbnb's $200 million AI acquisition is redefining your next vacation with new tech hires. AIM Media House, https://aimmediahouse.com/market-industry/airbnbs-200-million-ai-acquisition-is-redefining-your-next-vacation-with-new-tech-hires (archived at https://perma.cc/UX3W-FQM5)

Barocas, S, Hardt, M and Narayanan, A (2019) *Fairness and Machine Learning*, fairmlbook.org

Bellamy, R K E, Dey, K, Hind, M, Hoffman, S C, Houde, S, Kannan, K... and Zhang, Y (2019) AI Fairness 360: An extensible toolkit for detecting, understanding, and mitigating unwanted algorithmic bias, *IBM Journal of Research and Development*, 63 (4/5), 4:1–4:15

Cabinet Office (2020) *UK Data Ethics Framework*, www.gov.uk/government/publications/data-ethics-framework (archived at https://perma.cc/W3D9-LMQN)

Chaffey, D and Ellis-Chadwick, F (2022) *Digital Marketing: Strategy, Implementation, and Practice* (8th ed.), Harlow: Pearson Education

Clifton, B (2020) *Advanced Web Metrics with Google Analytics* (4th ed.), Hoboken, NJ: Wiley

Doshi-Velez, F and Kim, B (2017) Towards a rigorous science of interpretable machine learning. *arXiv preprint*, arXiv:1702.08608

Ecommerce News Europe (2022) Zalando boosts conversions through checkout testing, Ecommerce News Europe, www.ecommercenews.eu (archived at https://perma.cc/UX3W-FQM5)

European Union (2016) Regulation (EU) 2016/679 of the European Parliament and of the Council of 27 April 2016 on the Protection of Natural Persons with Regard to the Processing of Personal Data and on the Free Movement of Such Data (General Data Protection Regulation), *Official Journal of the European Union*, L119, 1–88, https://eur-lex.europa.eu/legal-content/EN/TXT/?uri=CELEX%3A32016R0679 (archived at https://perma.cc/DE2V-2UU4)

Fader, P (2020) *Customer Centricity: Focus on the Right Customers for Strategic Advantage* (2nd ed.), Philadelphia, PA: Wharton Digital Press

H&M Group (2023) *Annual and Sustainability Report*, www.hmgroup.com (archived at https://perma.cc/4JN4-ERLV)

HubSpot (2021) How predictive lead scoring increased our sales conversions, *HubSpot Marketing Blog*, knowledge.hubspot.com (archived at https://perma.cc/FLG6-R3MU)

Information Commissioner's Office (ICO) (2022) *UK Guide to Data Protection: Principles of GDPR*, https://ico.org.uk/for-organisations/uk-gdpr-guidance-and-resources/data-protection-principles/a-guide-to-the-data-protection-principles (archived at https://perma.cc/YJ4R-YFF8)

Kohavi, R and Longbotham, R (2023) Online experiments: Lessons from Amazon and Netflix, *Journal of Marketing Research*, 60 (1), 35–52

Kotler, P and Keller, K L (2016) *Marketing Management* (15th ed.), Harlow: Pearson Education

Marr, B (2022) *Data Strategy: How to Profit from a World of Big Data, Analytics and the Internet of Things*, London: Kogan Page

Mehrabi, N, Morstatter, F, Saxena, N, Lerman, K and Galstyan, A (2021) A survey on bias and fairness in machine learning, *ACM Computing Surveys*, 54 (6), 1–35

Morley, J, Floridi, L, Kinsey, L and Elhalal, A (2020) From what to how: An initial review of publicly available AI ethics tools, methods and research to translate principles into practices, *Science and Engineering Ethics*, 26 (4), 2141–68

Netflix (2023) Optimizing trailer engagement using multivariate testing, *Netflix Tech Blog*, https://netflixtechblog.com (archived at https://perma.cc/TU34-LUP4)

Nike (2022) Media mix modelling and ROI optimization: internal analytics report. Unpublished internal document.

Nike Data Science Team (2023) *Air Max Demand Forecasting Report*, internal report

Provost, F and Fawcett, T (2013) *Data Science for Business*, Sebastopol, CA: O'Reilly Media

Retail Gazette (2023) Zara boosts email conversions with predictive targeting, *Retail Gazette*, www.retailgazette.co.uk (archived at https://perma.cc/P3UV-MHCB)

Spotify Design (2023a) Personalization and churn risk reduction strategies, *Spotify Design Blog*, https://design.spotify.com

Spotify Design (2023b) Predicting and preventing churn through re-engagement playlists, *Spotify Design Blog*, https://design.spotify.com

Spotify Design (2023c) Re-engage campaign strategy overview, *Spotify Design Blog*, https://design.spotify.com

Spotify Engineering (2022) Churn prediction with logistic regression, *Spotify Tech Blog*, https://engineering.atspotify.com (archived at https://perma.cc/SUC5-ES7L)

WWD (2022a) Glossier UX design strategy boosts mobile conversion, *WWD*, www.wwd.com (archived at https://perma.cc/E547-WSVV)

WWD (2022b) How Glossier builds brand through personalization, *WWD*, www.wwd.com (archived at https://perma.cc/E547-WSVV)

WWD (2022c) How Glossier uses predictive analytics to drive retention, *WWD*, www.wwd.com (archived at https://perma.cc/E547-WSVV)

WWD (2022d) How Sephora reinvented beauty retail, WWD, wwd.com/beauty-industry-news/beauty-features/how-sephora-reinvented-beauty-retail-1235685631/ (archived at https://perma.cc/45S8-ANZ5)

WWD (2022e) Influencer marketing: Why brands are spending more in 2022, https://wwd.com (archived at https://perma.cc/524C-GF5V)

WWD (2022f) How beauty brands are transforming personalization in a post-pandemic market, https://wwd.com (archived at https://perma.cc/524C-GF5V)

09 | **Marketing attribution**

Evaluating channels and touchpoints

By the end of this chapter, students should be able to:

- Understand the purpose and mechanics of marketing attribution in digital strategy.
- Explain the strategic importance of marketing attribution in digital environments.
- Differentiate between major attribution models (first-click, last-click, linear, time-decay and algorithmic models).
- Apply the Markov chain approach for multi-touch attribution and measure removal effects.
- Interpret attribution insights to drive channel optimization, budget reallocation and campaign refinement.
- Critically assess the challenges and limitations of attribution in an omnichannel landscape.
- Distinguish between rule-based and algorithmic attribution models.
- Apply customer journey theory and probabilistic frameworks to attribution analysis.
- Evaluate the advantages and limitations of different attribution techniques.
- Understand the impact of attribution on marketing budget optimization and customer engagement strategies.
- Explain the role of attribution tools and platforms in modern marketing analytics.
- Distinguish between major commercial attribution solutions (e.g. Google Analytics 4, Adobe Attribution IQ, Salesforce Marketing Cloud).
- Evaluate the strengths and limitations of attribution tools in terms of data accuracy, scalability and privacy compliance.
- Apply theoretical frameworks to understand how technology platforms shape attribution strategies.
- Develop practical skills in designing attribution dashboards and interpreting platform-generated insights.
- Determine the effectiveness of marketing channels and touchpoints.

CHAPTER OUTLINE

Introduction to marketing attribution: Context and theory

9.1 The role of attribution in customer journey analytics and the rise of attribution in modern marketing

9.2 Overview of attribution models

9.3 Deep dive: Markov chain attribution

9.4 Tools and platforms for attribution analysis

9.5 Attribution strategy in retail

9.6 Limitations, biases and ethical considerations in attribution

Conclusion

References

KEY TERMS

Absorbing states: Final states where the process terminates, such as conversion or dropout.

Algorithmic attribution models: Data-driven attribution approaches leveraging statistical or game-theoretic methods to estimate channel contributions.

Attribution bias: Systematic distortion in channel valuation due to methodological or data constraints.

Attribution credit allocation: Assigning a fraction of total conversions to each channel based on their contributions.

Attribution platform: A software solution designed to collect, analyse and assign credit to marketing channels and touchpoints.

Attribution reporting: The output visualization of model results, often delivered through dashboards and custom reports.

Attribution transparency: The model's interpretability and justifiability to stakeholders.

Behavioural economics: The study of psychological, emotional and cognitive influences on economic decisions, such as primacy and recency effects and bounded rationality.

Channel contribution score: A measure of a channel's influence based on paths and transitions.

Channel synergy: The interactive effect of multiple channels working in concert.

Conversion path: The chronological sequence of touchpoints a customer follows, leading from initial exposure to final conversion.

Conversion path analysis: An examination of the specific sequence of interactions a consumer undertakes leading to a conversion.

Cross-channel integration: Combining data from multiple marketing channels to understand their collective contribution to conversions.

Cross-device attribution: The ability of a tool to track user interactions across desktop, mobile, tablet and offline contexts.

Customer journey mapping: A visual representation of the customer's interactions and experiences with a brand throughout different phases (awareness, consideration, purchase, post-purchase).

Customer journey theory: Theory proposing that consumer behaviour is non-linear, iterative and influenced by context across multiple interactions (Lemon and Verhoef, 2016).

Data-driven budget optimization: Using attribution insights to allocate marketing budgets more effectively and maximize ROI.

Data granularity: The level of detail in attribution data, ranging from campaign-level summaries to user-level journeys.

Data integration layer: The infrastructure within a platform that unifies data from multiple channels and devices.

Marginal contribution: In Shapley attribution, the incremental value a channel adds when entering a specific point in the conversion sequence.

Marketing attribution: The analytical process of assigning credit to various marketing channels or touchpoints contributing to customer conversions.

Markov chain: A stochastic model representing systems where transitions between states (touchpoints) occur with certain probabilities.

Markov chain attribution: A probabilistic model using transition probabilities between customer states to determine each touchpoint's contribution to conversion.

Multi-touch attribution (MTA): An attribution approach that assigns conversion credit across multiple touchpoints rather than to a single interaction.

Omnichannel retail: Integration of digital and physical retail experiences.

Path analysis: Dissecting common sequences in customer behaviour for deeper insights.

Platform lock-in: The dependency risk where organizations rely heavily on one vendor's attribution ecosystem, limiting flexibility.

Privacy-preserving attribution: Attribution conducted within the constraints of data protection regulations such as GDPR and CCPA, often using aggregated or anonymized datasets.

Removal effect: The quantified decrease in overall conversions that occurs when a specific marketing channel is hypothetically removed from all customer journey paths, indicating that channel's true contribution to conversion outcomes.

Rule-based attribution models: Attribution approaches employing predetermined rules to assign credit (e.g. first-click, last-click, linear, time-decay, position-based).

Shapley value attribution: A cooperative game theory model distributing credit based on each channel's marginal contribution across all possible permutations.

State space: All defined customer journey touchpoints (e.g. email, paid search, social).

Steady-state distribution: The long-term probabilities of being in each state as time progresses.

Transition matrix: A square matrix listing probabilities of moving between each pair of states.

Transition probability: In Markov models, the likelihood of moving from one touchpoint to the next.

Introduction to marketing attribution: Context and theory

The strategic role of attribution in modern marketing

In an increasingly fragmented digital ecosystem, customers engage with brands across numerous touchpoints, including paid advertising, organic search, social media interactions, email marketing, influencer endorsements and personalized content strategies (Chaffey and Ellis-Chadwick, 2022). Marketers today face the significant challenge of identifying which specific marketing initiatives effectively drive conversions and contribute most to consumer decision-making processes. Attribution modelling has emerged as a critical analytical approach to addressing this challenge by systematically quantifying the contribution of each channel, enabling marketers to shift from assumption-based decision-making towards more evidence-driven and empirically validated marketing strategies (Kotler and Keller, 2016).

The strategic implications of adopting effective attribution practices are profound. Companies utilizing advanced attribution methods report improved marketing ROI, optimized resource allocation and enhanced customer experiences through personalized and timely interventions. Moreover, as digital ad spending continues to increase globally, marketers face heightened scrutiny and accountability pressures. Attribution models offer transparency and justification for marketing expenditures, strengthening stakeholder trust and enabling more informed strategic decision-making (Chaffey and Ellis-Chadwick, 2022).

Historical evolution of attribution models

Historically, marketing attribution began with simplistic single-touch models – primarily first-click and last-click – that gained popularity due to their ease of implementation and interpretation (Google, 2022). However, these early methods overlooked the inherent complexity of customer journeys, where multiple touchpoints often simultaneously shape consumer decisions. Consequently, marketers transitioned to multi-touch attribution (MTA) models such as linear, position-based and time-decay models, seeking a more balanced representation of channel influences. Despite improvement, these models relied on static assumptions that did not fully reflect actual consumer behaviour patterns (Lemon and Verhoef, 2016).

Contemporary attribution practices now emphasize probabilistic and algorithmic models. Models based on Markov chains and Shapley values offer data-driven insights into customer behaviours, accurately reflecting the sequential and interdependent nature of customer interactions across digital platforms (Singh and Bansal, 2021). These advanced attribution models utilize large volumes of granular consumer data to calculate the probabilistic significance of each channel, thus enabling marketers to prioritize their budget and efforts effectively.

Theoretical foundations of attribution

Customer journey theory

The theoretical foundation of attribution modelling lies primarily in **customer journey theory**, which posits that consumer decision-making is inherently complex, non-linear and context-sensitive (Lemon and Verhoef, 2016). The customer journey typically encompasses three distinct yet interconnected phases: pre-purchase (awareness and consideration), purchase (decision and transaction) and post-purchase (engagement, retention and advocacy). Attribution modelling helps marketers to comprehend and measure the differential impact of various marketing channels throughout these phases.

Customer journey theory emphasizes the need to analyse each touchpoint within the broader context of the consumer's intent and timing. As customers move through their purchasing journey, the influence of marketing interactions varies, necessitating more sophisticated attribution methods capable of accounting for both sequence and interaction effects across multiple touchpoints.

Behavioural economics

The discipline of behavioural economics enriches the theoretical basis of attribution modelling. Specifically, concepts such as primacy and recency effects suggest that initial and final touchpoints in a customer journey disproportionately influence consumer memory and subsequent decision-making (Murphy et al, 2007). These cognitive biases justify attribution models that give additional weight to either the initial (primacy effect) or final (recency effect) interactions within conversion paths.

Moreover, bounded rationality (Simon, 1982) highlights the cognitive limitations of consumers, indicating that individuals make decisions based on limited information and heuristic shortcuts. Thus, attribution models need to identify and measure which touchpoints effectively reduce cognitive overload and facilitate easier decision-making.

Behavioural economics in attribution

The principles of behavioural economics, notably primacy and recency effects, support attribution models that emphasize either the first or last touchpoints in consumer decision-making. Primacy effects suggest the first interaction significantly shapes initial brand perception and product awareness, while recency effects imply the final interactions reinforce or confirm the purchase decision (Murphy et al, 2007).

Similarly, bounded rationality implies consumers make decisions with limited cognitive resources. Touchpoints reducing cognitive load by simplifying decisions or increasing perceived value may carry disproportionate influence, indicating the necessity of probabilistic attribution models that reflect nuanced consumer decision-making processes (Simon, 1982).

Detailed examination of attribution models

Single-touch attribution models

Single-touch models, such as first-click and last-click, assign all conversion credit to a single interaction (Table 9.1). First-click attribution emphasizes the entry point of the customer journey, highlighting brand discovery and awareness activities. Conversely, last-click attribution emphasizes final, conversion-oriented touchpoints. These models, while easy to implement, oversimplify customer journeys, potentially misdirecting budget allocations and neglecting critical intermediate touchpoints.

Multi-touch rule-based models

Multi-touch rule-based attribution models include linear, time-decay and position-based models (Table 9.2). Linear attribution distributes credit evenly across all touchpoints, offering a balanced view but potentially undervaluing influential interactions. Time-decay models prioritize recent interactions, aligning attribution with temporal proximity, while position-based (U-shaped) models emphasize the significance of both the initial and final interactions. Despite their improvements over single-touch models, these models still apply predetermined rules rather than reflecting actual consumer behaviour patterns.

Table 9.1 Single-touch attribution models

Component	Details
Definition	Models that assign 100% of conversion credit to a single touchpoint
Types	• **First click:** Credit to the initial interaction • **Last click:** Credit to the final interaction

(continued)

Table 9.1   (Continued)

Component	Details
Core focus	• **First click:** Awareness and brand discovery • **Last click:** Conversion and decision
Strengths	• Easy to implement and interpret • Useful for campaigns focused on top- or bottom-funnel outcomes
Limitations	• Ignores intermediate touchpoints • Oversimplifies complex journeys • May lead to budget misallocation
Ideal use cases	• Simple buyer journeys • Branding (first-click) or direct-response (last-click) campaigns
Theoretical basis	Linear causality; assumes a single point of impact is most influential

Table 9.2   Multi-touch rule-based models

Component	Details
Definition	Models that allocate credit across multiple touchpoints using predefined rules
Types	• **Linear**: Equal credit to all touchpoints • **Time-decay**: More credit to recent interactions • **Position-based (U-shaped):** Emphasizes first and last touchpoints
Core focus	Understands the full customer journey and values all participating touchpoints
Strengths	• More representative than single touch • Flexible depending on campaign goals • Rule transparency
Limitations	• Arbitrary weight assignments • Does not reflect actual consumer decision behaviour
Ideal use cases	• Multichannel campaigns • Mid-length buyer journeys with consistent engagement
Theoretical basis	Descriptive rules (heuristics) based on marketing logic, not data-driven behavioural patterns

Probabilistic and algorithmic models

Probabilistic attribution models (Table 9.3), notably the Markov chain model, adopt a data-driven approach by computing probabilities associated with consumer

Table 9.3   Probabilistic and algorithmic models

Component	Details
Definition	Data-driven models that use probability theory and algorithms to assign conversion credit
Types	• *Markov chain models* • Shapley value models • Machine learning-based attribution
Core focus	Identifies each touchpoint's true contribution based on modelled transition behaviour
Strengths	• Reflects actual user behaviour • Quantifies marginal impact (e.g. via removal effect) • Enables accurate ROI estimation
Limitations	• Requires large datasets • Complex to implement and interpret • Computationally intensive
Ideal use cases	• Long, multi-step customer journeys • Omnichannel marketing • Precision budget optimization
Theoretical basis	Stochastic processes, cooperative game theory and predictive modelling

transitions between touchpoints (Singh and Bansal, 2021). Markov chains evaluate customer interactions as states within a stochastic process, measuring the transition probabilities to subsequent interactions until conversion or dropout occurs. The removal effect – a central concept in Markov chain attribution – quantifies how conversions would diminish if a specific channel were removed, thus guiding precise budget adjustments.

Figure 9.1 summarizes the attribution models. The **layered pyramid** image (Figure 9.2) presents them in a hierarchy based on their complexity, accuracy and data requirements.

Base layer: Single-touch attribution models

- Includes: First-click, last-click.
- Description: Simplest models that assign all credit to one interaction (beginning or end).
- Strengths: Easy to implement and interpret.
- Limitations: Ignores intermediate steps; may misrepresent customer journeys.

Figure 9.1   Attribution models comparative matrix

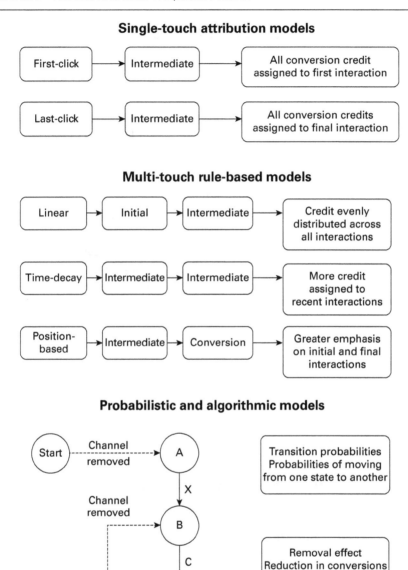

Single-touch attribution models

First-click → Intermediate → All conversion credit assigned to first interaction

Last-click → Intermediate → All conversion credits assigned to final interaction

Multi-touch rule-based models

Linear → Initial → Intermediate → Credit evenly distributed across all interactions

Time-decay → Intermediate → Intermediate → More credit assigned to recent interactions

Position-based → Intermediate → Conversion → Greater emphasis on initial and final interactions

Probabilistic and algorithmic models

Start --- Channel removed ---> A

Channel removed ---> B

Channel removed

A →(X) B →(C) C

Conversion

Transition probabilities
Probabilities of moving from one state to another

Removal effect
Reduction in conversions if a channel is removed

Middle layer: Multi-touch rule-based models

- Includes: Linear, time-decay, position-based (U-shaped).
- Description: Distributes credit across multiple touchpoints using preset rules.

Figure 9.2   Layered pyramid of attribution models

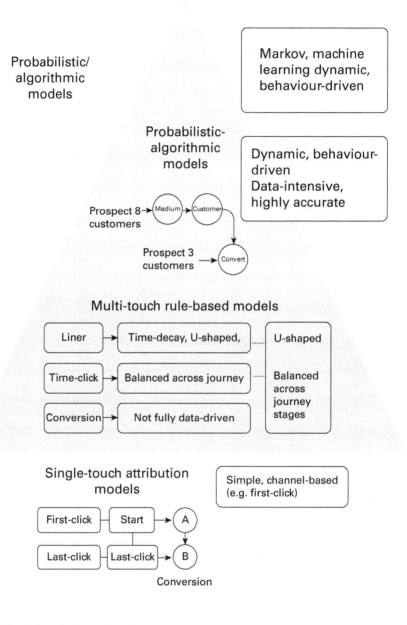

Attribution models

Probabilistic/
algorithmic
models

Markov, machine
learning dynamic,
behaviour-driven

Probabilistic-
algorithmic
models

Dynamic, behaviour-
driven
Data-intensive,
highly accurate

Prospect 8 → Medium → Customer
customers

Prospect 3 → Convert
customers

Multi-touch rule-based models

Liner	→	Time-decay, U-shaped,	U-shaped
Time-click	→	Balanced across journey	Balanced across journey stages
Conversion	→	Not fully data-driven	

Single-touch attribution
models

Simple, channel-based
(e.g. first-click)

First-click — Start → A

Last-click — Last-click → B

Conversion

- Strengths: More balanced; reflects customer journey structure.
- Limitations: Rules are arbitrary – not based on actual user behaviour.

Top layer: Probabilistic/algorithmic models

- Includes: Markov chains, machine learning models.
- Description: Uses data-driven algorithms to determine how each touchpoint contributes to conversion.
- Strengths: Highly accurate and behaviourally reflective.
- Limitations: Requires large datasets and technical expertise.

Interpretation: The higher up the pyramid, the more sophisticated and behaviourally accurate the model – ideal for organizations with advanced data capabilities.

Real-world examples of marketing attribution

Adidas: Transition to data-driven attribution

Adidas historically relied on a last-click attribution model, which provided limited insights and overvalued bottom-of-the-funnel channels like paid search and generic display ads. Upon switching to a probabilistic data-driven attribution model offered by Google Attribution, Adidas discovered that channels such as influencer marketing and branded search significantly contributed earlier in the customer journey yet were severely undervalued previously. By reallocating budgets towards these underappreciated touchpoints, Adidas achieved a notable improvement in marketing efficiency and a 30 per cent increase in return on advertising spend (ROAS) (Google, 2022).

Skyscanner: Multi-touch attribution implementation

Skyscanner implemented advanced multi-touch attribution to better understand user behaviour across various digital platforms, including mobile apps, email campaigns, push notifications, paid search and social media. The insights revealed that strategically timed push notifications and personalized email marketing significantly influenced user conversion behaviour. By integrating this data-driven insight into its campaign strategy, Skyscanner enhanced customer engagement, increased retention rates and improved overall marketing performance (Skyscanner Insights, 2023a and b).

Sephora: Omnichannel attribution integration

Beauty retailer Sephora utilized advanced algorithmic attribution models to measure the impact of online marketing activities on in-store purchasing behaviours. Integrating CRM data, mobile ad interactions and in-store sales information, Sephora accurately captured cross-channel customer journeys. The resulting insights demonstrated that mobile advertisements influenced approximately 19 per cent of in-store purchases indirectly, prompting Sephora to strategically shift budgets towards mobile channels and enhancing customer experience both digitally and physically (Liu and Viswanathan, 2021).

Technical and ethical challenges in attribution modelling

Attribution modelling encounters significant challenges, including data fragmentation, privacy constraints and potential attribution bias. Fragmented data across platforms such as CRM systems, advertising networks and offline channels complicate comprehensive attribution modelling. Simultaneously, increasing privacy regulations such as GDPR and Apple's App Tracking Transparency (ATT) policy limit tracking capabilities, necessitating innovative privacy-preserving attribution approaches.

Moreover, channels with greater ease of measurement (e.g. paid search) tend to be over-attributed, while less measurable yet influential channels like organic social media may be systematically undervalued, leading to skewed resource allocation decisions. Ensuring transparency and interpretability in advanced algorithmic attribution models also remains crucial, as opaque models can hinder trust among marketers and stakeholders (Wachter et al, 2017).

Attribution in marketing technology ecosystems

Attribution modelling is increasingly integrated into leading marketing technology platforms such as Google Analytics 4, Adobe Experience Cloud and Salesforce Marketing Cloud. These platforms provide comprehensive, built-in attribution solutions enabling marketers to execute sophisticated attribution analyses without extensive manual computations. Additionally, organizations leverage open-source frameworks in Python and R to build customized, highly granular attribution models suited to their unique industry contexts and data infrastructures.

EXERCISE

Applying attribution with Markov chain analysis

Scenario

You are a marketing analyst for an online fashion retailer, similar to H&M, with marketing campaigns across four primary channels:

1 Paid search (Google Ads)

2 Social media ads (Instagram, Facebook)

3 Email marketing campaigns

4 Influencer partnerships (Instagram, YouTube).

Your task is to analyse the customer conversion journey and optimize marketing spend.

Steps to conduct exercise

1 Collect data on customer interaction sequences over three months, tracking conversions.
2 Use Python or R to construct a Markov chain attribution model, estimating transition probabilities.
3 Calculate the 'removal effect' for each channel.
4 Identify which channel has the highest incremental impact on conversions.
5 Recommend adjustments to channel spend based on removal effect insights.

Questions to guide analysis

- Which channel has the highest contribution to conversions according to the Markov chain model?
- How would removing each channel individually affect total conversion rates?
- Which channels are currently overvalued or undervalued based on the removal effect?
- How should the marketing budget be reallocated to maximize overall ROI?

9.1 The role of attribution in customer journey analytics and the rise of attribution in modern marketing

Attribution has become a cornerstone of customer-journey analytics and strategic marketing because modern consumer paths are increasingly complex, fragmented and digital-first (Lemon and Verhoef, 2016). Rather than asking whether a single marketing touchpoint drives success, attribution enables marketers to assign value to multiple interactions across channels – search, social, email, programmatic advertising, content marketing, influencer engagements and more (Buhalis and Volchek, 2021). In this section, we explore how attribution supports a deeper understanding of the customer journey and trace its evolution into a central discipline in modern performance marketing, highlighting the methods, models and analytical frameworks that enable organizations to quantify contribution, optimize budget allocation and enhance marketing ROI (De Haan, 2022). As consumers move fluidly across devices and platforms, the need for robust, data-driven attribution systems has intensified, positioning attribution not only as a measurement tool but as a strategic capability that informs campaign design, channel investment, personalization initiatives and long-term customer value optimization (Mrad, 2024).

Customer journey analytics: A foundational framework

Customer journey analytics (CJA) refers to the multidisciplinary process of tracking, analysing and optimizing every interaction a customer has with a brand across digital and physical touchpoints (Lemon and Verhoef, 2016; Rawson et al, 2013). Its goal is to uncover behavioural patterns, friction points and conversion drivers to deliver seamless experiences. Attribution models operationalize CJA by attaching a quantitative value to each touchpoint within a journey, contributing to diagnostics such as:

- funnel drop-off identification
- path-to-purchase insights
- channel synergies and sequencing effects
- segment-level behaviour profiling.

In essence, attribution brings transparency to customer journeys by translating qualitative mapping into quantitative action.

From attribution to optimization: Strategic implications

Attribution plays a pivotal role in moving marketing from intuition to empiricism. Instead of relying on assumptions – such as 'emails drive awareness' or 'paid search drives final conversions' – attribution yields data-backed insights into how channels work together. This shift enables:

- **Performance accountability**: Teams can assign contribution metrics to each channel and prove ROI.
- **Budget optimization**: Channels with high removal effects can receive budget increases; underperformers can be deprioritized.
- **Experimentation and iteration**: Marketers can test adjusted channel mixes and measure incremental gains via attribution-based models.

In short, attribution is the linchpin in closing the gap between customer journey mapping and marketing optimization.

Historical evolution: Why attribution matters more than ever

Early era: Web analytics and single-touch models

In the early 2000s, marketing measurement hinged on metrics such as page views, clicks and conversions – most linked to a single channel. The **first-click** and **last-click** attribution models became defaults due to their simplicity and minimal data requirements. However, these models ignored the multiplicity of influences over a customer's path, and risks included over-crediting certain channels while neglecting real contributors.

Rise of multi-touch attribution (MTA)

As tracking capabilities improved, marketers embraced **multi-touch attribution**. Models like **linear, time-decay** and **position-based** allowed equal or weighted credit across journey touchpoints. These models improved on single-touch rules but still imposed static assumptions about channel importance.

Advent of algorithmic and probabilistic attribution

More recently, machine learning has enabled **algorithmic attribution models**, like Markov chains and Shapley-value models. These models use historical clickstream data to deduce channel transition probabilities and the marginal impact of each touchpoint (Singh and Bansal, 2021). They account for user sequences and channel interplay and produce **removal effects** that identify channels with the highest impact when omitted.

Conceptual theories underpinning attribution

1. Customer journey theory

As proposed by Lemon and Verhoef (2016), customer decisions unfold across the following stages:

- **Awareness**: Discovery of brand or product.
- **Consideration**: Evaluation via content, research.
- **Conversion**: Purchase or sign-up.
- **Retention/advocacy**: Repeat behaviour or referrals.

Attribution models must account for how touchpoints contribute variably at each stage to drive progression from awareness to advocacy.

2. Behavioural economics and cognitive biases

Attribution modelling intersects with behavioural economics: **primacy and recency effects** (Murphy et al, 2007) suggest that early and late touchpoints are more memorable and influential – hence U-shaped attribution models. Meanwhile, **bounded rationality** (Simon, 1955) implies that consumers make decisions with limited attention, so attribution must identify which touchpoints break through cognitive noise at critical junctures.

The modern attribution landscape: Industry adoption and platform support

Integrated attribution in major platforms

- **Google Analytics 4 (GA4)** offers both rule-based and data-driven attribution, using machine learning to distribute credit across channels.

- **Adobe Analytics Attribution IQ** enables customized attribution modelling with both heuristic and algorithmic options.
- **Salesforce Marketing Cloud** and **Tableau CRM** embed attribution insights into campaign dashboards for marketing executives.

These platforms are converging to serve as central hubs for attribution analytics, reducing reliance on ad hoc spreadsheets or offline calculations.

Enterprise adoption

Leading brands illustrate the strategic value of attribution:

- **Adidas** improved ROAS by realigning marketing efforts after discovery that branded search and influencer channels were undervalued (Google, 2022).
- **Skyscanner** embedded attribution into their decision-making across web, app and marketplace channels, improving forecast accuracy and planning (Skyscanner Insights, 2023).
- **Sephora** combined in-store and digital attribution data to highlight the role of mobile advertising in driving offline purchases (Liu and Viswanathan, 2021).

Attribution and measurement: Impacts on analytics practice

Attribution affects the entire analytics process:

- **Data integration:** Attribution requires unified streams from web analytics, CRM, email platforms, ad networks and potentially in-store systems.
- **Data cleaning and preprocessing:** Accurate path data demands de-duplicated user IDs, resolved cross-device tracking and normalized channel naming conventions.
- **Model selection:** Choice between rule-based or probabilistic models depends on data quality, organizational technologies and analytical maturity.
- **Interpretation and action:** Attribution exists to guide decisions – whether reallocating budgets, adjusting creative or shifting channel mix.

Attribution drives accountability and trade-offs: for instance, high-touch direct response channels may overshadow branding efforts whose influence is not immediately measurable.

Challenges, limitations and ethical considerations

Data silos and fragmentation

Even large enterprises suffer from disconnected data islands. Without unified data practices, attribution models can undercount touchpoints like offline ads or referral signals.

Tracking limitations and privacy constraints

Regulations like **GDPR, CCPA** and platform changes such as **Apple's ATT** diminish third-party tracking abilities. This complicates attribution modelling, especially across new cookieless environments.

Attribution bias

Channels that are more easily tracked (paid search, email) tend to inherit more conversion credit, while less measurable channels (organic social, word-of-mouth) get undervalued.

Ethical and interpretability concerns

Complex models like Shapley value or deep learning may deliver accuracy but lack transparency. Stakeholders must understand how decisions are derived from models and ensure fairness across demographics or segments (Wachter et al, 2017).

Future directions in attribution

- **Cross-channel identity resolution** using deterministic (e.g. login events) and probabilistic matching techniques to stitch user behaviour across devices and environments.

- **Unified marketing measurement (MMM plus MTA)**: blending long-term media mix modelling with real-time attribution insights.

- **Privacy-first attribution**: Using aggregated, anonymized data and differential privacy techniques to respect user consent while still deriving insight.

- **Real-time attribution**: With edge analytics and streaming data, attribution models will increasingly power personalization today – not just post hoc analysis.

9.2 Overview of attribution models

Attribution modelling is increasingly critical given complex, multichannel customer journeys. Understanding how to distribute credit across marketing channels affects not only ROI calculation but also strategic investment decisions. This section provides an academically grounded review of the main attribution methodologies – first examining traditional rule-based approaches and then evaluating advanced algorithmic models like **Markov chain attribution** and **Shapley value attribution**. The content integrates theoretical foundations, practical applications, real-world examples and a case exercise illustrating model selection and implementation.

Rule-based attribution models

First-click attribution

Definition   Allocates 100 per cent of the conversion credit to the first interaction in a customer journey.

Strengths

- Highlights acquisition and awareness channels.
- Simple to compute and explain to stakeholders.

Limitations

- Ignores downstream interactions that reinforce decision-making.
- Overvalues early-stage channels even when later interventions may be decisive.

Theoretical consideration   Aligns loosely with the primacy effect in behavioural economics – the tendency to give more weight to initial stimuli – but lacks empirical accuracy in complex journeys (Murphy et al, 2007).

Last-click attribution

Definition   Allocates full credit to the final touchpoint prior to conversion.

Advantages

- Emphasizes conversion actions.
- Common default in analytics platforms.

Drawbacks

- Neglects the role of earlier touchpoints that prime interest.
- Overvalues lower-funnel channels, misattributing influence.

Critique   This model can reinforce narrow tactical optimization – often at the expense of brand-building or awareness-led channels.

Linear attribution

Definition   Distributes equal credit across all touchpoints in the conversion path.

Pros

- Balanced view across journey phases.
- Simple to calculate.

Cons

- Assumes equal impact at each interaction.
- Fails to reflect real-world influence differences (e.g. mid-journey friction).

Critique   Linear attribution is useful as a neutral benchmark – it mitigates bias towards early or late events but oversimplifies dynamics.

Time-decay attribution

Definition   Allocates increasing weight to later touchpoints, based on configured decay parameters (e.g. half-life settings).

Advantages

- Acknowledges recency effects in decision-making.
- Reflects that later touchpoints often have more influence.

Weaknesses

- Weighting is arbitrary; requires subjective parameter setting.
- May undervalue high-impact early interactions.

Position-based (U-shaped) attribution

Definition   Allocates high weight to both first and last touchpoints, with lesser weight in the middle (e.g. 40 per cent / 20 per cent / 40 per cent).

Strengths

- Recognizes dual importance of brand discovery and conversion reinforcement.
- Institutionalizes insight into funnel roles.

Limitations

- Middle interactions often still play a critical role; this model may underrepresent them.
- Preset weight distribution may not reflect actual consumer dynamics.

Algorithmic attribution models

Rule-based models, while simple, do not account for interaction effects between channels, nor do they reflect real-world variability across customer journeys. Algorithmic attribution models address these limitations by using observed data to attribute each event's contribution dynamically.

Markov chain attribution

Fundamentals   Markov chain attribution models treat each touchpoint as a **state**, constructing a transition probability matrix that represents the likelihood of moving from one channel to the next, ending in conversion or dropout. The model requires large datasets to estimate transition frequencies accurately (Singh and Bansal, 2021).

See Figure 9.3 for a diagram illustrating a Markov chain attribution model for a customer journey.

Visual description

- **Nodes:** Represent marketing touchpoints such as email, social, paid search, conversion and dropout.
- **Edges:** Arrows indicate transitions between touchpoints, with probabilities (e.g. 0.4 from 'Start' to 'Email').
- **Purpose:** This flowchart demonstrates how customers transition between different touchpoints and either convert or drop out.
- **Application:** Used in algorithmic attribution modelling to compute each channel's contribution via transition analysis and 'removal effect'.

Figure 9.3   Customer journey – Markov chain attribution model

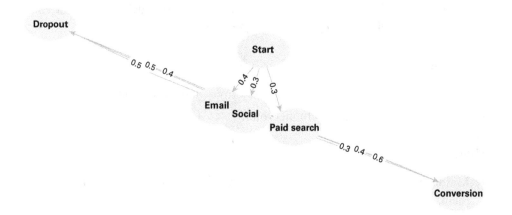

Removal effect   A key output of Markov modelling is the **removal effect** – if a given channel is removed from all paths and the model re-run, the resulting percentage decline in conversions indicates the channel's marginal contribution.

Advantages

- Empirical rather than arbitrary weighting.
- Reflects real customer behaviour sequences and channel dependencies.
- Transparent and interpretable in terms of transition probabilities.

Challenges

- Requires comprehensive journey-level data.
- Computational costs can be significant for large datasets.
- May underrepresent rare paths or less frequent touch sequences.

Example implementation   A video-streaming service might evaluate paths like:

Display ad → Social post → Email → Free trial → Subscription

By simulating the removal of the email channel, the model quantifies its removal effect – allowing marketers to determine whether re-investment is warranted.

Shapley value attribution

Theoretical basis   Originating in cooperative game theory, the Shapley value allocates credits based on the average marginal contribution of each participant (COP channels) across all permutations of a journey.

Calculation   For attribution, the Shapley value is computed as:

- Enumerate all permutations of channels in a conversion path.
- Calculate marginal lift when a channel is added to preceding events.
- Average these marginal contributions across all permutations.

Strengths

- **Fair** and **consistent**: Each channel's contribution is fairly distributed.
- Captures interaction effects among multiple channels.
- Theoretically grounded, objective.

Challenges

- Exponential computation complexity as channel count increases.
- Requires careful pathway sampling or approximation techniques.
- Less intuitive to interpret for non-technical stakeholders.

Use cases   Brands with sophisticated data engineering teams and high-channel complexity, such as B2B SaaS or multinational retailers, are prime candidates for Shapley value implementation.

EXERCISE

Applying attribution models in practice

Scenario

An omnichannel apparel company runs campaigns across four channels:

1 Paid search

2 Organic social

3 Email marketing

4 Influencer-based display ads.

Exercise steps

1 **Collect raw conversion path data** for a significant period (e.g. three months).

2 **Compute attribution** using three models:

   o Position-based (rule-based U-shaped)

   o Markov chain attribution

   o Shapley value attribution.

3 **Compare results**:

   o Which channel credit differs most from the U-shaped baseline?

   o How do Markov and Shapley attribute value across early, mid and late funnel?

4 **Budget recommendation** based on **removal effect** (Markov) or **marginal contribution** (Shapley).

5 **Reflect on transparency and interpretation**:

   o Which model offers the best balance of accuracy and stakeholder understanding?

REAL-WORLD EXAMPLES   Adidas (Google, 2022)

Adidas transitioned from last-click attribution to algorithmic attribution using Google's platform. This shift revealed that branded search and influencer marketing had been undervalued. By reallocating media spend accordingly, Adidas increased ROAS by approximately 30 per cent.

Skyscanner (Skyscanner Insights, 2023)

Skyscanner applied Markov chain attribution across web and app paths, discovering that email and push notifications had a strong cumulative influence that earlier models undercounted. As a result, engagement and conversion rates improved.

Sephora (Liu and Viswanathan, 2021)

Sephora integrated online and offline touchpoints, leveraging algorithmic attribution to determine that mobile ads indirectly influenced nearly 19 per cent of in-store purchases. This insight reshaped channel budget allocation and omni-shopping strategies.

Integrative insights

- **Rule-based models** remain valuable for quick, baseline analysis and when interpretability is paramount.
- **Algorithmic models** (Markov, Shapley) yield more nuanced, data-driven attribution insights that reflect actual consumer behaviour but require robust data infrastructure.
- Model selection should account for organizational analytics maturity, stakeholder needs and data availability.
- Combining rule-based and algorithmic approaches may offer a practical balance – starting with simpler models and progressing to probabilistic analysis as data sophistication improves.

9.3 Deep dive: Markov chain attribution

Markov chain attribution marks a significant methodological advancement beyond heuristic models. It is based on formal Markov chain theory, a branch of probability and statistics that models sequential, memoryless transitions (i.e. a future state depends only on the current state, not on the path taken to it). In marketing attribution, each customer touchpoint represents a state in the chain. The model captures how customers move from one interaction to another until they convert or abandon, enabling rigorous quantification of each touchpoint's relative contribution.

Theoretical foundations

At the heart of Markov chain attribution lies the **memoryless property**. In marketing terms, this implies that the probability of moving from one interaction (e.g. 'email') to the next (e.g. 'paid search') depends solely on the current interaction – not on how the consumer reached that point. While this abstraction simplifies real customer behaviour, it enables estimation of transition probabilities and the calculation of conversion likelihoods via matrix operations.

The mathematical elegance of this approach allows for 'what-if' analysis via the **removal effect** – calculating how removing a state (a channel) affects overall conversion probability. This positions Markov attribution as both analytically robust and strategically actionable.

Constructing the Markov chain attribution model

Define the state space

- Identify relevant touchpoints, e.g., home page, display ad, email, social media, paid search, conversion, dropout.

- Mark **conversion** and **dropout** as **absorbing states** – once entered, the process terminates.

Figure 9.4   Comparison of Markov chains and Shapley value attribution

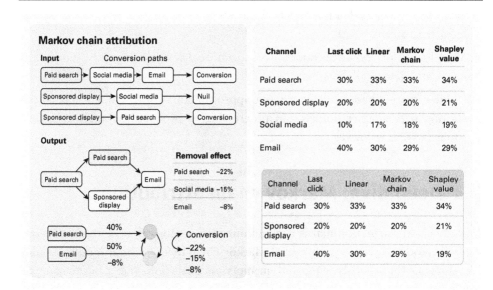

Markov chain attribution

Channel	Last click	Linear	Markov chain	Shapley value
Paid search	30%	33%	33%	34%
Sponsored display	20%	20%	20%	21%
Social media	10%	17%	18%	19%
Email	40%	30%	29%	29%

Channel	Last click	Linear	Markov chain	Shapley value
Paid search	30%	33%	33%	34%
Sponsored display	20%	20%	20%	21%
Email	40%	30%	29%	19%

Removal effect: Paid search −22%, Social media −15%, Email −8%

Estimate transition probabilities

Use customer journey logs to count transitions: e.g. from email to social = 200, email to conversion = 100, total from mail = 400 → probabilities: 0.5 to social, 0.25 to conversion, etc.

Build the transition matrix

- Create an $N \times N$ matrix , where N is the number of states.
- Populate rows with transition probabilities from each state to all others. Absorbing states have self-loop (probability 1) and zeros elsewhere.

Compute attribution via removal effect

- Baseline conversion probability (P0): Simulate a chain until absorption to conversion.
- For each channel, remove the corresponding state and adjust the matrix; recompute conversion probability (Pi). Removal effect = P0 − Pi.
- Normalize removal effects to distribute conversion credit across channels.

Practical modelling considerations

Data requirements and quality

- Requires comprehensive, deterministic user-level path data across channels and time.
- Sampling may bias transition probabilities if infrequent paths are underrepresented.

Handling multiple touch sequences

Aggregated sequences need careful preprocessing to ensure path integrity.

Computational complexity

Models scale linearly with the number of states and paths; with thousands of states, computation may become intensive.

Model interpretability

While results are data-driven, stakeholders may find probabilistic outputs less intuitive than fixed-rule models, requiring effective visualization and explanation.

EXAMPLES

Travel aggregator (e.g. Skyscanner)

Skyscanner applied Markov chain attribution across web, mobile app and email touchpoints. Removal analysis revealed that email interactions had outsized influence early in the purchase funnel – often catalysing flight searches. Reducing email support showed meaningful conversion decline, leading to retention of higher email traffic budgets (Skyscanner Insights, 2023).

Streaming service (e.g. Spotify)

Spotify traced user transitions from app open to content view, playlist creation and subscription. The 'email promo' state had a high removal effect even when not the last touchpoint. Based on this insight, Spotify increased retention email frequency, resulting in higher trial-to-subscription conversion.

EXERCISE

Scenario

A mid-sized fitness subscription brand markets via these channels:

- content blog (CB)
- social media ads (SM)
- email retargeting (ER)
- search ads (SA).

Task steps

1 **Data collection**: Gather anonymized visitor path sequences over 60 days.
2 **Transition matrix construction**: Compute touchpoint-to-touchpoint transition probabilities.
3 **Conversion baseline**: Simulate chain to estimate base conversion rate (e.g, 12 per cent).
4 **Removal effects**:
   o Remove ER channel; recalibrate transition matrix.
   o Check conversion rate decrease (e.g. from 12 per cent to 9 per cent → 3 per cent removal effect).
   o Repeat for SA, CB, SM.

5 **Normalize removal effects** to distribute equal 100 per cent of conversions across channels.

6 **Interpretation**:

   o Which channel contributes most?

   o Is the first or last interaction more impactful?

   o Recommend reallocation (e.g. boost email or SA budgets, cut SM).

Integration with marketing strategy

Markov chain attribution supports strategic decision-making by:

- Highlighting pivotal early journey channels often undervalued in rule-based models.

- Informing media mix optimization (e.g. increasing commitment to channels with high removal effects).

- Defining clear performance indicators (e.g. removal effect percentages) for channel monitoring.

- Supporting A/B tests (e.g. incremental lift) by offering predictions with and without specific channels.

Limitations and caveats

- **Simplification of memoryless behaviour:** In reality, customer decisions may be path-dependent.

- **Session segmentation errors:** Incorrectly identifying session boundaries can distort transition probabilities.

- **Limited offline integration:** In-store visits or cold-call influences may not appear in digital data.

- **Privacy restrictions:** GDPR and tracking opt-outs may limit the ability to compute accurate transition matrices.

- **Overfitting rare paths:** Outlier journey sequences may skew transition probabilities if not filtered.

Conclusion

Markov chain attribution represents a powerful and analytically rigorous method to allocate conversion credit across complex customer journeys. It leverages empirical data to estimate how users progress through touchpoints and how removing any channel impacts outcomes. While more resource-intensive than rule-based models, its insights are better aligned with real consumer behaviours. Applied effectively, Markov attribution can refine marketing investment, optimize omnichannel strategies and elevate measurement maturity.

9.4 Tools and platforms for attribution analysis

The role of technology in attribution analysis

Attribution analysis has evolved from a primarily statistical exercise into a **technology-enabled discipline** driven by cloud-based platforms, machine learning algorithms and integrated data ecosystems. As customer journeys grow more **multichannel, multi-device**, and **non-linear**, marketers increasingly depend on specialized platforms to synthesize disparate datasets into actionable attribution insights (Chaffey and Ellis-Chadwick, 2022). See Tables 9.4 and 9.5 for summaries.

Technology plays three critical roles in attribution analysis:

1 **Data integration** – aggregating signals from multiple touchpoints (search, email, social, display, in-app).

2 **Model application** – implementing rule-based and algorithmic models without requiring deep coding expertise.

3 **Insight visualization** – generating dashboards that communicate attribution findings for strategic decision-making.

Overview of attribution platforms

Google Analytics 4 (GA4)

GA4 represents a significant shift from Google's Universal Analytics, emphasizing **event-based tracking** and **data-driven attribution**. GA4's attribution module leverages **machine learning algorithms** to assign conversion credit dynamically, moving beyond fixed rule-based models.

Key features

- **Data-driven attribution (default)**: Uses algorithmic modelling to estimate channel contributions.
- **Cross-platform tracking**: Integrates app and web interactions.
- **Exploration tools**: Path analysis and funnel visualizations.
- **Privacy-first**: Adjusted for cookie deprecation and privacy regulation.

Use case   Adidas' transition to GA4 revealed underappreciated contributions from branded search and influencer marketing, driving a 30 per cent increase in ROAS when budgets were reallocated (Google, 2022).

Adobe Attribution IQ

Adobe Attribution IQ is part of **Adobe Analytics** and offers marketers flexibility in comparing multiple attribution models.

Key features

- **Multi-model comparison**: Users can run linear, time-decay, first-touch and algorithmic models side by side.
- **Custom weight settings**: Enables hybrid attribution strategies.
- **Integration with Adobe Experience Cloud**: Provides cross-channel campaign insights.
- **Advanced segmentation**: Filters attribution by audience cohorts, geographies or device type.

Use case   Sephora adopted Adobe Attribution IQ to analyse cross-channel contributions, discovering that mobile ads indirectly influenced in-store purchases by 19 per cent (Liu and Viswanathan, 2021).

Salesforce Marketing Cloud (SFMC)

SFMC's attribution tools are designed for **customer relationship management (CRM)-driven attribution**.

Key features

- **Journey builder integration**: Connects attribution directly to customer journey orchestration.
- **AI-powered insights**: Einstein attribution applies predictive modelling.
- **Omnichannel focus**: Tracks email, SMS, social and commerce in unified dashboards.
- **Closed-loop reporting**: Integrates attribution with sales pipeline performance.

Use case   Amazon deployed Salesforce Marketing Cloud attribution to connect advertising impressions with purchase events. This integration improved campaign targeting, boosting customer retention and repeat purchases.

HubSpot attribution reporting

HubSpot offers **attribution reporting** for small-to-medium enterprises (SMEs) seeking more accessible solutions.

Key features

- Pre-built multi-touch attribution reports.
- Integration with CRM and CMS.
- Simple interface for non-technical users.

Limitations include **restricted customization** and **limited algorithmic modelling**, but HubSpot provides an entry-level solution for firms without advanced analytics teams.

Other industry solutions

- **Adjust and AppsFlyer:** Focused on mobile attribution, widely used in app marketing.
- **Nielsen attribution:** Provides multi-touch attribution with panel data, often used by consumer goods and media companies.
- **Improvado, Ruler Analytics, Segment:** Emerging platforms emphasizing **API-driven integration** and **custom dashboarding**.

Theoretical perspectives on technology-enabled attribution

Socio-technical systems theory

Attribution platforms function as **socio-technical systems**, integrating human decision-making with algorithmic processing (Bostrom and Heinen, 1977). Their effectiveness depends on:

- **technical quality** (data accuracy, integration)
- **human adoption** (ease of use, interpretability).

Datafication and phantomization

Attribution exemplifies **datafication**, where marketing practices are transformed into quantifiable, algorithmic measures (Mayer-Schönberger and Cukier, 2013). Platforms like GA4 and Adobe facilitate **platformization** of analytics, embedding attribution within broader ecosystems that lock marketers into vendor infrastructures (Nieborg and Poell, 2018).

Table 9.4 Comparative evaluation of attribution tools

Criteria	Google Analytics 4	Adobe Attribution IQ	Salesforce Marketing Cloud	HubSpot Attribution
Modelling	Data-driven ML, rule-based	Multi-model comparison	AI-powered (Einstein)	Rule-based, simple
Integration	Web and app	Adobe Experience Cloud	CRM and omnichannel	CRM and CMS
Scalability	High (enterprise and SME)	Enterprise	Enterprise	SME focus
Privacy compliance	Strong (cookie-less future)	Strong (enterprise focus)	Strong (CRM-centric)	Moderate
Ease of use	Moderate	Advanced (requires training)	Moderate to high	High (non-technical)

Table 9.5 Comparison of attribution platforms

	Google Analytics 4	Adobe Attribution IQ	Salesforce Marketing Cloud
Modelling	Data-driven ML, rule-based	Multi-model comparison	AI-powered (Einstein)
Data integration	Web and app	Adobe Experience Cloud	CRM and omnichannel
Scalability	High (enterprise and SME)	Enterprise	Enterprise
Privacy compliance	Strong (cookie-less future)	Strong (enterprise focus)	Strong (CRM-centric)

EXAMPLES

Adidas (GA4)

Adidas adopted GA4's machine learning-based attribution to uncover undervalued channels, leading to reallocation from generic display ads to influencer partnerships. Result: 30 per cent% ROAS improvement (Google, 2022).

Sephora (Adobe Attribution IQ)

Sephora used Adobe Attribution IQ to merge online and offline sales attribution. Insights revealed mobile ads indirectly contributed to in-store purchases, reshaping budget allocations (Liu and Viswanathan, 2021).

Amazon (Salesforce Marketing Cloud)

Amazon implemented SFMC to connect customer journeys with purchase behaviours, enabling personalized, multi-touch marketing strategies that improved retention and loyalty.

Technical and ethical challenges

- **Data fragmentation:** Integrating offline data remains challenging.
- **Privacy constraints:** GA4 and Adobe must adapt to cookie deprecation.
- **Attribution bias:** Over-crediting easily trackable channels like paid search.
- **Platform lock-in:** Vendor ecosystems limit flexibility and raise switching costs.
- **Explainability:** AI-driven models like Salesforce Einstein lack interpretability, complicating trust.

EXERCISE

Building an attribution dashboard Using GA4

Scenario

Nike launches a multichannel campaign using social, email and paid search. The company wants to measure which touchpoints contributed most to purchases.

Tasks

1 Use GA4 to set up **event-based tracking** for campaign interactions.
2 Run attribution reports using:
   o last-click
   o data-driven attribution.
3 Export results into a dashboard.
4 Compare differences and recommend budget reallocations.

Guiding questions

- How does GA4's data-driven model differ from rule-based outputs?
- Which channels are undervalued by last-click attribution?
- What are the ethical implications of using GA4's user-level data?

9.5 Attribution strategy in retail

Retailers operate in one of the most dynamic and competitive marketing environments. The rise of **omnichannel retailing** – the seamless integration of online and offline shopping – has intensified the complexity of customer journeys. Modern consumers frequently move across digital channels (e.g. websites, apps, social media), physical environments (brick-and-mortar stores) and hybrid spaces (e.g. click-and-collect services). Each touchpoint influences eventual purchase behaviour, but attributing sales to specific channels remains one of the most challenging analytical tasks in retail marketing.

Marketing attribution provides a structured methodology to quantify the contribution of these touchpoints. For retail brands, attribution is not only about assigning credit for conversions but also about optimizing **budget allocation, pricing, promotion, personalization** and **customer relationship strategies**. Attribution thus serves as a bridge between marketing accountability and operational performance.

Strategic importance of attribution in retail marketing

Attribution in retail serves multiple strategic purposes:

- **Resource allocation:** Retailers like H&M and Zara invest heavily in paid search, programmatic advertising, influencer partnerships and email campaigns. Attribution models inform decisions on which channels to prioritize.

- **Customer experience management:** Attribution provides insights into the customer journey, supporting personalization strategies that improve satisfaction and retention.

- **Measurement of ROI:** In an era of heightened accountability, attribution enables retailers to justify marketing spend to stakeholders.

- **Omnichannel integration:** With offline and online channels converging, attribution helps retailers understand cross-channel synergies, e.g. how online ads influence in-store sales.

From a theoretical perspective, attribution aligns with **customer journey theory** (Lemon and Verhoef, 2016) and **service-dominant logic** (Vargo and Lusch, 2008), both emphasizing that value creation arises from complex, interactive processes rather than isolated exchanges.

Theoretical foundations: Customer journey and omnichannel retail

Attribution models are anchored in several theoretical frameworks:

- **Customer journey theory**
  - Consumers move through **pre-purchase, purchase** and **post-purchase stages** (Lemon and Verhoef, 2016).
  - Attribution identifies which touchpoints (e.g. Instagram ads in pre-purchase, email in purchase stage) drive progression across these phases.
- **Omnichannel retail framework:** Verhoef et al (2015) argue that modern retail requires seamless integration of channels. Attribution analysis provides visibility into how channels interact (e.g. paid search may generate awareness, while mobile apps finalize conversions).
- **Behavioural economics**
  - **Primacy and recency effects** influence attribution – early or final touchpoints may have disproportionate psychological weight.
  - **Bounded rationality:** (Simon, 1982) explains why consumers rely on heuristics when confronted with complex, multichannel journeys. Attribution models must account for these biases.

Together, these theoretical foundations highlight that attribution in retail is not just a statistical exercise but a reflection of consumer psychology and systemic retail design.

REAL-WORLD EXAMPLE   Application to retail strategy:
                          The case of H&M

H&M provides an illustrative case of how attribution informs retail strategy. (See also Figure 9.5.)

H&M's marketing context

As one of the world's largest fast-fashion retailers, H&M employs a multichannel strategy including:

- paid search campaigns on Google
- social media advertising on Instagram and TikTok
- influencer partnerships targeting Gen Z

- loyalty app-based promotions
- email marketing for personalized offers.

Attribution challenges

H&M faces several attribution challenges:

- **High channel overlap**: Customers may engage with multiple touchpoints before conversion.
- **Offline–online integration**: Many purchases occur in-store after exposure to digital campaigns.
- **Privacy constraints**: Regulations like GDPR restrict tracking of customer data across channels.

Attribution application

H&M has adopted **multi-touch attribution (MTA)** combined with **Markov chain modelling** to analyse customer journeys. By examining conversion paths across app interactions, social ads and email campaigns, H&M estimates the **removal effect** of each channel.
    For example:

- Social media ads drive early awareness.
- Email campaigns contribute heavily in the mid-funnel.
- Mobile app notifications trigger final conversions.

This analysis allows H&M to reallocate budgets dynamically, e.g. increasing investment in app engagement strategies while moderating spending on lower-performing display ads.

Strategic implications

- **Budget efficiency**: More accurate spend across channels.
- **Customer engagement**: Tailored campaigns for specific journey phases.
- **Cross-channel synergies**: Evidence that early-stage touchpoints (Instagram) indirectly support late-stage conversions (mobile app).

REAL-WORLD EXAMPLE   Adidas' transition from last-click
to data-driven

Attribution

Adidas offers a real-world case of how shifting attribution models impacts retail performance.

Previous model

- Relied on **last-click attribution**.

- Over-credited display advertising because it often represented the final interaction before purchase.

Transition to data-driven attribution

- Adopted Google's Data-Driven Attribution (DDA) model, powered by machine learning.
- This model analysed the entire sequence of touchpoints, redistributing credit more accurately.

Findings

- Branded search and influencer marketing were previously undervalued.
- Display advertising had been overvalued under last-click.

Outcomes

- **Budget reallocation**: Increased spending on branded search and influencer collaborations.
- **Performance gains**: Reported 30 per cent improvement in return on ad spend (ROAS) (Google, 2022).

Strategic lessons

- Moving away from simplistic models reveals hidden drivers of performance.
- Data-driven attribution supports innovation in channel strategy, particularly for fast-moving retail sectors like sportswear.

Figure 9.5   Attribution strategy in retail

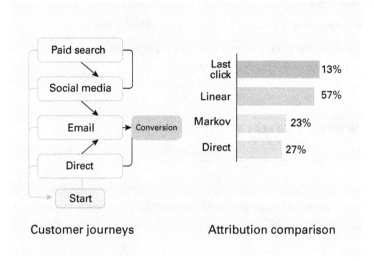

Customer journeys   Attribution comparison

9.6 Limitations, biases and ethical considerations in attribution

Despite advances, attribution modelling faces several **structural limitations** in retail contexts.

- **Data silos**: Retail data often resides in separate systems (POS, CRM, online analytics), limiting comprehensive journey visibility.
- **Offline attribution gaps**: Difficult to track in-store sales influenced by digital ads. Solutions like loyalty card integration help but remain imperfect.
- **Model assumptions**: Rule-based models (linear, U-shaped) rely on assumptions that may not match actual consumer behaviour.
- **Complexity vs interpretability**: Advanced models (Markov chains, Shapley values) offer precision but are often opaque to marketers.
- **Sample bias**: Attribution relies on observed data; unobserved touchpoints (e.g. word-of-mouth) are underrepresented.

These limitations highlight the need for a balanced approach: combining analytical sophistication with interpretability and business usability.

Attribution biases and methodological concerns

Attribution models are subject to various biases:

- **Trackability bias**: Channels easier to measure (search, email) receive more credit than harder-to-track channels (word-of-mouth, offline branding).
- **Recency bias**: Overweighting recent interactions, ignoring long-term brand-building effects.
- **Platform bias**: Vendors like Google or Meta design attribution models favoring their ecosystems (Muthukrishnan, 2020).
- **Data sparsity bias**: Rare but influential touchpoints may be underestimated in models requiring high data volume.

Addressing these biases requires methodological triangulation – using multiple attribution models in parallel to cross-validate insights.

Ethical considerations in attribution practices

Attribution also raises important ethical issues:

- **Privacy**
  - Attribution relies on tracking individual user data across channels. Regulations such as GDPR and CCPA mandate explicit consent and data minimization (ICO, 2021).
  - Apple's App Tracking Transparency policy reduces cross-app tracking, challenging traditional attribution.

- **Transparency:** Advanced attribution models (e.g. algorithmic models) are often opaque. Ethical marketing requires explainability to maintain stakeholder trust (Wachter et al, 2017).

- **Consumer autonomy:** Over-reliance on hyper-targeted attribution-driven strategies risks manipulative personalization, raising concerns about consumer autonomy and fairness.

Ethically sustainable attribution thus requires privacy-preserving methods, transparent reporting and customer-centric design.

Future directions in retail attribution

Emerging trends point towards more holistic and ethical attribution practices:

- **Privacy-preserving attribution:** Federated learning and differential privacy allow modelling without exposing raw user data.
- **Cross-channel identity resolution:** Integrating deterministic (login-based) and probabilistic (device-matching) methods to bridge online and offline data.
- **Hybrid models:** Combining rule-based, probabilistic and experimental approaches (e.g. A/B tests, geo experiments) to validate attribution outcomes.
- **AI-driven insights:** Machine learning models (e.g. deep learning for sequence modelling) offer predictive attribution capabilities.
- **Long-term brand impact measurement:** Moving beyond short-term conversions to measure lifetime value and brand equity in attribution.

Conclusion

Chapter 9 has demonstrated that marketing attribution is both a technical discipline and a strategic imperative, underpinning how firms evaluate and optimize their customer engagement across increasingly fragmented and non-linear journeys. From its origins in simple single-touch models to the development of sophisticated algorithmic approaches such as Markov chains and Shapley values, attribution has evolved into a powerful tool for evidence-based decision-making in digital marketing.

The review of theoretical foundations showed that attribution cannot be separated from broader frameworks such as **customer journey theory** (Lemon and Verhoef, 2016) and **behavioural economics** (Murphy et al, 2007; Simon, 1982). These perspectives highlight that consumer decision-making is iterative, influenced by context, and shaped by cognitive limitations such as primacy and recency effects. Attribution models thus serve not only as measurement tools but also as reflections of consumer psychology and systemic retail dynamics.

By distinguishing between **rule-based models** and **algorithmic models**, this chapter emphasized the trade-off between interpretability and accuracy. Rule-based models (first-click, last-click, linear, time-decay, U-shaped) remain useful for providing baseline insights and stakeholder-friendly explanations but risk oversimplification. In contrast, algorithmic methods such as Markov chain attribution and Shapley value attribution provide data-driven insights that more accurately capture channel interdependencies and marginal contributions. However, these methods demand robust data, technical expertise and careful interpretation to avoid opacity or bias.

The case examples of Adidas, Skyscanner, Sephora, H&M and Nike underscored the real-world significance of attribution in shaping marketing strategy. Adidas' shift from last-click to data-driven attribution demonstrated how overlooked channels like branded search and influencer marketing could be revalued, leading to a 30 per cent increase in ROAS. Similarly, Skyscanner's multi-touch approach and Sephora's integration of digital and offline attribution revealed the power of attribution to uncover hidden synergies across channels. These cases illustrate that attribution, when implemented rigorously, can directly enhance ROI, guide budget reallocations and improve customer experiences.

Nonetheless, the chapter also highlighted critical **limitations and challenges**. Attribution is constrained by data silos, offline measurement gaps and methodological biases that favour easily tracked channels. Privacy regulations such as GDPR and platform policies like Apple's App Tracking Transparency further complicate attribution practices, forcing marketers to adopt privacy-preserving methods and more aggregated approaches. Additionally, ethical concerns – including transparency, explainability and consumer autonomy – require attribution to be implemented responsibly, with accountability to both organizational stakeholders and end-users.

Looking ahead, attribution is moving towards **integrated, privacy-first** and **AI-driven approaches**. Hybrid measurement frameworks combining **multi-touch attribution** (MTA) with **media mix modelling (MMM)**, real-time identity resolution and predictive analytics will become standard practice. Importantly, firms will need to balance sophistication with accessibility – ensuring that attribution insights are not only technically accurate but also transparent, interpretable and actionable.

In summary, marketing attribution provides the essential link between data-driven analytics and strategic marketing execution. It equips organizations to move from assumption-based decision-making to **evidence-based optimization**, fostering efficiency, accountability and innovation. By embedding attribution within broader marketing technology ecosystems and aligning it with ethical and theoretical principles, firms can unlock its full potential as both a measurement framework and a driver of long-term competitive advantage.

KEY TAKEAWAYS

Attribution has become a **strategic necessity** in retail. By quantifying the contribution of diverse touchpoints, attribution enables retailers to allocate budgets effectively, improve ROI and design customer-centric strategies.

- The H&M case demonstrates how multi-touch and Markov chain attribution reveal channel synergies across the customer journey.

- The Adidas case illustrates the pitfalls of last-click attribution and the benefits of adopting data-driven approaches.

- Nonetheless, attribution faces limitations (data silos, offline attribution gaps), biases (recency, platform) and ethical challenges (privacy, transparency).

Recommendations for retailers

- Employ **multi-model strategies** (rule-based plus algorithmic plus experimental) to cross-validate attribution insights.

- Integrate offline and online data for a true omnichannel perspective.

- Balance sophistication with interpretability to ensure stakeholder buy-in.

- Adopt privacy-preserving technologies and maintain transparency in attribution reporting.

- Shift from short-term conversion metrics to **lifetime value-based attribution** for long-term strategy.

By embedding attribution within broader marketing analytics and retail strategy, companies can achieve both accountability and competitive advantage in an increasingly data-driven marketplace.

References

Bostrom, R P and Heinen, J S (1977) MIS problems and failures: A socio-technical perspective, *MIS Quarterly*, 1 (3), 17–32

Chaffey, D and Ellis-Chadwick, F (2022) *Digital Marketing: Strategy, Implementation, and Practice* (8th ed.), Harlow: Pearson Education

Google (2022) Adidas and data-driven attribution, *Think with Google*, www.thinkwithgoogle.com (archived at https://perma.cc/4PRA-T72S)

Information Commissioner's Office (ICO) (2021) *Guide to the UK General Data Protection Regulation (UK GDPR)*, Information Commissioner's Office, ico.org.uk (archived at https://perma.cc/BGG2-6UAP)

Kotler, P and Keller, K L (2016) *Marketing Management* (15th ed.), Pearson Education

Lemon, K N and Verhoef, P C (2016) Understanding customer experience throughout the customer journey, *Journal of Marketing*, 80 (6), 69–96

Liu, C and Viswanathan, V (2021) Cross-channel attribution in retail: A machine learning perspective, *Journal of Retail Analytics*, 17 (2), 55–67

Liu, H and Viswanathan, S (2021) Analyzing cross-channel marketing attribution, *Journal of Interactive Marketing*, 54, 35–49

Liu, T and Viswanathan, S (2021) Mobile targeting and offline sales: The cross-channel effects of mobile display advertising, *Management Science*, 67 (1), 131–152

Mayer-Schönberger, V and Cukier, K (2013) *Big Data: A Revolution that will Transform how We Live, Work, and Think*, Boston: Eamon Dolan/Houghton Mifflin Harcourt

Murphy, G L, Hofacker, C F and Mizerski, R (2007) Primacy and recency effects in memory-based consumer judgments, *Journal of Behavioural Decision Making*, 20 (1), 23–42

Muthukrishnan, S (2020) Ad exchanges: Research issues, *ACM SIGecom Exchanges*, 19 (1), 37–52

Nieborg, D B and Poell, T (2018) The platformization of cultural production: Theorizing the contingent cultural commodity, *New Media & Society*, 20 (11), 4275–92

Rawson, A, Duncan, E and Jones, C (2013) The truth about customer experience, *Harvard Business Review*, 91 (9), 90–98

Simon, H A (1955) A behavioural model of rational choice, *Quarterly Journal of Economics*, 69 (1), 99–118

Simon, H A (1982) *Models of Bounded Rationality*, Cambridge, MA: MIT Press

Singh, A and Bansal, S (2021) Marketing attribution using Markov chains: A case study, *International Journal of Marketing Analytics*, 9 (2), 101–18

Skyscanner Insights (2023a) Multi-touch attribution analysis: Improving customer engagement, *Skyscanner Partners*, www.skyscanner.net/partners/insights (archived at https://perma.cc/L2JQ-CQZH)

Skyscanner Insights (2023b) Omnichannel attribution in travel, *Skyscanner Partners*, www.skyscanner.net/insights (archived at https://perma.cc/L2JQ-CQZH)

Vargo, S L and Lusch, R F (2008) Service-dominant logic: Continuing the evolution, *Journal of the Academy of Marketing Science*, 36 (1), 1–10

Verhoef, P C, Kannan, P K and Inman, J J (2015) From multi-channel retailing to omni-channel retailing, *Journal of Retailing*, 91 (2), 174–81

Wachter, S, Mittelstadt, B and Floridi, L (2017) Why a right to explanation of automated decision-making does not exist in the General Data Protection Regulation, *International Data Privacy Law*, 7 (2), 76–99

10 | Machine learning for marketing

Automating and enhancing decisions

DR TAHERA KALSOOM

LEARNING OUTCOMES

By the end of this chapter, students should be able to:

- Understand the role of machine learning in marketing and how it transforms tasks such as prediction, personalization and automation compared to traditional approaches.

- Apply clustering algorithms to segment customers and analyse how segmentation insights can inform marketing strategies.

- Differentiate and assess between collaborative filtering, content-based and hybrid recommendation systems, identifying their applications, benefits and limitations in marketing contexts.

- Critically evaluate the opportunities and challenges of adopting machine learning in marketing, including ethical considerations, scalability and consumer privacy issues.

- Leverage artificial intelligence to automate marketing tasks and improve decision-making.

KEY TERMS

Clustering: An unsupervised learning technique used to group similar data points (e.g. customers) into clusters based on shared features.

Cold-start problem: A challenge in recommendation systems where insufficient user or item data leads to poor predictions.

Collaborative filtering: Suggesting items by finding similar users or items based on behaviour patterns.

Content-based filtering: Recommending items like what a user liked, based on item features.

Decision support systems (DSS): Tools that provide data-driven insights to support strategic and operational decision-making.

Hybrid models: Combining content-based and collaborative filtering techniques to improve accuracy and mitigate weaknesses.

Machine learning (ML): A branch of AI that enables systems to learn from data and improve their performance without being explicitly programmed.

Personalization: Customizing content, products or messaging for individual users based on behavioural or demographic data.

Predictive analytics: A data-driven process using ML and statistical models to forecast future behaviours or outcomes based on historical data.

Recommendation systems: Algorithms that predict and suggest relevant items to users, enhancing user engagement and sales.

Introduction

The rapid expansion of digital technologies has revolutionized the marketing land-scape. In the current data-driven economy, businesses operate in an ecosystem that is saturated with customer touchpoints, from online shopping portals, social media latforms, email campaigns and search engines to mobile applications, chatbots and customer service centres (Figure 10.1) (Zhuk and Yatskyi, 2024). Each of these interactions generates a wealth of data, including clicks, views, likes, shares, purchases, preferences and even sentiment.

With such an overwhelming volume and variety of data, traditional marketing approaches that relied on manual analysis or intuition have become insufficient. Marketers now face the imperative to extract actionable insights from big data to remain competitive, anticipate consumer behaviour and deliver personalized customer experiences (Zhuk and Yatskyi, 2024). This has led to the increasing adoption of machine learning (ML), a field within artificial intelligence (AI) that focuses on developing algorithms that learn from data and make data-driven predictions or decisions without being explicitly programmed (Ngai and Wu, 2022).

Machine learning plays a crucial role in transforming how marketing tasks are executed. It enables systems to automatically detect patterns, segment audiences, forecast trends, recommend products and optimize campaigns in real time (Herhausen et al, 2024; Talha, 2025). These capabilities go beyond automation; they empower marketers with predictive and prescriptive insights that drive measurable outcomes (Zhuk and Yatskyi, 2024). Whether it is determining the best time to send an email, identifying at-risk customers for retention initiatives or dynamically adjusting ad spending across platforms, ML allows for smarter, faster and more accurate decision-making (Agu et al, 2024).

One of the most significant advantages of ML in marketing is its ability to personalize at scale. Personalization is no longer a luxury; it is an expectation. Consumers are more likely to engage with brands that understand their preferences and deliver relevant content (Wen, 2025). ML facilitates this by constructing detailed customer profiles based on behaviour, demographics, preferences and purchase history, and then using these profiles to tailor messages and product offerings accordingly (Talha, 2025).

This chapter explores the intersection of machine learning and marketing, with a deep dive into two pivotal areas: clustering algorithms for customer segmentation and recommendation systems in e-commerce. Clustering enables marketers to identify distinct customer groups within a heterogeneous market, allowing for more precise targeting and communication. Recommendation systems, on the other hand, power the personalized shopping experiences that consumers encounter on platforms like Amazon, Netflix and Spotify.

We will begin by discussing the general applications of ML in marketing, followed by a detailed exploration of clustering techniques. The latter half of the chapter will introduce recommendation systems, examining their types, architecture and practical implementations. Through a combination of theoretical concepts and hands-on examples, this chapter aims to equip readers with the knowledge and tools to leverage ML in their marketing strategies effectively.

Figure 10.1   Evolution of machine learning in marketing

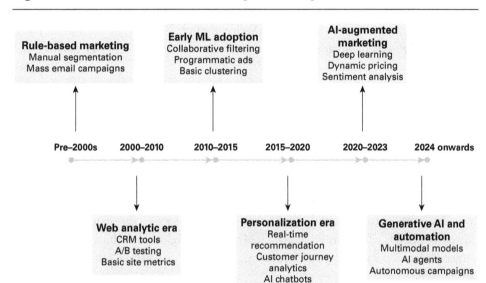

Ultimately, the goal is to highlight how machine learning, when thoughtfully applied, can unlock deeper customer insights, automate complex processes and significantly enhance the efficiency and effectiveness of marketing operations in today's fast-paced digital economy.

10.1 Machine learning in marketing

Machine learning enhances marketing efforts across multiple dimensions, transforming how businesses understand, reach and serve their customers (Thontirawong and Chinchanachokchai, 2021). Its integration into the marketing ecosystem is reshaping the tools marketers use and the strategies they deploy. ML enables brands to evolve from reactive to proactive and even prescriptive approaches by continuously learning from data, optimizing processes and uncovering insights that would be nearly impossible to detect manually (Thontirawong and Chinchanachokchai, 2021; Zhuk and Yatskyi, 2024).

One of the defining features of machine learning in marketing is its adaptability. As customer behaviour, market conditions and technological landscapes shift, ML systems can recalibrate in near real time, ensuring that strategies remain relevant and effective (Agu et al, 2024). Additionally, ML supports cross-functional alignment by bridging insights from sales, product development, customer service and finance, creating a unified view of customer experience (Ngai and Wu, 2022).

By integrating ML technologies, businesses not only streamline operations but also elevate customer engagement, drive conversion, reduce churn and ultimately achieve higher return on investment (ROI) (Kaličanin et al, 2019). These benefits span various aspects of marketing, from strategic planning to execution and encompass both B2B and B2C environments (Volkmar et al, 2022).

This section gives a detailed breakdown of the core areas where ML makes a significant impact.

Predictive analytics

Predictive analytics refers to the use of statistical techniques and ML algorithms to analyse historical data and forecast future events or behaviours (Fiorini, 2018). It empowers marketers to shift from reactive to proactive strategies by enabling data-driven foresight (Shalev-Shwartz and Ben-David, 2013). At its core, predictive analytics leverages patterns found in past data to make informed estimates about future customer actions (Zhuk and Yatskyi, 2024). These insights allow businesses to make targeted decisions with greater accuracy, improving marketing outcomes and resource allocation.

In marketing contexts, predictive analytics can be used to determine:

- which customers are most likely to make a purchase in the near future
- when a customer is likely to churn or stop engaging with the brand
- what products or services are expected to see increased demand
- how specific marketing actions are likely to impact customer response.

The strength of predictive analytics lies in its versatility (Agu et al, 2024). Techniques span from traditional statistical models such as linear and logistic regression to more sophisticated machine learning algorithms, including decision trees, random forests, gradient boosting machines, support vector machines (SVM) and deep learning neural networks (Volkmar et al, 2022). These models can handle complex, non-linear relationships and massive datasets, making them ideal for modern digital marketing environments (Wen, 2025).

Predictive models are trained using labelled datasets where the outcome variable (e.g. a purchase or a churn event) is known. The algorithm identifies patterns among the predictors, such as demographics, past behaviour, website interactions and transactional history, and generalizes these to make predictions on new, unseen data (Shalev-Shwartz and Ben-David, 2013; Amrita et al, 2024). With continuous learning, these models improve over time, especially when integrated with automated feedback loops.

Predictive analytics allows marketers to (Shalev-Shwartz and Ben-David, 2013):

- estimate customer lifetime value (CLV) based on past purchases and engagement levels
- forecast product demand and anticipate peak selling periods for better inventory planning

- predict customer churn and implement timely retention strategies
- identify high-conversion audience segments for targeted advertising
- personalize marketing content based on predicted user interests and behaviour.

Use case: An online retailer uses ML to predict customer lifetime value (CLV). By analysing past purchase data, browsing history, frequency of interactions and demographic details, the model identifies high-value customers. The marketing team then prioritizes these segments with tailored loyalty programmes, exclusive discounts and proactive customer service, thus enhancing retention and profitability (Thontirawong and Chinchanachokchai, 2021).

Personalization

Personalization is the process of delivering content, product recommendations and messaging that is uniquely tailored to individual users. In today's hyper-connected world, consumers are inundated with marketing messages and only those that are timely, relevant and meaningful truly stand out (Ngai and Wu, 2022; Volkmar et al, 2022). Consequently, personalization has moved from being a competitive advantage to a business imperative (Zhuk and Yatskyi, 2024).

Machine learning enables this level of personalization by ingesting and analysing large, diverse datasets, from browsing history and transaction logs to demographic data and social media behaviour (Huang and Rust, 2021; Wen, 2025). It processes these signals in real time to build highly granular customer profiles, which serve as the foundation for dynamic, context-aware engagement (Shalev-Shwartz and Ben-David, 2013). Unlike rule-based personalization that relies on static logic, ML-driven personalization adapts to each customer's evolving behaviours and preferences.

ML personalization capabilities include (Wen, 2025):

- real-time content and product recommendations tailored to browsing behaviour and past purchases
- dynamic website and app experiences that adjust layout, messaging or featured products based on user profile
- customized email marketing and promotions with optimized subject lines, timing and offers
- adaptive pricing models that respond to a user's likelihood to purchase, browsing patterns and competitive trends
- contextual advertising that reflects recent interests, search terms or social engagement.

With deep learning techniques, personalization can even incorporate emotional cues such as sentiment or tone, further enhancing message resonance (Talha, 2025).

Businesses also benefit from personalization engines embedded in customer relationship management (CRM) platforms, email marketing tools and content management systems (CMS), enabling seamless deployment across channels (Kaličanin et al, 2019).

The end result is a more engaging, intuitive and satisfying customer journey. Personalization not only drives immediate actions like clicks and purchases but also builds long-term loyalty by making users feel understood and valued (Arya, 2021).

Use case: Spotify leverages machine learning to analyse a user's listening history, skip patterns and favourite genres. This data feeds into a recommendation engine that curates personalized playlists such as 'Discover Weekly' or 'Release Radar'. This tailored experience keeps users engaged, increasing both user satisfaction and subscription retention.

Automation

Automation in marketing refers to the use of technology to perform repetitive, rule-based or time-consuming tasks without manual intervention. In a digital ecosystem where speed, precision and scalability are critical, automation becomes an essential tool for managing complex, multichannel campaigns (Arya, 2021; Volkmar et al, 2022). Machine learning elevates this concept by adding intelligence to automation; systems can learn from outcomes, adapt to changes and optimize decisions in real time (Thontirawong and Chinchanachokchai, 2021; Agu et al, 2024).

Unlike traditional automation tools that follow predefined instructions, ML-powered automation systems can dynamically adjust strategies based on new inputs, trends or anomalies (Huang and Rust, 2021; Talha, 2025). For example, rather than sending emails at fixed intervals, an ML model can identify the best time for each individual user based on historical open rates and behaviour patterns. Similarly, ad placements can be automatically refined based on ongoing performance metrics, audience segments or contextual relevance (Amrita et al, 2024; Wen, 2025).

Marketing automation powered by ML includes (Ngai and Wu 2022):

- **Dynamic ad bidding and placement:** Automatically adjusts bidding strategies in real time to target the most valuable impressions, using past performance data and predictive analytics.
- **Automated social media scheduling and sentiment analysis:** Schedules content based on optimal engagement windows and monitors user feedback to refine future content.
- **Real-time campaign adjustments:** Continuously evaluates campaign performance and reallocates resources (e.g. budget, creative, targeting) for maximum impact.
- **Email and content delivery optimization:** Sends personalized content based on recipient preferences, engagement history and current stage in the customer journey.

This level of automation allows marketers to scale their efforts significantly while maintaining precision and relevance. It also enhances agility, marketers can respond to changes in customer behaviour, market conditions or competitive actions with minimal delay (Kaličanin et al, 2019; Volkmar et al, 2022).

Use case: Google Ads uses ML to automate bid adjustments for ad placements based on user behaviour, historical conversion data, device usage, time of day and more. This intelligent automation maximizes return on ad spend (ROAS) by ensuring that ads are displayed to the right user at the optimal time and price.

Decision support

Machine learning supports decision-making by providing marketers with predictive and prescriptive insights that guide both tactical and strategic planning. In the age of information overload, making sense of vast and complex datasets in real time is a formidable challenge (Kaličanin et al, 2019; Thontirawong and Chinchanachokchai, 2021; Volkmar et al, 2022). ML addresses this by uncovering hidden patterns, identifying trends and generating recommendations that inform better decision-making across all levels of the marketing function (Kaličanin et al, 2019).

Decision support systems powered by ML not only present marketers with descriptive insights (what happened) but also predictive (what will happen) and prescriptive (what should be done) analytics (Kaličanin et al, 2019; Zhuk and Yatskyi, 2024). These insights empower organizations to make timely and evidence-based decisions that are aligned with business goals.

ML-driven decision support systems enhance marketing by enabling (Sana, 2018; Talha, 2025):

- **Real-time dashboards with KPI forecasting**: Visual interfaces that integrate predictive analytics to help marketers monitor campaign performance and anticipate future trends.

- **Customer sentiment analysis from reviews and social media**: Natural language processing (NLP) techniques automatically analyse unstructured text to assess public perception and identify emerging concerns or interests.

- **Market segmentation and positioning strategy development**: By analysing customer data and market trends, ML helps define distinct segments and craft competitive positioning strategies tailored to specific consumer needs.

- **Campaign performance benchmarking and attribution modelling**: ML algorithms can isolate the impact of different marketing channels and touchpoints, enabling more accurate ROI assessment and resource allocation (Zhuk and Yatskyi, 2024).

Incorporating ML into decision support systems also facilitates scenario analysis and forecasting (Volkmar et al, 2022; Herhausen et al, 2024). For example, marketers can simulate different pricing or promotional strategies and predict how each will affect conversion rates or customer acquisition costs. These simulations provide a valuable risk-mitigation framework, allowing businesses to plan confidently in uncertain environments (Kaličanin et al, 2019; Arya, 2021).

Moreover, ML supports personalization at the strategic level. By analysing which types of content or messaging perform best across different segments, decision makers can craft high-level marketing themes that resonate across diverse customer profiles (Huang and Rust, 2021; Thontirawong and Chinchanachokchai, 2021).

Use case: A fashion brand leverages NLP to process thousands of customer reviews, social media posts and survey responses. The ML model identifies common themes, such as preferences for sustainable fabrics or complaints about sizing inconsistencies. These insights inform product development and marketing campaigns, ensuring alignment with customer expectations.

Through these applications, machine learning not only improves operational efficiency but also fosters innovation and strategic foresight in marketing. In the following sections, we explore specific ML techniques – clustering and recommendation systems – that further illustrate the power and versatility of machine learning in marketing.

10.2 Clustering for customer segmentation

Customer segmentation is a cornerstone of modern marketing strategy, enabling firms to group customers based on shared characteristics such as behaviour, preferences and purchasing patterns (Amrita et al, 2024; Agu et al, 2024). Effective segmentation allows marketers to move beyond one-size-fits-all messaging towards tailored, highly relevant campaigns that resonate with specific audiences (Gomez-Uribe and Hunt, 2015; Talha, 2025). Traditionally, segmentation relied on demographics or psychographics, but such methods often fall short in capturing behavioural nuance. This is where machine learning, particularly clustering algorithms, comes into play, offering data-driven methods to automatically discover hidden patterns within customer data (Gomez-Uribe and Hunt, 2015; Wen, 2025).

Machine learning-based clustering techniques provide a scalable, objective and data-centric way to group customers, helping businesses uncover natural segments that might be invisible to human analysts (Talha, 2025). These clusters can then be used to refine marketing strategies, customize offerings and allocate resources more efficiently.

What is clustering?

Clustering is a fundamental technique in unsupervised machine learning that seeks to uncover the inherent structure in data by grouping similar data points into clusters without relying on predefined class labels (Kaličanin et al, 2019; Zhuk and

Yatskyi, 2024; Talha, 2025). Unlike supervised learning, which requires a labelled dataset to train a model for classification or regression, clustering works by identifying patterns and similarities within the input data itself (Ngai and Wu, 2022). This makes it particularly useful for situations where the categories or segments are unknown and need to be discovered organically.

The objective of clustering is twofold:

1 Intra-cluster similarity – maximize similarity within a cluster.

This means that all data points (e.g. customers) grouped into the same cluster should be as similar as possible to each other based on selected features (Zhuk and Yatskyi, 2024; Talha, 2025).

Example: A clothing retailer runs clustering on customer data using features like total spending, frequency of purchase, and preferred product categories. One resulting cluster includes customers who:

- shop every month
- spend between $200–$300 per month
- consistently buy women's formal wear.

These customers are behaviourally similar, so placing them in the same cluster achieves high intra-cluster similarity. Marketing to them with tailored ads for new formalwear collections is likely to be highly effective (Talha, 2025).

2 Inter-cluster dissimilarity – maximize difference between clusters.

This ensures that clusters are distinct from each other, representing different types of customers with minimal overlap in characteristics (Zhuk and Yatskyi, 2024; Talha, 2025).

Example: Continuing from the previous case, another cluster may consist of customers who:

- shop once or twice a year
- spend less than $50 per visit
- mostly purchase discounted casual wear.

These customers are clearly different from the monthly high spenders in the first cluster. This high inter-cluster dissimilarity allows marketers to treat each group uniquely, e.g, offering seasonal discounts to this casual, price-sensitive segment rather than sending them premium product promotions (Talha, 2025). By maximizing intra-cluster similarity, marketers ensure message relevance; by maximizing inter-cluster dissimilarity, they reduce wasted effort on generic campaigns (Table 10.1).

Figure 10.2 visually demonstrates both:

- **Intra-cluster similarity**: Customers within each cluster are tightly grouped, showing similar behaviour.
- **Inter-cluster dissimilarity**: There is a clear separation between the two clusters, highlighting different customer segments.

Table 10.1   Summary of clustering two-fold objectives

Cluster type	Characteristics	Marketing strategy
Cluster A (high intra-cluster similarity)	Frequent, high-spending formalwear buyers	Exclusive previews, loyalty rewards
Cluster B (high inter-cluster dissimilarity from A)	Infrequent, low-spending bargain shoppers	Sales notifications, win-back emails

Figure 10.2   Illustration of intra-cluster similarity and inter-cluster dissimilarity

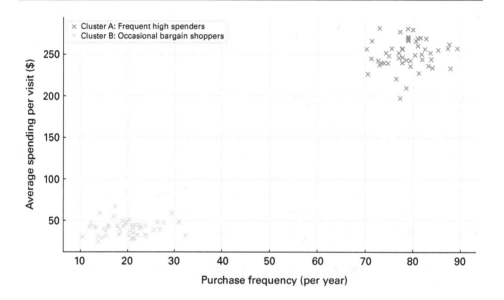

In technical terms, clustering algorithms often optimize objective functions such as minimizing within-cluster sum of squares (WCSS), maximizing silhouette scores or maximizing likelihoods depending on the method used (Kaličanin et al, 2019; Arya, 2021). Common similarity metrics include Euclidean distance, cosine similarity and Manhattan distance, which help define how 'close' or 'similar' data points are (Aryal et al, 2018).

Clustering serves as a cornerstone for **exploratory data analysis (EDA)**, enabling data scientists and marketers to uncover hidden structures, detect anomalies and simplify complex datasets (Kaličanin et al, 2019; Arya, 2021). In high-dimensional datasets, clustering can be paired with dimensionality reduction techniques such as **principal component analysis (PCA)** or **t-distributed stochastic neighbour embedding (t-SNE)** to visualize latent patterns and groupings more effectively (Arya, 2021).

Clustering in marketing contexts

In marketing, clustering is primarily employed for customer segmentation, a critical strategic activity aimed at dividing a diverse and heterogeneous customer base into distinct, homogenous subgroups (Kaličanin et al, 2019). These subgroups or segments consist of individuals who exhibit similar characteristics, needs or behaviours. Segmentation enables organizations to customize their marketing efforts, delivering the right message to the right audience at the right time, thereby improving engagement, satisfaction and conversion rates (Ngai and Wu, 2022; Agu et al, 2024; Wen, 2025).

Historically, customer segmentation was based on demographic (e.g. age, gender, income) or geographic (e.g. location, region) variables. While useful, such static categories often fail to capture the dynamic nature of customer behaviour and preferences in today's digital environment (Amrita et al, 2024; Agu et al, 2024). As a result, modern marketers are shifting towards behavioural segmentation, which leverages large-scale data generated from customer interactions across multiple channels, online and offline (Talha, 2025). These data include:

- purchase frequency and transaction history
- product affinities or category preferences
- engagement metrics from emails, websites or mobile apps
- browsing and clickstream behaviour
- customer service interactions and feedback
- device usage patterns and time-of-day preferences.

Clustering algorithms play a vital role in automating this behavioural segmentation, enabling marketers to uncover meaningful patterns that are too complex or subtle to detect through manual analysis (Arya, 2021; Zhuk and Yatskyi, 2024). Unlike rule-based methods, clustering adapts to the structure of the data and can discover segments that marketers might not have anticipated (Zhuk and Yatskyi, 2024).

One widely adopted method for behavioural clustering in retail and e-commerce is through RFM analysis, which segments customers based on (Talha, 2025):

- **Recency (R):** How recently a customer made a purchase. Recent purchasers are more likely to respond to marketing efforts.
- **Frequency (F):** How often the customer has made purchases over a defined period. Frequent buyers indicate brand loyalty and high engagement.
- **Monetary (M):** How much money the customer has spent. High spenders often represent valuable customers with strong revenue potential.

For instance, by applying a clustering algorithm to RFM data, a business may identify:

- 'Champions' who purchase frequently, recently and spend a lot – ideal for exclusive offers and brand advocacy programmes.
- 'Potential loyalists' who buy frequently but have not spent much yet – suitable for upselling or targeted incentives.
- 'At-risk' or 'Churning' customers who have not purchased in a while – these may require win-back campaigns or satisfaction surveys.

Such data-driven segmentation goes beyond assumptions, enabling marketers to develop precise strategies for customer retention, reactivation and value maximization.

In addition to RFM, clustering can be applied to multidimensional behavioural vectors that combine dozens or even hundreds of variables (Huang and Rust, 2021). For example, a streaming service might cluster users based on:

- genre preferences
- viewing time
- device usage
- skipping behaviour
- interaction with recommendations.

These clusters can inform highly personalized content suggestions, improve user experience and reduce churn. Similarly, in B2B marketing, firms can cluster leads or clients based on engagement history, deal size, conversion timeline and product interest – enhancing lead scoring and sales prioritization (Huang and Rust, 2021; Ngai and Wu, 2022; Herhausen et al, 2024).

Ultimately, clustering in marketing enables a shift from mass marketing to precision targeting, enhancing customer lifetime value (CLV), reducing acquisition costs and strengthening brand relationships (Huang and Rust, 2021; Thontirawong and Chinchanachokchai, 2021; Herhausen et al, 2024). It supports the creation of micro-segments, each with tailored value propositions, content strategies and communication cadences – driving both revenue and customer satisfaction in an increasingly competitive digital landscape (Zhuk and Yatskyi, 2024).

Clustering enables marketers to uncover nuanced and behaviourally rich customer segments that often go unnoticed in traditional demographic profiling. While age, gender or geographic location may offer some insight, they rarely capture the full complexity of customer intent, preferences or value (Thontirawong and Chinchanachokchai, 2021; Amrita et al, 2024). By analysing behavioural and transactional data, clustering reveals unconventional yet actionable groupings that align more closely with real-world consumer behaviour (Agu et al, 2024; Wen, 2025). For instance:

- **High-spending but infrequent shoppers:** These are customers who make large purchases but do so sporadically – perhaps only during seasonal sales, major life events or product launches. Despite their low frequency, they contribute significantly to revenue per transaction. Clustering helps isolate this segment, allowing marketers to design re-engagement strategies – such as exclusive previews, VIP loyalty programmes, or 'we miss you' campaigns with curated offerings – to nudge them into more regular engagement (Herhausen et al, 2024; Wen, 2025).

- **Frequent buyers of low-value items:** These customers demonstrate habitual purchasing behaviour, such as buying daily essentials, digital downloads or entry-level products. Though individual transactions are low in value, their cumulative behaviour reflects strong brand engagement. Clustering this group highlights opportunities for upselling or bundling strategies – for example, offering multi-pack discounts, suggesting premium alternatives or promoting subscription models that increase basket size and average order value (Zhuk and Yatskyi, 2024; Talha, 2025).

- **Browsers who abandon carts frequently:** These users show high intent but low follow-through, often leaving items in their carts or wish lists. Clustering algorithms can detect patterns in their browsing behaviour – such as timing, device use or category preferences – that reveal barriers to purchase. This segment is ideal for behavioural nudging, including cart abandonment emails, limited-time discounts, personalized remarketing ads or even chatbot interventions to answer potential concerns before checkout (Sana, 2018; Kaličanin et al, 2019).

- **Loyal repeat buyers of specific product lines:** These customers consistently return for certain products or categories (e.g. skincare, athletic gear or pet food). Clustering helps identify these loyalists, enabling cross-selling or premium upselling opportunities. For instance, if a customer regularly buys mid-range running shoes, the brand could recommend accessories, higher-end models or even fitness-related services – capitalizing on their established trust and brand alignment (Amrita et al, 2024; Zhuk and Yatskyi, 2024; Talha, 2025).

What makes these insights particularly powerful is that they cut across conventional segments (Talha, 2025). Two customers of the same age and income may behave entirely differently online and clustering captures these latent behavioural patterns. This empowers marketers to craft hyper-personalized campaigns, optimize recommendation systems and allocate marketing budgets more strategically, focusing efforts on the highest-value opportunities (Sana, 2018; Kaličanin et al, 2019).

Beyond customer segmentation, clustering has versatile applications across the marketing and business ecosystem:

- **Product taxonomy classification:** Automatically grouping similar products based on attributes or purchase behaviour to improve catalogue structure and site navigation (Kaličanin et al, 2019).

- **Content recommendation**: Clustering articles, videos or social posts based on engagement metrics and topic similarity to enhance content discovery (Kaličanin et al, 2019; Thontirawong and Chinchanachokchai, 2021).

- **Social media community detection**: Identifying clusters of users or influencers who interact frequently, enabling targeted messaging or community-building strategies (Talha, 2025).

- **Store location planning**: Segmenting regions based on foot traffic patterns, local purchasing behaviour and demographic mix to determine optimal physical store placement (Zhuk and Yatskyi, 2024; Talha, 2025).

In all these cases, clustering transforms raw data into structural intelligence, revealing how people or entities naturally organize themselves in relation to a product, brand or platform. This level of understanding enables not just better marketing but smarter, more customer-centric business decisions across the enterprise (Herhausen et al, 2024; Zhuk and Yatskyi, 2024).

The business value of clustering

From a strategic standpoint, the true value of clustering lies in its ability to convert raw, unlabelled and often chaotic customer data into actionable marketing intelligence (Talha, 2025). In today's omnichannel environment, where customers interact with brands across websites, apps, emails, social media and physical stores, understanding behavioural diversity is essential. Clustering acts as a bridge between data collection and decision-making, uncovering hidden relationships and segment-level behaviours that drive strategic marketing execution (Herhausen et al, 2024).

Clustering supports and enhances decision-making in several key areas:

- **Targeted advertising and retargeting strategies**: Clustering allows businesses to refine their advertising efforts by creating detailed behavioural segments. For example, a fashion retailer might use clustering to identify high-intent browsers who frequently view a specific product category but have not converted. Ads can then be tailored with dynamic creatives showcasing those exact items, potentially coupled with limited-time offers. Retargeting campaigns become more effective because they are built on behavioural intent rather than broad demographic assumptions (Ngai and Wu, 2022; Herhausen et al, 2024).

- **Customer journey optimization**: By clustering users by interaction patterns, such as time spent on site, click paths and content engagement, marketers can identify common journey stages and pain points (Huang and Rust, 2021; Wen, 2025). For instance, a SaaS platform might discover a cluster of users who frequently engage with tutorials but never activate the product, prompting the development of onboarding interventions. This insight enables marketers to deliver stage-specific nudges, content or support, smoothing the user journey and increasing conversion rates (Wen, 2025).

- **Dynamic pricing models:** Clustering can inform pricing strategies by identifying customer segments with varying price sensitivities, value perceptions or willingness to pay. For example, price-insensitive customers (e.g. brand loyalists or urgent buyers) may be segmented and presented with premium bundles, while price-conscious segments could be offered discounts or installment options (Thontirawong and Chinchanachokchai, 2021). This personalized pricing approach helps maximize revenue without undermining perceived value.

- **New product development based on demand clusters:** Analysing customer purchase behaviour and preferences through clustering reveals gaps and opportunities in existing product lines (Arya, 2021). For example, a beverage company might discover a growing segment that consistently purchases low-sugar, plant-based drinks across regions. This cluster insight can fuel ideation for new stock-keeping units, flavour variations or sustainable packaging, aligning product innovation with real consumer demand (Thontirawong and Chinchanachokchai, 2021; Amrita et al, 2024; Agu et al, 2024).

- **Market expansion planning:** Clustering geospatial and transactional data allows firms to identify promising regional clusters based on population behaviour, lifestyle indicators and consumption trends. For example, a fitness brand might use clustering to pinpoint neighbourhoods with a high concentration of active, wellness-focused consumers, guiding decisions on where to open new stores, host pop-up events or localize marketing efforts (Arya, 2021; Talha, 2025). This reduces risk and improves ROI when entering new markets.

In addition to these strategic use cases, the broader impact of clustering is its ability to shift marketing from reactive to proactive. Rather than waiting for trends to surface or problems to emerge, organizations can detect early signals of changing behaviour, such as declining engagement in a previously active cluster or sudden interest in a new product category (Huang and Rust, 2021). These real-time insights allow for agile responses, whether through promotions, personalized outreach or supply chain adjustments.

Clustering also enhances internal alignment by providing a unified customer view. Teams across marketing, sales, product and customer support can reference the same segments to coordinate strategy, messaging and service delivery (Huang and Rust, 2021; Zhuk and Yatskyi, 2024). This consistency improves the overall customer experience and drives better outcomes across the customer life cycle.

10.3 Recommendation systems

In the digital commerce landscape, recommendation systems have become indispensable tools for enhancing user experience, boosting engagement and driving sales

(Zhang and Chen, 2020). By analysing user behaviour, preferences and product attributes, these systems deliver personalized suggestions that help customers discover relevant items from a vast catalogue, increasing the likelihood of conversion and long-term retention (Beel et al, 2014).

E-commerce giants such as Amazon, Netflix and Alibaba have shown that well-designed recommendation engines not only increase average order value and customer lifetime value (CLV) but also reduce decision fatigue, improving user satisfaction (Gomez-Uribe and Hunt, 2015). For brands with large inventories and diverse customer bases, recommendation systems serve as a virtual personal shopper, curating items to individual tastes and contexts in real time.

Types of recommendation systems

Recommendation systems generally fall into three broad categories: collaborative filtering, content-based filtering and hybrid models (Ricci et al, 2011; Gomez-Uribe and Hunt, 2015; Zhang and Chen, 2020). Each has distinct mechanisms, advantages and limitations. See Table 10.2 for a summary.

1 Collaborative filtering

Collaborative filtering relies on user-item interaction data, such as ratings, purchases, likes, clicks or time spent viewing, to identify patterns and suggest items. It operates on the premise that users with similar behaviour or preferences will enjoy similar items (Shalev-Shwartz and Ben-David, 2013; Zhang and Chen, 2020). This approach is powerful because it does not require knowledge about the items themselves, only the interaction data (Ricci et al, 2011).

Subtypes

- **User-based collaborative filtering:** Recommends items to a user based on what similar users liked. Example: If User A and User B have both rated several items similarly, and User A liked a new product that User B has not seen, that product is recommended to User B.

- **Item-based collaborative filtering:** Recommends items similar to those the user has already liked or interacted with (Ricci et al, 2011; Zhang and Chen, 2020). Example: If many users who bought product X also bought product Y, then product Y is recommended to future buyers of product X.

Common techniques include:

- **K-Nearest Neighbours (k-NN):** Identifies the top-k users or items most similar to a target user or item.

- **Matrix factorization** (e.g. singular value decomposition – SVD): Reduces the dimensionality of user-item interaction matrices, uncovering latent factors that explain preferences and enabling scalable recommendations even with sparse data (Ricci et al, 2011; Zhang and Chen, 2020).

Advantages:

- Highly personalized.
- Learns from implicit signals like clicks or time spent.

Limitations:

- **Cold-start problem**: Difficult to make recommendations for new users (no history) or new items (no interactions) (Gomez-Uribe and Hunt, 2015).
- **Data sparsity**: Large platforms may have a vast number of items but relatively few interactions per user (Koren et al, 2009).

2 Content-based filtering

Content-based filtering recommends items based on their attributes or features, matched with a user's known preferences (Beel et al, 2014; Zhang and Chen, 2020). This method uses metadata (e.g. genre, brand, ingredients, author, colour) to determine item similarity.

How it works If a user frequently watches sci-fi movies or buys vegan skincare products, the system recommends other items with similar characteristics, even if no other users have interacted with them (Ricci et al, 2011).
  Techniques include:

- TF-IDF or word embeddings for text-based features (e.g. product descriptions).
- Cosine similarity or Euclidean distance to compare item vectors.
- Decision trees or Naïve Bayes for learning user preferences from labelled data.

Advantages:

- Does not rely on other users; good for niche interests.
- Effective for cold-start users with limited interaction data.

Limitations:

- Can lead to over-specialization – the system keeps recommending similar items, reducing diversity.
- Requires detailed and well-structured metadata.

3 Hybrid recommendation systems

Hybrid systems combine collaborative filtering and content-based filtering to leverage the strengths of both and overcome their limitations (Ricci et al, 2011; Shalev-Shwartz and Ben-David, 2013).

How they work

- Some hybrids blend predictions from both systems using weighted averages.
- Others switch between methods depending on the context or availability of data.
- More advanced models use machine learning algorithms (e.g, neural networks, gradient boosting) to integrate multiple sources of information – including user behaviour, content metadata, social influence and contextual data like time or location (Beel et al, 2014; Zhang and Chen, 2020).

Advantages:

- More accurate and robust recommendations.
- Reduces cold start and sparsity issues.
- Improves diversity and novelty in suggestions.

Netflix, for example, combines viewing history (collaborative filtering) with movie attributes like genre, actors and director (content-based) to recommend shows that align with both personal preferences and broader viewing patterns (Gomez-Uribe and Hunt, 2015).

Recommendation systems are a cornerstone of personalization in digital commerce and understanding these approaches helps marketers, data scientists and developers deploy solutions that deliver both commercial value and customer satisfaction (Ricci et al, 2011; Beel et al, 2014; Zhang and Chen, 2020).

Table 10.2 Summary of different recommendation systems

Type	Data used	Strengths	Weaknesses
Collaborative filtering	User–item interaction history	Learns complex user behaviour patterns	Cold start, sparsity
Content-based filtering	Item features and user preferences	Good for niche items and new users	Over-specialization
Hybrid models	Combined data from both sources	More accurate, adaptive and scalable	More complex to build and maintain

REAL-WORLD EXAMPLE   Amazon's hybrid recommendation
engine

Overview

Amazon has become synonymous with personalized e-commerce, in large part due to its industry-defining recommendation engine. Through real-time, individualized product suggestions, Amazon guides customers through its vast product catalogue, estimated to contain over 350 million items, making the shopping experience intuitive and highly efficient.

Its hybrid recommendation engine powers a variety of personalized features, including:

- 'Customers who bought this item also bought…' – based on aggregated co-purchase behaviour.

- 'Frequently bought together' – suggests bundles of items commonly purchased in the same transaction.

- 'Inspired by your browsing history' – tailors suggestions to individual users' clickstreams and views.

- 'Recommended for you' homepage modules – a personalized carousel of items generated for each user session.

According to a McKinsey report (2013), Amazon attributes up to 35 per cent of its total revenue to the effectiveness of these personalized recommendation systems, underscoring their immense commercial impact.

System design: A hybrid approach

Amazon's recommendation system exemplifies a hybrid architecture, combining collaborative filtering, content-based filtering and rule-based logic, each serving different user contexts, product scenarios and data availability challenges.

1 Collaborative filtering

Amazon primarily uses item-based collaborative filtering – an efficient alternative to user-based methods for large-scale systems. Instead of identifying similar users, the algorithm identifies items that frequently appear together in user interactions.
   Mechanism:

- Constructs a user-item interaction matrix.

- Measures item similarity using metrics like cosine similarity or Jaccard index.

- Recommends items that are statistically similar based on co-occurrence patterns.

Example: If users who purchased a DSLR camera also bought a tripod and a memory card, those items are recommended to future DSLR buyers.
   Advantages:

- Scales efficiently with millions of users and items.

- Works well for popular, high-traffic products with rich historical data.
- Learns from implicit feedback (e.g. clicks, time spent) as well as explicit ratings.

2 Content-based filtering

For long-tail or newly launched products with limited interaction data, Amazon relies on content-based filtering. This method uses product metadata and user profiles to match items with individual preferences.

Data features used:

- product titles, categories and tags
- brand reputation and manufacturer
- technical attributes (e.g. dimensions, material, compatibility)
- natural language descriptions and reviews, often processed with NLP techniques like TF-IDF or word embeddings.

Example: A customer who frequently buys noise-cancelling headphones is recommended other audio devices with similar features, such as over-ear design, Bluetooth 5.0 or premium noise isolation.

Advantages:

- Effective for cold-start problems (i.e. new users or products).
- Recommends niche or specialized items.
- Does not require collaborative behaviour from other users.

3 Personalization layer

Amazon's engine does not treat users uniformly. A dynamic personalization layer adjusts recommendations based on contextual, temporal and behavioural factors. It incorporates:

- **User behaviour**: Browsing history, purchase frequency, cart additions, wish lists, abandoned carts.
- **Contextual factors**: Time of day, device used (mobile vs desktop), location (urban vs rural) and weather (for seasonal products).
- **Customer segments**: Amazon Prime members, business customers, frequent buyers or first-time visitors.

This layer enables individualized recommendation sets for every user session – even for the same product pages – leveraging real-time data to orchestrate hyper-personalization at scale.

Business impact

Amazon's recommendation engine yields measurable and multidimensional business benefits that extend across marketing, operations and customer experience.

Cross-sell and upsell optimization:

- Recommending complementary products (e.g. camera plus lens plus SD card) increases basket size and average order value.
- Promotes premium or bundled versions of frequently viewed items.

Higher conversion rates:

- Reduces decision fatigue by surfacing relevant items early in the user journey.
- Empowers product discovery even when users do not have a specific intent.

Customer satisfaction and loyalty:

- Enhances the sense of being 'understood' by the platform.
- Builds habitual use and brand affinity as users return for a familiar and personalized experience.

Inventory and supply chain efficiency:

- Predictive recommendations help forecast product demand across segments and regions.
- Improves stock rotation, reduces dead inventory and enables better demand-driven logistics.

Applications in e-commerce

Recommendation systems are at the heart of personalized digital experiences and are widely implemented across various e-commerce and digital platforms. The following examples show how major brands use them strategically.

Amazon

Amazon leverages a sophisticated hybrid recommendation system that combines collaborative filtering, content-based filtering and rule-based logic. It analyses each user's purchase history, browsing behaviour, wish lists and frequently viewed products to deliver tailored product suggestions (Shalev-Shwartz and Ben-David, 2013; Fiorini, 2018). These are deployed in modules like 'Recommended for You', 'Customers who viewed this item also viewed' and 'Frequently Bought Together', all designed to increase average order value and customer engagement.

Netflix

Netflix uses a collaborative filtering engine enhanced by deep learning models to recommend TV shows and movies based on a user's viewing history, watch time, skip behaviour and genre preferences. The platform personalizes content selection, thumbnails and descriptions, testing which variant is most likely to drive engagement (Ricci et al, 2011; Gomez-Uribe and Hunt, 2015). The goal is to keep users watching longer, reducing churn and increasing subscription retention.

Spotify

Spotify applies both collaborative filtering and natural language processing to analyse listening patterns, song metadata and even lyrics. This powers features like 'Discover Weekly', 'Daily Mix' and 'Release Radar', where playlists are algorithmically generated based on user listening behaviour, track similarities and emerging trends. Spotify also analyses temporal patterns (e.g. what you listen to in the morning vs evening) to optimize playlist delivery (Beel et al, 2014; Gomez-Uribe and Hunt, 2015).

Zalando

Zalando, a major European fashion retailer, uses recommendation engines to personalize clothing suggestions based on style preferences, past purchases, return behaviour and sizing history (Gomez-Uribe and Hunt, 2015; Zhang and Chen, 2020). The system also accounts for fit predictions and seasonal trends, helping reduce return rates and improving the shopping experience. Zalando's model adapts to customer feedback (e.g. 'too small' or 'too large' reviews), refining size and style recommendations with each transaction (Shalev-Shwartz and Ben-David, 2013; Fiorini, 2018).

These applications demonstrate how recommendation systems drive not just conversion and retention, but also operational efficiency (e.g. size prediction at Zalando), content optimization (e.g. Netflix thumbnails) and habit formation (e.g. Spotify playlists).

Key components

To build a robust recommendation system, several core components and concepts must work together:

- **User-item matrix:** This matrix is the foundational dataset that captures interactions between users and items (Ricci et al, 2011; Zhang and Chen, 2020). Each row represents a user and each column represents an item (product, movie, track, etc.). Values in the matrix can be:
  - ○ **Explicit feedback:** Ratings or thumbs up/down.
  - ○ **Implicit feedback:** Clicks, purchases, time spent, cart additions.

Because real-world interaction data is often sparse (most users interact with only a small subset of items), algorithms must infer patterns from incomplete data (Ricci et al, 2011).

- **Similarity measures:** To recommend similar items or users, systems compute similarity using mathematical distance metrics:

  ○ **Cosine similarity:** Measures the cosine of the angle between two vectors; useful for high-dimensional and sparse data (e.g. text or ratings).

  ○ **Pearson correlation:** Measures linear correlation between two variables; commonly used for comparing user rating patterns.

  ○ **Euclidean distance:** Measures the straight-line distance between two vectors; more intuitive but sensitive to scale (Ricci et al, 2011; Beel et al, 2014; Zhang and Chen, 2020).

These metrics help determine which users or items are 'closest' in preference space and are crucial in both collaborative and content-based models (Ricci et al, 2011).

- **Model training:** Recommendation engines rely on trained algorithms to learn patterns from the user-item matrix (Koren et al, 2009; Gomez-Uribe and Hunt, 2015). Common training approaches include:

  ○ **ALS (alternating least squares):** A matrix factorization technique particularly useful for implicit feedback datasets. It decomposes the user–item matrix into lower-dimensional user and item factors.

  ○ **SVD++ (singular value decomposition++):** An extension of basic SVD that incorporates implicit signals to improve accuracy, especially in cold-start scenarios.

  ○ **Neural collaborative filtering:** Deep learning models that capture non-linear user-item interactions, used by platforms like YouTube and Pinterest.

- **Evaluation metrics:** Once trained, the model's effectiveness is assessed using performance metrics tailored to ranking and recommendation tasks:

  ○ **Precision:** Proportion of recommended items that are relevant.

  ○ **Recall:** Proportion of relevant items that were successfully recommended.

  ○ **F1 score:** Harmonic mean of precision and recall, balancing false positives and false negatives (Ricci et al, 2011; Beel et al, 2014).

  ○ **MAP (mean average precision):** Measures the quality of ranked recommendations, accounting for the position of relevant items in the recommendation list (Amrita et al, 2024).

These metrics help compare algorithms and tune models for optimal real-world performance, ensuring that users receive accurate, diverse and serendipitous recommendations.

10.4 Benefits and challenges

The integration of machine learning (ML) into marketing operations, especially through clustering and recommendation systems, offers transformational opportunities for businesses. However, these benefits come with challenges that must be carefully managed to ensure ethical, sustainable and effective deployment.

Benefits

Efficiency

Machine learning automates complex, repetitive and data-intensive marketing tasks that would otherwise require significant manual labour and time (Shalev-Shwartz and Ben-David, 2013; Fiorini, 2018). For instance, a recommendation engine can automatically generate individualized product suggestions for millions of users in real time, something impossible to do manually. Similarly, clustering algorithms can segment customers instantly based on thousands of behavioural attributes, enabling rapid campaign design, real-time A/B testing and quicker decision cycles (Koren et al, 2009; Thontirawong and Chinchanachokchai , 2021). This automation allows human marketers to focus on strategic creativity and oversight, rather than rule-based operations (Zhuk and Yatskyi, 2024).

Scalability

ML models are inherently scalable, capable of processing and learning from massive datasets spanning millions of users, products and transactions. As an organization grows, whether through expanding its product catalogue, customer base or geographic reach, machine learning systems can adapt to increased data volume with minimal additional overhead (Volkmar et al, 2022). For example, Spotify and Amazon scale their recommendation engines globally, serving personalized content to diverse markets and user segments without sacrificing performance or relevance.

Personalization

One of the most powerful benefits of ML in marketing is its ability to deliver granular, one-to-one personalization at scale. Rather than relying on broad demographic groups or generic messaging, ML models analyse real-time behaviour, preferences and contextual signals to tailor content, offers and communications (Thontirawong and Chinchanachokchai, 2021; Ngai and Wu, 2022). Personalization not only improves click-through rates, conversion and average order value but also enhances the overall customer experience, building brand trust and loyalty over time (Kaličanin et al, 2019; Talha, 2025).

Insight generation

Machine learning excels at uncovering hidden patterns and generating actionable insights from raw, high-dimensional data (Ngai and Wu, 2022). Clustering can reveal emerging customer segments or behavioural trends that were previously undetectable. Recommendation systems can surface underperforming or high-potential products based on interaction data. These insights enable data-driven decision-making across departments, informing product development, inventory planning, customer service and sales strategy (Zhuk and Yatskyi, 2024; Talha, 2025).

Challenges

Data privacy

With the increasing use of personal data in ML applications, organizations face mounting responsibility to ensure data privacy and protection. Laws such as the General Data Protection Regulation (GDPR) and the California Consumer Privacy Act (CCPA) impose strict requirements on how user data is collected, stored and used (Volkmar et al, 2022; Herhausen et al, 2024). Recommendation systems must avoid using sensitive or personally identifiable information unless clear consent has been given and data practices must be transparent. Violations can result in legal penalties, reputational damage and loss of consumer trust.

Bias and fairness

ML models are only as fair as the data they are trained on. If data contains biases related to gender, race, income or geography, the model may unintentionally reproduce or even amplify those biases (Thontirawong and Chinchanachokchai , 2021; Volkmar et al, 2022). For example, a recommendation system might underrepresent products popular with minority groups if they are less represented in the training data. This creates ethical concerns and may lead to exclusionary outcomes, reduced engagement or regulatory scrutiny (Shalev-Shwartz and Ben-David, 2013; Fiorini, 2018). Implementing bias detection, fairness audits and inclusive training datasets is essential.

Cold-start problem

Recommendation systems often struggle with cold-start scenarios, where there is little or no data about new users or new products (Gomez-Uribe and Hunt, 2015; Zhang and Chen, 2020). For instance, when a user first signs up for a streaming service or when a retailer adds a new product, the system lacks the interaction data needed to generate relevant suggestions. This limits short-term effectiveness and may lead to irrelevant or generic recommendations that reduce user engagement (Shalev-Shwartz and Ben-David, 2013; Beel et al, 2014; Zhang and Chen 2020). Solving this often requires hybrid models, initial onboarding surveys or content-based features.

Complexity

Deploying ML models in production environments involves more than just training an algorithm. It requires data infrastructure, model versioning, monitoring systems, periodic retraining and cross-functional collaboration between data scientists, engineers, marketers and compliance teams (Kaličanin et al, 2019; Volkmar et al, 2022). Over time, models may degrade in accuracy due to concept drift, when user behaviour or market dynamics change, necessitating continuous tuning and updating (Zhuk and Yatskyi, 2024). Integration with existing CRM, CMS and analytics systems can also be resource-intensive and require significant technical expertise.

EXAMPLES

Example 1: Coca-Cola's ML-driven personalization

Coca-Cola uses ML to analyse data from vending machines, social media and mobile apps to identify flavour preferences and regional trends. This data-driven approach helps launch limited edition products tailored to local tastes and optimize vending machine placements.

Example 2: Sephora's recommendation engine

Sephora uses a hybrid recommendation system combining collaborative and content-based filtering to suggest products based on skin type, purchase history and user reviews. The result is increased conversion and customer satisfaction.

Example 3: Netflix's dynamic thumbnails

Netflix uses ML not just to recommend shows, but also to personalize thumbnails based on users' viewing history. Users interested in romance might see a romantic scene highlighted in the thumbnail of a comedy movie, increasing click-through rates.

Example 4: Starbucks predictive analytics

Starbucks employs ML to forecast store demand, personalize mobile order suggestions and optimize stock levels across regions based on purchasing patterns, weather and local events.

REAL-WORLD EXAMPLE Spotify's behavioural segmentation with clustering

Background: Spotify aimed to increase user retention by understanding listening behaviours more granularly.

Method: Using k-means clustering on user behaviour data – skip rates, listening duration, playlist usage and time of day – Spotify identified multiple user segments:

- morning commuters
- sleep music listeners

- genre loyalists
- skippers (high skip rates).

Result: Spotify designed segment-specific strategies:

- push notifications in the morning for commuters
- personalized sleep playlists for night listeners
- 'you might like' features tailored for loyalists.

The campaign led to a measurable increase in weekly active users and playlist engagement.

EXERCISES

Exercise 1: Clustering practice for e-commerce

Scenario

You are a data analyst at an online fashion retailer. You have collected the following data from 1,000 customers:

- purchase frequency (per month)
- average order value
- preferred category (e.g. casual, formal, accessories).

Instructions

1 Use a k-means clustering algorithm to create three to five customer segments.
2 Visualize the clusters using a scatter plot (frequency vs value).
3 Analyse and describe the characteristics of each cluster.
4 Propose a personalized marketing strategy for each segment.

Expected outcome

- Distinct clusters such as:
  o high-value formal buyers
  o budget casual shoppers
  o accessory-only frequent buyers.
- Marketing recommendations:
  o Offer loyalty discounts to high-value buyers.

o Provide budget bundles for casual shoppers.

o Upsell to accessory buyers with combo deals.

Exercise 2: Build a simple recommendation system

Scenario

You work for an online bookstore. Your task is to build a basic content-based recommendation system.
Dataset: Each book includes:

- title
- genre
- author
- description
- tags (e.g. #thriller, #romance).

Instructions

1 Choose a book.
2 Convert text features (genre, tags, description) into vectors using TF-IDF.
3 Compute cosine similarity between books.
4 Recommend the top three similar books.

Extension

Introduce user ratings and attempt a collaborative filtering model using matrix factorization.

Goal

Understand the mechanics behind recommendation engines and appreciate how hybrid models increase personalization quality.

Conclusion

ML is no longer a futuristic concept in marketing; it is a present-day imperative that has fundamentally redefined how organizations understand, engage and serve their customers. In an era of data abundance, shrinking attention spans and rising customer expectations, ML offers the tools and intelligence needed to transform marketing from a reactive, intuition-driven function into a proactive, insight-led discipline.

By automating complex decision-making processes and uncovering patterns hidden within massive datasets, ML empowers marketers to work smarter, faster and more effectively. It facilitates:

- automation of time-intensive tasks such as customer segmentation, lead scoring and campaign optimization
- personalization of customer experiences at scale, through targeted content, offers and product recommendations
- predictive analytics that anticipate user behaviour, optimize resource allocation and improve strategic forecasting.

Two of the most powerful applications covered in this chapter, clustering and recommendation systems, demonstrate how ML drives tangible business value:

- Clustering algorithms reveal rich, behaviourally informed customer segments that go far beyond traditional demographic profiles. These insights enable more relevant messaging, better product–market alignment and deeper brand loyalty.
- Recommendation systems create frictionless digital experiences by surfacing the right product or content at the right time, enhancing engagement and boosting revenue.

While the benefits are substantial, responsible implementation is crucial. Challenges such as data privacy, algorithmic bias and cold-start limitations require careful attention, regulatory compliance and a commitment to fairness and transparency. Organizations must ensure that ML is used not just for efficiency but also ethically and inclusively, respecting user consent and fostering trust.

Looking ahead, the role of ML in marketing will only continue to grow. As algorithms become more sophisticated and computing power becomes more accessible, marketers will be expected to collaborate closely with data scientists, embrace AI-powered tools and stay attuned to emerging technologies such as generative AI, real-time personalization engines and multimodal recommendation systems.

Ultimately, the marketers who thrive in this evolving landscape will be not only those who adopt machine learning but those who understand how to use it strategically, balancing automation with empathy, data with creativity and scale with relevance. In doing so, they will lead the transformation of marketing from a support function into a core driver of growth, innovation and customer value in the digital economy.

References

Agu, Edith Ebele, Obiki-Osafiele, Anwuli Nkemchor and Chickezie, Njideka Rita (2024) Enhancing market analysis using artificial intelligence for strategic business decision-making, *World Journal of Engineering and Technology Research*, 3 (1), 038–045, doi: 10.53346/wjetr.2024.3.1.0053 (archived at https://perma.cc/45TG-UG2L)

Amrita, S, Chen, Y, Patel, R and Okafor, T (2024) The impact of artificial intelligence and machine learning in medical imaging', *Enhancing Medical Imaging with Emerging Technologies*, 13 (3), 221–49, doi: 10.4018/979-8-3693-5261-8.ch014 (archived at https://perma.cc/7RTK-62TU)

Arya, S (2021) A study on artificial intelligence in production management, *South Asian Journal of Marketing & Management Research*, 11 (11), 102–7, doi: 10.5958/2249-877x.2021.00118.1 (archived at https://perma.cc/ER4J-XUAY)

Aryal, A, Chaudhary, P, Searcy, C and Tiwari, S (2018) The emerging big data analytics and IoT in supply chain management: a systematic review, *Supply Chain Management*, (November), doi: 10.1108/SCM-03-2018-0149 (archived at https://perma.cc/MJU5-MDN5)

Beel, J, Gipp, B, Langer, S and Breitinger, C (2014) *Research Paper Recommender Systems: A Literature Survey*, 1–68, Preprint, https://isg.beel.org/pubs/2016%20IJDL%20---%20Research%20Paper%20Recommender%20Systems%20--%20A%20Literature%20Survey%20(preprint).pdf (archived at https://perma.cc/3TAK-LNGB)

Fiorini, L (2018) How artificial intelligence will change the future of bullion production, 42nd International Precious Metals Institute Annual Conference, IPMI 2018, *Journal of the Academy of Marketing Science*, 60–69

Gomez-Uribe, C A and Hunt, N (2015) The netflix recommender system: Algorithms, business value, and innovation, *ACM Transactions on Management Information Systems*, 6 (4), doi: 10.1145/2843948 (archived at https://perma.cc/3VVH-5WFE)

Herhausen, D, Wiesel, T, Thomasdsen, R, Kraft, F and Kraus, M (2024) Editorial for the Special Issue 'Machine Learning in Marketing', *Journal of Business Research*, Elsevier Inc., 170 (October 2023), 114254, doi: 10.1016/j.jbusres.2023.114254 (archived at https://perma.cc/XX9F-ZZAL)

Huang, M H and Rust, R T (2021) A strategic framework for artificial intelligence in marketing, *Journal of the Academy of Marketing Science*, 49 (1), 30–50, doi: 10.1007/s11747-020-00749-9 (archived at https://perma.cc/38RR-PCP9)

Kaličanin, K, Radosavljeć, M, Đorđević, A and Stanković, J (2019) Benefits of artificial intelligence and machine learning in marketing, *Proceedings of the International Scientific Conference Sinteza 2019*, 472–477, doi: 10.15308/sinteza-2019-472-477 (archived at https://perma.cc/N2YN-8VCZ)

Koren, Y, Bell, R and Volinsky, C (2009) Matrix factorization techniques for recommender systems, *IEEE Computer*, 42 (8), 30–37

Ngai, E W T and Wu, Y (2022) Machine learning in marketing: A literature review, conceptual framework, and research agenda, *Journal of Business Research*, Elsevier Inc., 145 (April 2021), 35–48, doi: 10.1016/j.jbusres.2022.02.049 (archived at https://perma.cc/CNA9-QUCN)

Ricci, F, Rokach, L and Shapira, B (2011) *Recommender Systems Handbook*, New York: Springer, doi: 10.1007/978-0-387-85820-3 (archived at https://perma.cc/NCT4-K3PF)

Sana, M (2018) Machine learning and artificial intelligence in radiology, *Journal of the American College of Radiology*, 15 (8), 1139–42, doi: 10.1016/j.jacr.2017.11.015 (archived at https://perma.cc/QCW2-C6JB)

Shalev-Shwartz, S and Ben-David, S (2013) *Understanding Machine Learning: From Theory to Algorithms*, Cambridge: Cambridge University Press, doi: 10.1017/CBO9781107298019 (archived at https://perma.cc/QTB5-DXBS)

Talha, M (2025) Optimizing digital marketing campaigns using artificial intelligence (AI) and social media analytics: A comparative study of machine learning algorithms, *International Journal of Scientific Research in Engineering and Management*, 09 (03), 1–9, doi: 10.55041/ijsrem42691 (archived at https://perma.cc/6BVQ-UGVW)

Thontirawong, P and Chinchanachokchai, S (2021) Teaching artificial intelligence and machine learning in marketing, *Marketing Education Review*, 31 (2), 58–63, doi: 10.1080/10528008.2021.1871849 (archived at https://perma.cc/WHQ7-93RW)

Volkmar, G, Fischer, P M and Reinecke, S (2022) Artificial intelligence and machine learning: Exploring drivers, barriers, and future developments in marketing management, *Journal of Business Research*, 149 (April 2021), 599–614, doi: 10.1016/j.jbusres.2022.04.007 (archived at https://perma.cc/Y77C-DSUK)

Wen, J (2025) Market forecasting model based on artificial intelligence and its application in marketing decision-making, *SHS Web of Conferences*, 213, 01020, doi: 10.1051/shsconf/202521301020 (archived at https://perma.cc/C3X7-2RDA)

Zhang, Y and Chen, X (2020) Explainable recommendation: A survey and new perspectives, *Foundations and Trends in Information Retrieval*, 14 (1), 1–101, doi: 10.1561/1500000066 (archived at https://perma.cc/UAV7-Y9DM)

Zhuk, A and Yatskyi, O (2024) The use of artificial intelligence and machine learning in e-commerce marketing, *Technology Audit and Production Reserves*, 3 (4(77)), 33–38, doi: 10.15587/2706-5448.2024.305280 (archived at https://perma.cc/9YC7-PNQV)

11 | The rise of generative AI in marketing

LEARNING OUTCOMES

By the end of this chapter, students should able to:

- Explain the core principles, functions and underlying mechanics of generative AI technologies in a marketing context.
- Assess the role of generative AI in transforming marketing practices, with emphasis on content creation, personalization and customer engagement.
- Apply theoretical frameworks to analyse how AI reshapes customer journey mapping and personalization strategies.
- Identify and critically discuss the ethical, legal and data governance challenges associated with generative AI applications.
- Examine and evaluate real-world case studies to extract best practices and lessons learned from generative AI implementation.
- Develop practical skills through hands-on exercises that involve applying generative AI tools to contemporary marketing scenarios.

CHAPTER OUTLINE

Introduction to generative AI

11.1 How generative AI works: Large language models

11.2 Content creation with generative AI

11.3 Personalization and customer experience with generative AI

11.4 Theories and frameworks supporting generative AI in marketing

11.5 Integrating generative AI into the marketing funnel

11.6 Ethical, legal and data governance considerations

Conclusion

References

Key terms

Term	Meaning	Marketing relevance
AIDA model	Attention, Interest, Desire, Action	Explains persuasive pathways for AI content
AI ethics	Principles ensuring fairness, transparency, justice	Safeguards responsible AI marketing practices
Attention mechanism	Technique in transformers that weighs the importance of each token relative to others	Allows context-aware messaging in brand storytelling
Chatbots	AI-powered conversational interfaces	Provide 24/7 customer service and product advice
Customer experience theory	Satisfaction arises from cumulative brand interactions	AI enhances seamless omnichannel CX
Deep learning	Multi-layered neural networks for complex patterns	Powers image, speech and advanced personalization tasks
Diffusion of innovations	Theory of how new tech spreads across adopters	Explains generative AI adoption patterns
Dynamic capabilities	Ability to adapt resources in fast-changing environments	Critical for long-term AI integration
Dynamic content	Content that adapts in real time to user behaviour	Used in personalized emails, websites and product offers
Few-shot learning	AI model performs tasks with only a few training examples	Quick adaptation to niche marketing copy needs
Fine-tuning	Additional training on domain-specific data	Custom LLMs trained on a brand's content for consistency

(continued)

(Continued)

Term	Meaning	Marketing relevance
GANs (generative adversarial networks)	Neural networks that generate realistic synthetic data	Used in ad creatives, product imagery and AR/VR try-ons
Generative AI	AI that produces new outputs (text, images, video, audio)	Enables scalable personalization and creative content generation
Hallucination	AI generates plausible but factually incorrect outputs	Ethical risk in marketing claims and compliance
LLMs (large language models)	Deep learning models trained on vast text corpora	Power conversational agents, blogs and marketing copy
Machine learning	Algorithms that learn from data to make predictions	Used in targeting, recommendations and pricing
NLP (natural language processing)	AI field enabling understanding and generation of human language	Underpins chatbots, content automation and sentiment analysis
Personalization	Tailoring experiences to individuals using data	Improves relevance, loyalty and CX
Prompt engineering	Crafting inputs to guide AI outputs effectively	Critical skill for marketers using tools like Jasper or ChatGPT
RACE framework	Reach, Act, Convert, Engage	Links AI personalization to campaign stages
Resource-based view	Competitive advantage arises from rare, valuable resources	Proprietary AI models and datasets as strategic assets
Sentiment analysis	Detecting emotional tone in text	Used for brand monitoring and adaptive communication
TAM (technology acceptance model)	Adoption depends on perceived ease and usefulness	Explains user acceptance of AI tools
Token	A unit of text (word, sub-word or character) used in LLM training	Determines cost and length of AI-generated content
Transformer networks	Deep learning architecture using self-attention	Foundation of GPT models for contextualized text generation
Zero-shot learning	Model performs tasks without prior examples	Automates campaign drafts with minimal input
5A framework	Awareness, Appeal, Ask, Act, Advocate	Guides AI use across the customer journey

Introduction to generative AI

In an era where digital transformation dictates competitive advantage, few technologies have captured marketers' attention like **generative artificial intelligence (AI)**. Generative AI refers to advanced artificial intelligence systems capable of producing original content – including text, images, audio and video – by learning from large datasets. These systems do not merely analyse or classify information like traditional AI; instead, they create novel content that closely resembles human creativity. In the marketing context, this means automatically writing blog articles, composing social media captions, generating product descriptions, personalizing email campaigns and even crafting visual advertisements.

Definition and scope in marketing

The central distinction of generative AI lies in its ability to **generate** rather than **react**. Unlike conventional automation, which executes predefined rules, generative AI employs **large language models (LLMs)** and **generative adversarial networks (GANs)** to emulate the nuances of human communication. A key example is ChatGPT, a conversational model developed by OpenAI, which is trained on billions of words from the internet and can produce coherent responses across a wide array of topics and tones (Brown et al, 2020). Other platforms such as DALL·E, Copy.ai, Jasper and Writesonic have brought generative AI to the forefront of content strategy in marketing departments.

In practical terms, generative AI is being used to:

- Automatically generate **tailored email content** for segmented audiences.
- Create **visual content and design mockups** using prompt-based image generation.
- Optimize **search engine-friendly** product descriptions at scale.
- Simulate **chat interactions** for customer support or product guidance.
- Perform **brand sentiment** and **review generation** to maintain tone consistency.

These tools do not merely increase efficiency; they reshape the creative process. Marketers can now experiment with hundreds of iterations of messaging and visuals in seconds, enabling A/B testing and multi-segment personalization with unprecedented speed and precision.

Historical context: The evolution of AI in marketing

The use of artificial intelligence in marketing is not a sudden phenomenon. It has evolved gradually, beginning with **rule-based systems** in the 1990s, moving through **predictive analytics** and **machine learning** in the 2000s and arriving at today's **generative AI capabilities**. Early AI implementations focused on **recommendation engines** – such as Amazon's 'Customers who bought this also bought…' feature – and **CRM-based personalization**. With the rise of **big data** and **cloud computing**, marketers began leveraging machine learning for **customer segmentation**, **churn prediction** and **ad targeting** (Davenport et al, 2020).

The emergence of **LLMs** marked a pivotal moment. These models, such as GPT-3, PaLM (Pathways Language Model by Google) and Llama (Meta), are trained on vast internet corpora and use transformer architectures to understand and generate language in a contextually relevant manner (Vaswani et al, 2017). Unlike prior generations of marketing AI, which required manually labelled data and extensive rule-coding, these models learn from unstructured data and can generalize across tasks.

This democratization of creativity, once the exclusive domain of copywriters and designers, now allows marketers without technical backgrounds to generate campaign-ready content with minimal input. The boundary between human creativity and machine augmentation is becoming increasingly blurred.

Generative AI in marketing today

Generative AI's applications in marketing are already mainstream. In 2023, Coca-Cola collaborated with OpenAI and Bain & Company to launch an AI-powered campaign allowing customers to create branded digital artwork using DALL·E. The campaign resulted in a 30 per cent increase in social media engagement, showcasing how AI can support user-generated content initiatives and strengthen brand identity (Bain & Company, 2023).

Similarly, Shopify's AI suite helps small and medium businesses write product descriptions and manage customer emails, dramatically reducing content creation time and increasing personalization. In email marketing, tools like Mailchimp's AI Content Optimizer analyse past campaign performance to recommend improved subject lines and copy, while HubSpot integrates GPT-based assistants to draft blog posts and outreach sequences based on customer behaviour data.

Generative AI is revolutionizing marketing by enhancing content creation, personalization and operational efficiency at scale. It empowers marketers to go beyond traditional segmentation and enter the era of **hyper-personalized experiences**, where messaging can be tailored to micro-audiences in real time. This increased agility not only accelerates campaign deployment but also amplifies engagement and conversion rates.

However, this innovation comes with **important ethical and practical considerations**. Questions around **bias**, **authenticity**, **data governance**, **intellectual property** and **customer consent** must be addressed to ensure responsible deployment. As marketing becomes more automated and data-driven, transparency and ethical governance are essential to maintaining consumer trust.

The dual nature of generative AI

The adoption of generative AI can be seen as a double-edged sword. On one hand, it enables cost savings, productivity boosts and consistent branding. On the other hand, there are risks associated with over-automation, content quality degradation and **loss of human authenticity**. Research has shown that audiences can often detect AI-generated content and may view it as less trustworthy if it lacks transparency (Mikalef et al, 2023).

Furthermore, regulatory bodies are beginning to monitor the use of AI in customer communications. The European Union's AI Act and the UK Data Ethics Framework encourage businesses to ensure fairness, transparency and explainability when deploying AI tools (UK Government, 2020; European Commission, 2023).

Setting the stage for this chapter

This chapter explores how generative AI is reshaping marketing practice, from content generation and customer journey personalization to real-time decision-making and campaign optimization. It critically examines both the **transformative potential** and **ethical implications** of this technology.

We will examine core technologies like LLMs, explore practical tools such as ChatGPT and Jasper, and apply marketing frameworks including **customer journey mapping** and **personalization matrices**. Case studies – like Coca-Cola's use of DALL·E – will illustrate real-world success stories, while exercises will give students the opportunity to use AI tools hands-on.

As we delve into the mechanics, applications and governance of generative AI in marketing, students will be encouraged to think critically about how to use this technology not just efficiently but responsibly.

11.1 How generative AI works: Large language models

Generative artificial intelligence (AI) represents one of the most transformative technological innovations shaping marketing in the digital era. Unlike traditional AI, which is typically limited to classification, prediction or optimization tasks, generative AI produces new outputs such as text, images, video and code by learning patterns from existing data (Dwivedi et al, 2023). In marketing, this translates into capabilities ranging from automated copywriting and personalized email campaigns to dynamic ad generation and conversational commerce.

At the heart of this revolution are large language models (LLMs) such as OpenAI's GPT (generative pre-trained transformer), Google's PaLM (Pathways Language Model) and Meta's Llama (Large Language Model Meta AI). These models leverage advances in deep learning architectures, particularly transformers, to achieve context awareness, adapt tone and style, and generalize tasks with minimal examples. Complementary technologies such as generative adversarial networks (GANs) and multimodal AI further expand the creative possibilities, allowing for the seamless integration of text, visuals and audio (Kietzmann et al, 2023).

This section provides a comprehensive exploration of how generative AI works in marketing. It introduces the core technologies and theories, defines key concepts and terms, examines real-world applications by brands, and outlines practical case exercises for students to apply their knowledge.

Foundations of generative AI

Generative AI rests on the convergence of several foundational domains in artificial intelligence, particularly **machine learning (ML), deep learning (DL)** and **natural language processing (NLP)**. At its essence, generative AI leverages neural networks – computational architectures inspired by the human brain – to recognize, model and reproduce complex patterns in data. By training on vast corpora of text, images and multimodal inputs, these systems can create novel outputs that are both statistically plausible and contextually relevant (Dwivedi et al, 2023).

The underlying foundations not only provide technical scaffolding but also shape the strategic marketing potential of generative AI. Each component – NLP, ML, DL and transformers – plays a distinct role in enabling marketers to automate creativity, personalize engagement and analyse consumer interactions at scale (see Figure 11.1).

Natural language processing (NLP)

Definition: NLP is a subfield of AI that equips machines with the ability to understand, interpret and generate human language in ways that are meaningful and contextually appropriate (Cambria and White, 2014).

Core concepts: NLP encompasses a wide range of techniques, including tokenization, part-of-speech tagging, named entity recognition (NER), sentiment analysis and machine translation. These functions enable AI to process unstructured text data, which constitutes the majority of marketing communications and consumer interactions online (Hirschberg and Manning, 2015).

Relevance to marketing:

- **Conversational AI:** NLP powers chatbots and virtual assistants such as Sephora's Virtual Artist and Amazon's Alexa, which provide real-time, personalized interactions with consumers.

Figure 11.1   Foundations of generative AI for marketing

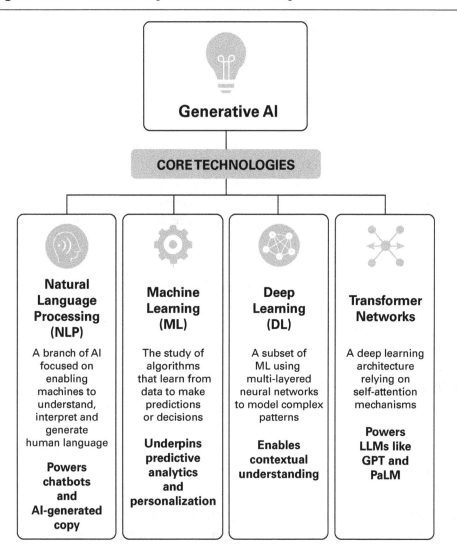

- **Sentiment analysis:** Platforms like Trustpilot and Twitter generate massive streams of consumer feedback. NLP allows brands to detect emotions and attitudes, identifying reputational risks and opportunities (Mostafa, 2013).

- **Content generation:** Tools like Jasper and Copy.ai use NLP models to draft product descriptions, ad copy and blog posts, reducing the cost and time of content production while maintaining tone consistency (Dwivedi et al, 2023).

- **Market research:** NLP-based topic modelling can extract insights from customer reviews or survey responses, informing product development and brand positioning.

By enabling real-time, human-like interactions, NLP directly contributes to **customer experience management**, reinforcing theories such as Lemon and Verhoef's (2016) customer journey framework, which emphasizes continuous engagement across touchpoints.

Machine learning (ML)

Definition: Machine learning is the study of computational algorithms that learn from data to make predictions or decisions without explicit rule-based programming (Jordan and Mitchell, 2015).

Core concepts: ML can be divided into supervised learning (training models on labelled data for tasks such as classification), unsupervised learning (discovering hidden structures, e.g. clustering) and reinforcement learning (optimizing decisions through feedback loops).

Relevance to marketing:

- **Predictive analytics:** ML models forecast consumer behaviour, such as churn probability, purchase intent or lifetime value (Wedel and Kannan, 2016).

- **Recommendation systems:** Platforms like Amazon and Netflix rely on ML to analyse browsing and purchase patterns, suggesting relevant items that drive sales (Gomez-Uribe and Hunt, 2015).

- **Dynamic pricing:** Airlines and e-commerce retailers employ ML algorithms to adjust prices based on demand fluctuations, customer profiles and competitor actions.

- **Targeted advertising:** ML models analyse demographic and behavioural data to deliver personalized ad experiences across platforms like Google Ads and Meta Ads Manager.

Generative AI builds on ML by moving beyond predictive functions into creative generation – not just forecasting what customers may buy, but crafting the persuasive messages and creative content that influence those decisions (Kietzmann et al, 2023).

Deep learning (DL)

Definition: Deep learning is a subset of machine learning that employs multi-layered artificial neural networks to identify and model intricate patterns within large, high-dimensional datasets (LeCun et al, 2015).

Core concepts: Unlike basic ML, which often relies on engineered features, DL models automatically learn hierarchical representations of data through multiple layers of abstraction. For example, in language tasks, initial layers might detect word embeddings, while deeper layers model semantic and contextual relationships.

Relevance to marketing:

- **Contextual understanding:** Deep learning enables AI models to grasp nuance, tone and intent, producing marketing content that resonates with consumers.

- **Image and video generation:** DL architectures such as convolutional neural networks (CNNs) underpin applications like AI-generated ads or product imagery.

- **Voice assistants and speech analysis:** DL models process audio inputs, allowing brands to deploy voice-based customer service or interactive campaigns (e.g. Domino's voice-activated ordering).

- **Behavioural prediction:** DL excels at analysing massive digital footprints, identifying subtle behavioural signals that may indicate churn, upsell potential or cross-sell opportunities.

In marketing strategy, DL aligns with the **resource-based view (RBV)** (Barney, 1991), where proprietary data and advanced learning models become strategic assets that deliver sustained competitive advantage.

Transformer networks

Definition: Transformers are a deep learning architecture introduced by Vaswani et al (2017) in their seminal paper, 'Attention is All You Need'. Unlike recurrent neural networks (RNNs), which process sequences sequentially, transformers use self-attention mechanisms to evaluate the relationships between all elements in a sequence simultaneously.

Core concepts:

- **Self-attention:** Assigns weights to tokens in a sequence based on their relevance to each other.

- **Parallel processing:** Improves efficiency by handling entire sequences simultaneously, allowing training on massive datasets.

- **Scalability:** Transformers scale effectively with more data and parameters, enabling breakthroughs in performance.

Relevance to marketing:

- **Large language models (LLMs):** GPT, PaLM and Llama – all transformer-based – enable the production of coherent long-form content, from blog posts to customer service scripts.

- **Contextual advertising:** Transformer-powered models generate ad copy tailored to user context and intent.

- **Brand voice consistency:** By capturing tone and style, transformers allow global brands such as Coca-Cola and Nike to maintain coherent messaging across diverse markets.

- **Multilingual marketing:** Transformers excel in machine translation, empowering brands to deliver campaigns across languages with cultural nuance (Johnson et al, 2017).

Transformers are the foundation of modern generative AI in marketing, bridging the technical underpinnings with strategic applications. They represent the transition from rule-based or statistical models towards fluid, human-like creativity at scale (Dwivedi et al, 2023).

Core technologies of generative AI

The emergence of generative AI is underpinned by three central technological foundations:

1 Large language models (LLMs)

2 Generative adversarial networks (GANs)

3 Multimodal AI.

These technologies represent the evolution of artificial intelligence from task-specific automation towards systems capable of generating novel, creative and contextually meaningful outputs. Each of these technologies contributes distinct capabilities:

- LLMs excel in textual generation and conversational interfaces.
- GANs are renowned for realistic synthetic imagery.
- Multimodal AI enables integration across text, image, audio and video streams.

Their combined use is rapidly transforming marketing practice, enabling unprecedented levels of personalization, scalability and interactivity (Dwivedi et al, 2023; Kietzmann et al, 2023).

Large language models (LLMs)

Large language models such as OpenAI's GPT series, Google's PaLM and Meta's Llama exemplify the advances made in deep learning and transformer architectures. These models are trained on massive corpora of text – ranging from books and journal articles to websites and social media interactions – containing trillions of tokens (Bommasani et al, 2021). Their ability to model statistical relationships between words and phrases enables them to generate coherent, contextually appropriate and stylistically adaptive outputs.

Key characteristics of LLMs

- **Context awareness:** By predicting the next token in a sequence using billions (or even trillions) of parameters, LLMs achieve sophisticated contextual understanding.

This allows them to generate long-form text, such as product descriptions or marketing blogs, while maintaining coherence and logical flow (Brown et al, 2020).

- **Tone and style adaptation**: LLMs can replicate specific stylistic registers, from the witty and informal tone of Wendy's Twitter campaigns to the professional and authoritative voice typical of B2B LinkedIn posts (Kaplan and Haenlein, 2020). This adaptability ensures brand consistency across digital touchpoints.

- **Few-shot and zero-shot learning**: LLMs demonstrate task generalization by producing relevant outputs with minimal or no training examples. For marketers, this enables rapid generation of SEO tags, ad copy or campaign slogans, reducing reliance on extensive labelled datasets (Bommasani et al, 2021).

Marketing applications of LLMs

- **Chatbots and virtual assistants**: Retailers like Sephora employ AI-driven chatbots, such as its Virtual Artist, to provide product advice and simulate in-store experiences online (Davenport et al, 2020).

- **Automated content creation**: Platforms like Shopify integrate GPT-based tools to auto-generate product descriptions, saving time for small businesses and ensuring optimized, keyword-rich copy.

- **Social media campaigns**: In 2023, Coca-Cola partnered with OpenAI and Bain & Company to launch creative campaigns powered by GPT-4 and DALL·E, demonstrating LLMs' ability to scale brand storytelling across global markets (Coca-Cola, 2023).

Generative adversarial networks (GANs)

Definition: Introduced by Goodfellow et al (2014), GANs consist of two competing neural networks – the generator, which creates synthetic data, and the discriminator, which evaluates whether outputs are real or artificial. Through iterative training, GANs produce increasingly realistic images, videos and other media.

Marketing applications of GANs

- **Synthetic ad creatives and product imagery**: GANs can create unique, photorealistic marketing visuals at scale. For instance, beauty and fashion brands use AI-generated images to supplement campaigns without costly photoshoots (Kietzmann et al, 2018).

- **Virtual try-ons**: Companies such as H&M and Gucci leverage GAN-driven systems to allow customers to digitally try on clothing or accessories, bridging the gap between online and offline retail (Cai et al, 2022).

- **Synthetic consumer insights:** GANs can simulate focus groups or survey responses by generating synthetic data that approximates consumer preferences, offering quicker and less costly alternatives for exploratory research (Dwivedi et al, 2023).

GANs thus complement the text-based capabilities of LLMs, providing the visual creative power necessary for integrated multimedia marketing campaigns.

Multimodal AI

Definition: Multimodal AI integrates data and representations across multiple modalities – text, images, video and audio – into unified models. Recent innovations include OpenAI's GPT-4V (Vision), which combines natural language understanding with visual interpretation, and Google's Gemini, which extends multimodal reasoning across diverse input formats (OpenAI, 2023; Google DeepMind, 2023).

Marketing applications of multimodal AI

- **Interactive shopping assistants:** Multimodal AI enables virtual assistants to respond not only to text queries but also to images. For instance, a customer could upload a photo of a shoe and receive suggestions for matching outfits.
- **Cross-channel personalization:** By merging text, image and audio capabilities, brands can generate coherent campaigns spanning Instagram posts, YouTube ads and podcasts, maintaining consistency in message and tone (Kietzmann et al, 2023).
- **Augmented and virtual reality (AR/VR):** Multimodal AI enhances immersive experiences. For example, furniture retailers like IKEA employ AI-driven AR applications that allow users to visualize products in their homes with realistic textures and lighting (Dwivedi et al, 2023).

Together, LLMs, GANs and multimodal AI constitute the core technologies driving generative AI in marketing. LLMs provide linguistic and stylistic adaptability; GANs offer high-quality synthetic imagery and creativity; and multimodal AI integrates these strengths into unified, interactive experiences (see Figure 11.2). Their adoption is reshaping customer engagement strategies, content production pipelines and creative design processes.

Theoretical frameworks

Diffusion of innovations theory (Rogers, 2003)

The **diffusion of innovations (DOI) theory,** developed by Rogers (2003), is a well-established framework for understanding how new ideas and technologies spread within a social system. The theory identifies five categories of adopters – innovators, early adopters, early majority, late majority and laggards – each of which plays a role in the

Figure 11.2   Core technologies of generative AI

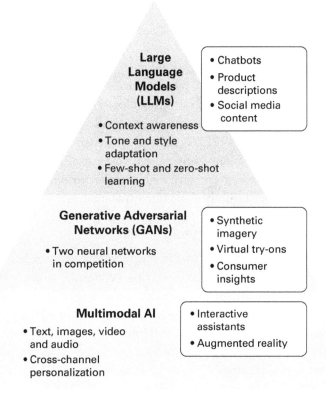

diffusion process. Adoption typically follows an S-shaped curve, starting with a small group of risk-taking innovators and culminating in widespread acceptance among the majority (Rogers, 2003).

In the context of generative AI, this framework helps explain the trajectory of adoption across industries. Tech startups and AI-focused firms often act as innovators, experimenting with generative AI for novel applications such as automated design, content creation and synthetic data generation (Dwivedi et al, 2023). Large consumer brands such as Coca-Cola and Nike were early adopters, leveraging generative AI to enhance marketing campaigns, personalization and creative storytelling (McKinsey, 2023). Over time, generative AI is expected to diffuse into the early and late majority segments, becoming a mainstream tool embedded within marketing, healthcare, education and other sectors (Bughin et al, 2019). Thus, DOI provides a useful lens for analysing adoption patterns and anticipating barriers such as organizational resistance, ethical concerns or infrastructure challenges.

Resource-based view (Barney, 1991)

The **resource-based view (RBV)** argues that a firm's sustained competitive advantage arises from its ability to acquire, develop and leverage resources and capabilities that are valuable, rare, inimitable and non-substitutable (VRIN) (Barney, 1991). Within the domain of generative AI, proprietary large language models (LLMs), algorithmic expertise and unique datasets can represent strategic resources that underpin differentiation. For example, firms with access to domain-specific training data or custom fine-tuned models can produce more contextually relevant outputs than competitors relying solely on general-purpose AI (Kaplan and Haenlein, 2020).

Generative AI thus extends RBV by transforming intangible assets such as knowledge, creativity and brand equity into technologically mediated capabilities. Firms that strategically integrate AI into content personalization, product innovation and customer engagement are more likely to develop dynamic capabilities – the ability to reconfigure resources in rapidly evolving environments (Teece, 2018). This suggests that beyond simply adopting generative AI, organizations must embed it into their strategic resource base to sustain competitive advantage.

Customer experience (CX) theory

Customer experience theory posits that customer satisfaction and loyalty derive from the cumulative journey of interactions between a consumer and a brand, spanning digital and physical touchpoints (Lemon and Verhoef, 2016). In competitive markets, CX serves as a differentiator, shaping perceptions, emotional connections, and long-term customer value (Homburg et al, 2017).

Generative AI offers transformative opportunities for CX enhancement. By enabling real-time personalization, AI-powered systems can tailor content, recommendations and product offerings to individual preferences, thereby increasing perceived relevance (Chatterjee et al, 2023). Conversational AI agents, such as chatbots and virtual assistants, create human-like interactions that improve service accessibility and responsiveness (Grewal et al, 2020). Furthermore, the integration of AI across omnichannel ecosystems – from social media to physical retail – enables seamless customer journeys and fosters stronger brand–consumer relationships.

In this sense, generative AI does not merely automate customer engagement but redefines the CX paradigm, shifting from transactional exchanges to personalized, co-created experiences that align with consumer expectations of convenience, immediacy and relevance.

Technology acceptance model (Davis, 1989)

The **technology acceptance model (TAM)**, introduced by Davis (1989), explains user adoption of new technologies through two main constructs: **perceived usefulness** and **perceived ease of use**. TAM has been widely applied in digital marketing and information systems research as a predictor of technology adoption (Venkatesh and Davis, 2000).

In the generative AI context, adoption by employees, customers and organizations depends on whether AI tools are perceived as useful (e.g. improving efficiency, personalization or creativity) and easy to use (e.g. user-friendly interfaces, seamless integration into workflows). For instance, OpenAI's ChatGPT adoption has been accelerated by its accessibility and ease of interaction, while enterprise-grade AI tools like Jasper and MidJourney appeal to professionals because of their clear productivity benefits (Dwivedi et al, 2023). Extending TAM to generative AI adoption underscores the importance of design, usability and trust in driving acceptance.

Dynamic capabilities theory (Teece et al, 1997; Teece, 2018)

The **dynamic capabilities theory** extends RBV by emphasizing a firm's ability to integrate, build and reconfigure internal and external competencies to address rapidly changing environments (Teece et al, 1997). Whereas RBV focuses on static resources, dynamic capabilities highlight adaptability and responsiveness as sources of long-term advantage.

In the context of generative AI, dynamic capabilities include the ability to rapidly adopt AI systems, train employees, experiment with new business models and scale successful applications. Firms that continuously learn and evolve their AI use – such as Amazon integrating AI into logistics, product recommendations and voice assistants – demonstrate the capacity to transform capabilities into sustained value creation (Teece, 2018). Dynamic capabilities are therefore critical in ensuring that generative AI adoption is not a one-time investment but an ongoing process of organizational renewal.

Integrated theoretical model of generative AI adoption and impact

Together, these frameworks create a holistic model where:

- Generative AI adoption is shaped by both **market diffusion patterns** and **user acceptance factors**.
- Competitive advantage depends on how well firms **embed AI into resources** and **adapt dynamically** to technological change.
- The ultimate outcome is **improved customer experience**, which reinforces adoption and competitive advantage in a **feedback loop**.

Figure 11.3 shows how the five frameworks interconnect:

- **Left side (adoption drivers)**:
  - Diffusion of innovations → Market-level spread
  - Technology acceptance model → User/firm-level adoption
- **Middle (organizational advantage)**:
  - Resource-based view → Strategic resources
  - Dynamic capabilities → Adaptability over time

Figure 11.3   Integrated theoretical model of generative AI adoption and impact

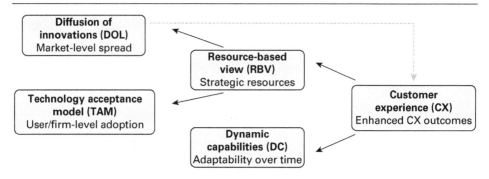

- **Right side (outcomes):**
  - Customer experience theory → Enhanced CX (personalization, conversational AI, omnichannel integration)
- **Arrows:**
  - DOI + TAM → influence RBV/dynamic capabilities (firms adopt and embed AI).
  - RBV + dynamic capabilities → enable superior CX.
  - CX outcomes → feed back into adoption (positive reinforcement loop).

This creates a **process model:**

Adoption drivers → Strategic integration → Customer outcomes → Reinforcement of adoption.

EXAMPLES

Coca-Cola – 'Create Real Magic' campaign

In 2023, Coca-Cola partnered with OpenAI and Bain & Company to integrate GPT-4 and DALL·E into its global marketing campaigns. Customers could co-create branded artwork and copy, which Coca-Cola then showcased in Times Square. This demonstrated co-creation at scale, blending consumer creativity with brand control.

Sephora – conversational AI for Beauty

Sephora deployed LLM-powered chatbots to provide personalized beauty consultations. By integrating NLP and recommendation systems, Sephora improved online engagement and boosted e-commerce sales, particularly during the pandemic (McKinsey, 2021).

Nike – personalized storytelling

Nike uses AI-driven storytelling to generate personalized content for its members, leveraging customer data to create tailored workout recommendations, motivational emails and social campaigns. LLMs ensure tone consistency with Nike's inspirational brand voice.

EXERCISE

Prompt engineering for marketing campaigns

1 Choose a product (e.g. eco-friendly sneakers).

2 Write three different prompts to generate ad copy using an LLM (ChatGPT, Jasper or Copy.ai).

o Prompt 1: Focus on sustainability benefits.

o Prompt 2: Target Gen Z with casual tone.

o Prompt 3: Emphasize performance and durability.

3 Compare outputs and analyse:

o How does tone change across prompts?

o Which version best fits your target segment?

o What risks of inaccuracy or bias emerge?

Learning outcome: To develop practical skills in guiding LLMs to produce brand-consistent outputs.

Practical and ethical implications

The adoption of large language models (LLMs) and generative adversarial networks (GANs) offers organizations opportunities for efficiency, personalization and innovation in marketing, customer engagement and content creation. However, their deployment raises several practical and ethical concerns that require critical attention.

Bias and fairness

Generative AI systems are trained on large-scale datasets that often contain historical and societal biases. As a result, they may inadvertently reproduce or amplify stereotypes related to gender, race or culture (Bender et al, 2021; Mehrabi et al, 2021). For example, AI-generated marketing content could unintentionally reinforce discriminatory representations, thereby damaging brand equity and leading to reputational risks. Addressing bias requires robust dataset curation, ongoing monitoring and the use of fairness-aware algorithms (Floridi and Cowls, 2019).

Transparency and explainability

A further challenge relates to the opacity of AI-generated outputs. Customers may be unaware that they are interacting with an algorithm rather than a human, raising issues of informed consent and trust (Shin, 2021). Black-box models such as LLMs also present difficulties in providing explainable reasoning for generated recommendations or responses (Doshi-Velez and Kim, 2017). Lack of transparency can undermine user confidence and poses regulatory risks, particularly in industries where accountability is critical (European Commission, 2021).

Intellectual property (IP) and ownership

Generative AI outputs, such as images, music or text, blur the boundaries of authorship and copyright. Legal debates persist as to whether AI-generated works qualify for protection and if so, whether ownership resides with the developer, the user or the AI system itself (Gervais, 2020; Samuelson, 2022). For example, the US Copyright Office has ruled that works created solely by AI are not eligible for copyright, complicating their commercial use. Firms deploying generative AI must therefore navigate complex IP landscapes, including the risk of infringing existing copyrighted materials embedded in training data (Elgammal, 2023).

Over-reliance and authenticity

While automation enhances efficiency, excessive reliance on AI-generated content risks eroding brand authenticity and diluting unique creative voices (Kaplan and Haenlein, 2020). Consumers increasingly value human and authentic brand storytelling, and overuse of AI in communications may trigger perceptions of artificiality or inauthentic engagement (Dwivedi et al, 2023). Furthermore, dependence on AI tools may lead to skill atrophy within creative teams, reducing firms' capacity for originality outside algorithmic outputs. Achieving a balance between AI augmentation and human creativity is therefore critical.

The practical and ethical implications of generative AI highlight the need for firms to adopt a responsible AI governance framework, integrating ethical guidelines, regulatory compliance and human oversight. By addressing issues of bias, transparency, intellectual property and authenticity, organizations can maximize the benefits of LLMs and GANs while minimizing risks to stakeholders and society.

Marketers must balance efficiency with ethical responsibility, guided by frameworks such as the EU AI Act (2023) and organizational governance policies.

Generative AI operates at the nexus of large-scale data, deep learning architectures and advanced algorithms, with LLMs, GANs and transformer networks as its foundation. In marketing, these technologies reconfigure how brands generate content, personalize experiences and engage with customers. Real-world examples such as Coca-Cola, Nike and Sephora demonstrate both the creative potential and strategic value of generative AI.

However, successful adoption requires not just technical understanding but also theoretical grounding, ethical reflection and practical skills. By engaging with frameworks such as **diffusion of innovations, resource-based view** and **customer experience theory,** marketers can align generative AI adoption with broader strategic objectives. Ultimately, generative AI is not simply a tool for efficiency – it is a driver of innovation, personalization and co-creation in the evolving landscape of digital marketing.

11.2 Content creation with generative AI

The rise of generative artificial intelligence (AI), particularly through large language models (LLMs) and generative adversarial networks (GANs), has transformed marketing content creation. By leveraging deep learning and natural language processing (NLP), brands can automate the production of personalized, scalable and contextually relevant content across multiple channels. Unlike traditional rule-based automation, generative AI produces original and adaptive outputs, ranging from blog articles and email campaigns to social media captions and dynamic product descriptions (Dwivedi et al, 2023).

In marketing, content serves as the bridge between brands and consumers, shaping brand identity, communicating value propositions and nurturing customer relationships. Generative AI enhances this process by reducing production time, improving personalization, and scaling engagement strategies (Kaplan and Haenlein, 2020). However, its application also raises ethical, creative and strategic considerations, including authenticity, copyright ownership and over-reliance on automation (Bender et al, 2021).

This section explores the applications, benefits and challenges of generative AI in marketing content creation, illustrated through real-world examples and case studies.

Key concepts

Before analysing applications, it is essential to define core concepts underpinning AI-driven content creation.

- **Generative AI:** A class of AI techniques that create new data – such as text, images, audio or video – based on training data. LLMs (e.g. GPT-4) specialize in text generation, while GANs generate visual and multimedia content (Goodfellow et al, 2014).

- **Content automation:** The process of automating repetitive or large-scale content creation tasks, such as generating product descriptions or campaign variations (Chatterjee et al, 2023).

- **Personalization:** Tailoring content to individual consumer preferences, contexts or behaviours, often powered by customer data and machine learning (Wedel and Kannan, 2016).

- **Dynamic content:** Content that adapts in real time to user behaviour, device or environment, often employed in websites, recommendation systems and email marketing (Rust, 2020).

- **Conversational AI:** AI-powered systems that simulate human dialogue, such as chatbots and virtual assistants, enabling interactive customer engagement (Grewal et al, 2020).

These concepts provide the theoretical foundation for understanding how AI integrates into content strategies.

Applications of generative AI in content creation

Blog posts and articles

Generative AI can draft long-form content, including blog articles, white papers and reports. AI-driven tools (e.g. Jasper, Writesonic) help marketers generate keyword-optimized content for search engine optimization (SEO).

- **Efficiency:** Reduces drafting time for routine topics.
- **Scalability:** Enables brands to publish more frequently across niches.
- **Challenges:** Risks of generic tone, factual inaccuracies or lack of originality (Zhang et al, 2023).

Social media content

Social media requires high-volume, short-form content that resonates with diverse audiences. AI can generate:

- caption variations for A/B testing

- hashtag suggestions to improve discoverability
- image and video generation (e.g. Canva AI, DALL·E).

This enhances engagement and allows brands to adapt content to emerging cultural trends in real time. However, overuse may dilute authentic brand voice (Kaplan and Haenlein, 2020).

Email marketing campaigns

Generative AI enables personalized email campaigns at scale. By analysing customer data, AI can craft subject lines, calls-to-action and dynamic body text.

- **Improved open rates**: AI-optimized subject lines increase engagement (Chatterjee et al, 2023).
- **Personalization**: AI tailors messages to customer segments.
- **Automation**: Enables trigger-based campaigns (e.g. cart abandonment reminders).

Ad copywriting

Advertising copy is a critical driver of click-through rates (CTR). Generative AI assists marketers by producing copy variants tailored to different audiences. Tools like Persado use natural language generation (NLG) to craft emotionally resonant ad content (Grewal et al, 2020).

Product descriptions

E-commerce platforms rely heavily on product descriptions to influence purchase decisions. AI tools can automatically generate thousands of descriptions, tailored for SEO and personalization.

- Amazon uses AI to standardize and localize product descriptions (Bughin et al, 2019).
- Fashion retailers apply AI to match tone with brand identity, ensuring alignment with customer expectations.

Customer segmentation and personalization

Generative AI integrates with customer data platforms (CDPs) to segment audiences and offer personalized recommendations. By analysing historical behaviour, AI suggests content variations likely to resonate with each segment (Wedel and Kannan, 2016).

Chatbots and virtual assistants

Conversational AI enables real-time engagement, improving customer service efficiency. Examples include:

- **Chatbots**: Automating FAQs and transactional queries.

- **Virtual assistants:** Providing guided shopping or personalized advice.
- **Sentiment analysis:** Detecting customer emotions to adjust responses (Shin, 2021).

These tools create seamless omnichannel experiences but require transparency to avoid consumer distrust.

REAL-WORLD EXAMPLES   Cases

Coca-Cola's generative AI campaign

Coca-Cola has been one of the most prominent adopters of generative AI in content creation. In 2023, the company launched the 'Create Real Magic' campaign, inviting consumers to co-create branded art using OpenAI's DALL·E and GPT models.

- **Application**: Consumers generated personalized Coca-Cola artwork, which was shared on social media and digital billboards.
- **Outcome**: The campaign increased brand engagement by fostering co-creation and interactivity (McKinsey, 2023).
- **Ethical Considerations**: Coca-Cola implemented disclosure measures, clarifying AI involvement in content generation.

This case highlights how generative AI can serve as both a marketing tool and a customer engagement platform, reinforcing authenticity through co-creation rather than replacing it.

Case 2: Nike's AI-powered personalization

Nike leverages generative AI for storytelling in its digital campaigns, customizing content (videos, training suggestions, social posts) to individual customer fitness journeys. This hybrid model of AI plus athlete ambassadors strengthens authenticity (Dwivedi et al, 2023).

Case 3: Sephora's chatbots and AR

Sephora's chatbot integrates with generative AI to simulate personalized beauty advice. The Sephora Virtual Artist combines AI content generation with AR to allow consumers to 'try before they buy' (Grewal et al, 2020).

Case 4: Netflix and Spotify as personalization leaders

Netflix personalizes movie titles, thumbnails and descriptions through generative AI, while Spotify's 'Wrapped' campaign personalizes year-end narratives. These reinforce CX differentiation through creative co-creation.

Practical considerations

While generative AI enhances efficiency, it requires careful governance:

- **Bias management** (Bender et al, 2021).
- **Transparency in AI-human collaboration** (Shin, 2021).
- **Copyright compliance** (Gervais, 2020).
- **Balancing automation and authenticity** (Kaplan and Haenlein, 2020).

Firms must embed generative AI within responsible marketing strategies, ensuring that automation complements rather than replaces human creativity.

EXERCISES

Exercise 1: Designing a generative AI-enhanced marketing campaign

Objective: To develop practical skills in integrating generative AI into content creation.

1 Select a brand of your choice (e.g. Nike, Spotify, Starbucks).
2 Using AI tools (e.g. ChatGPT, Canva AI), generate the following content:
   o a personalized **email campaign**
   o at least three **social media posts** tailored for different platforms (Instagram, LinkedIn, Twitter/X)
   o a **product description** optimized for SEO
   o a **chatbot script** for customer service interaction.
3 Critically evaluate the AI-generated content:
   o Does it align with brand voice?
   o What ethical risks are present?
   o How can human creativity enhance the outputs?
4 Present findings in a short report (1,000 words), including screenshots of generated content.

Exercise 2: Bias testing in AI-generated content

1 Use an AI tool to generate product descriptions for luxury fashion.
2 Analyse whether outputs show **gender**, **cultural** or **class biases**.
3 Redraft to make content more inclusive.

Learning outcome: To recognize risks of bias and apply corrective editing.

Exercise 3: Comparative case analysis

Compare two brands (e.g. Nike and Adidas) in their adoption of generative AI. Evaluate:

- o strategic fit
- o customer experience impact
- o ethical governance.

Learning outcome: To gain hands-on experience in AI-assisted content creation and critically assess its benefits and limitations.

Generative AI has fundamentally altered content creation in marketing, enabling hyper-personalization, scalability and real-time engagement across multiple channels. Applications span blogs, social media, emails, ads, product descriptions, personalization engines and chatbots, each offering measurable efficiencies.

However, the technology also presents risks: biases embedded in training data, lack of transparency in customer interactions, unresolved copyright disputes and the erosion of authentic brand storytelling. The most successful cases – Coca-Cola, Nike, Sephora, Netflix, Spotify – illustrate that AI works best when it complements rather than replaces human creativity.

Future trajectories suggest:

- greater integration with **predictive analytics** for proactive personalization
- stronger **regulatory frameworks** (EU AI Act)
- movement towards **AI–human co-creation models**, where consumers co-design content alongside AI.

Thus, the competitive advantage of generative AI lies not in automation alone but in **responsible, creative** and **ethical integration into brand strategies**.

11.3 Personalization and customer experience with generative AI

In the digital age, personalization has emerged as a cornerstone of effective marketing and customer experience (CX) strategy. Consumers increasingly expect brands to recognize their preferences, anticipate their needs and deliver seamless interactions across touchpoints (Lemon and Verhoef, 2016). Traditional segmentation methods based on demographics have given way to AI-driven personalization, which leverages vast datasets and predictive models to deliver real-time, individualized content (Wedel and Kannan, 2016).

Generative AI enhances this evolution by enabling not only recommendations and targeting but also the creation of tailored content – emails, product descriptions, ads and conversational interactions – at scale (Chatterjee et al, 2023). This section explores the role of generative AI in personalization and CX, structured around AI-driven segmentation, predictive analytics and real-time targeting, before applying established marketing frameworks (5A, RACE, AIDA) to illustrate practical implementations.

Key concepts

Table 11.1   Key concepts relevant to AI personalization

Concept	Definition	Relevance to AI personalization
Customer experience (CX)	The sum of interactions a customer has with a brand across the journey (Lemon and Verhoef, 2016)	Generative AI enhances CX via personalized content and conversational AI
AI-driven segmentation	Using machine learning to cluster customers based on behaviours, preferences and predictive signals	Enables micro-segmentation beyond demographics
Predictive analytics	Use of historical and real-time data to forecast customer behaviour (Wedel and Kannan, 2016)	Allows proactive targeting and personalization
Real-time targeting	Delivering tailored messages instantly based on current context (Rust, 2020)	Improves relevance and engagement
Generative AI in CX	Use of LLMs, GANs and deep learning to create adaptive content	Powers personalized recommendations, dialogue and storytelling

Applications of generative AI in personalization and CX

AI-driven segmentation

Traditional segmentation divides markets by demographics, psychographics or geography. However, digital environments demand granular, dynamic segmentation based on real-time data and behavioural signals (Wedel and Kannan, 2016).

Generative AI facilitates micro-segmentation by analysing clickstream data, purchase histories and social media behaviours to cluster consumers with similar predictive patterns. For example:

- **Retailers**: Use clustering algorithms to group shoppers by likelihood of conversion.
- **Streaming platforms**: Segment audiences by genre preferences, time of engagement and device usage.

KEY CONCEPT

Hyper-personalization refers to tailoring content at the individual level, leveraging AI and data to move beyond segment averages (Kaplan and Haenlein, 2020).

Predictive analytics and real-time targeting

Predictive analytics enables marketers to forecast consumer behaviour (e.g. churn risk, purchase intent) and deploy interventions. Real-time targeting ensures that messages are sent at the optimal moment and context.

- E-commerce: Generative AI predicts cart abandonment and triggers personalized recovery emails.
- Banking: AI anticipates customer service needs and provides proactive chatbot assistance.
- Hospitality: Hotels use AI to push dynamic offers based on browsing patterns and location data.

Real-time personalization has been shown to significantly improve conversion rates and customer satisfaction (Rust, 2020).

Frameworks for implementing generative AI in marketing

To understand how personalization and CX strategies can be structured, it is useful to integrate generative AI applications into established marketing frameworks.

The 5A framework (Kotler et al, 2017)

1 **Aware** – AI enables targeted brand discovery through personalized ad placements and SEO-optimized AI-generated content.

2 **Appeal** – generative AI crafts emotionally resonant campaigns aligned with customer values. Example: Coca-Cola's AI co-creation campaigns.

3 **Ask** – conversational AI chatbots answer customer queries instantly, providing informational transparency.

4 **Act** – predictive analytics nudges consumers towards purchase with personalized offers.

5 **Advocate** – AI monitors sentiment and encourages user-generated content (UGC), enhancing advocacy loops.

The RACE framework (Chaffey and Ellis-Chadwick, 2019)

1 **Reach** – generative AI creates personalized ad copy across channels.

2 **Act** – AI-driven segmentation tailors landing page content dynamically.

3 **Convert** – predictive targeting optimizes checkout offers (e.g. discounts for high-intent users).

4 **Engage** – AI-powered recommendation engines sustain customer relationships through continuous personalization.

The AIDA model (Strong, 1925)

- **Attention** – AI-generated visuals and copy grab user attention (GAN-based creatives).
- **Interest** – personalized product recommendations sustain interest.
- **Desire** – predictive analytics identifies cross-selling opportunities to heighten desire.
- **Action** – real-time targeting ensures customers receive timely prompts to act (e.g. push notifications).

Figure 11.4 illustrates how generative AI applications – AI-driven segmentation, predictive analytics and real-time targeting – integrate with established marketing frameworks (5A, RACE and AIDA) to enhance customer experience (CX). By aligning AI capabilities with customer journey frameworks, firms can systematically deliver personalized content, improve engagement and foster loyalty and advocacy.

Figure 11.4   Conceptual model of generative AI in personalization and customer experience

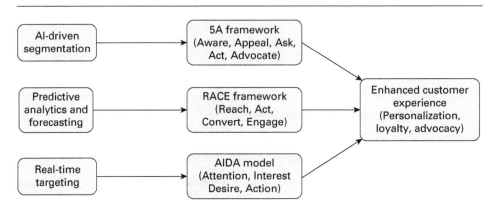

- Left side (applications):
  - ○ **AI-driven segmentation**: Groups customers into dynamic clusters beyond demographics.
  - ○ **Predictive analytics**: Forecasts customer behaviour and future needs.
  - ○ **Real-time targeting**: Delivers content instantly at the right moment.
- Middle (frameworks):
  - ○ **5A framework** (Aware, Appeal, Ask, Act, Advocate) shows how AI personalizes each stage of the journey.
  - ○ **RACE framework** (Reach, Act, Convert, Engage) links personalization to digital campaign management.
  - ○ **AIDA model** (Attention, Interest, Desire, Action) illustrates AI's role in persuasion.
- Right side (outcome):
  - ○ The result is **enhanced customer experience (CX)** through personalization, loyalty and advocacy.

REAL-WORLD EXAMPLES   Netflix and Amazon

Netflix – personalized entertainment experiences

- **Segmentation**: Netflix employs machine learning and generative AI to segment viewers based on micro-behaviours (e.g. watch duration, skips, rewinds).

- **Predictive analytics**: AI forecasts which shows users will enjoy, powering its recommendation engine.
- **CX outcome**: 75–80 per cent of viewing is driven by personalized recommendations (McKinsey, 2023).

Amazon – dynamic personalization in e-commerce

- **Segmentation**: Customer purchase and browsing histories feed into personalized storefronts.
- **Predictive analytics**: Anticipates purchase intent and suggests complementary products.
- **Real-time targeting**: Pushes personalized offers, reminders and email triggers.
- **CX outcome**: Amazon attributes significant revenue uplift to AI-driven personalization (Bughin et al, 2019)

Practical and ethical considerations

- Bias in segmentation: Risk of exclusionary practices (Bender et al, 2021).
- Privacy concerns: Real-time targeting relies on sensitive behavioural data (Floridi and Cowls, 2019).
- Transparency: Need to disclose AI personalization to maintain trust (Shin, 2021).
- Over-personalization: Excessive targeting may feel invasive ('creepy marketing effect') (Aguirre et al, 2015).

EXERCISES

Exercise 1: AI-powered segmentation simulation

- **Task**: Using sample datasets (e.g. retail transactions), apply clustering techniques to create AI-driven customer segments.
- **Deliverable**: Identify three segment types and design one personalized campaign per segment.

Exercise 2: Real-time targeting campaign

- **Task**: Choose a brand (e.g. Nike, Starbucks). Design a predictive targeting campaign using generative AI tools (e.g. ChatGPT for copy, Canva AI for visuals).
- **Deliverable**: Campaign outline showing awareness, personalization touchpoints and conversion triggers.

Exercise 3: Framework application

- **Task**: Apply the 5A, RACE and AIDA models to analyse how Netflix or Amazon uses generative AI in personalization.
- **Deliverable**: Comparative report (1,000 words).

Generative AI enables AI-driven segmentation, predictive analytics and real-time targeting, reshaping personalization and CX strategies. By embedding AI into 5A, RACE and AIDA frameworks, marketers can systematically apply personalization across the customer journey.

Case studies from Netflix and Amazon highlight how personalization drives engagement, loyalty and revenue. However, ethical challenges – including bias, privacy, transparency and over-personalization – require responsible AI governance.

Future developments point towards hyper-personalization ecosystems, where AI continuously adapts CX based on real-time signals, co-created with consumers. Firms that balance AI efficiency with authenticity and ethical responsibility will secure sustainable competitive advantage.

11.4 Theories and frameworks supporting generative AI in marketing

The integration of generative artificial intelligence (AI) into marketing practice is transforming how brands design, deliver and personalize content. While much of the focus has been on technological affordances, the strategic application of AI requires grounding in established theories and frameworks. Cognitive psychology, communication theory and consumer behaviour models provide critical insights into how AI-generated content influences perception, engagement and decision-making.

This section explores three key theories – **cognitive load theory, elaboration likelihood model (ELM)** and **uses and gratifications theory** – and three frameworks – **customer journey mapping**, the **personalization matrix** and **AI ethics frameworks**. Together, these perspectives help marketers design AI-driven strategies that balance efficiency, personalization and ethical responsibility.

Theories supporting generative AI in marketing

Cognitive load theory (Sweller, 1988)

Definition: Cognitive load theory (CLT) posits that human working memory has a limited capacity. Excessive or poorly structured information creates cognitive overload, impairing learning and decision-making (Sweller, 1988).

Relevance to generative AI in marketing:

- Generative AI reduces cognitive complexity by presenting information in structured, simplified formats (e.g. personalized product summaries).

- AI chatbots can filter and tailor information to avoid overwhelming consumers with irrelevant details.

- For e-commerce, AI-generated descriptions and recommendations help reduce choice overload, increasing decision efficiency.

Example: Amazon's AI-powered recommendation engine simplifies shopping by narrowing thousands of product options into personalized shortlists, reducing consumer effort (Bughin et al, 2019).

KEY CONCEPT

By aligning with CLT, generative AI enhances decision-making through clarity, relevance and simplicity, particularly in environments with information abundance.

Elaboration likelihood model (ELM) (Petty and Cacioppo, 1986)

Definition: The elaboration likelihood model (ELM) explains persuasion via two routes:

1 **Central route:** Consumers engage in deep, rational evaluation of information.

2 **Peripheral route:** Consumers rely on superficial cues (e.g. visuals, tone, credibility).

Relevance to generative AI in marketing:

- Generative AI allows marketers to target both routes simultaneously.

- Central route personalization: AI crafts in-depth product comparisons, data-driven blogs or educational content for high-involvement decisions.

- Peripheral route personalization: AI generates catchy social media captions, emotional imagery or humour-driven ads.

Example: Nike uses AI to personalize content differently for high-involvement customers (e.g. product performance data for athletes) versus casual buyers (visual storytelling on Instagram).

KEY CONCEPT

Generative AI enhances message tailoring across persuasion routes, increasing conversion effectiveness.

Uses and gratifications theory (Katz et al, 1973)

Definition: Uses and gratifications theory (UGT) suggests that audiences actively choose media to satisfy psychological and social needs, including information, entertainment, personal identity and social integration (Katz et al, 1973).

Relevance to generative AI in marketing:

- Generative AI allows brands to align content with consumer motives:
  - **Information:** AI-powered blogs and Q&A chatbots.
  - **Entertainment:** AI-generated interactive campaigns (e.g. Coca-Cola 'Real Magic').
  - **Identity:** Personalized Spotify Wrapped experiences.
  - **Social integration:** AI-driven community engagement on platforms like TikTok.

Example: Spotify's Wrapped campaign leverages AI personalization to satisfy users' need for identity expression and social sharing, resulting in viral global engagement (Dwivedi et al, 2023).

KEY CONCEPT

Generative AI supports UGT by enabling interactive, engaging and need-fulfilling experiences.

Frameworks for implementing generative AI in marketing

Customer journey mapping (Lemon and Verhoef, 2016)

Customer journey mapping (CJM) visualizes all touchpoints between a consumer and brand across pre-purchase, purchase and post-purchase stages.

Application of generative AI:

- **Pre-purchase**: Personalized ads, AI-generated blog content and targeted awareness campaigns.
- **Purchase**: Dynamic product descriptions, chatbot guidance and predictive pricing.
- **Post-purchase**: AI-powered loyalty emails, sentiment analysis and automated customer support.

Example: Sephora uses AI chatbots during purchase (Virtual Artist) and AI-generated follow-up emails post-purchase, ensuring seamless CX.

Personalization matrix (Wedel and Kannan, 2016)

The personalization matrix categorizes personalization along two dimensions:

- Content-based vs collaborative filtering.
- Static vs dynamic personalization.

Generative AI enhances all quadrants:

- **Static content-based**: Automated email greetings.
- **Dynamic content-based**: Real-time personalized recommendations.
- **Static collaborative**: Segment-based product offers.
- **Dynamic collaborative**: Streaming platforms predicting preferences (e.g. Netflix).

Brand example: Netflix exemplifies the dynamic collaborative quadrant, where AI generates unique thumbnails and copy per user (McKinsey, 2023).

AI ethics frameworks (Floridi and Cowls, 2019; EU AI Act, 2021)

Responsible adoption of AI in marketing requires adherence to ethical frameworks. **Key principles** (Floridi and Cowls, 2019):

- **Beneficence** – AI should enhance well-being.
- **Non-maleficence** – avoid harm (bias, misinformation).
- **Autonomy** – respect consumer agency.
- **Justice** – ensure fairness and inclusion.
- **Explicability** – transparency and accountability.

Application in marketing:

- Transparency in AI-generated customer service responses.
- Monitoring bias in AI-driven segmentation.
- Disclosing AI involvement in content creation.

Example: Unilever has adopted AI ethical guidelines ensuring transparency in chatbots and data-driven campaigns.

REAL-WORLD EXAMPLE   Coca-Cola 'Create Real Magic'

Coca-Cola's 2023 'Create Real Magic' campaign illustrates the convergence of theories and frameworks:

- **Cognitive load theory**: Simplified participation via user-friendly AI platforms.
- **ELM**: Engaged both central (AI creative process) and peripheral (visual appeal) routes.
- **UGT**: Fulfilled needs for entertainment, identity expression and social sharing.
- **Customer journey mapping**: Engaged consumers across pre-purchase (awareness via ads), purchase (in-store displays) and post-purchase (UGC advocacy).
- **Personalization matrix**: Allowed dynamic, user-generated personalization.
- **AI ethics framework**: Ensured disclosure that AI was used in content creation.

The campaign resulted in millions of social impressions and positioned Coca-Cola as a leader in AI-driven consumer co-creation (McKinsey, 2023).

EXERCISES

Exercise 1: Theory-driven campaign design

- **Task**: Design a generative AI marketing campaign applying CLT, ELM and UGT.
- **Deliverable**: 1,000-word campaign plan showing how AI personalization reduces cognitive load, tailors persuasion and fulfils user gratifications.

Exercise 2: Customer journey mapping with AI

- **Task**: Map a customer journey for a chosen brand (e.g. Nike, Sephora). Identify at least three points where generative AI enhances CX.
- **Deliverable**: A visual journey map with explanatory notes.

Exercise 3: AI ethics audit

- **Task**: Evaluate an AI-powered brand campaign against Floridi and Cowls' ethical principles.
- **Deliverable**: 1,000-word critical essay assessing ethical strengths and risks.

The integration of generative AI into marketing is best understood through the lens of supporting theories and frameworks. Cognitive load theory explains how AI reduces complexity, ELM highlights how AI tailors persuasion routes and UGT emphasizes how AI fulfils consumer needs for information, identity and entertainment.

Frameworks such as customer journey mapping, the personalization matrix and AI ethics frameworks provide practical tools for systematically embedding AI into marketing strategies. Real brand applications, such as Coca-Cola's 'Create Real Magic', Netflix's dynamic personalization and Sephora's chatbot experiences, illustrate the value of theory-informed AI strategies.

Ultimately, generative AI in marketing succeeds when it balances efficiency, personalization and ethics, creating customer experiences that are not only engaging and effective but also trustworthy and inclusive.

The conceptual framework diagram (Figure 11.5) shows how:

- Theories (CLT, ELM, UGT) provide psychological and communication foundations.
- These theories feed into frameworks (customer journey mapping, personalization matrix, AI ethics).
- The frameworks collectively enable AI-powered customer experiences (personalization, trust, loyalty, advocacy).

This framework illustrates how theories – **cognitive load theory (CLT)**, **elaboration likelihood model (ELM)**, and **uses and gratifications theory (UGT)** – inform

Figure 11.5   Theories and frameworks supporting generative AI in marketing

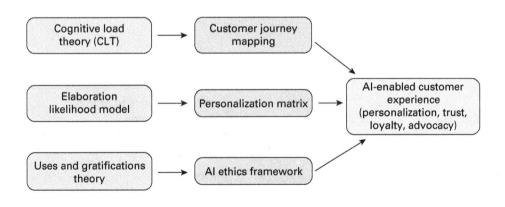

the design of frameworks such as **customer journey mapping**, the **personalization matrix**, and **AI ethics frameworks**. Together, these guide the responsible implementation of generative AI to create AI-enabled customer experiences characterized by personalization, trust, loyalty and advocacy.

11.5 Integrating generative AI into the marketing funnel

The marketing funnel is one of the most enduring models in marketing strategy, illustrating how consumers move from awareness of a brand to advocacy and loyalty. Traditionally conceptualized as a linear pathway – **Awareness** → **Interest** → **Consideration** → **Conversion** → **Retention** → **Advocacy** – it has evolved into a more dynamic, multi-touch process in the digital era (Kotler et al, 2017; Lemon and Verhoef, 2016).

The rise of generative artificial intelligence (AI) has accelerated this transformation. By leveraging large language models (LLMs), generative adversarial networks (GANs) and reinforcement learning, brands can create personalized, scalable and context-aware marketing interventions at each funnel stage. Generative AI not only automates tasks (e.g. content production) but also augments strategic decision-making by predicting consumer behaviour, tailoring content and optimizing real-time targeting (Chatterjee et al, 2023).

This section examines how generative AI integrates across the marketing funnel, supported by key concepts, real-world brand applications and critical reflections on opportunities and risks.

Key concepts

Table 11.2   Key concepts and relevance to funnel integration

Concept	Definition	Relevance to funnel integration
Marketing funnel	Model illustrating stages of customer journey from awareness to advocacy (Kotler et al, 2017)	Provides structure for AI-enabled interventions
Generative AI	AI that creates novel outputs (text, images, audio, video) using machine learning (Goodfellow et al, 2014)	Powers personalized content and targeting

(continued)

Table 11.2 (Continued)

Concept	Definition	Relevance to funnel integration
Personalization	Tailoring messages/content to individual consumers based on data-driven insights (Wedel and Kannan, 2016)	Enhances engagement at each funnel stage
Predictive analytics	AI-driven forecasting of customer behaviours such as churn or purchase intent (Rust, 2020)	Supports targeting and conversion strategies
Customer experience (CX)	The sum of interactions shaping consumer perceptions of a brand (Lemon and Verhoef, 2016)	AI enhances CX through seamless, real-time personalization
Conversational AI	Chatbots and virtual assistants simulating human dialogue (Grewal et al, 2020)	Engages consumers in consideration and retention stages

Generative AI in the marketing funnel

Awareness stage

Goal: The awareness stage represents the top of the marketing funnel, where the primary objective is to capture consumer attention, build recognition and establish initial brand visibility (Kotler et al, 2017). At this stage, consumers are not yet considering purchase decisions; rather, they are being introduced to the brand and forming early impressions. In the digital age, characterized by content saturation and short attention spans, awareness generation requires both creativity and personalization to stand out. Generative AI offers novel solutions by automating content creation, enhancing targeting precision and producing unique designs that resonate with diverse audiences.

Generative AI applications:

1 **Content generation:** Generative AI models such as GPT-4 can create SEO-optimized blogs, social media posts and video scripts tailored to audience preferences. By analysing trending keywords and consumer interests, AI ensures that content is discoverable in search engines and appealing across social platforms (Chatterjee et al, 2023).

   o **Example:** A retail brand can deploy AI to generate multiple blog posts around seasonal fashion trends, each optimized for different geographies and demographics. This allows the brand to increase organic visibility while reducing manual content creation costs.

- Theoretical link: Cognitive load theory (Sweller, 1988) supports this application by showing how well-structured AI-generated summaries and bite-sized content reduce the mental effort required for consumers to process information.

2 **Hyper-targeted advertising:** One of the most significant advantages of generative AI is the ability to produce hundreds of ad variants simultaneously, each personalized for a micro-segment. AI systems analyse consumer data (e.g. browsing history, demographic profiles and behavioural signals) to craft ad copy and visuals that are highly relevant to each audience cluster (Wedel and Kannan, 2016).

- Example: An e-commerce platform can deploy AI to generate distinct ad creatives for eco-conscious shoppers versus high-spending premium buyers, thus improving click-through rates and engagement.
- Theoretical link: The elaboration likelihood model (Petty and Cacioppo, 1986) suggests that consumers persuaded via the peripheral route (e.g. visual appeal, relatable tone) may engage more readily with targeted ads than with generic campaigns.

3 **AI-powered creative design:** Generative adversarial networks (GANs) allow brands to develop unique, visually compelling campaign materials that break through the clutter. Unlike stock imagery, GAN-generated visuals can be designed to reflect the brand identity, audience values or campaign themes (Goodfellow et al, 2014).

- Example: Fashion brands can generate AI-driven lookbooks and campaign visuals that align with current aesthetic trends, providing a competitive edge in visual storytelling.
- Theoretical link: Uses and gratifications theory (Katz et al, 1973) highlights that consumers often engage with brand content for entertainment and identity reinforcement; AI-generated creative assets directly support these gratifications by offering novelty and personalization.

REAL-WORLD EXAMPLE   Coca-Cola

Coca-Cola's 'Create Real Magic' campaign (2023) provides a vivid example of generative AI in the awareness stage. Partnering with OpenAI and Bain & Company, Coca-Cola enabled consumers to co-create branded visuals using DALL·E (image generation) and GPT (copywriting) tools. Participants were invited to submit their AI-generated artwork, which was then showcased on billboards in New York's Times Square and London's Piccadilly Circus.

Impact

- The campaign achieved millions of impressions on social media, with user-generated content fuelling further reach.
- Coca-Cola positioned itself as a pioneer of AI creativity, reinforcing its reputation for innovation and consumer engagement.
- By merging co-creation and personalization, the campaign aligned with UGT principles, satisfying consumers' needs for entertainment, identity expression and social sharing (Dwivedi et al, 2023).

Generative AI at the awareness stage allows brands to scale content without compromising personalization. However, risks include over-automation (leading to generic or repetitive messaging) and ethical concerns around transparency (consumers may be unaware that content was AI-generated). The most effective use of AI in this stage involves human–AI collaboration, where marketers use AI for scale and optimization while ensuring creativity, brand voice and authenticity remain intact.

Interest stage

Goal: The interest stage is where consumers begin to engage more deeply with brand offerings after initial exposure. The objective is to spark curiosity, sustain attention and create emotional connections that motivate consumers to seek further information (Kotler et al, 2017).

Generative AI applications:

1 **Personalized email campaigns**: AI-driven tools craft subject lines, body text and calls-to-action (CTAs) tailored to specific consumer segments. By analysing browsing history, purchase behaviour, and engagement metrics, AI generates emails that resonate on a personal level.

   ○ **Example:** A fitness brand can generate distinct email campaigns for athletes versus casual gym-goers, optimizing open and click-through rates.

   ○ **Theory link:** Cognitive load theory (Sweller, 1988) supports AI's role in simplifying communication, ensuring relevance without overwhelming recipients.

2 **Dynamic social media posts**: Generative AI tools adapt captions, hashtags and imagery in real time, based on audience demographics, cultural trends or platform dynamics. This ensures maximum engagement and cultural resonance.

   ○ **Example:** AI might create multiple TikTok captions tailored for humour-driven Gen Z audiences versus an aspirational tone for millennials.

   ○ **Theory link:** The elaboration likelihood model (Petty and Cacioppo, 1986) highlights that engaging visuals and emotionally resonant posts act as peripheral cues, driving audience interest.

3 Conversational content: Chatbots and AI-powered assistants offer interactive dialogue with users, addressing FAQs and product queries. This two-way engagement builds trust and fosters further exploration.

   o **Example:** A fashion retailer's chatbot can recommend outfits and instantly answer style-related queries.

   o **Theory link:** Uses and gratifications theory (Katz et al, 1973) shows that conversational content satisfies consumer needs for information and interactivity.

REAL-WORLD EXAMPLE   Nike

Nike employs AI for personalized social storytelling, tailoring Instagram and TikTok posts to reflect individual fitness goals. For example, AI-generated workout tips and motivational captions align with consumer aspirations, deepening emotional connections (Dwivedi et al, 2023).

Critical insight

Generative AI amplifies consumer interest by blending personal relevance with interactivity. However, over-targeting may feel intrusive, leading to the 'creepy marketing' effect (Aguirre et al, 2015).

Consideration stage

Goal: The consideration stage focuses on influencing evaluation and moving customers closer to purchase decisions. Consumers compare options, assess brand credibility and seek reassurance.

   Generative AI applications:

1 AI-generated product comparisons: LLMs produce side-by-side comparisons, highlighting unique selling propositions (USPs) for different products. This helps simplify decision-making and reduce choice overload.

2 Recommendation systems: Generative AI analyses behavioural data to suggest relevant products, dynamically adapting to browsing context.

   o **Example:** Streaming services suggest new shows based on recent viewing patterns.

3 Customer support chatbots: AI-powered assistants answer pre-purchase queries in real time, reducing friction. They can simulate personalized advice traditionally given by in-store representatives.

Theory link: The ELM's central route processing applies here, as consumers seek rational, detailed information before committing (Petty and Cacioppo, 1986).

REAL-WORLD EXAMPLE   Sephora

The Sephora Virtual Artist chatbot combines AI recommendations with AR simulations, allowing users to try on cosmetics virtually. This reduces uncertainty and increases confidence in purchase decisions (Grewal et al, 2020).

Critical insight

Generative AI reduces barriers in consideration, but reliance on AI must not obscure transparency – consumers should be aware they are interacting with AI (Shin, 2021).

Conversion stage

Goal: The conversion stage aims to secure transactions and maximize purchase value. Here, personalization directly influences buying decisions.

Generative AI applications:

1 **Predictive targeting:** AI forecasts purchase intent and delivers timely offers such as discounts or product bundles.

   ○ **Example:** Cart abandonment triggers emails with tailored incentives.

2 **Dynamic pricing models:** Generative AI supports personalized discounts based on real-time demand and customer history.

3 **Optimized checkout experience:** AI-generated nudges such as 'Only two items left in stock' or '10 other shoppers are viewing this product' create urgency.

Theory link: Persuasive triggers align with UGT's gratification of reassurance and efficiency, encouraging decisive action (Katz et al, 1973).

REAL-WORLD EXAMPLE   Amazon

Amazon integrates AI in its recommendation engine to propose complementary products, bundles and personalized promotions, significantly enhancing conversion rates (Bughin et al, 2019).

Critical insight

AI-driven nudges enhance conversion efficiency but raise ethical concerns around manipulation (Floridi and Cowls, 2019). Transparency in how recommendations are generated is essential.

Retention stage

Goal: Retention focuses on building long-term relationships and encouraging repeat purchases, ensuring the lifetime value (LTV) of customers.

Generative AI applications:

1 **Personalized loyalty emails:** AI crafts individualized thank-you messages, birthday rewards or tailored loyalty programme updates.

2 **Sentiment analysis:** AI monitors reviews, surveys and social mentions to gauge customer satisfaction and identify potential churn.

3 **Content automation:** Post-purchase tutorials, how-to blogs or personalized guides keep customers engaged with products.

Theory link: CLT highlights that simplified, timely guidance reduces customer effort and enhances satisfaction (Sweller, 1988).

REAL-WORLD EXAMPLE   Netflix

Netflix applies AI to personalize post-subscription experiences, generating tailored movie thumbnails, show descriptions and recommendations that sustain engagement.

Approximately 75–80 per cent of viewing activity is AI-driven (Kieser et al, 2023).

Critical insight

Generative AI fosters retention by continuously tailoring engagement. However, excessive personalization risks narrowing consumer choice ('filter bubbles'), potentially reducing discovery and variety (Zhang et al, 2023a).

Advocacy stage

Goal: The advocacy stage converts loyal customers into brand ambassadors, encouraging them to promote the brand through word-of-mouth and social sharing.

Generative AI applications:

1 **UGC co-creation:** AI tools empower consumers to generate branded content (e.g. custom designs, music playlists).

2 **Personalized sharing campaigns:** Campaigns like Spotify Wrapped encourage viral engagement by personalizing experiences for social sharing.

3 **AI-driven sentiment analysis:** AI identifies potential brand advocates by analysing positive reviews and high engagement patterns, enabling targeted ambassador programmes.

Theory link: UGT shows that advocacy satisfies the need for identity expression and social integration (Katz et al, 1973).

REAL-WORLD EXAMPLE   Spotify

The Spotify Wrapped campaign uses generative AI to create personalized listening narratives, which users eagerly share across social platforms. The campaign has become a global cultural phenomenon, driving advocacy and reinforcing Spotify's market leadership (Dwivedi et al, 2023).

Critical insight

AI amplifies advocacy by fuelling co-creation and social engagement. Yet, marketers must safeguard authenticity, as overly engineered campaigns risk being perceived as manipulative rather than genuine.

This framework illustrates how generative AI applications align with each funnel stage (Figure 11.6). At the awareness stage, AI generates ads and branded content (e.g. Coca-Cola). During interest and consideration, AI delivers personalized emails,

Figure 11.6   Generative AI integration in the marketing funnel

Awareness
AI-generated ads, blogs, creative visuals
(e.g. CoCa-Cola 'Create Real Magic')

Interest
Personalized emails, social media posts,
chatbots for product queries
(e.g. Nike personalization)

Consideration
Product comparisons, recommendations,
virtual assistants (e.g. Sephora Virtual Artist)

Conversion
Predictive targeting, dynamic pricing,
checkout nudges (e.g. Amazon)

Retention
Loyalty emails, tutorials,
sentiment analysis
(e.g. Netflix personalization)

Advocacy
UGC co-creation, viral
sharing campaigns
(e.g. Spotify Wrapped)

social media posts and chatbots (e.g. Nike, Sephora). At conversion, predictive targeting and dynamic pricing drive purchase (e.g. Amazon). Retention is supported by loyalty communications and recommendations (e.g. Netflix), while advocacy leverages AI-powered co-creation and sharing campaigns (e.g. Spotify).

Benefits of integrating generative AI into the funnel

- **Scalability**: Automates content creation across channels.
- **Personalization**: Enhances relevance at every stage.
- **Efficiency**: Reduces time and cost of campaign development.
- **CX enhancement**: Creates seamless omnichannel experiences.
- **Strategic insight**: Predictive analytics supports proactive decision-making.

Risks and ethical considerations

- **Bias in content generation**: Reinforcing stereotypes (Bender et al, 2021).
- **Transparency issues**: Lack of disclosure about AI involvement (Shin, 2021).
- **Copyright/IP concerns**: Ambiguity over ownership of AI-generated work (Gervais, 2020).
- **Authenticity risks**: Over-reliance on automation dilutes human creativity (Kaplan and Haenlein, 2020).
- **Privacy challenges**: Predictive targeting relies on sensitive behavioural data (Floridi and Cowls, 2019).

REAL-WORLD EXAMPLE   Integrating AI in the funnel – Nike

Nike has been a pioneer in integrating generative AI throughout the funnel:

- **Awareness**: AI-generated campaign visuals (e.g. AI-driven sneaker designs).
- **Interest**: Personalized storytelling across Instagram and TikTok.
- **Consideration**: AI chatbots for product advice.
- **Conversion**: Predictive analytics powering targeted discounts.
- **Retention**: Personalized training content via Nike Run Club app.
- **Advocacy**: Co-creation campaigns encouraging customers to share AI-generated sneaker art.

Nike's AI strategy demonstrates how end-to-end funnel integration drives engagement, conversions and loyalty.

EXERCISES ⬈

Exercise 1: Funnel mapping with generative AI

- **Task**: Choose a brand (e.g. Starbucks, Adidas). Map how generative AI could be used at each funnel stage.
- **Deliverable**: 1,500-word report with funnel visualization.

Exercise 2: AI ethics in the funnel

- **Task**: Evaluate potential ethical risks of AI at three funnel stages for a chosen brand.
- **Deliverable**: Short essay (1,000 words) with recommendations for governance.

Exercise 3: Campaign design workshop

- **Task**: In teams, design an AI-powered marketing campaign that integrates across the funnel. Use generative tools (e.g. ChatGPT, Canva AI).
- **Deliverable**: Campaign presentation including AI-generated examples.

Generative AI has redefined the marketing funnel, offering new tools for awareness, interest, consideration, conversion, retention and advocacy. By automating content creation, enabling personalization and supporting predictive targeting, AI provides marketers with unprecedented opportunities for scalable, customer-centric strategies.

Yet, as case studies from Coca-Cola, Nike, Sephora, Amazon, Netflix and Spotify demonstrate, AI's impact is maximized when integrated responsibly, balancing automation with creativity and ethical oversight. The future of the marketing funnel lies in AI-human collaboration, where generative AI amplifies human storytelling while respecting consumer trust, privacy and authenticity.

11.6 Ethical, legal and data governance considerations

The adoption of generative artificial intelligence (AI) in marketing raises not only opportunities for efficiency, personalization and innovation but also complex challenges around ethics, law and data governance. While organizations embrace AI for content creation, customer segmentation and predictive targeting, the risks of bias, manipulation, data breaches and regulatory non-compliance are increasingly evident (Floridi and Cowls, 2019; Dwivedi et al, 2023).

To build consumer trust and achieve sustainable competitive advantage, firms must adopt responsible AI frameworks, ensuring that generative AI deployment aligns with principles of fairness, transparency, accountability and legality (European Commission, 2021). This section explores ethical considerations, legal obligations and data governance challenges associated with generative AI in marketing, supported by key concepts, brand examples and student activities.

Ethical considerations

Algorithmic bias and fairness

Generative AI systems are trained on vast datasets that may embed historical, social or cultural biases. When applied to marketing, this can lead to discriminatory outcomes, such as reinforcing gender stereotypes in product ads or excluding minority groups from targeted campaigns (Bender et al, 2021).

- **Brand example:** In 2019, Amazon abandoned an AI recruitment tool after discovering gender bias in its algorithms (Dastin, 2018). Though not marketing-specific, the case illustrates the risk of biased AI undermining inclusivity.
- **Key insight:** Organizations must use bias audits, fairness-aware algorithms and diverse datasets to mitigate risks.

Transparency and explainability

Consumers may be unaware when they are engaging with AI-generated content, raising questions of trust and informed decision-making (Shin, 2021). Black-box AI models like LLMs present challenges in explaining how specific outcomes are generated (Doshi-Velez and Kim, 2017).

- **Brand example:** Meta (Facebook) has faced criticism for its opaque ad targeting systems, which made it difficult for users to understand why they were seeing specific ads (Mittelstadt, 2019).
- **Key insight:** Transparent disclosure (e.g. labelling AI-generated content) enhances trust and regulatory compliance.

Authenticity and over-reliance

While automation enhances efficiency, excessive reliance on generative AI risks diluting brand authenticity. Consumers may perceive AI-generated messages as generic or manipulative if not balanced with human creativity (Kaplan and Haenlein, 2020).

- **Brand example:** Coca-Cola's 'Create Real Magic' campaign (2023) succeeded because it blended human creativity and AI tools, rather than replacing human input.
- **Key insight:** AI should augment, not replace, human brand storytelling.

Manipulation and consumer autonomy

Generative AI enables hyper-personalized persuasion but risks exploiting psychological vulnerabilities. This 'dark personalization' undermines consumer autonomy and raises ethical red flags (Zarsky, 2019).

- **Key insight:** Ethical AI governance requires balancing personalization with respect for consumer agency.

Legal considerations

Data protection laws (GDPR, CCPA)

The EU General Data Protection Regulation (GDPR) and the California Consumer Privacy Act (CCPA) establish strict rules around data consent, access and erasure. Marketers using AI must ensure that data is collected and used lawfully, transparently and with explicit consent.

- **Key insight:** Violations can result in heavy fines (up to €20 million or 4 per cent of turnover under GDPR).

Intellectual property and copyright

A key challenge lies in determining ownership of AI-generated outputs. Current legal systems often deny copyright to works created solely by AI, raising questions about commercial use (Gervais, 2020; Samuelson, 2022).

- **Brand example:** Getty Images sued Stability AI in 2023 for alleged copyright infringement, arguing that its training data included copyrighted images without permission.
- **Key insight:** Firms must audit training datasets and clarify ownership of AI-generated marketing assets.

Liability and accountability

If an AI system generates misleading or harmful content, determining liability becomes complex. Should responsibility fall on the developer, deploying company or end user (Morse, 2021)?

- **Key insight:** Clear accountability frameworks are required to address consumer harm caused by AI marketing practices.

Emerging AI regulations

The EU AI Act (2021) classifies AI applications by risk levels, imposing stricter obligations on high-risk systems (e.g. credit scoring). While marketing is not deemed 'high risk,' systems involving personal profiling may face stricter oversight.

- **Key insight:** Firms must prepare for increasing global regulatory harmonization (OECD, 2021).

Data governance considerations

Data quality and integrity

AI effectiveness depends on data completeness, accuracy and representativeness. Poor data governance undermines personalization quality and increases bias risk (Wedel and Kannan, 2016).

Consent management

Consumers must provide informed consent for data collection and AI usage. Dynamic consent platforms enable users to manage preferences in real time.

Data security

Generative AI applications pose cybersecurity risks, including data leaks, adversarial attacks and synthetic identity fraud.

- **Brand example:** In 2023, Samsung banned employee use of ChatGPT after data leaks involving proprietary code (*Financial Times*, 2023).

Governance frameworks

Industry bodies such as ISO, IEEE and OECD have proposed AI governance principles emphasizing accountability, fairness and transparency. Companies are increasingly adopting AI ethics boards and third-party audits.

REAL-WORLD EXAMPLES Cases

Case 1: Unilever and responsible AI

Unilever has adopted an internal AI ethics framework ensuring transparency in data-driven campaigns. The company invests in bias testing and emphasizes human oversight, positioning itself as a leader in ethical AI branding.

Case 2: IBM Watson and data governance

IBM has pioneered AI governance platforms that monitor model transparency, bias and compliance. This supports clients in adopting responsible AI marketing systems.

Case 3: Meta and ethical controversies

Meta's opaque ad targeting practices highlight the risks of low transparency, leading to regulatory scrutiny. The company has since increased ad transparency tools, though trust remains an issue.

EXERCISES

Exercise 1: Ethical AI audit

- **Task**: Choose a recent AI marketing campaign (e.g. Coca-Cola, Nike). Evaluate its ethical dimensions using Floridi and Cowls' (2019) principles.
- **Deliverable**: 1,500-word critical report.

Exercise 2: Legal case analysis

- **Task**: Research a recent copyright or data privacy lawsuit involving AI (e.g. Getty vs Stability AI). Discuss implications for marketing.
- **Deliverable**: 1,000-word essay.

Exercise 3: Data governance workshop

- **Task**: Design a data governance framework for an e-commerce company adopting generative AI. Include rules for consent, transparency and accountability.
- **Deliverable**: Group presentation.

Generative AI in marketing offers unprecedented opportunities for personalization, efficiency and engagement. Yet its use raises profound ethical, legal and governance challenges. Addressing algorithmic bias, transparency, data privacy, intellectual property and accountability is essential for sustainable adoption.

Real-world cases – ranging from Coca-Cola's innovative campaigns to Meta's transparency controversies and Samsung's data governance measures – illustrate both the potential and pitfalls of generative AI in marketing.

Ultimately, responsible AI adoption requires integrating ethical frameworks, complying with evolving legal standards and establishing robust data governance structures. Marketers who achieve this balance will not only build consumer trust but also secure a durable competitive edge.

Ethical (bias, transparency, authenticity), legal (data protection, IP, liability) and data governance (quality, consent, security) considerations flow into →

responsible generative AI in marketing (human–AI collaboration, fairness, transparency), which leads to →

outcomes (consumer trust, loyalty, sustainable competitive advantage).

Figure 11.7 illustrates how ethical (bias, transparency, authenticity, autonomy), legal (data protection, intellectual property, liability, regulations) and data governance (quality, consent, security, oversight) considerations intersect to shape responsible generative AI in marketing. When managed effectively, these factors lead to positive outcomes, including consumer trust, brand loyalty and sustainable competitive advantage.

Figure 11.7   Framework: Ethical, legal and data governance in generative AI marketing

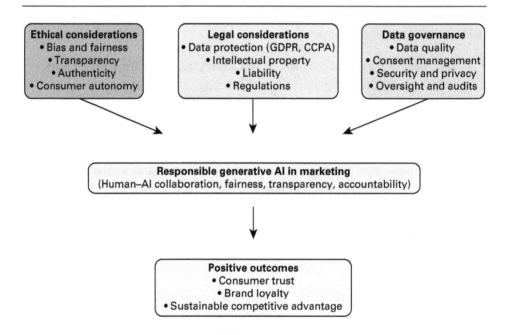

Conclusion

Generative artificial intelligence (AI) represents a transformative force in marketing, reshaping how brands conceptualize, create and deliver value to customers. Unlike traditional automation, generative AI enables scalable personalization, dynamic content creation and predictive engagement across the entire customer journey. The integration of large language models (LLMs), generative adversarial networks (GANs), and multimodal AI empowers organizations to move from static communication to hyper-personalized, interactive and co-created experiences.

Theories such as **diffusion of innovations** (Rogers, 2003), **resource-based view** (Barney, 1991), **cognitive load theory** (Sweller, 1988), **elaboration likelihood model** (Petty and Cacioppo, 1986) and **uses and gratifications** theory (Katz et al, 1973) provide critical insights into adoption, persuasion and customer engagement. Frameworks including **customer journey mapping** (Lemon and Verhoef, 2016), the **personalization matrix** (Wedel and Kannan, 2016) and **AI ethics principles** (Floridi and Cowls, 2019; EU AI Act, 2023) enable structured and responsible integration into marketing strategies.

Real-world cases – such as Coca-Cola's 'Create Real Magic' campaign, Nike's personalized storytelling, Sephora's AI-driven beauty consultations, Netflix's recommendation engine and Spotify Wrapped – illustrate the dual nature of generative AI: it is both a catalyst for engagement and a source of ethical complexity.

Alongside opportunities, risks persist: bias, lack of transparency, intellectual property concerns and over-reliance on automation may compromise authenticity and consumer trust. To achieve sustainable competitive advantage, firms must embed generative AI within robust ethical, legal and data governance frameworks.

Ultimately, generative AI should not replace human creativity but augment and amplify it. The competitive edge lies in human–AI collaboration: leveraging AI's scale and efficiency while maintaining human originality, empathy and authenticity. Marketers who balance these dimensions will build trust, foster loyalty and ensure long-term relevance in the evolving digital economy.

References

Aguirre, E, Mahr, D, Grewal, D, de Ruyter, K and Wetzels, M (2015) Unraveling the personalization paradox: The effect of information collection and trust-building strategies on online advertisement effectiveness, *Journal of Retailing*, 91 (1), 34–49

Amed, I, Berg, A, Berthelot, S, et al. (2020) How COVID-19 is changing the world of beauty. McKinsey & Company. https://www.mckinsey.com/industries/consumer-packaged-goods/our-insights/how-covid-19-is-changing-the-world-of-beauty (archived at https://perma.cc/96BS-KDPA)

Bain & Company (2023) Coca-Cola's partnership with OpenAI: Redefining creative marketing, www.bain.com (archived at https://perma.cc/A5YK-Q4KB)

Barney, J (1991) Firm resources and sustained competitive advantage, *Journal of Management*, 17 (1), 99–120

Bender, E M, Gebru, T, McMillan-Major, A and Shmitchell, S (2021) On the dangers of stochastic parrots: Can language models be too big? *Proceedings of the 2021 ACM Conference on Fairness, Accountability, and Transparency*, 610–23

Bommasani, R, Hudson, D A, Adeli, E, Altman, R, Arora, S, von Arx, S. et al (2021) On the opportunities and risks of foundation models, *arXiv preprint*, arXiv:2108.07258

Brown, T, Mann, B, Ryder, N, Subbiah, M, Kaplan, J, Dhariwal, P et al (2020) Language models are few-shot learners, *Advances in Neural Information Processing Systems*, 33, 1877–1901

Bughin, J, Seong, J, Manyika, J, Chui, M and Joshi, R (2019) *Notes from the AI Frontier: Tackling Europe's Gap in Digital and AI*, McKinsey Global Institute.

Cambria, E and White, B (2014) Jumping NLP curves: A review of natural language processing research, *IEEE Computational Intelligence Magazine*, 9 (2), 48–57

Cai, Y, Wohn, D Y and Menon, R G V (2022) Try-on experiences in fashion retail: The role of AI in shaping consumer perceptions, *Journal of Retailing and Consumer Services*, 64, 102803

Chaffey, D and Ellis-Chadwick, F (2019) *Digital Marketing: Strategy, Implementation, and Practice* (7th ed.), Harlow: Pearson Education

Chatterjee, S, Rana, N P, Tamilmani, K, Sharma, A and Dwivedi, Y K (2023) The role of generative artificial intelligence in reshaping digital marketing: Conceptual framework and research agenda, *Journal of Business Research*, 162, 113862

Coca-Cola (2023) Coca-Cola partners with OpenAI and Bain & Company to launch AI-powered marketing [Press release], www.coca-colacompany.com (archived at https://perma.cc/5YKV-SN2D)

Dastin, J (2018) Amazon scraps secret AI recruiting tool that showed bias against women, Reuters, 10 October, www.reuters.com (archived at https://perma.cc/Q4Y2-XT4E)

Davenport, T H, Guha, A, Grewal, D and Bressgott, T (2020) How artificial intelligence will change the future of marketing, *Journal of the Academy of Marketing Science*, 48 (1), 24–42

Davis, F D (1989) Perceived usefulness, perceived ease of use, and user acceptance of information technology, *MIS Quarterly*, 13 (3), 319–40

Doshi-Velez, F and Kim, B (2017) Towards a rigorous science of interpretable machine learning, *arXiv preprint*, arXiv:1702.08608

Dwivedi, Y K, Hughes, L, Baabdullah, A M, Ribeiro-Navarrete, S, Giannakis, M, Al-Debei, M M et al (2023a) Metaverse beyond the hype: Multidisciplinary perspectives on emerging challenges, opportunities, and agenda for research, practice and policy, *International Journal of Information Management*, 71, 102642

Dwivedi, Y K, Hughes, L, Baabdullah, A M, Ribeiro-Navarrete, S, Giannakis, M, Al-Debei, M M et al (2023b) Metaverse marketing: How the metaverse will shape the future of consumer research and practice, *Psychology & Marketing*, 40 (4), 777–97

Elgammal, A (2023) Generative AI and copyright: The challenges ahead, *Communications of the ACM*, 66 (4), 22–24

European Commission (2021) *Proposal for a Regulation of the European Parliament and of the Council Laying Down Harmonised Rules on Artificial ntelligence (Artificial Intelligence Act)*, Brussels: European Commission, ec.europa.eu (archived at https://perma.cc/8V3C-KYWM)

European Commission (2023) *Proposal for a Regulation on Artificial Intelligence (AI Act)*, Brussels: European Commission, ec.europa.eu (archived at https://perma.cc/8V3C-KYWM)

Financial Times (2023) Samsung bans staff from using ChatGPT after data leak, *Financial Times*, 2 May, www.ft.com (archived at https://perma.cc/G5DA-8QXF)

Floridi, L and Cowls, J (2019) A unified framework of five principles for AI in society, *Harvard Data Science Review*, 1 (1), 1–15

Gervais, D J (2020) The machine as author, *Iowa Law Review*, 105 (5), 2053–106

Gomez-Uribe, C A and Hunt, N (2016) The Netflix recommender system: Algorithms, business value, and innovation, *ACM Transactions on Management Information Systems*, 6 (4), 1–19

Goodfellow, I, Pouget-Abadie, J, Mirza, M, Xu, B, Warde-Farley, D, Ozair, S, Courville, A and Bengio, Y (2014) Generative adversarial nets, *Advances in Neural Information Processing Systems*, 27, 2672–80

Google DeepMind (2023) Introducing Gemini: A multimodal foundation model, deepmind. google (archived at https://perma.cc/9MBP-WLND)

Grewal, D, Roggeveen, A L and Nordfält, J (2020) The future of retailing, *Journal of Retailing*, 96 (1), 80–88

Hirschberg, J and Manning, C D (2015) Advances in natural language processing, *Science*, 349 (6245), 261–266

Homburg, C, Jozić, D and Kuehnl, C (2017) Customer experience management: Toward implementing an evolving marketing concept, *Journal of the Academy of Marketing Science*, 45 (3), 377–401

Johnson, M, Schuster, M, Le, Q V, Krikun, M, Wu, Y, Chen, Z, Thorat, N, Viégas, F, Wattenberg, M, Corrado, G, Hughes, M and Dean, J (2017) Google's multilingual neural machine translation system: Enabling zero-shot translation, *Transactions of the Association for Computational Linguistics*, 5, 339–351

Jordan, M I and Mitchell, T M (2015) Machine learning: Trends, perspectives, and prospects, *Science*, 349 (6245), 255–260

Kaplan, A M and Haenlein, M (2020) Rulers of the world, unite! The challenges and opportunities of artificial intelligence, *Business Horizons*, 63 (1), 37–50

Katz, E, Blumler, J G and Gurevitch, M (1973) Uses and gratifications research, *Public Opinion Quarterly*, 37 (4), 509–23

Kieser, J, Naumann, J, and Schaninger, B (2023) Insurer of the future: Are Asian insurers keeping up with AI advances? www.mckinsey.com (archived at https://www.mckinsey.com/industries/financial-services/our-insights/insurer-of-the-future-are-asian-insurers-keeping-up-with-ai-advances)

Kietzmann, J, Paschen, J and Treen, E (2018) Artificial intelligence in advertising: How marketers can leverage AI along the consumer journey, *Journal of Advertising Research*, 58 (3), 263–67

Kietzmann, J, Paschen, J and Treen, E (2023) Artificial intelligence in marketing: Practical applications and ethical concerns, *Journal of Business Research*, 152, 137–48

Kotler, P, Kartajaya, H and Setiawan, I (2017) *Marketing 4.0: Moving from Traditional to Digital*, Hoboken, NJ: Wiley

LeCun, Y, Bengio, Y and Hinton, G, (2015) Deep learning, *Nature*, 521 (7553), 436–444

Lemon, K N and Verhoef, P C (2016) Understanding customer experience throughout the customer journey, *Journal of Marketing*, 80 (6), 69–96

McKinsey (2023) The state of AI in 2023: Generative AI's breakout year, McKinsey & Company, www.mckinsey.com (archived at https://perma.cc/TF29-Q24B)

Mehrabi, N, Morstatter, F, Saxena, N, Lerman, K and Galstyan, A (2021) A survey on bias and fairness in machine learning, *ACM Computing Surveys*, 54 (6), 1–35

Mikalef, P, Krogstie, J and Pappas, I O (2023) Artificial intelligence in business: An ethical perspective, *Information Systems Frontiers*, 25 (1), 1–14

Mittelstadt, B (2019) Principles alone cannot guarantee ethical AI, *Nature Machine Intelligence*, 1 (11), 501–507

Morse, S C (2021) AI liability: Who is responsible when artificial intelligence causes harm? *Harvard Journal of Law & Technology*, 34 (2), 457–93

Organisation for Economic Co-operation and Development (OECD) (2021) International Regulatory Co-operation: Best Practice Principles, Paris: OECD Publishing

OpenAI (2023) GPT-4V(ision): Expanding multimodal capabilities in AI [Technical report], openai.com (archived at https://perma.cc/XM22-CJHB)

Petty, R E and Cacioppo, J T (1986) *Communication and Persuasion: Central and Peripheral Routes to Attitude Change*, New York: Springer

Rogers, E M (2003) *Diffusion of Innovations* (5th ed.), New York: Free Press

Rust, R T (2020) The future of marketing, *International Journal of Research in Marketing*, 37 (1), 15–26

Samuelson, P (2022) Copyright implications of generative AI, *Journal of the Copyright Society of the USA*, 69 (2), 203–36

Shin, D (2021) The effects of explainability and causability on perception, trust, and acceptance: Implications for explainable AI, *International Journal of Human-Computer Studies*, 146, 102551

Strong, E K (1925) *Theories of Selling*, New York: McGraw-Hill

Sweller, J (1988) Cognitive load during problem solving: Effects on learning, *Cognitive Science*, 12 (2), 257–85

Teece, D J (2018) Business models and dynamic capabilities, *Long Range Planning*, 51 (1), 40–49

Teece, D J, Pisano, G and Shuen, A (1997) Dynamic capabilities and strategic management, *Strategic Management Journal*, 18 (7), 509–33

UK Government (2020) *Data Ethics Framework*, www.gov.uk/government/publications/data-ethics-framework (archived at https://perma.cc/AK85-PFK8)

Vaswani, A, Shazeer, N, Parmar, N, Uszkoreit, J, Jones, L, Gomez, A N, Kaiser, Ł and Polosukhin, I (2017) Attention is all you need, *Advances in Neural Information Processing Systems*, 30

Venkatesh, V and Davis, F D (2000) A theoretical extension of the technology acceptance model: Four longitudinal field studies, *Management Science*, 46 (2), 186–204

Wedel, M and Kannan, P K (2016) Marketing analytics for data-rich environments, *Journal of Marketing*, 80 (6), 97–121

Zarsky, T (2019) Incompatible: The GDPR in the age of big data, *Seton Hall Law Review*, 49 (4), 995–1025

Zhang, B, Sheng, J and Yao, L (2023a) Algorithmic curation and filter bubbles: Risks for consumer autonomy, *Journal of Consumer Research*, 50 (3), 511–29

Zhang, Y, Deng, S, Wang, H and Xu, S (2023b) AI-generated content: Opportunities, challenges, and future research directions, *Electronic Commerce Research and Applications*, 57, 101245

ANSWERS TO THE MULTIPLE-CHOICE QUIZZES

CHAPTER 1: MULTIPLE-CHOICE QUIZ

Q1 What is the primary purpose of marketing analytics?

Answer: B – To measure, manage and analyse marketing performance

Q2 Which of the following best describes customer lifetime value (CLV)?

Answer: B – The predicted net profit attributed to a customer over their entire relationship with a company

Q3 Which theory suggests that firms must continuously adapt their analytics practices to remain competitive?

Answer C – Dynamic capabilities theory

Q4 Netflix's recommendation system is an example of which analytics application?

Answer: B – Predictive analytics and personalization

Q5 Which of the following is **not** a challenge in marketing analytics?

Answer: D – Improved customer segmentation

Q6 Real-time marketing analytics provides businesses with which key advantage?

Answer: B – Ability to adapt campaigns quickly to changing conditions

Q7 According to Kotler and Keller (2016), one of the foundations of modern marketing analytics is:

Answer: A – Market research methods like sampling and regression

CHAPTER 2: MULTIPLE-CHOICE QUIZ

Q1 Which of the following is an example of secondary data?

Answer: B – Industry reports

Q2 Qualitative data is best used to understand:

Answer: B – Customer attitudes and motivations

Q3 Which principle of database design reduces redundancy and improves data organization?

Answer: B – Normalization

Q4 Starbucks uses loyalty card and app data to segment customers. This is an example of:

Answer: C – Primary quantitative data

Q5 GDPR and CCPA primarily concern:

Answer: B – Data security and privacy

INDEX

Note: Page numbers in *italics* refer to figures or tables.

Looking for another book?

Explore our award-winning
books from global business
experts in Marketing and Sales

Scan the code to browse

www.koganpage.com/marketing

More from Kogan Page

ISBN: 9781398622869

ISBN: 9781398623637

ISBN: 9781398625259

ISBN: 9781398623149

From 4 December 2025 the EU Responsible Person (GPSR) is:
eucomply oÜ, Pärnu mnt. 139b – 14, 11317 Tallinn, Estonia
www.eucompliancepartner.com

www.ingramcontent.com/pod-product-compliance
Lightning Source LLC
Chambersburg PA
CBHW080548060326
40689CB00021B/4782